Data Structures and Algorithms in Java

Data Structures and Algorithms in Java

Peter Drake

Upper Saddle River, NJ 07458

Library of Congress Cataloging-in-Publication Data

Drake, Peter.
    Data structures and algorithms in Java / Peter Drake.
       p. cm.
    Includes bibliographical references and index.
    ISBN 0-13-146914-2
       1. Java (Computer program language) 2. Data structures (Computer science)
    3. Computer algorithms. I. Title.

QA76.73.J38D693 2005
005.13'3--dc22

                                        2005050807

Vice President and Editorial Director, ECS: *Marcia J. Horton*
Senior Acquisitions Editor: *Tracy Dunkelberger*
Assistant Editor: *Carole Snyder*
Editorial Assistant: *Christianna Lee*
Executive Managing Editor: *Vince O'Brien*
Managing Editor: *Camille Trentacoste*
Production Editor: *Donna Crilly*
Director of Creative Services: *Paul Belfanti*
Art Director and Cover Manager: *Jayne Conte*
Cover Designer: *Bruce Kenselaar*
Managing Editor, AV Management and Production: *Patricia Burns*
Art Editor: *Gregory Dulles*
Manager, Cover Visual Research and Permissions: *Karen Sanatar*
Manufacturing Manager, ESM: *Alexis Heydt-Long*
Manufacturing Buyer: *Lisa McDowell*
Executive Marketing Manager: *Robin O'Brien*
Marketing Assistant: *Barrie Reinhold*

Cover Image: *Russel Illig / Photodisc / Getty Images, Inc.*

© 2006, Pearson Education, Inc.
Pearson Prentice Hall
Pearson Education, Inc.
Upper Saddle River, New Jersey 07458

The author and publisher of this book have used their best efforts in preparing this book. These efforts include the development, research, and testing of the theories and programs to determine their effectiveness. The author and publisher make no warranty of any kind, expressed or implied, with regard to these programs or the documentation contained in this book. The author and publisher shall not be liable in any event for incidental or consequential damages in connection with, or arising out of, the furnishing, performance, or use of these programs.

Printed in the United States of America

10 9 8 7 6 5 4 3 2 1

ISBN 0-13-146914-2

Pearson Education Ltd., *London*
Pearson Education Australia Pty. Ltd., *Sydney*
Pearson Education Singapore, Pte. Ltd.
Pearson Education North Asia Ltd., *Hong Kong*
Pearson Education Canada, Inc., *Toronto*
Pearson Educación de Mexico, S.A. de C.V.
Pearson Education—Japan, *Tokyo*
Pearson Education Malaysia, Pte. Ltd.
Pearson Education, Inc., *Upper Saddle River, New Jersey*

Table of Contents

Preface

Intended Audience

This book is intended for a second undergraduate course in computer science. I assume that the reader is familiar with the basic control structures of Java or C and with elementary concepts such as variables and decomposing a problem into functions (methods). Only a pre-calculus level of mathematics is expected.

Why Choose This Book?

This book has everything you would ever want in a data structures textbook: plentiful exercises, crystal-clear prose, code available on-line, and just the right amount of depth. Of course, every author claims as much. What makes this book different?

This book is distinguished by the following features:

- Use of new Java 1.5 features
- An unusually large number of diagrams, drawn in the Unified Modeling Language (UML)
- "Inverted pyramid" style, with the most important material up front
- Gradual introduction of abstract concepts
- Extensive use of games as examples

Version 1.5 of Java adds several long-awaited features to the language. These new features are explained and used in many examples throughout this book. Specifically:

- The new enhanced for loop allows a programmer to concisely say, "For each element of this array or Collection...." This is discussed in Appendix A and, for Collections, in Chapter 5.

- Primitives are now automatically boxed and unboxed, freeing programmers from the awkward

  ```
  ((Integer)(numbers.get(i))).intValue()
  ```

  construction. This is covered in Chapter 2 in the discussion of reference types.

- The new java.util.Scanner class (Appendix A) finally makes it possible to read input from the keyboard without a ridiculous amount of code.

- The biggest change is probably the introduction of generic types (Chapter 4), which allow a programmer to specify the element type of a collection, improving both program clarity and type safety.

In explaining concepts, I use many diagrams. Long stretches of text, code, and equations make for dry reading. A good diagram can explain a new concept clearly, provide an instant review, and serve as a landmark when reviewing the text. Since the Unified Modeling Language has become the de facto standard for software diagrams, the diagrams in this book are drawn in a subset of the UML. I have deliberately left out even intermediate UML features, such as access level tags and aggregation diamonds, as I feel they would cause more confusion than clarity. This notation is introduced gradually (mostly in the first part of the book) and reviewed in Appendix B.

A related graphic feature is the use of fonts for emphasis in code. Many texts either provide no font highlighting or use fonts to highlight keywords. This syntax highlighting is useful when typing code (helping to prevent typographical errors), but it neither makes code easier to read nor emphasizes important passages. I use bold italic text to highlight parts of the code which are of particular interest in the current discussion. If nothing in particular is being emphasized, I highlight method and field names to delineate the major sections of a class.

This book is written in the "inverted pyramid" style taught to journalists: the most important material is at the front, with finer details and more advanced topics introduced with each chapter. A course could reasonably be stopped after any chapter. This gives instructors the freedom to speed up or slow down as necessary, without fear of not getting to an important topic before the end of the course.

Many texts overwhelm the reader with too much abstraction up front. This is an easy mistake to make for fully trained computer scientists, who *prefer* to read about the big picture before delving into details. On the other hand, students who must absorb inheritance, polymorphism, recursion, and analysis of algorithms before they've written a single "real" program are likely to lose interest, if not consciousness. I constantly hear students asking for more concrete examples, and I've never heard one complain about too many examples.

With this tension in mind, I have tried to provide examples early in each chapter. Let the students have complete, working programs to mess with as soon as possible. Abstract concepts are much easier to absorb in the context of a concrete problem.

Difficult concepts are also introduced as gradually as possible. For example, the call stack is discussed before it appears in the context of recursion.

Most of my examples are games, often involving dice, cards, and boards. Games capture the students' imagination, giving them some reason to care about the data structure or algorithm being discussed. While simple enough to program without pages and pages of code, games offer a more realistic challenge than antiseptic tasks such as finding a greatest common divisor. Near the midpoint of the text, games involving a dictionary of tens of thousands of words provide compelling motivation for efficient data structures and algorithms.

Especially near the beginning of the book, I work through the development of each project, often providing multiple versions of the code and considering alternate designs. Students thus experience the *process* of crafting programs, rather than just the results. While no vital parts of the program are left out, some enhancements (such as checking for valid input) are left as problems.

Complete, working code for every program is printed in the book and available on-line. I recall, as a student, being annoyed when the hard part of an algorithm or data structure was left as an exercise. It's all here, even code for B-trees; I know of no other undergraduate text that presents this material at this level of completeness.

No classes have to be downloaded in advance to use the code in this book. Later classes make use of earlier classes. If desired, these later classes can be easily adapted to use built-in classes from the Java collections framework; the method names for the classes developed in the book are congruent.

My hope is that, by the end of the text, the reader will have gained considerable skill in rapidly developing correct, efficient, general-purpose programs.

Organization

This book is divided into five parts: object-oriented programming, linear structures, algorithms, trees and collections, and advanced topics.

Part I introduces object-oriented programming, with one chapter on each of the three major principles: encapsulation, polymorphism, and inheritance. Use of this part of the book may vary greatly from one institution to another. Where objects are taught in CS1, this part may be covered very quickly or skipped altogether (although there are few students who wouldn't benefit from a review of this material). At other institutions, where CS1 is taught in C or some other language, more time may be spent on this material. Alternately, this part of the book (along with Appendix A) is good for a short course introducing object-oriented programming.

Part II covers stacks, queues, and lists, in both array-based and linked implementations. The reader is shown how these structures are used and how to build them, then where to find them in the Java collections framework.

In Part III, the reader begins the journey from mere programming to computer science. Analysis of algorithms is introduced, including asymptotic notation and a step-by-step procedure for analyzing simple algorithms. After this difficult material, the reader gets a break with a relatively short chapter on the simplest searching and sorting algorithms. By the time recursion is introduced, the reader has been prepared with an understanding of the call stack, an understanding of the sorting problem, and the ability to appreciate the better performance provided by recursive algorithms such as merge sort and Quicksort.

Part IV focuses on data structures, covering trees and set implementations (ordered lists, binary search trees, and hash tables).

Advanced topics are addressed in Part V, from which instructors may freely choose their favorites. Among the choices are advanced linear structures, strings, advanced trees, graphs, memory management, and issues involved with disk storage.

Exercises, Problems, and Projects

Exercises are provided at the end of most sections. These should not take more than a couple of minutes to solve. Exercises are good questions to pose during class or on exams.

Problems are provided at the end of each chapter. These are slightly more involved, taking perhaps 5 or 10 minutes to solve. These are good for exams and homework.

Finally, one or more projects are given at the end of each chapter. These will usually take an hour or more, and make good stand-alone homework or lab assignments.

Acknowledgments

I wish to thank: my wife Heather, for proofreading above and beyond the call of duty and for reminding me to eat; Dan Friedman, for convincing me that I wasn't joking when I began writing an early version of this book in graduate school; James Ernest (the Sid Sackson of the twenty-first century), for allowing me to use his game designs; Alan Apt, for his guidance and for giving me a shot at the big time; Paul Purdom and David Wise, for illuminating some of the darker corners of data structures and algorithms; and all those who have provided comments, suggestions, and proofreading through the years, including Kevin and Rebecca Djang, Jerry Franke, Matt Jadud, Sid Kitchel, Jim Levenick, countless computer science students both at Indiana University and at Lewis & Clark College, and the anonymous reviewers.

PETER DRAKE
Portland, Oregon

Object-Oriented Programming

I

1

Encapsulation

This chapter introduces the object-oriented approach to software development. Section 1.1 discusses the software development process and the idea of encapsulation: dividing a program into distinct components which have limited interaction. In Sections 1.2 and 1.3, we develop a program to play the game of Beetle. Section 1.2 introduces terminology and concepts related to objects as we write a class to model the die used in the game. Section 1.3 expands on this, developing two more classes to complete the program.

Some readers may wish to read Appendix A before beginning this chapter.

1.1 Software Development

Good Programs

What are the features of a good computer program? It is essential that the program be *correct*, doing what it is supposed to do and containing no bugs. The program should be *efficient*, using no more time or memory than is necessary. The program should be *general-purpose*, so that we don't have to start from scratch the next time we build a similar program. Finally, all other things being equal, the program should be *rapidly developed*. While there are some changes which will further one of these goals at no cost, it is often necessary to make tradeoffs, as suggested by Figure 1–1.

3

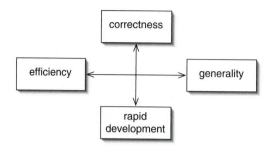

Figure 1-1: There are often tradeoffs between the features of a good computer program.

We would like all of our programs to be perfectly correct. In some applications, such as medical equipment, aircraft navigation, and nuclear power plant control, lives may literally depend on the correctness of software. In others, such as games and web browsers, the occasional crash may be merely an annoyance. The best way to ensure correctness is to precisely specify how the program is supposed to behave and then thoroughly test the program to verify that it does so. Unfortunately, this can take a prohibitive amount of time. Practical concerns often lead to the release of buggy software.

Much of this book concerns choosing data structures and algorithms to make programs more efficient. A *data structure* is a way of organizing information (numbers, text, pictures, and so on) in a computer. An *algorithm* is a step-by-step process for doing something, written either in plain English or in a programming language. (We study *algorithms* rather than *programs* because, while programming languages change every few years, good algorithms stay around for decades or even millennia.)

Data structures and algorithms are intimately intertwined. A data structure may support efficient algorithms for some operations (such as checking whether some item is present) but not for others (such as removing an item). Conversely, a fast algorithm may require that data be stored in a particular way. To make the best choices, we would like to know as much as possible about how our program will be used. What kinds of data are we likely to encounter? Which operations will be most common? Some of the most efficient data structures and algorithms are limited to specific tasks, so choosing them makes our programs less general-purpose.

If a program is to be used very heavily, it may be worth spending some time to *optimize* it, that is, fine-tune it to maximize efficiency given the expected data, the hardware on which it will run, and so on. This trades development time and generality for efficiency.

Once we have a certain amount of programming experience, we realize that we are writing roughly the same programs over and over again. We can save development time by cutting and pasting code from previous programs. Sometimes the new program requires changes to the code. To minimize the time we spend changing our old code, we try to write general-purpose components. For example, rather than writing a method to sort an array of five numbers, we write a method which can sort an array of any length, containing any values of any comparable type (numbers, letters, strings, and so on). This general-purpose code tends to be less efficient than code written for a specific use. It can also take a little more time to make sure it is correct. On the other hand, once it is written *and thoroughly documented* we never need to think about its inner workings again—it is a trusty power tool that we can bring out whenever we need it. Established programming languages like Java have huge, general-purpose libraries for graphics, file handling, networking, and so on.

Development time is a precious resource to employers (who must pay their programmers) and students (who are notorious for procrastination). As you have probably learned by now from bitter experience, most development time is spent debugging. The way to reduce debugging time is to invest time in design and testing. The urge to sit down and start writing code is powerful, even for experienced programmers, but a hastily thrown together program will invariably turn on its creator.

While development time may seem irrelevant to the final program—who cares how long the Mona Lisa took to paint?—many of the techniques for reducing development time also reduce the time needed for program maintenance by making our programs more correct and general-purpose.

Encapsulation

It is difficult to write correct, efficient, general-purpose programs in a reasonable amount of time because computer programs are among the most complex things people have ever constructed. Computer scientists have put a great deal of thought into dealing with this complexity. The approach used by the Java programming language is ***object-oriented programming***. Object-oriented programming is characterized by three principles:

- ***Encapsulation*** is the division of a program into distinct components which have limited interaction. A method is an example of an encapsulated component: other methods interact with it only through the arguments they pass to it and the value it returns. Each component can be tested separately, improving correctness, and components can be recombined into new programs, improving generality and development speed. This chapter focuses on encapsulation.

- ***Polymorphism*** is the ability of the same word or symbol to mean different things in different contexts. For example, in Java, the symbol + means one thing (addition) when dealing with numbers, but means something else (concatenation) when dealing with Strings. Polymorphism greatly improves generality, which in turn improves correctness and development speed. Polymorphism is discussed in Chapter 2.

- ***Inheritance*** is the ability to specify that a program is similar to another program, delineating only the differences. To draw an example from nature, a platypus is pretty much like any other mammal, except that it lays eggs. Inheritance makes code reuse easier, improving correctness, generality, and development speed. Inheritance is the subject of Chapter 3.

None of these features directly improves efficiency. Indeed, there may be some loss of efficiency. The consensus among object-oriented programmers is that this price is well worth paying. The trouble with software today is not that it runs too slowly, but that it is buggy and takes too long to develop.

The first principle of object-oriented programming, encapsulation, is analogous to division of labor in an organization. A grocery store, for example, might have one person in charge of stocking the shelves and another in charge of purchasing. When the stocker notices that the store's supply of rutabagas is running low, she only needs to notify the purchaser, who then orders more. The stocker doesn't have to know how much rutabagas cost or where they come from. The purchaser doesn't have to know which aisle they are displayed on. Both jobs are made easier through encapsulation.

Encapsulation makes it easier to rapidly develop correct programs because a programmer only has to consider a few things when writing any one component of the program. This is particularly important in projects involving several programmers: once the programmers have agreed on how the components will interact, each is free to do whatever he wants within his component.

Generality is improved, both because components can be reused in their entirety and because understanding one component does not require one to understand the entire program. In fact, very large programs would be effectively impossible to write, debug, and maintain without encapsulation.

The relation between encapsulation and efficiency is less clear. Encapsulation prevents certain efficiency improvements which depend on understanding several parts of a program. Suppose the purchaser in the grocery store always has new merchandise delivered to the back of the store. It might be more efficient to park the rutabaga truck in front if rutabagas are displayed near the entrance, but the purchaser isn't aware of this detail. On the other hand, by simplifying individual program components, encapsulation can give a programmer freedom to make improvements *within* a component. If the stocker had to think about purchasing, running the cash register, and so on, then she might not have time to learn to balance five crates of rutabagas on a handtruck.

We have already seen encapsulation in at least one sense. By dividing a class into methods, we can concentrate on one method at a time. Any variables declared inside a method are visible only inside that method. When we invoke another method, we only need to know the information in the method signature (what arguments it expects and what it returns) and associated documentation. We don't have to know what happens inside the method.

We don't merely have the *option* to ignore the innards of a method. We actually *cannot access* variables declared inside a method from outside that method. This is in keeping with the principle of ***information hiding***: the workings of a component should not be visible from the outside. Information hiding enforces encapsulation. Continuing the grocery store analogy, we don't give the stocker access to the bank account and we don't give the purchaser the keys to the forklift.

Information hiding may seem counterintuitive. Isn't it better for everyone to have as much information as possible? Experience has shown that the answer is "no." If someone can see the inner workings of a component, they may be tempted to take shortcuts in the name of efficiency. With access to the bank account, the stocker may reason, "The purchaser is on vacation this week. I'll just order more rutabagas myself." If she does not follow proper accounting procedures, or does not realize that the purchaser has already ordered more rutabagas as part of the regular monthly vegetable order, she could cause problems. We shudder to think what might happen if the purchaser got behind the wheel of the forklift.

The Software Development Cycle

Software engineering is the study of how to develop correct, efficient, general-purpose programs in a reasonable amount of time. There is a vast body of literature, techniques, jargon, and competing philosophies about software engineering. Much of it is devoted to the largest, most challenging programs, which are written by teams of dozens of programmers working for years. These elaborate techniques are not appropriate for the relatively small programs we will write in this book. On the other hand, our programs are now sufficiently sophisticated that some examination of the software development process is in order. If we just sit down and start writing code, we will likely get into trouble.

We can think of the process of writing a program in terms of the *software development cycle* (Figure 1–2). We divide the process into three major phases: design, implementation, and testing. (Many software engineers divide the process into more phases.)

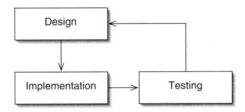

Figure 1-2: The software development cycle.

In the *design* phase, we decide what the program is going to look like. This includes *problem specification*, the task of stating precisely what a program is supposed to do. In a programming class, the problem specification is often given as the assignment. In real life, problem specification involves working with the end user (for example, the customer, employer, or scientific community) to decide what the program should do.

The design phase also includes breaking the program down into components. What are the major components of the program? What is each component supposed to do? How do the components interact? It is a good idea to write a comment for each component at this point, so that we have a very clear understanding of what the component does. Commenting first also avoids the danger that we'll put off commenting until our program has become hopelessly complicated.

The *implementation* phase is the writing of code. This is where we move from a *description* of a program to a (hopefully) working program. Many students erroneously believe that this is the only phase in which actual programming is occurring, so the other two phases are unimportant. In fact, the more time spent on the other two phases, the less is needed in implementation. If we rush to the keyboard to start coding, we may end up having to throw away some of our work because it doesn't fit in with the rest of the program or doesn't meet the problem specification.

In the *testing* phase, we run our program and verify that it does what it is supposed to do. After a long session of programming, it is tempting to believe that our program is correct if it compiles and runs on one test case. We must be careful to test our program thoroughly. For example, when testing a method to search for some item in an array, we should consider cases where the target is the first element of the array, where it is somewhere in the middle, where it is the last element, and where it is not present at all.

The French poet Paul Valéry wrote, "A poem is never finished, only abandoned." The same can be said of computer programs. There is some point when the software is released, but there is often *maintenance* to be performed: changes to make, new features to add, bugs to fix. This maintenance is just more iterations of the software development cycle. This is why the cycle has no point labeled "end" or "finished." In a programming course, assignments are often completely abandoned after they are handed in, but general-purpose components may need some maintenance if they are to be reused in future assignments.

Some software engineers argue that there should be, in effect, only one iteration of the cycle: the entire program should be designed in exquisite detail, then implemented, then tested. Proponents of this *top-down* approach argue that, by making all design decisions up front, we avoid wasting time implementing components that won't fit into the final program.

Other software engineers advocate many iterations: design some simple component, implement it, test it, expand the design very slightly, and so on. Proponents of this *bottom-up* approach argue that this allows us to start testing before we have accumulated a huge body of code. Furthermore, because we put off our design decisions, we avoid wasting time redesigning the program if we discover that, for example, we misunderstood the problem specification.

In practice, most software development falls between these two extremes. In this chapter, we will lean toward the bottom-up end of the spectrum. When we are first learning to program, we don't yet have the experience to envision the structure of an entire program. We are also likely to make a lot of coding errors, so we should test early and often.

Encapsulation allows us to break up the software development cycle (Figure 1–3).

Once we divide the program into encapsulated components, we can work on each one separately. In a project with several programmers, multiple components can be developed at the same time. Even if we are working alone, the ability to concentrate on a single component makes it much easier to rapidly develop correct, efficient, general-purpose code. Once the components are "complete," we integrate them in a high-level implementation phase and then test the entire system.

Exercises

1.1   What have you done in the past to make one of your programs more correct? More efficient? More general-purpose? More rapidly developed?

1.2   Discuss the extent to which your college education has consisted of encapsulated courses.

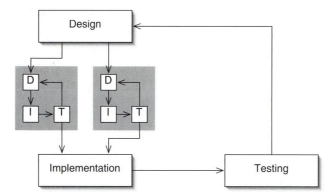

Figure 1-3: The construction of each encapsulated component (shaded) involves one or more iterations of the software development cycle. The initial design phase involves breaking the program into components, each of which can be developed separately. These components are combined in the implementation phase.

1.3 Discuss whether a top-down or a bottom-up approach to software development is more likely to produce a correct program. Which is likely to produce a more efficient program? More general-purpose? More rapidly developed? Which approach do you prefer?

1.4 Discuss whether assertions (Appendix A) should be considered part of design, part of implementation, or part of testing.

1.5 Where do comments fit into the development cycle? How do they affect correctness, efficiency, generality, and development speed?

1.2 Classes and Objects

This section illustrates the software development cycle and introduces some concepts from object-oriented programming. As an extended example, we develop a program to play the game of Beetle (Figure 1–4).

Classes

In Appendix A, we use the word "class" as a rough synonym for "program." While each program needs to have a main() method in some class, many classes are not programs. In object-oriented programming, a *class* is predominantly a description of a set of similar objects, such as the class of birds, the class of insurance claims, or the class of dice. A class is an encapsulated component of the program.

Beetle

Players: 2 or more

Object: To be the first player with a complete beetle. A complete beetle has a body, a head, six legs, two eyes, two feelers, and a tail.

Setup: Each player starts with no parts on her beetle.

Play: On your turn, roll a die, and act on the result:

1.   If your beetle already has a body, pass the die to the next player. Otherwise, add a body and roll again.

2.   If your beetle already has a head or has no body, pass the die to the next player. Otherwise, add a head and roll again.

3.   If your beetle already has six legs or has no body, pass the die to the next player. Otherwise, add two legs and roll again.

4.   If your beetle already has two eyes or has no head, pass the die to the next player. Otherwise, add an eye and roll again.

5.   If your beetle already has two feelers or has no head, pass the die to the next player. Otherwise, add a feeler and roll again.

6.   If your beetle already has a tail or has no body, pass the die to the next player. Otherwise, add a tail and roll again.

Figure 1–4: Beetle, also known as Bug or Cootie, is a children's game of pure luck. Our implementation handles only two players.

We can create multiple *instances* of a class. Each instance is a different *object*, but they have things in common with the other members of their class. In the Beetle game, we'll eventually have to create two instances of the class of beetles—one for each player. We will also create one instance of the class of dice.

Breaking our program down into classes is the first step in design. For the Beetle game, we will need three classes: the class of beetles, the class of dice, and the class of Beetle games. (We create one instance of the last class each time we play the game.) This organization is illustrated in Figure 1–5. This type of diagram is called a *UML class diagram*. The UML (Unified Modeling Language) is a widely used set of notations for diagramming many aspects of software development, from user interactions to relationships between methods. Most of the UML is beyond the scope of this book, but we will use these class diagrams as well as (later in this section) instance diagrams. UML notation is introduced gradually over the course of the book and summarized in Appendix B.

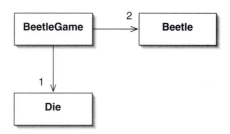

Figure 1–5: UML class diagram for the Beetle game program. This diagram says that one instance of BeetleGame is associated with two instances of Beetle and one instance of Die.

In Java, the name of a class traditionally begins with an upper-case letter. The three classes we need to build are therefore called Die, Beetle, and BeetleGame. Each class is defined in a separate file, which must have the same name as the class and a .java extension. The first drafts of these files are shown in Figures 1–6 through 1–8.

```
1 /** Beetle with parts for the Beetle game. */
2 public class Beetle {
3 }
```
Figure 1–6: The file `Beetle.java`.

```
1 /** The game of Beetle for two players. */
2 public class BeetleGame {
3 }
```
Figure 1–7: The file `BeetleGame.java`.

```
1 /** A six-sided die for use in games. */
2 public class Die {
3 }
```
Figure 1–8: The file `Die.java`.

Objects, Fields, and Methods

We now focus on the simplest class of objects, the Die class.

What exactly is an object? An object has two kinds of components:

- The *fields* of the object represent its current state. In a Die, there will be one field indicating which face of the Die is on top. Field values vary from one instance to another. One Die might have the 2 showing, another the 6.

- The *methods* of the object are actions it can perform. In object-oriented programming, we don't do things to objects. Instead, we *ask objects to do things to themselves*. We don't roll a die, we ask it to roll itself. All instances of a given class have the same methods.

In order to make our development cycle for the Die class as short as possible, we start by thinking, "It will have to keep track of which face is on top." We'll design other features, such as the method for rolling, later. In a top-down approach to software development, on the other hand, we would specify all of the methods before thinking about implementation details such as fields.

A first shot at implementing the Die class is shown in Figure 1–9.

```
1 /** A six-sided die for use in games. */
2 public class Die {
3
4   /** The face of this Die that is showing. */
5   private int topFace;
6
7 }
```

Figure 1-9: A first shot at implementing the Die class. It compiles, but it doesn't run.

This class compiles, but it doesn't run. The problem is that there is no `main()` method. Before we fix this, notice a couple of things about the field `topFace`.

First, the field is not declared static. This means that it can have a different value for each instance of Die. A field like this is called an *instance field* or *instance variable*. Since this is the most common kind of field, it is often simply called a field.

Second, the field is declared *private*. Instance fields are normally declared private. This means that they cannot be accessed by methods in other classes. When other classes do things with Die instances, code in those classes can't access private fields directly. This is an example of information hiding.

Let's put in an empty `main()` method (Figure 1–10).

```
1 /** A six-sided die for use in games. */
2 public class Die {
3
4   /** The face of the die that is showing. */
5   private int topFace;
6
7   /** Doesn't do anything yet. */
8   public static void main(String[] args) {
9   }
10
11 }
```

Figure 1-10: The class can now be run, although it still doesn't do anything.

Was there any point in doing this? Yes: we now have a program that we can run. After each change we make from now on, we can check if the program still runs. If not, the bug is most likely in the new code. By making such small, incremental changes to the code, we can avoid spending a lot of time hunting for bugs.

We have now completed one iteration of the software development cycle—design, implementation, and testing—for the Die class.

Constructors

Returning to design, the next thing our class needs is a ***constructor***. A constructor is a method that initializes all of the fields of an object. It always has the same name as the class. We decide that, whenever a new instance of the Die is created, it will have the 1 as the top face.

Our design so far can be summed up in a more detailed UML class diagram (Figure 1–11). Since the Die class is an encapsulated component, we don't include the boxes for the other two classes in the program in the diagram.

```
              Die
  topFace:int
  Die()
  main(String[]):void
```

Figure 1–11: UML class diagram for the Die class. This diagram says that there is one field, **topFace**, which is of type int. There are two methods: the constructor **Die()** and the method **main()**. The constructor takes no arguments and, like all constructors, has no return type. The **main()** method takes an array of Strings as an argument and has a return type of void. This method is underlined because it is static—more on this later.

The implementation of the class, including the constructor, is shown in Figure 1–12. The constructor, on lines 7–10, is easily recognized because (a) it has the same name as the class and (b) it has no return type. Its job is to initialize the **topFace** field of every new instance of Die to 1.

```
 1 /** A six-sided die for use in games. */
 2 public class Die {
 3
 4   /** The face of this Die that is showing. */
 5   private int topFace;
 6
 7   /** Initialize the top face to 1. */
 8   public Die() {
 9     this.topFace = 1;
10 }
11
```

Figure 1–12: The constructor initializes the field **topFace** to 1. (Part 1 of 2)

```
12   /**
13    * Create a Die, print the top face, set the top face to 6, and
14    * print it again.
15    */
16   public static void main(String[] args) {
17     Die d = new Die();
18     System.out.println(d.topFace);
19     d.topFace = 6;
20     System.out.println(d.topFace);
21   }
22
23 }
```

Figure 1–12: The constructor initializes the field `topFace` to 1. (Part 2 of 2)

To create a new instance of the Die class, we use the expression:

`new Die();`

On line 17, the `main()` method creates such an instance. This line may seem a bit cryptic, but it is no stranger than a line like:

`int x = 3;`

Line 17 declares and initializes a variable of type Die. New types are defined in Java by creating classes. The name of the variable is d. The initial value of d is the result of the expression `new Die()`.

Once we have an instance, we can access its `topFace` field. In the `main()` method, the instance is called d, so the field is accessed as `d.topFace`. Within a nonstatic method such as our constructor, we can refer to the current object as `this`.

Information hiding prevents us from referring to `d.topFace` within the constructor, because d is a variable inside the `main()` method. The constructor can still do things to the object (such as setting its `topFace` field), because `this` and d are *references* to the same instance.

This situation is illustrated in Figure 1–13, which is called a ***UML instance diagram***. In an instance diagram, we show the values of the fields within an instance. While there is only one instance in

Figure 1–13: In a UML instance diagram, the (nonstatic) fields of each instance are shown, but the methods are not. In this diagram, `this` and d are both references to the same instance of Die.

this particular diagram, we will later see instance diagrams containing multiple instances of the same class. In a class diagram, on the other hand, each class appears only once. We do not show the methods in an instance diagram, because all instances of the same class have the same methods.

If we fail to initialize a field in an object, Java gives it a ***default value***. For number types such as int and double, the default value is 0. For booleans, the default value is false. For chars, the default value is the unprintable character with the ASCII and Unicode value 0. For arrays and all object types, the default value is the special value ***null***. A null reference does not point to anything in particular. We'll discuss null in more detail in Chapter 2.

This automatic initialization of fields is an unusual feature of Java. If we rely on it, we should include a comment to this effect, in case someone some day wants to translate our code into another language, such as C, which does not have this feature.

We now compile and run our program. It produces the output:

```
1
6
```

This is exactly what we expected. On to the next iteration of the development cycle!

Accessors, Mutators, and this

Referring to the `topFace` field as `d.topFace` is fine while we're working within the Die class, but eventually other classes (like BeetleGame) will have to know which face is showing on a Die. It would violate encapsulation for a method in another class to directly access this field. In fact, since we declared `topFace` to be private, Java won't let us do this. This is information hiding enforcing encapsulation.

Other classes should be able to get at the fields of an object only through methods. Two particularly common types of methods are accessors and mutators. An ***accessor***, also known as a ***getter***, returns the value of some field. A ***mutator***, also known as a ***setter***, changes (mutates) the value of some field within the object.

We add an accessor `getTopFace()` and a mutator `setTopFace()` to the design of the Die class in Figure 1–14.

```
┌─────────────────────────┐
│           Die           │
├─────────────────────────┤
│ topFace:int             │
├─────────────────────────┤
│ Die()                   │
│ getTopFace():int        │
│ setTopFace(int):void    │
│ main(String[]):void     │
└─────────────────────────┘
```

Figure 1–14: Adding an accessor and a mutator to the UML class diagram for the Die class.

The code for these two methods, as well as the revised `main()` method, is shown in Figure 1–15.

```
1 /** Return the top face of this Die. */
2 public int getTopFace() {
3    return this.topFace;
4 }
5
6 /** Set the top face to the specified value. */
7 public void setTopFace(int topFace) {
8    this.topFace = topFace;
9 }
10
11 /**
12  * Create a Die, print the top face, set the top face to 6, and
13  * print it again.
14  */
15 public static void main(String[] args) {
16    Die d = new Die();
17    System.out.println(d.getTopFace());
18    d.setTopFace(6);
19    System.out.println(d.getTopFace());
20 }
```

Figure 1-15: Accessor, mutator, and revised `main()` method for the Die class. Since the rest of the class is unchanged, it is not shown in this Figure.

Notice the statement

```
this.topFace = topFace;
```

on line 8. The use of `this` distinguishes between the *field* `topFace` (on the left) and the *argument* `topFace` (on the right).

Static vs. Nonstatic

Whenever we refer to a nonstatic field or invoke a nonstatic method, we must indicate a particular instance. For example, we can't just say `getTopFace()`; we have to say something like `d.getTopFace()` or `this.getTopFace()`. (We'll see a way to implicitly indicate `this` in Section 1.3.) We can use `this` only within nonstatic methods, because only nonstatic methods are invoked on a particular instance of the class. For example, we cannot say

```
System.out.println(this.getTopFace());
```

in `main()` because `main()` is a **static method**. A static method is about the *entire class*, rather than about an individual instance. Static methods are sometimes called **class methods**. Nonstatic methods are sometimes called **instance methods**. In UML class diagrams, static methods are underlined.

The `main()` method of any class *must* be static. This is because it can be the first method run. It can't be invoked on a particular instance because there might not yet be any instances of the class.

Static methods are invoked on a class (such as the Math class, which we'll use momentarily) rather than on a specific instance. While it is legal to invoke a static method on an instance, doing so can lead to some surprising results, so it is a bad idea.

Completing the Die Class

We will need one more method to roll the Die. The expanded class diagram is shown in Figure 1–16.

Die
topFace:int
Die() getTopFace():int roll():void setTopFace(int):void main(String[]):void

Figure 1–16: The `roll()` method takes no arguments and has a return type of void.

The implementation involves the static `random()` method from the built-in Math class. This method returns a random double which is at least 0 and less than 1. If we multiply the result by 6, throw away any fractional part by casting it to an int, and add 1, we get a random int between 1 and 6 inclusive.

The `roll()` method, along with a `main()` method to test it, is shown in Figure 1–17. We should run this one a few times, because it does not always produce the same output.

```
 1 /**
 2  * Set the top face to a random integer between 1 and 6, inclusive.
 3  */
 4 public void roll() {
 5   this.topFace = ((int)(Math.random() * 6)) + 1;
 6 }
 7
 8 /** Create a Die, print it, roll it, and print it again. */
 9 public static void main(String[] args) {
10   Die d = new Die();
11   System.out.println("Before rolling: " + d.getTopFace());
12   d.roll();
13   System.out.println("After rolling: " + d.getTopFace());
14 }
```

Figure 1–17: The `roll()` method and a `main()` method to test it.

We are done with the Die class for now. We can generate automatic documentation with the command:

```
javadoc -public Die.java
```

Notice that in the resulting file `Die.html`, the private field is not shown. This is encapsulation at work again. If someone comes along later to write another game involving the Die class, she doesn't have to look at our code. The documentation tells her everything she needs to use Die objects.

Exercises

1.6   Remove the statement

```
this.topFace = 1;
```

from the Die constructor (line 9 in Figure 1–12). Does the class still compile and run correctly? Explain.

1.7   Explain why accessors and mutators are not needed for constants. (Constants are explained in Appendix A.)

1.8   Consider the statement:

```
System.out.println("Practice what you preach.");
```

What sort of thing is `System`? (Is it a class, a static method, an instance method, or something else?) What is `System.out`? What is `System.out.println()`?

1.9   Add an assertion to the `setTopFace()` method to prevent anyone from setting a Die's `topFace` field to a value less than 1 or greater than 6.

1.3 Using Objects

We now complete our program by building the Beetle and BeetleGame classes.

The Beetle Class

For variety, we develop the Beetle class in a more top-down fashion. We begin by thinking about what a Beetle can do.

We will need methods to add various body parts. This might not always succeed. For example, the rules of the game don't allow a player to add an eye if his beetle doesn't have a head yet. Since the success of an addition earns the player another turn, the BeetleGame class will need to know whether the addition succeeded. These methods should therefore return a boolean value.

We need a method to indicate whether the Beetle is complete. The BeetleGame class will need this information to determine when the game is over.

We also need a constructor (a newly constructed Beetle has no parts) and a `main()` method to test the class.

What about fields? We'll need one for each of the different body part types. Some of them are booleans (either a Beetle has a head or it doesn't) while others are ints (a Beetle may have from 0 to 6 legs).

This design is summed up in Figure 1–18. We don't need a `main()` method because we aren't going to run this class. We're just going to use it when we run the BeetleGame class. (It would still be a good idea to include a `main()` method for testing; this is left as Exercise 1.12.)

```
                    Beetle
         body:boolean
         eyes:int
         feelers:int
         head:boolean
         legs:int
         tail:boolean
         Beetle()
         addBody():boolean
         addEye():boolean
         addFeeler():boolean
         addHead():boolean
         addLeg():boolean
         addTail():boolean
         isComplete():boolean
```

Figure 1–18: UML class diagram for the Beetle class.

We could try to implement all of this at once, but it is a better idea to implement one field and the corresponding method and then test the program. This way, if we make a mistake, we'll only have to fix it once instead of once for each kind of body part. A first draft is shown in Figure 1–19.

```
 1 /** Beetle with parts for the Beetle game. */
 2 public class Beetle {
 3
 4   /** True if this Beetle has a body. */
 5   private boolean body;
 6
 7   /** A new Beetle has no parts. */
 8   public Beetle() {
 9     body = false;
10   }
11
```

Figure 1–19: Beginning to implement the Beetle class. (Part 1 of 2)

```
12  /** Try to add a body and return whether this succeeded. */
13  public boolean addBody() {
14    if (body) {
15      return false;
16    } else {
17      body = true;
18      return true;
19    }
20  }
21
22 }
```

Figure 1-19: Beginning to implement the Beetle class. (Part 2 of 2)

Notice that, on lines 9, 14, and 17, we refer to body instead of this.body. Since we refer to fields so often, Java does not require us to explicitly name this. We occasionally need to use this to distinguish a field from a variable or argument with the same name, as on line 8 of Figure 1–15.

To test what we've got so far, we'll need a main() method. As we start to implement this, we realize that we have a hurdle to overcome. We will often need to print out the state of a Beetle instance, both for testing purposes and to let the players know how they are doing. This is going to take more than a few lines of code.

The toString() Method

Whenever we are going to need some nontrivial piece of code more than once, we should think seriously about moving it off into a separate encapsulated component. In this case, we add a method toString() to the Beetle class. This method returns a String representation of the current state of the Beetle, which can then be printed.

What should the toString() method return? We could just print out the value of each field, so a complete Beetle would be displayed like this:

```
body: true
eyes: 2
feelers: 2
head: true
legs: 6
tail: true
```

It would be much more entertaining to give a visual representation:

```
\ /
o0o
-#-
-#-
-#-
 v
```

Encapsulation gives us the freedom to put off this decision. We could implement the first version (which is easier) and later, time permitting, come back and write the second version. Since the description of the method's behavior ("print a text representation of this Beetle") hasn't changed, changing the code for this method won't break anything in the rest of the program.

If we have a variable bug referring to an instance of Beetle, we can print it with the statement:

```
System.out.println(bug.toString());
```

Since writing toString() methods is so common, the println() method allows us to simplify this to:

```
System.out.println(bug);
```

Java's built-in string concatenation operator + has the same property, so we can say something like:

```
System.out.println("The beetle looks like this:\n" + bug);
```

The fancy implementation of the toString() method for the Beetle class is shown in Figure 1–20. Since the description of the toString() method in any class is *always*, "Return a String representation of this object," we take the liberty of omitting the comment.

```
1 public String toString() {
2   if (body) {
3     String result = "";
4     if (feelers > 0) {
5       result += "\\";
6       if (feelers == 2) {
7         result += " /";
8       }
9       result += "\n";
10    }
11    if (head) {
12      if (eyes > 0) {
13        result += "o";
14      } else {
15        result += " ";
16      }
17      result += "O";
18      if (eyes == 2) { result += "o"; }
19      result += "\n";
20    }
```

Figure 1–20: The toString() method for the Beetle class returns a String representation of the instance. (Part 1 of 2)

```
21    if (legs > 0) {
22       result += "-";
23    } else {
24       result += " ";
25    }
26    result += "#";
27    if (legs > 1) {
28       result += "-";
29    }
30    result += "\n";
31    if (legs > 2) {
32       result += "-";
33    } else {
34       result += " ";
35    }
36    result += "#";
37    if (legs > 3) {
38       result += "-";
39    }
40    result += "\n";
41    if (legs > 4) {
42       result += "-";
43    } else {
44       result += " ";
45    }
46    result += "#";
47    if (legs > 5) {
48       result += "-";
49    }
50    if (tail) {
51       result += "\n v";
52    }
53    return result;
54  } else {
55    return "(no parts yet)";
56  }
57 }
```

Figure 1-20: The `toString()` method for the Beetle class returns a String representation of the instance. (Part 2 of 2)

We can also add a `toString()` method to the Die class (Figure 1–21). This method takes advantage of the fact that, when we use + to combine a String (in this case an empty String) with an int, Java converts the int to a String.

```
1 public String toString() {
2   return "" + topFace;
3 }
```

Figure 1-21: The toString() method for the Die class.

The rest of the Beetle class is shown in Figure 1–22.

```
1 /** Beetle with parts for the Beetle game. */
2 public class Beetle {
3
4   /** True if this Beetle has a body. */
5   private boolean body;
6
7   /** Number of eyes this Beetle has, from 0-2. */
8   private int eyes;
9
10  /** Number of feelers this Beetle has, from 0-2. */
11  private int feelers;
12
13  /** True if this Beetle has a head. */
14  private boolean head;
15
16  /** Number of legs this Beetle has, from 0-6. */
17  private int legs;
18
19  /** True if this Beetle has a tail. */
20  private boolean tail;
21
22  /** A new Beetle has no parts. */
23  public Beetle() {
24    body = false;
25    eyes = 0;
26    feelers = 0;
27    head = false;
28    legs = 0;
29    tail = false;
30  }
31
32  /** Try to add a body and return whether this succeeded. */
33  public boolean addBody() {
34    if (body) {
35      return false;
36    } else {
37      body = true;
38      return true;
39    }
40  }
```

Figure 1-22: The Beetle class. (Part 1 of 3)

```
41
42   /** Try to add an eye and return whether this succeeded. */
43   public boolean addEye() {
44     if (head && (eyes < 2)) {
45       eyes++;
46       return true;
47     } else {
48       return false;
49     }
50   }
51
52   /** Try to add a head and return whether this succeeded. */
53   public boolean addHead() {
54     if (body && !head) {
55       head = true;
56       return true;
57     } else {
58       return false;
59     }
60   }
61
62   /** Try to add a feeler and return whether this succeeded. */
63   public boolean addFeeler() {
64     if (head && (feelers < 2)) {
65       feelers++;
66       return true;
67     } else {
68       return false;
69     }
70   }
71
72   /** Try to add a leg and return whether this succeeded. */
73   public boolean addLeg() {
74     if (body && (legs < 6)) {
75       legs++;
76       return true;
77     } else {
78       return false;
79     }
80   }
81
```

Figure 1-22: The Beetle class. (Part 2 of 3)

```
82    /** Try to add a tail and return whether this succeeded. */
83    public boolean addTail() {
84      if (body && !tail) {
85        tail = true;
86        return true;
87      } else {
88        return false;
89      }
90    }
91
92    /** Return true if this Beetle has all of its parts. */
93    public boolean isComplete() {
94      return body && (eyes == 2) && (feelers == 2)
95        && head && (legs == 6) && tail;
96    }
97
98    // See Figure 1-20 for the toString() method.
99
100 }
```

Figure 1-22: The Beetle class. (Part 3 of 3)

The BeetleGame Class

We tie everything together with the BeetleGame class. We're certainly going to need a `main()` method, a constructor, and a few fields (Figure 1-23). Since we're going to take input from the user (a command to roll the die), we also need a `java.util.Scanner` (see Appendix A).

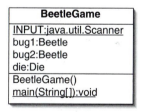

Figure 1-23: Class diagram for BeetleGame. The field `INPUT` is underlined because it is static.

A first draft of the implementation is shown in Figure 1-24.

```
 1 /** The game of Beetle for two players. */
 2 public class BeetleGame {
 3
 4   /** For reading from the console. */
 5   public static final java.util.Scanner INPUT
 6     = new java.util.Scanner(System.in);
 7
 8   /** Player 1's Beetle. */
 9   private Beetle bug1;
10
11   /** Player 2's Beetle. */
12   private Beetle bug2;
13
14   /** A die. */
15   private Die die;
16
17   /** Create the Die and Beetles. */
18   public BeetleGame() {
19     bug1 = new Beetle();
20     bug2 = new Beetle();
21     die = new Die();
22   }
23
24   /** Create the game. */
25   public static void main(String[] args) {
26     System.out.println("Welcome to Beetle.");
27     BeetleGame game = new BeetleGame();
28   }
29
30 }
```

Figure 1–24: First draft of the BeetleGame class.

What is the state of the program after line 27 in the main() method? There is one instance of BeetleGame, called game. This contains references to an instance of Die, called die, and two instances of Beetle, called bug1 and bug2. This is best illustrated by a UML instance diagram (Figure 1–25).

Running the main() method in Figure 1–24 is a (weak) test of the constructor. Satisfied that the program doesn't crash, we do another design phase. What else should an instance of Beetle-Game be able to do? Play itself, of course! We add a play() method and invoke it from main() (Figure 1–26).

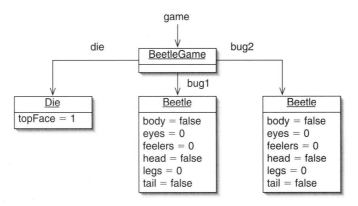

Figure 1–25: Instance diagram of the situation after line 27 in Figure 1–24.

```
1 /** Play until someone wins. */
2 public void play() {
3    int player = 1;
4    Beetle bug = bug1;
5    while (!(bug.isComplete())) {
6      if (!(takeTurn(player, bug))) {
7        if (player == 1) {
8          player = 2;
9          bug = bug2;
10       } else {
11         player = 1;
12         bug = bug1;
13       }
14     }
15   }
16   System.out.println("\nPlayer " + player + " wins!");
17   System.out.println(bug);
18 }
19
20 /** Create and play the game. */
21 public static void main(String[] args) {
22   System.out.println("Welcome to Beetle.");
23   BeetleGame game = new BeetleGame();
24   game.play();
25 }
```

Figure 1–26: The main() method invokes the play() method.

We could have put all of this code directly in the `main()` method, but breaking it into two pieces makes each method shorter and easier to understand. Similarly, the process of taking a single turn is moved off into yet another method, `takeTurn()`, which is invoked on line 6. We'll write that method in a moment.

The main loop of the program, on lines 5–15, runs until the current player's beetle is complete. Within the loop, `takeTurn()` is invoked. If this returns false (because the player did not earn a bonus turn by adding a part to their beetle), the other player becomes the main player. It is necessary to keep track of both the number of the current player (for printing) and the current player's Beetle instance (so that methods can be invoked on it).

A snapshot of the state of the program after one pass through the loop is shown in Figure 1–27.

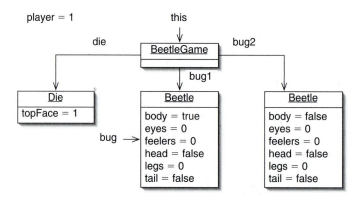

Figure 1–27: Instance diagram of the situation after the first pass through the loop in `play()`. The first player rolled a 1, so the corresponding Beetle now has a body. The BeetleGame instance to which **this** refers is also known as **game**, but that name is visible only inside the `main()` method.

The `takeTurn()` method (Figure 1–28) asks `die` to roll itself and then acts on the result, using a long switch statement. Imagine how long and complicated this method would be if we had not written all of those methods for adding parts in the Beetle class!

```
1 /**
2  * Take a turn for the current player.  Return true if the player
3  * earned a bonus turn.
4  */
5 public boolean takeTurn(int player, Beetle bug) {
6   System.out.println("\nPlayer " + player + ", your beetle:");
7   System.out.println(bug);
8   System.out.print("Hit return to roll: ");
9   INPUT.nextLine();
```

Figure 1–28: The `takeTurn()` method. (Part 1 of 2)

```
10   die.roll();
11   System.out.print("You rolled a " + die.getTopFace());
12   switch (die.getTopFace()) {
13     case 1:
14       System.out.println(" (body)");
15       return bug.addBody();
16     case 2:
17       System.out.println(" (head)");
18       return bug.addHead();
19     case 3:
20       System.out.println(" (leg)");
21       return bug.addLeg();
22     case 4:
23       System.out.println(" (eye)");
24       return bug.addEye();
25     case 5:
26       System.out.println(" (feeler)");
27       return bug.addFeeler();
28     default:
29       System.out.println(" (tail)");
30       return bug.addTail();
31   }
32 }
```

Figure 1-28: The takeTurn() method. (Part 2 of 2)

We are now in a position to test the entire program by compiling and running the BeetleGame class. The first few turns of one game are shown in Figure 1–29. A game usually runs for many turns; we should play it out (probably holding down the return key) to make sure that the program handles the end of the game properly.

The complete structure of our program can be summarized by a UML class diagram (Figure 1–30).

We can generate javadoc documentation for all of our classes with the command:

```
javadoc -public *.java
```

This generates a number of files, including index.html, which contains links to the documentation for each class.

Similar documentation is available, at http://java.sun.com, for all of Java's hundreds of built-in classes. This is called the *application programming interface* or *API*. Any time you can't remember the exact name of some method in a built-in class, the API is a good place to start.

```
 1 Welcome to Beetle.
 2
 3 Player 1, your beetle:
 4 (no parts yet)
 5 Hit return to roll
 6 You rolled a 5 (feeler)
 7
 8 Player 2, your beetle:
 9 (no parts yet)
10 Hit return to roll
11 You rolled a 1 (body)
12
13 Player 2, your beetle:
14   #
15   #
16   #
17 Hit return to roll
18 You rolled a 3 (leg)
19
20 Player 2, your beetle:
21 -#
22   #
23   #
```

Figure 1-29: First few turns of the Beetle game.

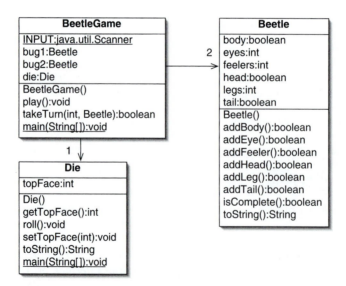

Figure 1-30: UML class diagram for the entire Beetle program.

Exercises

1.10   Add an accessor for each field in the Beetle class.

1.11   Add a mutator for each field in the Beetle class. Use assertions (see Appendix A) to ensure that these mutators cannot be used to put the Beetle into an inconsistent state, such as having legs but no body.

1.12   Write a `main()` method to test the Beetle class.

1.13   Change the type of the `topFace` field in the Die class from int to double. What other modifications do you have to make to the Die class to get it to compile? The Beetle-Game class should run without any modifications when you are finished.

1.14   Remove the `main()` method from the Die class. Does the Die class still compile and run correctly? Does the BeetleGame class still compile and run correctly? Explain.

1.15   At which places in the Die class can we avoid mentioning `this` explicitly?

1.16   Suppose we declare the field `head` in the Beetle class to be public instead of private. We could then replace the line

```
return bug.addHead();
```

in the `takeTurn()` method of BeetleGame (line 18 of Figure 1–28) with:

```
bug.head = true;
return true;
```

What problem is caused by this violation of encapsulation? (Hint: What happens if the first die roll of the game is a 2?)

1.17   Modify the constructor for the BeetleGame class as shown in Figure 1–31. Draw a UML instance diagram, similar to Figure 1–25, showing the situation after line 23 of the `main()` method in Figure 1–26. Does the program still compile and run correctly? Explain.

```
1 /** Create the Die and Beetles. */
2 public BeetleGame() {
3   bug1 = new Beetle();
4   bug2 = bug1;
5   die = new Die();
6 }
```

Figure 1–31: Modified constructor for the BeetleGame class, used in Exercise 1.17.

1.18   Look up the Point class in the Java API. What are the methods and fields of this class? In what way is encapsulation violated?

Summary

Good programs are correct, efficient, general-purpose, and rapidly developed. It is often necessary to make tradeoffs between these desired features. For example, a general-purpose program is usually not as efficient at a particular task as a program that has been optimized for that task. Much of this book, especially after Part I, concerns choosing efficient data structures and algorithms.

Object-oriented programming is a powerful technique for rapidly developing correct, efficient, general-purpose software. It is characterized by three principles: encapsulation, polymorphism, and inheritance. Encapsulation, discussed in this chapter, is the division of a program into distinct components (such as methods and classes) which have limited interaction.

The software development cycle has three phases: design, implementation, and testing. The top-down approach to software development advocates thoroughly designing the entire program before implementing anything, effectively performing only one iteration of the cycle. The bottom-up approach advocates many short iterations of the cycle. Encapsulation allows us to develop each component separately.

One important encapsulated component is a class of objects. An object consists of fields, which hold the current state of the object, and methods, which are actions the object can perform. All objects in a class have the same methods, but their field values may differ. Static methods and fields pertain to the class as a whole rather than to individual instances.

Encapsulation is enforced by information hiding, which prevents external access to the internal details of a component. Specifically, private fields of an object can be accessed only within the object's class. A properly encapsulated object can be accessed only through its methods, which may include accessors and mutators for its fields.

Vocabulary

accessor. Method that returns the value of a field.

algorithm. Step-by-step process for doing something. An algorithm can be expressed as a program.

application programming interface (API). Specification of the behavior of a code library. In this book, "the API" refers to the javadoc documentation for the standard Java libraries.

bottom-up. Software engineering approach where there are many short passes through the development cycle.

class. Description of a set of similar objects.

constructor. Method for initializing a new instance of a class.

correctness. Desired feature of software: that it performs as specified and contains no bugs.

data structure. Way of organizing information in a computer.

default value. Value given to a field which is not initialized. 0 for numeric types, false for booleans, and null for array and object types.

design. Phase of the software development cycle in which the software is designed.

efficiency. Desired feature of software: that it uses no more time or memory than necessary.

encapsulation. Division of a program into distinct components which have limited interaction.

field. Part of an object holding a value, much like a variable. An object's fields represent its current state.

generality. Desired feature of software: that it can be used for a variety of purposes.

getter. Accessor.

implementation. Phase of the software development cycle in which code is actually written.

information hiding. Preventing external access to the details of a software component. Information hiding enforces encapsulation.

inheritance. Ability to specify that a class is similar to another class, delineating only the differences. See Chapter 3.

instance. Individual object in a class. Of a field or method, pertaining to an individual instance, that is, nonstatic.

instance variable. Instance field.

maintenance. Debugging, improvement, and alteration of software after the software is released.

method. Part of an object expressing an algorithm. An object's methods specify what the object can do.

mutator. Method that changes the value of a field.

null. Reference to nothing. Default value for array and object types.

object. Instance of some class.

object-oriented programming. Approach to programming characterized by encapsulation, polymorphism, and inheritance.

optimize. "Fine-tune" software to maximize efficiency under expected conditions.

polymorphism. Ability of the same word or symbol to mean different things in different contexts. See Chapter 2.

private. Accessible only within the current class. See Chapter 3.

problem specification. Precise statement of what a piece of software is supposed to do. Part of the design phase of the software development cycle.

rapid development. Desired feature of software: that it is produced as quickly as possible.

reference. Pointer to a particular object or array. See Chapter 2.

setter. Mutator.

software development cycle. Process of developing software involving three phases: design, implementation, and testing.

software engineering. Study of how to develop correct, efficient, general-purpose programs in a reasonable amount of time.

static. Of a field or method, pertaining to a class as a whole rather than to each instance.

testing. Phase of the software development cycle in which the software is checked for correctness by running it on various inputs.

top-down. Software engineering approach in which there is only one pass through the development cycle.

Unified Modeling Language (UML). Set of notations for diagramming software. See Appendix B.

UML class diagram. Diagram showing the fields and methods of classes, the relationships between classes, or both.

UML instance diagram. Diagram showing the field values of objects (class instances) and any references between them. Variables and arrays may also be shown.

Problems

1.19 In plain English, write an algorithm for making a peanut butter and jelly sandwich. Hand these instructions to a partner, who must then follow them to the letter while misinterpreting their intent as much as possible.

1.20 Write a class to represent a complex number of the form $a + bi$, where i is the imaginary square root of 1. The constructor should accept two doubles as arguments: the real part a and the imaginary part b. Use an assertion in the constructor to ensure that both of these numbers are positive. The methods you must provide are summarized in Figure 1–32. You may want to include others, such as a `main()` method for testing. One good test is to create the number $3 + 4i$ and print its magnitude:

```
ComplexNumber x = new ComplexNumber(3, 4);
System.out.println(x.getMagnitude());
```

This should print 5.0.

Hint: The built-in Math class contains static methods `sqrt()` (to find a square root) and `atan()` (to find an arctangent).

1.21   Repeat Problem 1.20, but with fields `angle` and `magnitude` instead of `imaginary-Part` and `realPart`. Your new class should behave exactly the same as the previous one.

1.22   Rewrite the `takeTurn()` method from BeetleGame (Figure 1–28) using if statements instead of a switch statement. Discuss which version is easier to understand.

1.23   Modify the BeetleGame program so that it handles three players.

ComplexNumber
imaginaryPart:double realPart:double
ComplexNumber(double,double) add(ComplexNumber):ComplexNumber getAngle():double getImaginaryPart():double getMagnitude():double getRealPart():double

Figure 1–32: UML class diagram for the ComplexNumber class in Exercise 1.20.

Projects

1.24   Implement the game of Craps (Figure 1–33). You do not need to modify the Die class to do this.

Craps

Players: 1

Play: Declare how much money you wish to bet, then roll two dice. If the sum is 7 or 11, you win the amount you bet. If the sum is 2, 3, or 12, you lose this amount. Otherwise, the sum is your point. Roll until either you roll your point again (in which case you win) or you roll a 7 (in which case you lose).

For simplicity, the various side bets involved in the casino version of craps are omitted here.

Figure 1–33: Craps is a traditional dice game of pure luck.

1.25   Implement the game of Pennywise (Figure 1–34). Your implementation has to handle only two players. (Hint: Create a CoinSet class, which keeps track of the number of pennies, nickels, dimes, and quarters a player has. Another instance of this class can be used to keep track of what's in the pot.)

Pennywise

Players: 2–6

Object: To be the last player with any coins.

Setup: Each player starts with four pennies, three nickels, two dimes, and a quarter. The pot is empty at the beginning of the game.

Play: On your turn, put one of your coins into the pot. You may then take change from the pot, up to one cent less than the value of the coin you played. For example, if you put in a dime, you may take out up to nine cents worth of coins.

Figure 1-34: Pennywise is a game of pure skill designed by James Ernest. Used with permission of the designer.

2

Polymorphism

This chapter discusses polymorphism, the second principle of object-oriented programming. Polymorphism is the ability for a word or symbol to mean different things in different contexts.

In Section 2.1, we explore references. References allow for polymorphic types—that is, types of variables which can hold more than one kind of value. In the context of checking for equality of such variables, we introduce the Object type, which can hold *almost* anything. Some details about primitive types and Strings are also pointed out.

Arrays are particularly interesting reference types. Section 2.2 deals with arrays, including multidimensional arrays. The game of Domineering is presented as an example.

Interfaces, which specify the behavior of a class without getting into the details of its implementation, are covered in Section 2.3. An interface is also a polymorphic type.

Section 2.4 discusses overloading, the ability of a method name to mean different things depending on the types of its arguments.

2.1 Reference Types

Java has eight primitive types. Only four of these are commonly used: boolean, char, double, and int. The other four are byte, float, long, and short. A variable (or field or argument) of a primitive type holds its value directly. In other words, if we declare

```
int x;
```

then Java sets aside a certain amount of memory to hold the bits of this number. When we ask for the value of x, Java simply looks in this location.

All other types, including array types and object types, are ***reference types***. A variable of a reference type holds a reference to an array or object. If we declare

```
int[] numbers;
```

then Java *can't* set aside enough memory to hold the array, because we haven't specified how big the array is. Instead, Java sets aside enough memory to hold the reference, which is the address of *another* location in memory. Later, when we actually create the array, this reference is altered to point to the array's location. This ability of the variable numbers to refer sometimes to an array of 10 ints and sometimes to an array of 100 ints is an example of polymorphism.

Similarly, if we declare

```
Beetle bug;
```

then Java sets aside enough memory for a reference. When we initialize the variable with

```
bug = new Beetle();
```

the reference is set to point to this new instance.

The assiduous reader may think, "Okay, I see the need for references when using arrays, but why is it necessary with objects? Don't all Beetles take up exactly the same amount of memory?"

Surprisingly, the answer is, "not necessarily"—more on that later. In the meantime, consider what happens when we pass an object as an argument to a method. We did this in the takeTurn() method of the BeetleGame class (Figure 1–28). If we didn't use a reference, we would have to copy all of the fields of the Beetle in question into the area of memory set aside for the argument bug. Not only would this waste time, but any methods invoked on bug would affect the copy instead of the original!

Most of the time, the distinction between "the variable v contains something" and "the variable v contains *a reference to* something" is unimportant. There are, however, a few things to watch out for.

Null

As mentioned in Chapter 1, the default value of a field with a reference type is null. Null is a reference to nothing in particular. We must be careful never to follow a null reference. For example, we cannot invoke a method on null. If we try to do so, our program will crash with an error message like this:

```
Exception in thread "main" java.lang.NullPointerException
```

(***Pointer*** is just another word for reference, as is ***link***.) This message is often a sign that we have forgotten to initialize one of our fields.

References and Equality

Suppose we have rolled two dice and want to determine if we rolled doubles. In other words, we want to know if the dice are equal. What does it mean for two Die instances to be equal? The answer is not as simple as it appears.

Suppose we evaluate the code in Figure 2–1. The resulting situation is shown in Figure 2–2.

```
1 Die die1 = new Die();
2 Die die2 = die1;
3 Die die3 = new Die();
```

Figure 2–1: Code producing the situation in Figure 2–2.

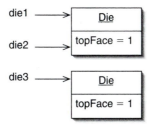

Figure 2–2: UML instance diagram of the situation after executing the code in Figure 2–1.

The variables `die1` and `die2` are equal in a strong sense: they are references to the same object. The variables `die2` and `die3` are equal in a weaker sense: they are references to two different objects which happen to be identical.

The == operator checks for equality in the strong sense. Thus,

`die1 == die2`

is true, but

`die2 == die3`

is false.

If we want to check whether two objects are identical, we have to check the fields. In this example,

`die2.getTopFace() == die3.getTopFace()`

is true.

This is all well and good for the Die class, but what about a more complicated class like Beetle? We would have to compare six different fields every time we wanted to see if two Beetles were identical. This sort of work should be done in a method of the Beetle class.

The method to do this checking is always called `equals()`. In our example,

```
die2.equals(die3)
```

is true. We will write the `equals()` method for the Die class in a moment.

The Polymorphic Type Object

The `equals()` method takes one argument. For reasons that will be explained in Chapter 3, the type of this argument must always be Object. A variable of type Object can hold a reference to an instance of *any* class or even to an array. For example, it is perfectly legal to say:

```
Object it;
it = new Beetle();
it = new double[10];
it = new Die();
```

Because a variable of type Object can hold a reference to any of a wide variety of things, Object is called a ***polymorphic type***. A polymorphic type must be a reference type, because it is not clear when the variable is declared how much memory will be needed to hold the value to which it will refer.

It is important to distinguish between the *type of a variable* and the actual *class of the instance* to which it refers. These might be the same, but with a polymorphic type they might not. Java can't tell, at compile time, what methods are available for `it`. If we want to invoke a method on `it`, we generally have to cast the value to a specific class:

```
((Die)it).roll();
```

There are a few things we can do with an Object without casting. These are explained in Chapter 3.

Returning to `equals()`, a first shot at writing the method for the Die class is shown in Figure 2–3.

```
1 /** Return true if that Die has the same top face as this one. */
2 public boolean equals(Object that) {
3   return topFace == ((Die)that).topFace;
4 }
```

Figure 2-3: This version of `equals()` is not good enough.

This seems reasonable enough, but there are some problems.

- If `this` == `that`, we should return `true` immediately. If there are a lot of fields, this can save considerable time.

- If `that` is `null`, we should return `false` immediately rather than trying to follow the null reference.

- The argument `that` might not be an instance of the same class as `this`. In this case, we should return `false` immediately.

A more robust version of the method is given in Figure 2–4. This makes use of the method `get-Class()`, which can be invoked on any Object. It returns a representation of Object's class. Two instances of the same class return the same representation, so

```
a.getClass() == b.getClass()
```

exactly when a and b are instances of the same class.

```
1 /** Return true if that Die has the same top face as this one. */
2 public boolean equals(Object that) {
3   if (this == that) {
4     return true;
5   }
6   if (that == null) {
7     return false;
8   }
9   if (getClass() != that.getClass()) {
10     return false;
11   }
12   Die thatDie = (Die)that;
13   return topFace == thatDie.topFace;
14 }
```

Figure 2-4: A much better version of `equals()`. Only the parts in bold (and the comment) need to change from one class to another.

For other classes, the `equals()` method looks almost identical. Figure 2–5 shows the method for the Beetle class.

Primitives and Wrappers

A variable of type Object can hold any object or array, but it can't hold a value of a primitive type. This appears to present a problem: what if we've created a general-purpose data structure to hold Objects, and we want to put integers in it?

To deal with this situation, Java provides a **_wrapper class_** for each of the primitive types. The wrapper classes are Boolean, Byte, Character, Double, Float, Integer, Long, and Short. The upper-case letter at the beginning of each class name helps distinguish it from the corresponding primitive type.

If we want to store a primitive value in a variable of type Object, we can first wrap it in a new instance of the appropriate class:

```
Object number = new Integer(23);
```

Each wrapper class has a method to extract the original primitive value. For example, the method in the Integer class is `intValue()`. Of course, for a variable of type Object, we must first cast the reference to an Integer before we can use this method.

```
 1 /** Return true if that Beetle has the same parts as this one. */
 2 public boolean equals(Object that) {
 3   if (this == that) {
 4     return true;
 5   }
 6   if (that == null) {
 7     return false;
 8   }
 9   if (getClass() != that.getClass()) {
10     return false;
11   }
12   Beetle thatBeetle = (Beetle)that;
13   return body == thatBeetle.body
14     && eyes == thatBeetle.eyes
15     && feelers == thatBeetle.feelers
16     && head == thatBeetle.head
17     && legs == thatBeetle.legs
18     && tail == thatBeetle.tail;
19 }
```

Figure 2-5: The equals() method for the Beetle class.

```
int n = ((Integer)number).intValue();
```

Before Java 1.5, code was often cluttered with wrapping and unwrapping, also called *boxing* and *unboxing*. Java is now smart enough to do this automatically, so we can do things like:

```
Object number = 5;
int n = (Integer)number;
```

If the type of number were Integer, we wouldn't even need the cast:

```
Integer number = 5;
int n = number;
```

This makes our code much clearer, but we should still be aware that boxing and unboxing takes time. A wrapped Integer also uses considerably more memory than a primitive int. The tradeoff here is between generality (writing code once to handle all sorts of Objects) and efficiency (using the primitive types to save time and memory).

In Chapter 4, we will discuss Java's new generic type feature, which provides an even more powerful way to write general-purpose code without casting all over the place.

Strings

We usually want to use equals() instead of == to compare objects. This is especially true for Strings, because Java sometimes reuses Strings.

Suppose we execute this code:

```
String s1 = "weinerdog";
String s2 = "weinerdog";
```

Java creates a single instance of the String class, with s1 and s2 containing references to the *same instance*, so s1 == s2. This saves some space. There is no danger that invoking a method on s1 will alter s2, because Java Strings are *immutable*—their fields cannot change. (There is another class, called StringBuilder, for mutable Strings. We'll discuss that in Chapter 13.)

Unfortunately, Java cannot always tell if two Strings are identical. Specifically, if we execute the code

```
String s3 = "weiner";
s3 += "dog";
```

then s3 refers to an instance which happens to be identical to s1 and s2. Thus, while s1.equals(s3), it is not true that s1 == s3.

Because the behavior of == is difficult to predict when Strings are involved, we should always use equals() to compare Strings.

Exercises

2.1   Is int a polymorphic type? Explain.

2.2   How could we convert the String "25" into the primitive int 25? (Hint: Look up the Integer class in the API.)

2.3   Is it ever necessary to assert that this != null? Explain.

2.4   Suppose we have two Die variables d1 and d2. Can the method invocation d1.roll() affect the state of d2 if d1 == d2? What if d1 != d2?

2.5   If two objects are equal in the sense of ==, are they automatically equal in the sense of equals()? What about vice versa?

2.6   Suppose we have two references, foo and bar. After evaluating the statement

```
foo = bar;
```

is it definitely true, possibly true, or definitely false that foo == bar? What about foo.equals(bar)?

2.7   Through experimentation, determine whether equals() can be used to compare arrays.

2.8   The robust equals() method in Figure 2–5 will produce the same output if lines 3–5 are omitted. What is the point of these lines?

2.9   Write an equals() method for the complex number class you wrote in Problem 1.20.

2.2 Arrays

Declaration, Allocation, and Initialization

Before it can be used, a variable must be both declared (to specify its type) and initialized (to give it an initial value). For a variable of an array type, there are *three* steps we must perform: declaration, allocation, and initialization. First, we must declare the variable. For example:

```
int[] nums;
```

The second step is to ***allocate*** space for the array. We have to tell Java how many elements the array will have so that it can set aside the appropriate amount of memory. The syntax for allocation uses the keyword new:

```
nums = new int[4];
```

The array now exists, but the elements themselves have not yet been initialized. They have default values—in this case, they are all 0. We often use a for loop to initialize the elements:

```
for (int i = 0; i < nums.length; i++) {
  nums[i] = i * 2;
}
```

The effects of these steps are summarized in Figure 2–6.

We can perform all three of these steps in a single statement by explicitly supplying the values of the array elements. This is reasonable only for relatively short arrays:

```
int[] nums = new int[] {0, 2, 4, 6};
```

The ability of a variable of an array type to hold an array of any size is another example of polymorphism.

Multidimensional Arrays

We can declare an array of anything. An array of Die objects would be declared like this:

```
Die[] dice;
```

An array of ints would be declared like this:

```
int[] nums;
```

We can even declare an array of *arrays of ints*, like this:

```
int[][] rows;
```

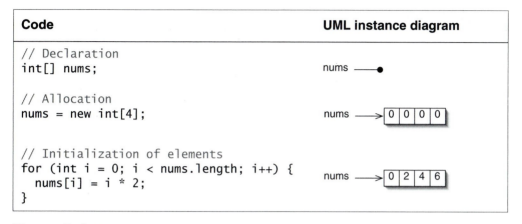

Code	UML instance diagram
```// Declaration``` ```int[] nums;```	nums
```// Allocation``` ```nums = new int[4];```	nums → 0 0 0 0

```// Initialization of elements```
```for (int i = 0; i < nums.length; i++) {```
``` nums[i] = i * 2;```
```}```
	nums → 0 2 4 6

Figure 2-6: Declaration, allocation, and initialization of an array variable. In the first diagram, the line ending in a dot indicates a null reference.

An array of arrays is called a ***multidimensional array***. Specifically, rows is a two-dimensional array, analogous to a Chess board. If we allocate rows with the statement

```
rows = new int[3][4];
```

then we get the data structure shown in Figure 2–7.

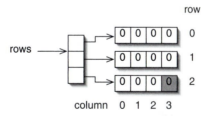

Figure 2-7: Instance diagram showing a two-dimensional array. The shaded element is rows[2][3].

The array rows is said to have ***dimensionality*** 2, because we have to specify two indices to get at a particular element. The ***dimensions*** of the array are 3 (the number of rows) and 4 (the number of columns).

While it would be difficult to draw, we could declare and allocate an array of dimensionality 4:

```
int[][][][] tesseract = new int[2][5][4][3];
```

This array has dimensions 2, 5, 4, and 3. It is rare to see dimensionalities greater than 3, because such arrays quickly become impractically large. Even `tesseract` has 120 elements!

This array-of-arrays representation allows for several interesting tricks. If we supply only one index for `rows`, we get a reference to a single row of the array. For example, if we say

```
int[] middleRow = rows[1];
```

we get the situation in Figure 2–8.

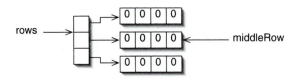

Figure 2-8: A reference to a single row of a two-dimensional array.

We can also allocate an array one part at a time. For example,

```
int[][] rows = new int[3][];
```

allocates the *spine* of the array, but not any of the rows. Since the elements of this array are references, they get the default value `null`. This is shown in Figure 2–9.

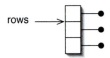

Figure 2-9: A two-dimensional array with only the spine allocated.

Now we can allocate the first row with

```
rows[0] = new int[4];
```

giving the situation shown in Figure 2–10.

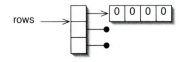

Figure 2-10: A two-dimensional array with the first row allocated.

There is no reason the other rows have to have the same length. If we now allocate

```
rows[1] = new int[2];
rows[2] = new int[3];
```

we get a ***ragged array***, as shown in Figure 2–11.

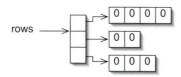

Figure 2–11: In a ragged array, different rows have different lengths.

Example: Domineering

To illustrate the use of arrays, we now write a program to let two people play the game of Domineering (Figure 2–12).

Domineering

Players: 2, one playing horizontally and one vertically.

Object: To be the last player with a legal move.

Board: The board is an 8 × 8 square grid, as in Chess or Checkers. It is initially empty.

Play: On a turn, a player places a domino on the board to occupy two adjacent squares. One player places his dominoes horizontally (east-west), the other vertically (north-south). The dots on the dominoes are ignored, but a domino cannot overlap any previously played dominoes.

Figure 2–12: The game of Domineering, also known as Crosscram, was invented by Göran Andersson.

What classes will we need? An initial sketch (Figure 2–13) suggests that we'll need a Domineering object, one Board object, and a number of Domino objects.

Further thought reveals that this is overkill. While Domineering involves dominoes, they don't have any interesting state. We don't even care what numbers are on them. All they do is take up space on the board. As long as we keep track of which board squares are occupied, we don't really need a Domino class for this game.

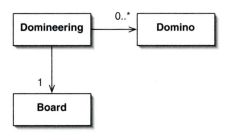

Figure 2-13: This UML class diagram says that a Domineering object is associated with one Board object and 0 to many Domino objects. The asterisk denotes "many." Our actual program will *not* have this structure.

In fact, the board is such a simple thing that we can represent it with a two-dimensional array of booleans. An individual element is true if that square is occupied. We can implement Domineering with a single class (Figure 2–14).

Domineering
INPUT:java.util.Scanner HORIZONTAL:boolean = false VERTICAL:boolean = true squares:boolean[][]
Domineering() getSquare(int,int):boolean hasLegalMoveFor(boolean):boolean play():void playAt(int,int,boolean):void setSquare(int,int,boolean):void toString():String main(String[]):void

Figure 2-14: The Domineering game can be implemented with a single class. As always, static fields and methods are underlined. It is not yet obvious what all of the fields and methods are for, but we show them here for completeness.

The field `squares`, the constructor, and the `main()` method are shown in Figure 2–15.

After allocating `squares`, we could have initialized the elements with the code

```
for (int row = 0; row < 8; row++) {
  for (int column = 0; column < 8; column++) {
    squares[row][column] = false;
  }
}
```

but, since false is the default value for booleans, we don't have to do this.

```
 1 /** The game of Domineering. */
 2 public class Domineering {
 3
 4   /** Array of board squares, true if occupied. */
 5   private boolean[][] squares;
 6
 7   /** The board is initially empty. */
 8   public Domineering() {
 9     squares = new boolean[8][8];
10     // Java initializes all array elements to false
11   }
12
13   /** Create and play the game. */
14   public static void main(String[] args) {
15     System.out.println("Welcome to Domineering.");
16     Domineering game = new Domineering();
17     game.play();
18   }
19
20 }
```

Figure 2–15: A field, constructor, and `main()` method for Domineering.

The `toString()` method (Figure 2–16) uses nested `for` loops.

```
 1 public String toString() {
 2   String result = "   0 1 2 3 4 5 6 7";
 3   for (int row = 0; row < 8; row++) {
 4     result += "\n" + row;
 5     for (int column = 0; column < 8; column++) {
 6       if (squares[row][column]) {
 7         result += " #";
 8       } else {
 9         result += " .";
10       }
11     }
12   }
13   return result;
14 }
```

Figure 2–16: The `toString()` method uses nested `for` loops.

Figure 2–17 shows a String the method might return for a board where one horizontal and one vertical domino have been placed.

As in BeetleGame, the `play()` method contains a loop which repeats until the game is over. This method must keep track of who the current player is. Rather than numbering the players and trying to remember which one plays horizontally and which one vertically, we define two

```
 1    0 1 2 3 4 5 6 7
 2 0  . # . . . . . .
 3 1  . # . . . . . .
 4 2  . . . . . . . .
 5 3  . . . . . . . .
 6 4  . . . . . . . .
 7 5  . . . . . # # .
 8 6  . . . . . . . .
 9 7  . . . . . . . .
```

Figure 2-17: Typical output of the `toString()` method.

constants HORIZONTAL and VERTICAL. This makes the code easier to read. Since there are only two choices, we can use the boolean values `false` and `true` for these constants.

An added advantage of this representation is that we can switch players with the simple statement:

`player = !player;`

The `play()` method and these constants are shown in Figure 2–18.

```
 1 /** For reading from the console. */
 2 public static final java.util.Scanner INPUT
 3   = new java.util.Scanner(System.in);
 4
 5 /** The player who plays their dominoes horizontally. */
 6 public static final boolean HORIZONTAL = false;
 7
 8 /** The player who plays their dominoes vertically. */
 9 public static final boolean VERTICAL = true;
10
11 /** Play until someone wins. */
12 public void play() {
13   boolean player = HORIZONTAL;
14   while (true) {
15     System.out.println("\n" + this);
16     if (player == HORIZONTAL) {
17       System.out.println("Horizontal to play");
18     } else {
19       System.out.println("Vertical to play");
20     }
21     if (!(hasLegalMoveFor(player))) {
22       System.out.println("No legal moves -- you lose!");
23       return;
24     }
```

Figure 2-18: The `play()` method and associated constants. On line 15, we want to print a blank line above the diagram of the board. We do this by adding the newline String "\n" to `this` (which is implicitly `this.toString()`) and passing the result to `System.out.println()`. (Part 1 of 2)

```
25      System.out.print("Row: ");
26      int row = INPUT.nextInt();
27      System.out.print("Column: ");
28      int column = INPUT.nextInt();
29      playAt(row, column, player);
30      player = !player;
31   }
32 }
```

Figure 2-18: The play() method and associated constants. On line 15, we want to print a blank line above the diagram of the board. We do this by adding the newline String "\n" to this (which is implicitly this.toString()) and passing the result to System.out.println(). (Part 2 of 2)

The play() method invokes two other methods, hasLegalMoveFor() and playAt(). The first determines if there is any legal move left for the current player—if not, the game is over. The second actually updates the array squares.

We present playAt() first, as it is simpler. This method (Figure 2–19) sets two elements of squares to true.

```
1 /**
2  * Play a domino with its upper left corner at row, column.
3  */
4 public void playAt(int row, int column, boolean player) {
5    squares[row][column] = true;
6    if (player == HORIZONTAL) {
7      squares[row][column + 1] = true;
8    } else {
9      squares[row + 1][column] = true;
10   }
11 }
```

Figure 2-19: The playAt() method actually modifies the elements of squares. Two elements are modified: one in line 5 and one in either line 7 or line 9.

The hasLegalMoveFor() method is more complicated, because it has to act slightly differently depending on the current player. If it is looking for horizontal moves, it has to check rows 0 through 7 and columns 0 through 6, making sure that both

squares[row][column]

and

squares[*row*][*column + 1*]

are unoccupied. On the other hand, when looking for vertical moves, it has to check rows 0 through 6 and columns 0 through 7, making sure that both

```
squares[row][column]
```

and

```
squares[row + 1][column]
```

are unoccupied. Rather than write loops for each of these very similar cases, we write the loops once, using variables `rowOffset` and `columnOffset` to control which version we use. Thus, the second square we check is:

```
squares[row + rowOffset][column + columnOffset]
```

If `player` is HORIZONTAL, rowOffset is 0 and `columnOffset` is 1. If `player` is VERTICAL, rowOffset is 1 and `columnOffset` is 0.

These variables are also used in the termination tests in the `for` loops. The `hasLegalMove-For()` method is shown in Figure 2–20.

```
1 /**
2  * Return true if there is a legal move for the specified player.
3  */
4 public boolean hasLegalMoveFor(boolean player) {
5    int rowOffset = 0;
6    int columnOffset = 0;
7    if (player == HORIZONTAL) {
8      columnOffset = 1;
9    } else {
10     rowOffset = 1;
11   }
12   for (int row = 0; row < (8 - rowOffset); row++) {
13     for (int column = 0; column < (8 - columnOffset); column++) {
14       if (!(squares[row][column]
15            || squares[row + rowOffset][column + columnOffset])) {
16         return true;
17       }
18     }
19   }
20   return false;
21 }
```

Figure 2-20: The exact behavior of the nested `for` loop in lines 12–19 of `hasLegalMoveFor()` is controlled by the variables `rowOffset` and `columnOffset`.

We conclude the example with testing. The first few turns of a game of Domineering are shown in Figure 2–21.

```
1 Welcome to Domineering.
2
3   0 1 2 3 4 5 6 7
4 0 . . . . . . . .
5 1 . . . . . . . .
6 2 . . . . . . . .
7 3 . . . . . . . .
8 4 . . . . . . . .
9 5 . . . . . . . .
10 6 . . . . . . . .
11 7 . . . . . . . .
12 Horizontal to play
13 Row: 1
14 Column: 0
15
16   0 1 2 3 4 5 6 7
17 0 . . . . . . . .
18 1 # # . . . . . .
19 2 . . . . . . . .
20 3 . . . . . . . .
21 4 . . . . . . . .
22 5 . . . . . . . .
23 6 . . . . . . . .
24 7 . . . . . . . .
25 Vertical to play
26 Row: 5
27 Column: 6
28
29   0 1 2 3 4 5 6 7
30 0 . . . . . . . .
31 1 # # . . . . . .
32 2 . . . . . . . .
33 3 . . . . . . . .
34 4 . . . . . . . .
35 5 . . . . . . # .
36 6 . . . . . . # .
37 7 . . . . . . . .
38 Horizontal to play
```

Figure 2-21: Beginning a game of Domineering. Text typed by the user is in grey.

Exercises

2.10   Draw a UML instance diagram of the situation after evaluating the code below.

```
int[] arr = new int[6];
int[] avast = new int[6];
int[] shiverMeTimbers = arr;
int[] yoHoHo;
arr[2] = 5;
avast[3] = 8;
```

2.11   Draw a UML instance diagram of the data structure produced by the code below.

```
int[][] triangle = new int[][] {{1, 2, 3}, {4, 5}, {6}};
```

2.12   Suppose we need to store a table of distances between cities, as found in a road atlas. One obvious approach would be to use a square array `distances`, where `distances[i][j]` is the distance between city `i` and city `j`. Explain how to use a ragged array to cut the amount of memory needed for this data structure roughly in half.

2.13   If the array `arr` has dimensions 3 and 7, what is `arr.length`?

2.14   Is the statement below legal? Explain.

```
Object[] ref = new int[10][10];
```

2.15   Arrays are not objects, so we can't invoke methods on them. This can make it awkward to, for example, test two arrays for equality. The built-in java.util.Arrays class provides several static methods that work on arrays. Look this class up in the API. Explain the difference between the `equals()` and `deepEquals()` methods and between the `toString()` and `deepToString()` methods. (If you use it in code, you must refer to the Arrays class as java.util.Arrays, for reasons explained in Chapter 3.)

2.16   Draw a UML instance diagram of the data structures that exist just before exiting the `main()` method in Figure 2–22.

```
1 public static void main(String[] args) {
2   int[][] numbers = new int[5][];
3   int[] row = new int[] {0, 1, 2, 3};
4   for (int i = 0; i < numbers.length; i++) {
5     numbers[i] = row;
6   }
7 }
```

Figure 2-22: Code for Exercise 2.16.

2.17   Suppose we provided an accessor `getSquares()` for the Domineering class. A method in another class, given an instance `game`, might do this:

```
game.getSquares()[2][5] = true;
```

Discuss whether this violates encapsulation.

2.18   As written, the Domineering program does not verify that a player has chosen a valid location. A player may place a domino so that it overlaps an existing one. Also, if the player places a domino so that part of it is off the board, the program will crash. Modify the program to fix both these problems. (If the player enters invalid coordinates, give her a chance to enter valid ones.)

2.19   Domineering is normally played on an 8 × 8 board, but there is no reason it couldn't be played on a 4 × 4 or 10 × 10 board. Modify the program to allow the user to specify the board size. You will need to eliminate all mention of the magic number 8 from the program. (Hint: Instead of storing the board size in a separate field, you can simply use `squares.length`.)

2.3 Interfaces

An *interface* is a very similar to a class, except that (a) it contains no fields, and (b) its methods have no bodies. In other words, it specifies how a class *behaves* (what methods it provides) without commenting on how the class is *implemented*. An example of an interface, to represent a domino, is given in Figure 2–23. (We didn't need to represent dominoes in this much detail in Domineering, but this might be useful in other games.)

```
1  /** A domino. */
2  public interface Domino {
3
4      /** Swap the left and right numbers on the Domino. */
5      public void flip();
6
7      /** Return the number on the left side of the Domino. */
8      public int getLeft();
9
10     /** Return the number on the right side of the Domino. */
11     public int getRight();
12
13 }
```

Figure 2-23: In an interface, there are no fields or method bodies.

A class which provides methods with these signatures can be said to *implement* the interface. The FieldDomino class (Figure 2–24) implements the Domino interface. Beware of the potential confusion between this Java-specific meaning of the word "implement" and its more general meaning of "provide code for," as in, "Implement this algorithm."

It is okay to leave off comments for the methods specified in the interface—javadoc is smart enough to copy them from the interface. Indeed, putting the comment in only one place (the interface) reduces the chance that inconsistent comments will appear.

It is possible for more than one class to implement the same interface. The ArrayDomino class (Figure 2–25) represents a domino in a different way. It is also possible for a class to implement

```
1 /** A domino. */
2 public class FieldDomino implements Domino {
3
4   /** The number on the left end of the Domino. */
5   private int left;
6
7   /** The number on the right end of the Domino. */
8   private int right;
9
10  /** Initialize the left and right numbers on the Domino. */
11  public FieldDomino(int left, int right) {
12    this.left = left;
13    this.right = right;
14  }
15
16  public void flip() {
17    int swap = left;
18    left = right;
19    right = swap;
20  }
21
22  public int getLeft() {
23    return left;
24  }
25
26  public int getRight() {
27    return right;
28  }
29
30  public String toString() {
31    return left + "-" + right;
32  }
33
34 }
```

Figure 2-24: The FieldDomino class uses two fields to hold the left and right numbers on the domino.

more than one interface, as long as it provides all of the methods specified by each of those interfaces.

Domino is a polymorphic type, which can hold a reference to an instance of any class which implements the Domino interface. Thus, if we declare a variable

```
Domino bone;
```

we can say either

```
bone = new FieldDomino(2, 3);
```

```
1 /** A domino. */
2 public class ArrayDomino implements Domino {
3
4   /** The numbers on the Domino. */
5   int[] numbers;
6
7   /** Index of the left number.  The other is the right number. */
8   int leftIndex;
9
10  /** Initialize the left and right numbers on the Domino. */
11  public ArrayDomino(int left, int right) {
12    numbers = new int[] {left, right};
13    leftIndex = 0;
14  }
15
16  public void flip() {
17    leftIndex = 1 - leftIndex;
18  }
19
20  public int getLeft() {
21    return numbers[leftIndex];
22  }
23
24  public int getRight() {
25    return numbers[1 - leftIndex];
26  }
27
28  public String toString() {
29    return numbers[leftIndex] + "-" + numbers[1 - leftIndex];
30  }
31
32 }
```

Figure 2-25: The ArrayDomino class uses an array of two ints instead of two int fields.

or:

```
bone = new ArrayDomino(2, 3);
```

The relationship between the Domino interface and the FieldDomino and ArrayDomino classes is shown in Figure 2–26. It is not necessary to list the interface methods in the boxes for the classes.

An interface used to specify all of the important methods of any implementing class is sometimes called an *abstract data type* or *ADT*. If you are going to write a class involving variables of

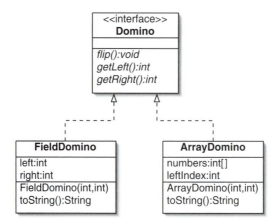

Figure 2-26: UML class diagram showing the relationship between the Domino interface and the FieldDomino and ArrayDomino classes. The dashed, hollow-headed arrows say that both classes implement the interface. The methods in the Domino interface are in italic to emphasize that they are only required, not provided, by the interface.

type Domino and I am going to write an implementation of the Domino interface, we can start by writing the ADT. As long as I provide the required methods and you do not expect any others, our classes will work together perfectly when they are done.

Many software engineers argue that a class implementing an abstract data type should provide *only* the methods required by the interface. (There are a few exceptions: constructors, nonpublic methods, common methods like `toString()`, and `main()` methods for testing.) If an implementation provides some other public method (say, `isDoublet()` to determine if both numbers on a Domino are the same), any code which takes advantage of this method will break if we switch to a different implementation which does not provide it.

There are other uses for interfaces besides specifying abstract data types. For example, the Comparable interface (Chapter 8) is used to specify that an object can be compared to other instances of its class. Since Comparable is a polymorphic type, it is possible to write one sorting method which works on any array of Comparables. The interface requires only one method, `compareTo()`, but nobody would expect a class to have only this method. Classes such as Integer and String are designed for other purposes and also implement Comparable.

Exercises

2.20   Draw UML instance diagrams of the objects created by the expressions

```
new FieldDomino(0, 6)
```

and

```
new ArrayDomino(0, 6)
```

2.21   Through experimentation, determine whether we have to say `implements Domino` at the top of FieldDomino in order to make (a reference to) an instance of FieldDomino a legitimate value for a variable of type Domino. Is it enough to supply methods with the correct signatures?

2.22   Discuss whether it makes sense for an interface to implement another interface. How about a class implementing another class?

2.23   Through experimentation, determine whether, when a class provides a method required by an interface, the argument names in the class have to match those in the interface.

2.24   Discuss whether it makes sense for an interface to include a constructor.

2.4 Overloading

Interfaces, the Object type, and array types are polymorphic types. A different kind of polymorphism is *overloading*: the ability of a method to do different things depending on the types of its arguments.

In Java, the + operator is overloaded. When given numeric arguments, it performs addition. When given Strings, it performs concatenation.

It is acceptable to have two different methods in the same class with the same name as long as their signatures specify different argument types. For example, in the Domineering class, we could have called the `playAt()` method `play()`, giving it the signature:

```
public void play(int row, int column, boolean player)
```

This is acceptable because the sequence of argument types is different from that in the existing method with the signature

```
public void play()
```

which happens to take no arguments whatsoever. When we invoke an overloaded method, Java figures out which version we mean, based on the number and types of arguments we provide.

We should not overload a method so that the same arguments would be acceptable to two different versions. For example, we should not declare one method with the signature

```
public void zorch(Object it)
```

and another with the signature

```
public void zorch(Beetle it)
```

because either one would be legitimate if we passed in an argument of type Beetle. The compiler will not complain if we overload a method like this, but it can lead to unexpected behavior (see Problem 2.29).

The value of overloading is that it reduces the number of method names we have to keep track of. For example, if we have a class to represent a matrix, we might want methods to multiply by another matrix, by a vector, and by a scalar. Without overloading, these would have to have the signatures:

```
public Matrix timesMatrix(Matrix m)
public Vector timesVector(Vector v)
public Matrix timesScalar(double s)
```

With overloading, we can just use one, shorter name:

```
public Matrix times(Matrix m)
public Vector times(Vector v)
public Matrix times(double s)
```

Exercises

2.25   Is it okay for a class to have two methods with the same name as long as their signatures differ in any way? Explain.

2.26   Write a class with two overloaded static methods, one of which takes an int as an argument and one of which takes an Object. Which version is used if the argument is 3? What if it is (Integer)3?

2.27   What is printed by the program in Figure 2–27?

```
 1 public class OverloadExample {
 2
 3   public static double zorch(double x) {
 4     return x / 2;
 5   }
 6
 7   public static double zorch(int x) {
 8     return x * 2;
 9   }
10
11   public static void main(String[] args) {
12     System.out.println(zorch(3));
13     System.out.println(zorch(3.0));
14     System.out.println(zorch(3 + 3.0));
15   }
16
17 }
```

Figure 2-27: A program with an overloaded method, for Exercise 2.27.

Summary

Except for the eight primitive types, all types in Java are reference types. Reference types include array types, class types, the Object type, and interface types. The default value for any reference type is the special value `null`.

Since the `==` operator determines only whether two references are to the exact same object or array, it should not be used to compare reference types. Instead, classes should provide an `equals()` method. This is especially true of Strings, because Java's reuse of Strings makes the behavior of the `==` operator difficult to predict.

A variable of the polymorphic type Object can contain any reference. It is usually necessary to cast the value of such a variable before invoking a method on it. Such a variable cannot hold a primitive value such as an int, but wrapper classes are provided for this purpose. In Java 1.5, this boxing and unboxing is done automatically.

A variable of an array type must be declared, allocated, and initialized before it can be used. Multidimensional arrays are represented as arrays of arrays.

An interface specifies the behavior of a class without commenting on how the class is implemented. An interface can define an abstract data type, so that implementations of the interface can be used interchangeably. Alternately, an interface may just specify a small number of methods, which implementing classes must provide.

An overloaded method is one with several different versions which differ in the number and types of arguments they take. Java uses the arguments passed to the method to determine which version to use.

Vocabulary

abstract data type (ADT). Description of the behavior of a class, but not its inner workings. In Java, interfaces can be abstract data types.

allocate. Set aside memory for. After declaring a variable of an array type, we must allocate space for it before we can initialize its contents.

box. Enclose a primitive value in an instance of the corresponding wrapper class.

dimensionality. Number of dimensions an array has. For example, a flat grid is two-dimensional.

dimensions. Sizes of the rows, columns, etc. of an array.

immutable. Unchangeable. In Java, Strings are immutable.

implement. In Java specifically, provide methods required by an interface. In general, write code for a described algorithm or data structure.

interface. Classlike code file that provides signatures of require methods, but no fields or method bodies.

link. Reference.

multidimensional array. Array of arrays. A common example is a two-dimensional table.

overload. Provide multiple methods in the same class which have the same name, but accept different arguments. Java uses the argument types to determine which version to use.

pointer. Reference.

polymorphic type. Type that can hold more than one kind of value.

ragged array. Multidimensional array where the subarrays (for example, rows) are not all the same size.

reference type. Any type that is not a primitive type. All array and object types are reference types.

spine. In a multidimensional array, the array that contains the subarrays (for example, rows).

unbox. Extract a primitive value from an instance of the corresponding wrapper class.

wrapper class. Class corresponding to one of the eight primitive types. For example, Integer is the wrapper class for ints.

Problems

2.28   Write a class to represent a hotel. Its one field should be a String[ ] holding the name of the person in each hotel room. (All of the rooms are singles.) Provide a method `checkIn()` which accepts a String and an int and puts the named person in the specified room. Use an assertion to verify that the room is not already occupied. Provide a method `checkOut()` to clear a room. Finally, provide a method `isFull()` which returns true if all of the rooms are occupied.

2.29   Write a program which provides two overloaded versions of a method. One takes an argument of type Object, the other an argument of type String. In the `main()` method, declare a variable:

```
Object thing = "this is a String";
```

Through experimentation, determine which version of the overloaded method is used when `thing` is passed as an argument to the overloaded method. In other words, does Java use the *type of the variable* or the *class of the instance* to decide which version of the overloaded method to use? What happens if you pass in `(String)thing`?

Projects

2.30   Write Vector and Matrix classes consistent with Figure 2–28.

2.31   Implement the game of Reversi (Figure 2–29).

Vector
numbers:double[]
Vector(int) dotProduct(Vector):double get(int):double plus(Vector):Vector set(int,double):void times(double):Vector

Matrix
numbers:double[][]
Matrix(int,int) get(int,int):double plus(Matrix):Matrix set(int,int,double):void times(double):Matrix times(Matrix):Matrix times(Vector):Vector

Figure 2-28: UML class diagram of the classes for Exercise 2.30. Since a particular Vector is not associated with a particular Matrix, nor vice versa, there is no arrow connecting the classes.

Reversi

Players: 2, black and white.

Object: To have the most pieces of your color on the board at the end of the game.

Board: The board is an 8 × 8 square grid. The initial setup is shown below.

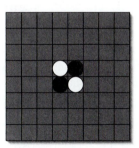

Play: On a turn, a player places one of her pieces on an empty board square. Every line (horizontal, vertical, or diagonal) of the opponent's pieces which is bounded on one end by the just-played piece and on the other end by another friendly piece is captured; all of the captured pieces change color. For example, in the diagram below, a white piece played on the square marked "a" would cause the two black stones marked "b" to become white.

Figure 2-29: The game of Reversi is sold commercially as Othello. (Part 1 of 2)

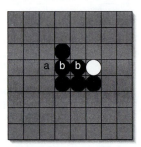

A player must capture if possible. If no capturing move is available, the player must pass, giving the opponent another turn.

Game End: The game is over when neither player has a legal move, usually because the board is full.

Figure 2–29: The game of Reversi is sold commercially as Othello. (Part 2 of 2)

2.32　　Implement the game of Go-Moku (Figure 2–30).

Go-Moku

Players: 2, black and white.

Object: To be the first to get five pieces in a row horizontally, vertically, or diagonally.

Board: The board is a square grid of 19 × 19 lines, initially empty. Pieces are played at the intersections of the lines, rather than in the squares.

Play: On a turn, a player places one of her pieces at any empty intersection.

Figure 2–30: The ancient Asian game of Go-Moku.

2.33　　Implement the game of Mancala (Figure 2–31). (Hint: Use a one-dimensional array of ints to represent the board. Number the pits counterclockwise. When sowing pebbles, if you are currently at pit i, the next pit is at position (i + 1) % 14, although your program must remember to skip this pit if it is the opponent's mancala.)

Mancala

Players: 2

Object: To have the most pebbles in your mancala (goal) at the end of the game.

Board: The Mancala board consists of 14 pits, each holding a number of pebbles. The starting position is shown below.

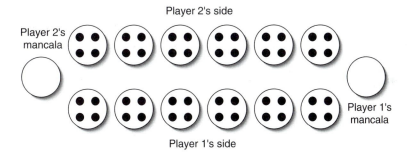

Play: On your turn, pick up all of the pebbles in any nonempty pit on your side of the board. Proceeding counterclockwise, sow one pebble in each pit until you run out. When sowing pebbles, include your own mancala, but skip your opponent's. An example of a first move is shown below.

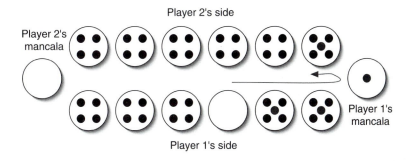

Figure 2–31: The traditional African game of Mancala. (Part 1 of 2)

Free Move: If the last pebble you sow lands in your own Mancala, you get to move again.

Capture: If the last pebble you sow lands in a previously empty pit on your side of the board, you move that pebble, as well as any pebbles in the pit directly across the board, into your mancala.

Game End: The game ends when, after either player's move, one player has no pebbles left in any of the six pits on her side of the board. The other player moves all of the pebbles left on his side of the board to his mancala.

Figure 2–31: The traditional African game of Mancala. (Part 2 of 2)

2.34   The Mancala rules in Figure 2–31 are the Egyptian rules. The Ethiopian rules make two changes: players may choose to sow pebbles either clockwise or counterclockwise around the board, and a move may not start from a pit containing only one pebble. The game ends when one player has no legal move. Modify the program from Project 2.33 to use the Ethiopian rules. (Hint: Remember that the % operator does not behave as modulo when the first operand is negative. This will be a problem if you evaluate (pit - 1) % 14 when pit is 0. You can get around this by first adding 14 to ensure that the first operand to % is positive.)

Inheritance

3

This third and final chapter on object-oriented programming covers inheritance, the ability to specify that a class is "just like that other one, except ...." Section 3.1 explains how and when to create a subclass that inherits code from the class it extends. The Object class, from which all other classes are ultimately derived, is described in Section 3.2. Section 3.3 discusses packages (collections of classes) and access levels, which give us finer control over who can see which parts of our classes.

3.1 Extending a Class

Suppose we want to implement the game of Cram, which is identical to Domineering except that a player can play each domino either horizontally or vertically. We could write a new program that looks very similar to the old one. A better solution is to use inheritance. We write a new class Cram which *extends* Domineering (Figure 3–1). This new class specifies only the things that are different.

Cram is called a *subclass* of Domineering. Conversely, Domineering is a *superclass* of Cram. The relationship between the two classes is shown in Figure 3–2.

```
 1 /** The game of Cram. */
 2 public class Cram extends Domineering {
 3
 4   /** No special initialization is required. */
 5   public Cram() {
 6     super();
 7   }
 8
 9   /** Play until someone wins. */
10   public void play() {
11     int player = 1;
12     while (true) {
13       System.out.println("\n" + this);
14       System.out.println("Player " + player + " to play");
15       if (!(hasLegalMoveFor(HORIZONTAL)
16             || hasLegalMoveFor(VERTICAL))) {
17         System.out.println("No legal moves -- you lose!");
18         return;
19       }
20       System.out.print("Row: ");
21       int row = INPUT.nextInt();
22       System.out.print("Column: ");
23       int column = INPUT.nextInt();
24       INPUT.nextLine();           // To clear out input
25       System.out.print("Play horizontally (y/n)? ");
26       boolean direction;
27       if (INPUT.nextLine().charAt(0) == 'y') {
28         direction = HORIZONTAL;
29       } else {
30         direction = VERTICAL;
31       }
32       playAt(row, column, direction);
33       player = 3 - player;
34     }
35   }
36
37   /** Create and play the game. */
38   public static void main(String[] args) {
39     System.out.println("Welcome to Cram.");
40     Cram game = new Cram();
41     game.play();
42   }
43
44 }
```

Figure 3-1: With inheritance, the Cram class is surprisingly short. Line 24 is necessary to clear out the input line after reading the column number. The method `charAt()`, invoked on the String `INPUT.nextLine()`, returns the character at a particular index.

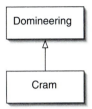

Figure 3–2: UML class diagram showing that Cram is a subclass of Domineering. The arrow for class extension uses the same hollow head as the one for interface implementation, but has a solid instead of a dashed line.

The fields and methods not listed in the code for the Cram class are ***inherited*** from the Domineering class. If we invoke a method like `playAt()` or `hasLegalMoveFor()` on an instance of Cram, the method from the Domineering class is used. Inherited fields and methods make a Cram instance *similar* to a Domineering instance.

We can provide additional fields and methods, although the Cram class does not do so. The Cram class does ***override*** two methods, `play()` and `main()`. When we invoke the `play()` method on an instance of Cram, the new version is used. Additional fields and methods, along with overridden methods, make a Cram instance *different* from a Domineering instance.

The difference between *overloading* and *overriding* is a subtle one. When we overload a method name, Java decides which version to use based on the *arguments which are passed to the method*. When we override a method, Java decides which version to use based on the *object on which the method is invoked*. If two methods with the same name are in the *same class* but have different signatures, the method name is overloaded. If two methods with the same name and signature are in *different classes* (one a subclass of the other), the method in the subclass overrides the one in the superclass.

The invocation

```
super();
```

on line 6 in the constructor says, "Do whatever you would do to set up an instance of Domineering." A constructor in a subclass must always begin by invoking a constructor from the class it extends, although, as we will see later in this chapter, this invocation can often be implicit. In this case, the constructor from Domineering initializes the field that holds the board. Notice that it doesn't matter if we've forgotten how that field was initialized or even what it was called. Inheritance allows us to extend an encapsulated class without thinking about its inner workings. This allows us to develop correct software much more rapidly.

Extending a class is similar to implementing an interface. The key difference is that a superclass provides functionality, while an interface merely makes promises. A class can implement many interfaces, but it can only have one superclass. If a subclass had two superclasses, there would be problems if both of them provided some method which the subclass did not—it would not be clear which version should be inherited.

Polymorphism and Inheritance

As a second example of inheritance, consider the class Light (Figure 3–3). This very simple class has only one field: a boolean indicating whether it is on or off. The `toString()` method returns the String "O" if the Light is on and "." if it is off.

```
1 /** A light bulb. */
2 public class Light {
3
4   /** Whether the Light is on. */
5   private boolean on;
6
7   /** A Light is off by default. */
8   public Light() {
9     on = false;
10  }
11
12  /** Return true if the Light is on. */
13  public boolean isOn() {
14     return on;
15  }
16
17  /** Set whether the Light is on. */
18  public void setOn(boolean on) {
19     this.on = on;
20  }
21
22  public String toString() {
23     if (on) {
24       return "O";
25     } else {
26       return ".";
27     }
28  }
29
30 }
```

Figure 3–3: The class Light models a light bulb.

The Light class is extended by the ColoredLight class (Figure 3–4), which also has a char indicating its color. The color is determined randomly in the constructor. A ColoredLight looks the same as a Light when it is off, but `toString()` returns "R", "G", or "B", respectively, for red, green, or blue ColoredLights.

```
 1 /** A colored light bulb. */
 2 public class ColoredLight extends Light {
 3
 4   /** Color of the ColoredLight. */
 5   private char color;
 6
 7   /** Set the color randomly to one of 'R', 'G', or 'B'. */
 8   public ColoredLight() {
 9     super();
10     int x = (int)(Math.random() * 3);
11     switch (x) {
12       case 0:
13         color = 'R';
14         break;
15       case 1:
16         color = 'G';
17         break;
18       default:
19         color = 'B';
20     }
21   }
22
23   /** Return the color of this ColoredLight. */
24   public char getColor() {
25     return color;
26   }
27
28   public String toString() {
29     if (isOn()) {
30       return "" + color;
31     } else {
32       return ".";
33     }
34   }
35
36 }
```

Figure 3-4: ColoredLight is a subclass of Light.

ColoredLight inherits the field on and adds a new field color. It inherits the methods isOn() and setOn(). It overrides the toString() method and adds a new method, getColor(). This is illustrated in Figure 3–5.

Although ColoredLight inherits the field on, it does not have direct access to the field. On line 29, the toString() method must work through the inherited method isOn() because the field on is private in Light. The private status of this field means that no other class, not even a subclass of Light, has direct access to on. This is information hiding enforcing encapsulation.

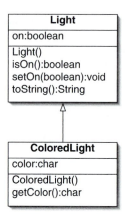

Figure 3-5: UML class diagram showing that ColoredLight extends Light. Only new fields and methods are shown in the subclass. Inherited or overridden fields can be read from the superclass.

A variable of type Light can hold an instance of Light *or of any subclass of Light*. It is therefore a polymorphic type. Thus, it is perfectly legal to say:

```
Light bulb = new ColoredLight();
```

Why not simply cut to the chase and declare `bulb` to be of type Object? By declaring it to be of type Light, we guarantee that all of the methods defined in the Light class are available. Every method in Light has to be either inherited or overridden, so it is safe to call such a method on `bulb`. We can turn `bulb` off without knowing its exact class:

```
bulb.setOn(false);
```

If `bulb` were of type Object, we would have to cast it in order to do this.

If we invoke `toString()` on bulb, Java uses the *class of the instance* (ColoredLight) instead of the *type of the variable* (Light) to determine which version of the method to use. This process is called **dynamic dispatch**, because the decision is made dynamically at run time rather than once and for all at compile time.

Chains of Inheritance

Can we make a subclass of a subclass? Sure! The class FlashingColoredLight (Figure 3–6) extends ColoredLight. It turns itself on or off every time `toString()` is invoked. (This is slightly bad style, because we normally don't expect `toString()` to change an object's state.)

```
1 /** A flashing, colored light bulb. */
2 public class FlashingColoredLight extends ColoredLight {
3
4   /** No special initialization is required. */
5   public FlashingColoredLight() {
6     super();
7   }
8
9   /** Toggle the light's on status after returning a String. */
10  public String toString() {
11    String result;
12    if (isOn()) {
13      result = "" + getColor();
14    } else {
15      result = ".";
16    }
17    setOn(!isOn());
18    return result;
19  }
20
21 }
```

Figure 3-6: FlashingColoredLight extends ColoredLight.

Inheritance is transitive, so FlashingColoredLight inherits every field and method from Light except for those methods overridden by ColoredLight.

The relationship between the three classes is shown in Figure 3–7. We can say that ColoredLight and FlashingColoredLight are *proper descendants* of Light. Strictly speaking, the *descendants* of Light are itself plus its proper descendants. This is consistent with the concepts of subset and proper subset from set theory. Conversely, Light and ColoredLight are *proper ancestors* of FlashingColoredLight. All three classes are *ancestors* of FlashingColoredLight.

Alternately, we can say that ColoredLight and FlashingColoredLight are both subclasses of Light, but only ColoredLight is a *direct subclass*. Conversely, both Light and ColoredLight are superclasses of FlashingColoredLight, but ColoredLight is the *direct superclass*.

We will omit the words "proper" and "direct" when there is no danger of confusion.

Is-a vs Has-a

It takes some experience to know when to extend a class. For example, suppose we want to model a string of Christmas lights. Should we extend the Light class?

To resolve this question, we should think about the relation between the new class and the one we're considering extending. If an instance of the new class *is* just like an instance of the old class, with a few modifications, we should extend. If an instance of the new class merely *has* an instance of the old class as a component, we should not. For example, a ColoredLight *is* a Light, but with the added feature of color, so extension is appropriate. On the other hand, an

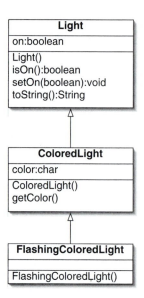

Figure 3-7: A chain of inheritance.

instance of BeetleGame merely *has* two beetles, so it is not appropriate for it to extend Beetle. Object-oriented programmers refer to these as *is-a* and *has-a* relationships.

A string of Christmas lights has several lights, so it should not extend Light. Instead, it should contain an array of Lights in a field. The LightString class is shown in Figure 3–8.

```
1 /** A string of Lights, as used in Christmas decorating. */
2 public class LightString {
3
4   /** The Lights in this LightString. */
5   private Light[] bulbs;
6
7   /** Every other Light is a ColoredLight. */
8   public LightString(int size) {
9     bulbs = new Light[size];
10    for (int i = 0; i < size; i++) {
11      if (i % 2 == 0) {
12        bulbs[i] = new Light();
13      } else {
14        bulbs[i] = new ColoredLight();
15      }
16    }
17  }
18
```

Figure 3-8: A LightString contains some Lights, but it is not a special kind of Light, so extension is not appropriate. The enhanced **for** loop used in lines 21–23 and 28–30 is explained in Appendix A. (Part 1 of 2)

```
19  /** Turn all of the Lights in the LightString on or off. */
20  public void setOn(boolean on) {
21    for (Light b : bulbs) {
22      b.setOn(on);
23    }
24  }
25
26  public String toString() {
27    String result = "";
28    for (Light b : bulbs) {
29      result += b;
30    }
31    return result;
32  }
33
34  /**
35   * Create a LightString, print it, turn it on, and print it
36   * again.
37   */
38  public static void main(String[] args) {
39    LightString lights = new LightString(20);
40    System.out.println(lights);
41    lights.setOn(true);
42    System.out.println(lights);
43  }
44
45 }
```

Figure 3–8: A LightString contains some Lights, but it is not a special kind of Light, so extension is not appropriate. The enhanced **for** loop used in lines 21–23 and 28–30 is explained in Appendix A. (Part 2 of 2)

Even though the LightString class has a method isOn(), it does not make sense to say this method overrides the one in Light, because LightString is not a subclass of Light.

The LightString class uses polymorphism to store both Lights and ColoredLights in the same array. The constructor uses the % operator to put Lights in even-numbered positions and ColoredLights in odd-numbered ones. (The first index is 0, which is even.) The keyword **new** is used both to allocate the array bulb and to create each individual object within that array.

When we run the LightString class, the output looks like this (colors will vary on each run):

```
. . . . . . . . . . . . . . . . . . . .
OROBOGOGOGOGOGOBOGOROR
```

The relationship between all four of the Light-related classes is shown in Figure 3–9.

Beginning object-oriented programmers often overuse inheritance. Inheritance should be used only when an instance of the subclass can stand in for an instance of the superclass. For example,

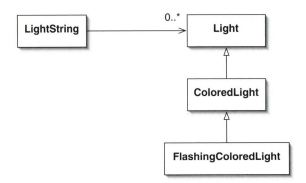

Figure 3–9: A LightString contains 0 or more Lights, some of which may actually be ColoredLights or FlashingColoredLights.

suppose we have a class Bicycle with a method `pedal()`. We should not define Motorcycle to extend Bicycle, because the `pedal()` method wouldn't make sense for a Motorcycle. Since Bicycle is a polymorphic type, any method that accepts a Bicycle might receive an instance of a subclass of Bicycle instead. To prevent such code from breaking, an instance of any subclass should work in place of a regular Bicycle. We might reasonably extend Bicycle with ElectricBicycle (the kind that can be pedaled or powered with an electric motor), but not with Motorcycle.

Exercises

3.1   Draw a detailed UML class diagram showing the relationship between the Domineering and Cram classes, showing fields and methods.

3.2   Recall your answer to Problem 2.29. Does Java use dynamic dispatch when deciding which version of an *overloaded* method to use?

3.3   Discuss what it would mean for an interface to extend another interface.

3.4   Discuss whether each pair below has an is-a or a has-a relationship.

        bicycle, vehicle

        bicycle, tire

        triangle, polygon

        rutabaga, vegetable

        person, bank account

        general, soldier

3.5   Is it possible for an is-a relationship to be symmetric, so that every A is a B and vice versa? What about a has-a relationship? Explain.

3.2 The Object Class

As we saw in Chapter 2, there is a polymorphic type Object which can hold a reference to any object. As you may have surmised from the fact that Object starts with an upper-case letter, there is in fact an Object class. The Object class is an ancestor of *every* other class. A very small part of the Object family tree is shown in Figure 3–10.

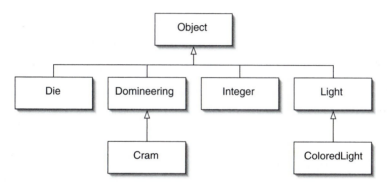

Figure 3–10: The Object class and a few of its descendants.

Since we extend Object so often, Java allows us to omit `extends Object` from the top of a class. If a class doesn't say that it extends some other class, it extends Object.

Methods of the Object Class

While we usually have to cast in order to invoke a method on a variable of type Object, the Object class does have a few methods of its own. These are usually overridden, but they are guaranteed to be present, so they can be invoked without casting.

The Object class has a constructor which takes no arguments. It is legal, though not terribly useful, to create an instance of the Object class:

```
Object it = new Object();
```

The `equals()` method for the Object class behaves exactly like ==. If we define a subclass of Object and fail to override `equals()`, then for two instances a and b of this subclass, `a.equals(b)` exactly when a == b. It is especially important to provide a valid `equals()` method for classes which implement the Comparable interface (Chapter 8).

In order to override the `equals()` method, we must provide a method with the same signature:

```
public boolean equals(Object that)
```

If we use a different argument type, we are not *overriding* the method, but merely *overloading* the name with a method accepting a different argument type. The version from Object is still inherited. Since an instance of any class other than Object might work as an argument for either version, this can cause unexpected behavior.

As we mentioned earlier, the method `getClass()` returns a representation of an object's class. This happens automatically—there is no need to override `getClass()`.

The `toString()` method for the Object class returns a String like:

```
java.lang.Object@9c26f5
```

The part to the left of the @ is the class of the instance. The part to the right has to do with the location in memory where the instance is stored and varies from one instance to another. If we fail to override `toString()` in a subclass, this method is smart enough to use the name of the subclass. For example, if we omitted the `toString()` method from Light, printing an instance of Light would produce a String like:

```
Light@4d3343
```

The last important method of the Object class, `hashCode()`, is discussed in Chapter 11. For now, we note that `equals()` and `hashCode()` interact. If a class overrides one of these methods, it should override both of them.

Implicit Constructors

If the Light class implicitly extends Object, then shouldn't its constructor begin by invoking a constructor from Object? Yes, and while it is not explicit, the constructor does this. Since it is so common for constructors to begin with

```
super();
```

Java allows us to omit this line. For example, we could have omitted line 9 in Figure 3–4.

We can go even farther than this. Every class *that does not provide an explicit constructor* gets an implicit zero-argument constructor which does nothing but invoke the zero-argument super constructor. This means that we could have left out the constructors in the Cram class (Figure 3–1) and the FlashingColoredLight class (Figure 3–6).

Exercise

3.6   Through experimentation, determine what happens if we print an array of ints. What about an array of Lights? What about a multidimensional array?

3.7   Make the superclass and constructor for the Thingamabob class (Figure 3–11) explicit.

```
1 public class Thingamabob {
2
3   private int x;
4
5   public void setX(int x) {
6     this.x = x;
7   }
8
9 }
```

Figure 3-11: The Thingamabob class for Exercise 3.7.

3.8   Consider the classes Doohickey (Figure 3–12) and Whatsis (Figure 3–13). Explain why Whatsis does not compile.

```
1 public class Doohickey extends Thingamabob {
2
3   public Doohickey(int x) {
4     super();
5     setX(x);
6   }
7
8 }
```

Figure 3-12: The Doohickey class for Exercise 3.8.

```
1 public class Whatsis extends Doohickey {
2 }
```

Figure 3-13: The Whatsis class for Exercise 3.8.

3.3 Packages and Access Levels

A method encapsulates an algorithm. A class encapsulates state (fields) and behavior (methods). A *package*, which contains a number of classes, provides encapsulation on an even larger scale. When many programmers are writing many classes, dividing them into packages helps keep the classes organized. Furthermore, it gives programmers more freedom in choosing names. If one programmer writes a Date class modeling a fruit, while another writes a Date class modeling a romantic evening, this does not cause a problem as long as the two Date classes are in different packages.

Over 100 packages are included with Sun's Java software development kit. Figure 3–14 shows some of the most commonly used packages.

Package	Purpose
java.awt	Graphic user interfaces
java.awt.event	Handling events such as mouse clicks
java.io	Input and output, as with files
java.lang	Basic classes such as Object, Integer, String, and Math
java.util	Data structures

Figure 3-14: Some of the most commonly used Java packages.

The full name of a class includes both its package name and its class name. For example, the full name of the Object class is java.lang.Object. Within a package, the package name can be dropped.

Continuing our example, we might have two packages called fruit and social.relationships. The two Date classes would then be fruit.Date and social.relationships.Date. Within the fruit package, the first one can be referred to simply as Date.

Outside of a package, the full name must be used, with a few exceptions. The first exception is that Java doesn't requires us to explicitly name the java.lang package because the classes in this package are used so often. The second exception is that there is no package name for the *default package*, the package containing all classes which are not part of any other package. All of the classes we have written so far are in the default package.

The third exception is that a class can be *imported* into another package. For example, we often use the Scanner class from the java.util package. We can import this class by including the line

```
import java.util.Scanner;
```

at the top of one of our programs, above the beginning of the class. Now, any reference to the Scanner class inside our class will be treated as a reference to java.util.Scanner.

If we want to use several classes from the java.util package, it is easier to import the entire package:

```
import java.util.*;
```

C programmers should note that this is not the same thing as a `#include` statement. That C statement copies the entire text of the included file into the current one before compiling. The Java import statement merely tells the compiler where to look for classes.

To put a class in a particular package, we must do two things. First, we must add a line at the top of the file where the class is defined, even before any import statements. If we want to put a Date class in the fruit package, for example, we say

```
package fruit;
```

at the beginning of `Date.java`.

Second, Sun's Java compiler insists that the package structure be reflected in the directory structure where the files are stored. In our example, our file must be in the `fruit` subdirectory of the directory where the compile command is given. The command, therefore, has to be:

```
javac fruit/Date.java
```

Package names with dots in them correspond to nested directories. Classes in the social.relationships package must be in the `relationships` subdirectory of the `social` subdirectory.

As another example, the classes in the java.awt.event package are in the event subdirectory of the directory containing the java.awt classes. This is the only relationship between these packages. Importing java.awt.* does *not* automatically import java.awt.event.*.

Access Levels

Every field or method has an ***access level***, indicating which classes can access it. Access levels provide information hiding. We have seen two access levels so far: private and public.

A private field or method is visible only within the class where it is declared. We have declared all of our nonconstant fields private.

A public field or method is visible everywhere. We have so far declared all of our methods and constants public.

There are two other access levels between these two. If we declare a field or method to be ***protected***, it is visible to any class which either is in the same package or is a descendant. If a method is not important to most users of a class, it is reasonable to declare it protected. For example, the `playAt()` method in the Domineering class might reasonably be declared protected.

Because we don't know when a class will be extended, it is a good idea to include protected accessors and mutators for each field, so that subclasses can get at private fields. These methods can ensure that the object stays in a consistent state, so this is a better approach than declaring the field itself protected.

Finally, if we don't specify an access level, a field or method gets the default ***package*** level, which makes it visible to all classes in the same package.

The four access levels are summarized in Figure 3–15.

Level	Visible To
private	same class only
(package)	same package only
protected	same package and descendants
public	all classes

Figure 3–15: Protection levels. The package level is specified by not providing one of the other keywords.

The levels can be better understood by looking at Figure 3–16. Suppose there is a method get-Seed() within Strawberry. If it is private, it can be accessed only within the Strawberry class. If no protection level is specified, it gets the default package level of protection, so it can be accessed only from Date and Strawberry. If it is protected, it can be accessed from Date, Strawberry, and ChocolateCoveredStrawberry. Finally, if it is public, all four classes can access the method.

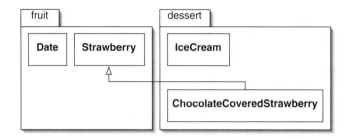

Figure 3-16: The fruit package contains the classes Date and Strawberry. The dessert package contains the classes ChocolateCoveredStrawberry (a subclass of Strawberry) and IceCream.

It may seem strange to have a class that extends a class in another package. This is perfectly reasonable if we use packages written by someone else. When we write our own package, we might want to extend one of their classes. In fact, we do this all the time when we write classes that extend Object, which is in the java.lang package.

Exercises

3.9   Through experimentation, determine whether it is acceptable for a method to have a more restrictive access level than the one it overrides. What about less restrictive? Why do you think the rules are set up this way?

3.10   Write a class with a private field and at least one method with each of the other three access levels. Through experimentation, determine how the documentation generated by javadoc changes if we replace the command-line option -public with -private. How about -protected? What if we omit this option altogether?

Summary

Every class (except for the Object class itself) extends one other class. If a class does not explicitly extend some other class, it extends Object. Every class is a polymorphic type; a variable of a class type can hold a reference to an instance of a subclass. Java distinguishes between the type of a variable and the class of the instance to which it refers.

A subclass inherits the methods and fields of its superclass, but it can also override methods in the superclass and add new fields and methods. We should extend only when it makes sense to say that an instance of the subclass is a (special kind of) instance of the superclass.

Classes can be grouped into packages. Access levels for fields and methods range from private (visible only in the same class) to public (visible in all classes in all packages). Choosing intermediate access levels gives us finer control over encapsulation.

Vocabulary

access level. One of four levels of information hiding: private, package, protected, and public.

ancestor. Any of a class, its direct superclass, the direct superclass of that class, and so on. All of these except for the class itself are proper ancestors.

default package. Nameless package containing all classes not explicitly placed in any other package. All of the programs in this book are in the default package.

descendant. Any of a class, its direct subclasses, their direct subclasses, and so on. All of these except for the class itself are proper descendants.

direct. Of a subclass or superclass, extending in a single step rather than through a chain of intervening classes.

dynamic dispatch. Process by which Java decides which version of a method to use, based on the class of the object on which the method is invoked.

extend. Define a subclass of. Every class except Object directly extends exactly one other class.

has-a. Relationship between a class and the class of one of its fields.

import. Specify that a class in another package may be referred to in this class without using the package name.

inherit. Possess by virtue of extending another class. Fields and methods may be inherited.

is-a. Relationship between a subclass and a superclass.

override. Redefine to prevent inheritance. Methods may be overridden.

package. Collection of classes. Also the default access level, granting access to all classes in the same package.

protected. Access level granting access to subclasses and to other classes in the same package.

subclass. A class that extends another class.

superclass. The class that is extended by another class.

Problems

3.11   Write a class LoadedDie which extends Die. A LoadedDie is just like a Die, but always comes up 6 whenever it is rolled.

3.12   Write a class PolyhedralDie which extends Die. A PolyhedralDie may have a number of sides other than 6. The number of sides should be an argument to the constructor.

Projects

3.13   Implement the game of Bogart (Figure 3–17). Your implementation has to handle only two players. (Hint: Create a class FourSidedDie which extends Die. Alternately, if you have done Exercise 3.12, you can use the PolyhedralDie class.)

Bogart

Players: 2–6

Object: To be the first to either accumulate 30 chips or roll all five dice at once without rolling a 1.

Setup: The pot is initially empty and all players start with no chips. New chips will be added to the pot from an inexhaustible bank.

Play: When your turn begins, add one chip from the bank to the pot. Roll a four-sided die. If you get a 1, you have aced out and your turn ends. Otherwise, you may either take the pot or keep going. If you keep going, add two chips to the pot and roll two dice. If you roll a 1 on either die, you have aced out. Otherwise, you may keep going, this time adding three chips and rolling three dice. Continue until you either ace out, decide to take the pot, or successfully roll all five dice without acing out.

Figure 3–17: Like Pennywise, the game of Bogart is an invention of James Ernest. Used with permission of the designer.

II

Linear Structures

4

Stacks and Queues

This chapter introduces two important interfaces, Stack and Queue. Each corresponds to a data structure holding a collection of objects, ordered by when they were inserted into the structure. A stack gives us access to only the newest (most recently inserted) object, whereas a queue gives us access to only the oldest object.

Section 4.1 introduces the Stack interface. We discuss how a stack behaves, putting off the implementation until later chapters. Generic classes, new to Java 1.5, are introduced in this section. We use stacks in the solitaire card game Idiot's Delight. Section 4.2 explores another important stack application: the call stack, which Java uses to keep track of all of the methods running at a given time. Knowing about the call stack helps us to understand many other principles and Java features, such as exceptions. Exceptions, introduced in Section 4.3, provide a way to recover gracefully from errors. Section 4.4 discusses the Queue interface and uses it in the game of War.

4.1 The Stack Interface

A *stack* is a data structure holding several items. As seen in Figure 4–1, we can think of the items in a stack as being arranged vertically. When a new item is added, it is added to the top of the stack. This is called *pushing* an item onto the stack. We can *pop* the stack to extract the topmost item. We can also *peek* at the top item or check if the stack is empty.

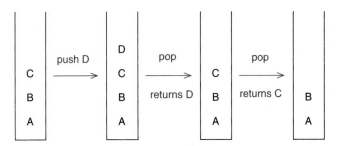

Figure 4-1: A stack changes as various operations are performed on it. Peeking at the final (rightmost) stack would return B, but not alter the stack. A real stack would start out empty, but we included a few items here to make the example more interesting.

Since the most recently pushed item is always on top of the stack (and hence available for popping), a stack is said to follow a ***last-in, first-out*** or ***LIFO*** policy. One consequence is that if we push a sequence of ten items onto a stack and then pop the stack ten times, the items are returned in reverse order. The standard analogy for a stack is a spring-loaded stack of plates found in a cafeteria: we can push a new plate on top or we can pop off the top plate, but we can't (directly) get at the plates underneath.

We can formalize the stack abstract data type in the Stack interface (Figure 4–2). We will explain lines 9 and 15 later in this chapter. There is more than one way to implement this interface. We will see one way in Chapter 5 and a very different one in Chapter 6.

```
 1 /** A last-in, first-out stack of Objects. */
 2 public interface Stack {
 3
 4    /** Return true if this Stack is empty. */
 5    public boolean isEmpty();
 6
 7    /**
 8     * Return the top Object on this Stack. Do not modify the Stack.
 9     * @throws EmptyStructureException if this Stack is empty.
10     */
11    public Object peek();
12
```

Figure 4-2: First draft of the Stack interface. (Part 1 of 2)

```
13   /**
14    * Remove and return the top Object on this Stack.
15    * @throws EmptyStructureException if this Stack is empty.
16    */
17   public Object pop();
18
19   /** Add target to the top of the Stack. */
20   public void push(Object target);
21
22 }
```

Figure 4-2: First draft of the Stack interface. (Part 2 of 2)

Before moving on to an example of using a Stack, we introduce a new feature of Java 1.5 that allows us to avoid some casting.

Generics

The Stack interface in Figure 4–2 describes a stack of Objects. We can push any kind of Object onto a Stack. For example, if s is a Stack:

```
s.push(new Die(3));
```

When we pop a Stack, on the other hand, we get back an Object. Even if we remember that the item on the Stack is an instance of some more specific class, we have to remind Java of this fact by casting:

```
((Die)(s.pop())).roll();
```

This is not only inconvenient, it is slightly unsafe. If we misremember what we put on the Stack, we might try to cast something that is not really a Die to be a Die. This would crash our program.

Java 1.5 introduces a new solution: *generic* classes and interfaces. A generic class or interface has one or more *type parameters*, indicating what sorts of things it holds. Every time we use a generic type, we have to specify a type for each type parameter. In the case of Stacks, there is only type parameter: the type of the elements stored on the Stack. To make a Stack of Die instances, we say:

```
Stack<Die> s = new Stack<Die>();
```

Now we can safely do:

```
s.push(new Die());
s.pop().roll();
```

Java won't let us push anything of the wrong type onto this Stack. Furthermore, the pop() method's return type is specified by the type parameter. In our example, the return type is Die.

The revised Stack interface is shown in Figure 4–3.

```
 1 /** A last-in, first-out stack. */
 2 public interface Stack<E> {
 3
 4   /** Return true if this Stack is empty. */
 5   public boolean isEmpty();
 6
 7   /**
 8    * Return the top item on this Stack, but do not modify the Stack.
 9    * @throws EmptyStructureException if this Stack is empty.
10    */
11   public E peek();
12
13   /**
14    * Remove and return the top item on this Stack.
15    * @throws EmptyStructureException if this Stack is empty.
16    */
17   public E pop();
18
19   /** Add target to the top of the Stack. */
20   public void push(E target);
21
22 }
```

Figure 4-3: Generic version of the Stack interface. The type parameter is E, which stands for 'element'.

In UML diagrams, type parameters are shown in dashed boxes at the upper right of a class, interface, or instance (Figure 4–4).

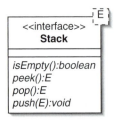

Figure 4-4: UML class diagram of the generic Stack interface.

Example: Idiot's Delight

One advantage of specifying an abstract data type is that we can write programs which use the ADT before we've implemented it. We now use the Stack interface to implement some parts of the game of Idiot's Delight (Figure 4–5).

Idiot's Delight

Players: 1

Object: To clear all the cards off the table.

Setup: Shuffle a deck of cards and deal four cards face up in a row, forming four stacks.

Play: On your turn, you may do any *one* of the following:

- If there are two cards of the same rank showing, discard *both of them*.
- If there are two cards of the same suit showing, discard *the one with lower rank*.
- Deal four new cards, one on top of each stack.

Figure 4-5: Idiot's Delight is a solitaire card game. As in all the card games in this book, the rank of ace is below 2.

A game of Idiot's Delight involves a Deck, which in turn includes up to 52 Cards. (There are fewer than 52, once some have been dealt from the Deck.) The game also needs four Stacks, each of which contains 0 or more Cards. This is illustrated in Figure 4–6.

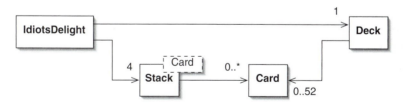

Figure 4-6: UML class diagram of the Idiot's Delight program.

The fields and `main()` method of the IdiotsDelight class are shown in Figure 4–7. Note that the field `stacks` contains an array of Stacks of Cards. Also, importing the Scanner class allows us to declare and initialize the constant INPUT more concisely.

The constructor, shown in Figure 4–8, is the most complicated constructor we've written yet. Line 3 invokes the constructor for the Deck class, which we'll write later. Line 4 invokes the `shuffle()` method from that class. Shuffling is something a Deck should know how to do, not part of this game in particular, so it is encapsulated inside the Deck class.

```
 1 import java.util.Scanner;
 2
 3 /** The solitaire card game Idiot's Delight. */
 4 public class IdiotsDelight {
 5
 6   /** For reading from the console. */
 7   public static final Scanner INPUT = new Scanner(System.in);
 8
 9   /** The four Stacks of Cards. */
10   private Stack<Card>[] stacks;
11
12   /** The Deck of Cards. */
13   private Deck deck;
14
15   /** Create and play the game. */
16   public static void main(String[] args) {
17     System.out.println("Welcome to Idiot's Delight.");
18     IdiotsDelight game = new IdiotsDelight();
19     game.play();
20   }
21
22 }
```

Figure 4-7: Fields and `main()` method for IdiotsDelight.

```
 1 /** Create and shuffle the Deck.  Deal one Card to each Stack. */
 2 public IdiotsDelight() {
 3   deck = new Deck();
 4   deck.shuffle();
 5   stacks = new Stack[4]; // This causes a compiler warning
 6   for (int i = 0; i < 4; i++) {
 7     stacks[i] = new ArrayStack<Card>();
 8   }
 9   deal();
10 }
```

Figure 4-8: Constructor for the IdiotsDelight class.

Line 5 allocates the array `stacks`, but each element of that array still has the default value `null`. The `for` loop on lines 6–8 is needed to initialize the elements. Line 7 invokes the constructor for the ArrayStack class. This class, which we will write in Chapter 5, uses an array to implement the Stack interface.

In a stroke of bad luck, the ugliest feature of generics rears its head here: generics do not play well with arrays. We can declare an array field or variable involving type parameters, like the field `stacks` in Figure 4–7. For complicated reasons involving the Java compiler, however, we cannot actually allocate an array involving a type parameter. We would like line 5 of Figure 4–8 to read

```
stacks = new Stack<Card>[4];
```

but Java will not let us do this. If we leave the line as it is in Figure 4–8, we get the following cryptic message when we try to compile the program:

```
Note: IdiotsDelight.java uses unchecked or unsafe operations.
Note: Recompile with -Xlint:unchecked for details.
```

Following these instructions, we invoke the command

```
javac -Xlint:unchecked IdiotsDelight.java
```

and get the following:

```
IdiotsDelight.java:20: warning: [unchecked] unchecked conversion
found    : Stack[]
required: Stack<Card>[]
    stacks = new Stack[4]; // This causes a compiler warning
             ^
1 warning
```

Significantly, this is a *warning*, not an *error*. The compiler is telling us, "I think this is a bad idea, but I'm not going to stop you from doing it." Surprisingly, this is the best we can do. By the end of Chapter 5, we'll have hidden this unpleasantness behind a layer of encapsulation.

Returning to the task at hand, line 9 of Figure 4–8 calls the `deal()` method from the Idiots-Delight class. This method, shown in Figure 4–9, deals one card onto each Stack.

```
1 /** Deal one Card from the Deck onto each Stack. */
2 public void deal() {
3   for (Stack<Card> s : stacks) {
4     s.push(deck.deal());
5   }
6 }
```

Figure 4–9: The `deal()` method from the IdiotsDelight class.

Line 4 does a lot of work. The expression `deck.deal()` invokes the `deal()` method of `deck`, which removes and returns the top Card in `deck`. The value of the expression is therefore of type Card. We pass this as an argument to the `push()` method from `s`, which is a Stack of Cards.

The play() method (Figure 4–10) is by far the longest in the class. In addition to invoking deal(), it invokes two other methods, removeLowCard() and removePair(). Notice that play() uses the isEmpty() Stack method.

```
 1 /** Play the game. */
 2 public void play() {
 3   while (true) {
 4     // Print game state
 5     System.out.println("\n" + this);
 6     // Check for victory
 7     boolean done = true;
 8     for (Stack<Card> s : stacks) {
 9       if (!(s.isEmpty())) {
10         done = false;
11         break;
12       }
13     }
14     if (done) {
15       System.out.println("You win!");
16       return;
17     }
18     // Get command
19     System.out.print("Your command (pair, suit, deal, or quit)? ");
20     String command = INPUT.nextLine();
21     // Handle command
22     if (command.equals("pair")) {
23       removePair();
24     } else if (command.equals("suit")) {
25       removeLowCard();
26     } else if (command.equals("deal")) {
27       deal();
28     } else {
29       return;
30     }
31   }
32 }
```

Figure 4-10: The play() method.

Both removeLowCard() and removePair() (Figure 4–11) use pop(). The pop() method returns a value, but we don't use that value in this particular program.

Since we print the IdiotsDelight instance on line 5 of play(), we need to provide a toString() method. This method, shown in Figure 4–12, uses peek() to look at the top card on each Stack.

```
 1 /**
 2  * Remove the lower of two Cards of the same suit, as specified by
 3  * the user.
 4  */
 5 public void removeLowCard() throws IllegalMoveException {
 6   System.out.print("Location (1-4) of low card? ");
 7   int i = INPUT.nextInt();
 8   System.out.print("Location (1-4) of high card? ");
 9   int j = INPUT.nextInt();
10   INPUT.nextLine();          // To clear out input
11   stacks[i - 1].pop();
12 }
13
14 /**
15  * Remove two Cards of the same rank, as specified by the user.
16  */
17 public void removePair() throws IllegalMoveException {
18   System.out.print("Location (1-4) of first card? ");
19   int i = INPUT.nextInt();
20   System.out.print("Location (1-4) of second card? ");
21   int j = INPUT.nextInt();
22   INPUT.nextLine();          // To clear out input
23   stacks[i - 1].pop();
24   stacks[j - 1].pop();
25 }
```

Figure 4-11: The removeLowCard() and removePair() methods.

```
 1 public String toString() {
 2   String result = "";
 3   for (int i = 0; i < 4; i++) {
 4     if (stacks[i].isEmpty()) {
 5       result += "-- ";
 6     } else {
 7       result += stacks[i].peek() + " ";
 8     }
 9   }
10   return result + "\n" + deck.size() + " cards left in the deck";
11 }
```

Figure 4-12: The toString() method.

We'll write the Card, Deck, and ArrayStack classes in Chapter 5. We will certainly have to provide the methods we've invoked on instances of these classes. Our knowledge of the program so far is shown in Figure 4–13.

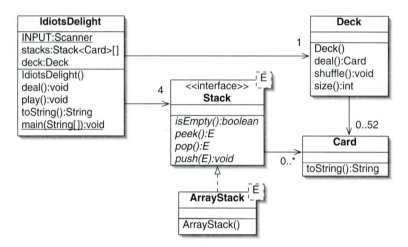

Figure 4-13: UML class diagram of the Idiot's Delight program so far. The four Stacks to which an instance of IdiotsDelight is related are actually instances of the ArrayStack class, which implements the Stack interface.

While we cannot actually run our program at this stage, Figure 4–14 shows how it will behave when it's done.

```
 1 Welcome to Idiot's Delight.
 2
 3 3c 7h Kd As
 4 48 cards left in the deck
 5 Your command (pair, suit, deal, or quit)? deal
 6
 7 9h 9s 2d Tc
 8 44 cards left in the deck
 9 Your command (pair, suit, deal, or quit)? pair
10 Location (1-4) of first card? 1
11 Location (1-4) of second card? 2
12
13 3c 7h 2d Tc
14 44 cards left in the deck
15 Your command (pair, suit, deal, or quit)? suit
16 Location (1-4) of low card? 1
17 Location (1-4) of high card? 4
18
19 -- 7h 2d Tc
20 44 cards left in the deck
```

Figure 4-14: The first few turns of a game of IdiotsDelight. Tc stands for "10 of clubs."

Exercises

4.1   The following sequence of methods are to be invoked on an initially empty stack. Draw
        the state of the stack (in the style of Figure 4–1) after each step. Indicate what is
        returned by any methods that return values.

```
push("a");
push("b");
push("c");
pop();
push("d");
push("e");
peek();
pop();
pop();
```

4.2   Discuss whether a PEZ candy dispenser is a good analogy for a stack.

4.3   Both the IdiotsDelight class and the Deck class have a method called deal(). Is this an
        example of overloading, overriding, neither, or both?

4.4   Discuss whether line 11 in the play() method (Figure 4–10) is necessary.

4.2 The Call Stack

Figure 4–15 shows a program for computing the length of the hypotenuse of a right triangle,
given the lengths of the other two sides.

```
1  /** Compute the hypotenuse of a right triangle. */
2  public class Hypotenuse {
3
4    /** Return the square of the number x. */
5    public static double square(double x) {
6      return x * x;
7    }
8
9    /**
10    * Return the hypotenuse of a right triangle with side lengths x
11    * and y.
12    */
13   public static double hypotenuse(double x, double y) {
```

Figure 4-15: To keep things simple, all of the methods in the Hypotenuse class are
static. (Part 1 of 2)

```
14      double x2 = square(x);
15      double y2 = square(y);
16      return Math.sqrt(x2 + y2);
17   }
18
19   /** Test the methods. */
20   public static void main(String[] args) {
21      double result = hypotenuse(3, 4);
22      System.out.println(result);
23   }
24
25 }
```

Figure 4–15: To keep things simple, all of the methods in the Hypotenuse class are static. (Part 2 of 2)

The hypotenuse() method invokes the square() method twice: once on line 13 and once on line 14. When Java finishes an invocation of square(), how does it know where to go next? Should it invoke square() again or go on to Math.sqrt()?

The vague answer is that Java somehow "keeps track of" what it was doing before the invocation started. How? Using a stack.

This stack, called the ***call stack***, exists behind the scenes. It is not an object that we can access, but we can understand it now that we know about stacks.

Every time a method is invoked, a behind-the-scenes object called a ***call frame*** is created. The call frame keeps track of the current state of the method. Specifically, it stores any arguments or variables for the method. It also keeps track of how far along the method has proceeded.

The history of the call stack for this program is illustrated in Figure 4–16. When Java first starts up, the call stack is empty. When main() is invoked, a new call frame is created and pushed onto the stack. This call frame stores the value of args (which we ignore in this example) and result, as well as the fact that we are at the beginning of the main() method (that is, line 20). (The author has carefully crafted the Hypotenuse program so that only one method invocation happens on each line. In a more complicated program, Java would break each line into multiple steps.)

On line 20, the main() method invokes hypotenuse(3, 4). Java creates a call frame for hypotenuse() and pushes it onto the stack. In this new call frame, x is 3, y is 4, and the method is at the beginning, on line 13. The variables x2 and y2 have not yet been initialized.

The hypotenuse() method then needs square(3), which causes yet another call frame to be pushed onto the stack. At any point, only the top frame on the call stack is active. The others are waiting for answers from methods they invoked. This clears up any confusion between arguments and variables with the same name in different methods, or in different invocations of the same method.

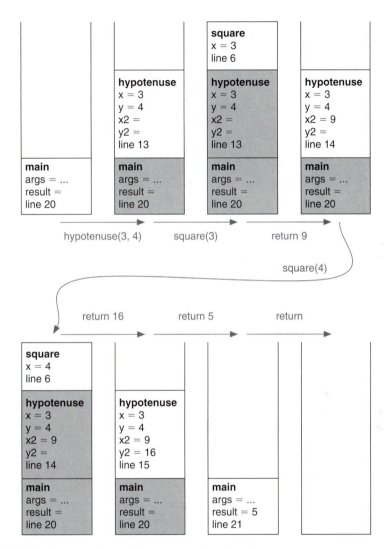

Figure 4-16: History of the call stack for the Hypotenuse program.

When `square()` finishes, its call frame is popped off the stack. The next frame down, the invocation of `hypotenuse()`, stores the returned value 9 in the variable `x2` and moves on to ask for `square(4)`.

Eventually, `main()` finishes, the last call frame is popped off the stack, and the program is done.

This was a lot of work, and we can be thankful that Java does it for us. We normally don't even have to think about the call stack, although it will be useful knowledge when we discuss recursion in Chapter 9.

Knowledge of the call stack also helps us understand some of Java's error messages. Suppose we are playing Idiot's Delight and decide to deal out all of the cards before discarding any. Unfortunately, we aren't paying attention to the number of cards left and we try to deal from any empty deck. The program crashes with a message like the one shown in Figure 4–17.

```
1 Exception in thread "main"
2  java.lang.ArrayIndexOutOfBoundsException: -1
3         at Deck.deal(Deck.java:25)
4         at IdiotsDelight.deal(IdiotsDelight.java:24)
5         at IdiotsDelight.play(IdiotsDelight.java:58)
6         at IdiotsDelight.main(IdiotsDelight.java:81)
```
Figure 4–17: Stack trace in an error message from Java.

The error message shows a ***stack trace*** (a snapshot of the call stack) indicating what was going on when the program crashed. The actual error occurred in the `deal()` method of the Deck class, so the top call frame was an invocation of this method. It was invoked in line 24 of the `deal()` method from the IdiotsDelight class, which was invoked on line 58 of the `play()` method, which was invoked on line 81 of the `main()` method. (These line numbers are from the complete files, so they won't match the numbers in our figures. Your numbers may differ due to whitespace, comments, and so on.)

Examining a stack trace makes our debugging much easier, because we can immediately tell that the `deal()` method from Deck either contains a bug or (as in this example) was called inappropriately. The next section discusses how to deal with such bad input without crashing the program.

Exercises

4.5   Can two call frames ever be waiting for each other? Explain.

4.6   Every method invocation involves pushing a frame onto the call stack, which takes up time and memory. Discuss whether we should avoid this by writing every program in a single, monolithic `main()` method.

4.3 Exceptions

Assertions (Appendix A) provide one way to verify assumptions we make during our programs. Unfortunately, if an assertion check fails, the program crashes. This is useful for debugging, but it is not acceptable behavior for a polished program. Exceptions enable us to recover gracefully from errors.

An ***exception*** is an unusual event that occurs during the operation of a program, such as an attempt to divide by zero, to follow a null reference, or to look at element −1 of an array. The operation that causes the exception is said to ***throw*** the exception. Once an exception is thrown, it must be ***caught*** by some method or the program will crash.

In Java, exceptions are represented by objects—instances of classes which descend from the built-in Exception class. Each class corresponds to a different kind of exception. A few of the built-in exception classes are shown in Figure 4–18.

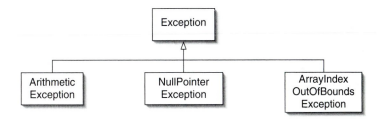

Figure 4-18: A few of the built-in exception classes. There are many more, and these three subclasses shown are not actually direct subclasses of Exception (see Figure 4–28).

An exception class doesn't have to be very complicated. All it needs is a constructor, and since we can have an implicit zero-argument constructor, the body of the class can be empty. An example is the IllegalMoveException class shown in Figure 4–19.

```
1 /** Thrown when a player attempts an illegal move in a game. */
2 public class IllegalMoveException extends Exception {
3 }
```

Figure 4-19: The body of the IllegalMoveException class is empty.

We want the `deal()` method from IdiotsDelight to throw an IllegalMoveException if it is invoked when `deck` is empty. We must do three things:

1. Add the declaration `throws IllegalMoveException` to the end of the method's signature. This warns any method calling `deal()` that such an exception might occur.

2. Mention this fact in the comment for `deal()`, explaining under what conditions an exception is thrown.

3. Add code to the body of `deal()` to check if `deck` is empty and throw an IllegalMove exception if it is.

The revised `deal()` method is shown in Figure 4–20. The special notation `@throws` in the comment helps javadoc make a link in the documentation to the page describing the Illegal-MoveException class.

```
 1 /**
 2  * Deal one Card from the Deck onto each Stack.
 3  * @throws IllegalMoveException if the Deck is empty.
 4  */
 5 public void deal() throws IllegalMoveException {
 6   if (deck.isEmpty()) {
 7     throw new IllegalMoveException();
 8   }
 9   for (Stack<Card> s : stacks) {
10     s.push(deck.deal());
11   }
12 }
```

Figure 4-20: The `deal()` method can throw an IllegalMoveException.

When this method is invoked, if `deck` is empty, it immediately stops and throws an exception. The code on lines 9–11 is not executed. This is similar to a return statement, but the method doesn't even return normally. It passes the exception to the next frame down in the call stack, which must handle it one way or another.

If we try to compile the program now, Java will complain with messages like this:

```
IdiotsDelight.java:19: unreported exception IllegalMoveException;
must be caught or declared to be thrown
      deal();
      ^
IdiotsDelight.java:63: unreported exception IllegalMoveException;
must be caught or declared to be thrown
        deal();
        ^
```

The problem is that when the constructor and the `play()` method invoke `deal()`, they don't deal with the possible exception. There are two ways to deal with an exception. The first is to pass the buck. If we declare that `play()` might throw an IllegalMoveException, then if `play()` receives such an exception, it is passed on to the next call frame down—an invocation of the method that invoked `play()`, namely `main()`.

We can get the program to compile and run by adding `throws IllegalMoveException` to the signatures of the constructor, `play()`, and `main()`.

If we try to deal from an empty deck, the `deal()` method throws an IllegalMoveException. The `play()` method receives it and passes it on to `main()`. Finally, `main()` passes the exception on to the Java system (which invoked `main()`), causing the program to crash. The stack trace in Figure 4–21 is printed. This is slightly better than the one in Figure 4–17, because it tells us that an illegal move was attempted.

```
1 Exception in thread "main" IllegalMoveException
2         at IdiotsDelight.deal(IdiotsDelight.java:30)
3         at IdiotsDelight.play(IdiotsDelight.java:63)
4         at IdiotsDelight.main(IdiotsDelight.java:124)
```

Figure 4-21: The stack trace from the new program is slightly more enlightening.

Rather than passing on an exception, a method can catch it. This is done with a try/catch block. As shown in Figure 4–22, this consists of the keyword try, a bunch of statements between curly braces, the keyword catch, the declaration of a variable of an exception type in parentheses, and another bunch of statements between curly braces.

```
 1 /** Play the game. */
 2 public void play() {
 3   while (true) {
 4     try {
 5       // Print game state
 6       System.out.println("\n" + this);
 7       // Check for victory
 8       boolean done = true;
 9       for (Stack<Card> s : stacks) {
10         if (!(s.isEmpty())) {
11           done = false;
12           break;
13         }
14       }
15       if (done) {
16         System.out.println("You win!");
17         return;
18       }
19       // Get command
20       System.out.print
21         ("Your command (pair, suit, deal, or quit)? ");
22       String command = INPUT.nextLine();
23       // Handle command
24       if (command.equals("pair")) {
25         removePair();
26       } else if (command.equals("suit")) {
27         removeLowCard();
```

Figure 4-22: Revised version of play() including a try/catch block. (Part 1 of 2)

```
28        } else if (command.equals("deal")) {
29            deal();
30        } else {
31            return;
32        }
33    } catch (IllegalMoveException e) {
34        System.out.println("I'm sorry, that's not a legal move.");
35    }
36  }
37 }
```

Figure 4-22: Revised version of `play()` including a try/catch block. (Part 2 of 2)

When this method is run, it tries to do everything in the `try` block (lines 4–32). If no exception occurs, the `catch` block (lines 32–34) is ignored. If an exception does occur, the method immediately jumps down to the `catch` block, executes the code there, and then picks up after the end of the `catch` block. In this example, the next thing after the `catch` block is the right curly brace on line 35, so after handling the exception the method begins another pass through the `while` loop.

There is sometimes no reasonable way to handle an exception. For example, in the constructor for IdiotsDelight, if the invocation of `deal()` throws an IllegalMoveException, something is seriously wrong with the program—the deck shouldn't be empty at this point! We could declare that the constructor and any methods which invoke it (such as `main()`) are capable of throwing IllegalMoveExceptions, but this would be a lot of clutter in our code for a situation which we never expect to occur. A better alternative is to simply catch the exception, print a stack trace (so we'll know that the exception occurred if there *is* a bug in our program), and bring the program to a screeching halt with `System.exit(1)`. The stack trace can be printed by invoking the `printStackTrace()` method on the instance `e` (Figure 4–23).

```
1 /** Create and shuffle the Deck.  Deal one Card to each Stack. */
2 public IdiotsDelight() {
3   deck = new Deck();
4   deck.shuffle();
5   stacks = new Stack[4]; // This causes a compiler warning
6   for (int i = 0; i < 4; i++) {
7     stacks[i] = new ArrayStack<Card>();
8   }
9   try {
10    deal();
11  } catch (IllegalMoveException e) {
12    e.printStackTrace();
13    System.exit(1);
14  }
15 }
```

Figure 4-23: We never expect `deal()` to throw an exception when invoked from the constructor. If it does, a stack trace is printed and the program crashes.

The removePair() method might also throw an IllegalMoveException. A revised version of this method is shown in Figure 4–24. On line 14, we assume Card has an equals() method which returns true for two cards of the same rank, ignoring suit. This is reasonable, because while many card games compare the ranks of cards, only a few unusual games involving multiple decks check to see if two cards have the same rank *and suit*.

```
1 /**
2  * Remove two Cards of the same rank, as specified by the user.
3  * @throws IllegalMoveException if the cards are not of the same
4  * rank.
5  */
6 public void removePair() throws IllegalMoveException {
7    System.out.print("Location (1-4) of first card? ");
8    int i = INPUT.nextInt();
9    System.out.print("Location (1-4) of second card? ");
10   int j = INPUT.nextInt();
11   INPUT.nextLine();              // To clear out input
12   Card card1 = stacks[i - 1].peek();
13   Card card2 = stacks[j - 1].peek();
14   if (!(card1.equals(card2))) {
15      throw new IllegalMoveException();
16   }
17   stacks[i - 1].pop();
18   stacks[j - 1].pop();
19 }
```

Figure 4-24: The revised removePair() method verifies that the cards chosen by the user have the same rank. If not, an exception is thrown.

We don't have to modify play(), because a single try/catch block can deal with an exception occurring anywhere in the block.

The removeLowCard() method (Figure 4–25) can also throw an IllegalMoveException. This invokes the getSuit() and getRank() methods from the Card class.

The behavior of the improved Idiot's Delight program is illustrated in Figure 4–26.

There are some classes of exceptions that can be thrown in so many places that catching them or passing them on would be an enormous nuisance. For example, any method which performs arithmetic might conceivably throw an ArithmeticException. Java does not require that exceptions of these classes, which descend from the RuntimeException subclass of Exception, be declared in method signatures. The built-in classes ArithmeticException, NullPointerException, and ArrayIndexOutOfBoundsException all descend from RuntimeException.

```
 1 /**
 2  * Remove the lower of two cards of the same suit, as specified by
 3  * the user.
 4  * @throws IllegalMoveException if the low card is not of the same
 5  * suit as, and of lower rank than, the high card.
 6  */
 7 public void removeLowCard() throws IllegalMoveException {
 8   System.out.print("Location (1-4) of low card? ");
 9   int i = INPUT.nextInt();
10   System.out.print("Location (1-4) of high card? ");
11   int j = INPUT.nextInt();
12   INPUT.nextLine();            // To clear out input
13   Card lowCard = stacks[i - 1].peek();
14   Card highCard = stacks[j - 1].peek();
15   if ((lowCard.getSuit() != highCard.getSuit())
16       || ( lowCard.getRank() > highCard.getRank())) {
17     throw new IllegalMoveException();
18   }
19   stacks[i - 1].pop();
20 }
```

Figure 4-25: The revised removeLowCard() method can also throw an IllegalMoveException.

```
 1 Welcome to Idiot's Delight.
 2
 3 7h Tc Th 4h
 4 48 cards left in the deck
 5 Your command (pair, suit, deal, or quit)? suit
 6 Location (1-4) of low card? 1
 7 Location (1-4) of high card? 2
 8 I'm sorry, that's not a legal move.
 9
10 7h Tc Th 4h
11 48 cards left in the deck
12 Your command (pair, suit, deal, or quit)?
```

Figure 4-26: Now, when we make an illegal move, the program neither crashes nor lets us get away with it.

RuntimeExceptions are preventable, so they should never occur in a program which checks for valid input. For example, by checking whether deck is empty before invoking its deal() method on line 8 of Figure 4–20, we prevent deck.deal() from throwing an ArrayIndexOutOfBoundsException. If a RuntimeException *does* occur, it is normally passed all the way back to the system, causing a program crash.

Returning to the Stack interface (Figure 4–2), we see that the comments for peek() and pop() mention that they might throw EmptyStructureExceptions, but the method signatures do not declare such a possibility. This is because the EmptyStructureException class extends Runtime-Exception. An EmptyStructureException is preventable, because we can use isEmpty() to check whether a Stack is empty before peeking at it or popping it. The EmptyStructureException class is shown in Figure 4–27.

```
1 /**
2  * Thrown when an attempt is made to access an element in a
3  * structure which contains no elements.
4  */
5 public class EmptyStructureException extends RuntimeException {
6 }
```

Figure 4-27: The EmptyStructureException class.

Figure 4–28 shows the inheritance hierarchy of all of the exception classes we have seen.

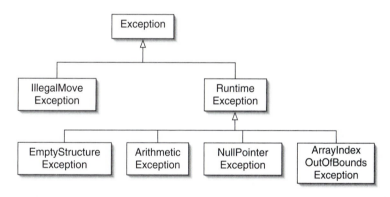

Figure 4-28: Since RuntimeExceptions are preventable, the possibility of throwing them does not have to be declared in method signatures.

Exercises

4.7 Discuss whether it makes sense for a method to be capable of throwing more than one kind of exception.

4.8 On line 12 of Figure 4–23, the constructor invokes the printStackTrace() method on e, which is an instance of IllegalMoveException. Speculate on how Java knows that e has such a method.

4.9   The Idiot's Delight program can still be crashed if the user specifies an invalid stack number such as 0 or 5. Describe how to fix the program.

4.10   The Idiot's Delight program does not prevent the user from giving the command `pair` and then entering the same stack number twice. What happens if the user does this? Describe how to fix the program.

4.11   Can the user cheat in Idiot's Delight by giving the command `suit` and then entering the same stack number twice? If so, fix the program. If not, explain why not.

4.4 The Queue Interface

A *queue* (pronounced like the letter Q) is very similar to a stack, except that items are inserted in one end (the back) and removed from the other end (the front). A queue therefore follows a *first-in, first-out* or *FIFO* policy. The standard analogy for a queue is a line of people at a ticket office. The behavior of a queue is illustrated in Figure 4–29.

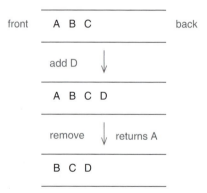

Figure 4–29: In a queue, objects are added to the back and removed from the front.

The Queue interface is shown in Figure 4–30. We will provide one implementation (Array-Queue) in Chapter 5 and another (LinkedQueue) in Chapter 6.

Example: War

Queues appear in many contexts, such as storing a sequence of documents to be printed. We will use them to implement the game of War (Figure 4–31). Each player's hand is a queue, because cards won are added at the bottom but cards played are removed from the top. Note that "bottom" and "top" are concepts from the game; as far as queues are concerned, these are actually the back and front of each player's queue of cards.

```
1 /** A first-in, first-out queue of Objects. */
2 public interface Queue<E> {
3
4    /** Add target to the back of this Queue. */
5    public void add(E target);
6
7    /** Return true if this Queue is empty. */
8    public boolean isEmpty();
9
10   /**
11    * Remove and return the front item from this Queue.
12    * @throws EmptyStructureException if the Queue is empty.
13    */
14   public E remove();
15
16 }
```

Figure 4-30: The Queue interface, like the Stack interface, is generic.

War

Players: 2

Object: To force the other player to run out of cards.

Setup: Deal out the entire deck, 26 cards to each player. Each player's cards are kept in a face-down pile.

Play: In each round, each player turns up the top card on his pile. The player with the higher-ranking card takes both cards and adds them to the bottom of his pile. A tie is resolved by a "war": each player plays three cards from his pile face-down and another face-up. The high card among these last two wins all ten cards. Subsequent ties are handled similarly, with the eventual winner of the round taking an even larger pile of cards.

Game End: If a player is unable to play a card (even during a war), he loses.

Figure 4-31: The children's card game War can take a very long time to play.

Like Idiot's Delight, this program involves a Deck and some Cards. The relationship between the classes involved is shown in Figure 4–32.

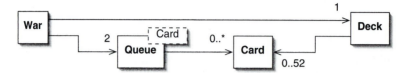

Figure 4–32: The class structure of the War program is very similar to that of the Idiot's Delight program.

We begin with the fields, constructor, and `main()` method (Figure 4–33). It seems a little strange to deal cards to the *bottom* of the players' hands, but it achieves the goal of distributing the shuffled cards into two equal-sized hands.

```
1 import java.util.Scanner;
2
3 /** The card game War for two players. */
4 public class War {
5
6   /** For reading from the Console. */
7   public static final Scanner INPUT = new Scanner(System.in);
8
9   /** Player 1's pile of Cards. */
10  private Queue<Card> hand1;
11
12  /** Player 2's pile of Cards. */
13  private Queue<Card> hand2;
14
15  /** Deal all the Cards out to the players. */
16  public War() {
17    hand1 = new ArrayQueue<Card>();
18    hand2 = new ArrayQueue<Card>();
19    Deck deck = new Deck();
20    deck.shuffle();
21    while (!(deck.isEmpty())) {
22      hand1.add(deck.deal());
23      hand2.add(deck.deal());
24    }
25  }
26
27  /** Create and play the game. */
28  public static void main(String[] args) {
29    System.out.println("Welcome to War.");
```

Figure 4-33: First parts of the War class. (Part 1 of 2)

```
30        War game = new War();
31        game.play();
32    }
33
34 }
```

Figure 4-33: First parts of the War class. (Part 2 of 2)

The play() method (Figure 4–34) takes care of checking for victory, but it shoves the work of playing the cards off onto playRound().

```
 1 /** Play until one player runs out of Cards. */
 2 public void play() {
 3   while (!(hand1.isEmpty() || hand2.isEmpty())) {
 4     System.out.print("\nHit return to play round: ");
 5     INPUT.nextLine();
 6     playRound();
 7     if (hand1.isEmpty()) {
 8       System.out.println("Player 2 wins!");
 9     }
10     if (hand2.isEmpty()) {
11       System.out.println("Player 1 wins!");
12     }
13   }
14 }
```

Figure 4-34: The play() method.

In playRound() (Figure 4–35), we use two Stacks to keep track of the pile of played cards in front of each player. This is appropriate because new cards are added to these piles only at the top. Lines 3–4 create these Stacks. Lines 5–6 have each player play one card to their Stack. The main loop on lines 7–18 compares the top cards on the two Stacks; if one is greater, someone has won the hand. Otherwise, we hold a war and check again. Since the war might end the game by causing one player to run out of cards, the method settledByWar() returns a boolean value indicating whether this happened. If so, playRound() ends.

```
 1 /** Play one round. */
 2 public void playRound() {
 3   Stack<Card> stack1 = new ArrayStack<Card>();
 4   Stack<Card> stack2 = new ArrayStack<Card>();
 5   stack1.push(hand1.remove());
 6   stack2.push(hand2.remove());
```

Figure 4-35: The playRound() method uses two Stacks. (Part 1 of 2)

```
 7  do {
 8    Card card1 = stack1.peek();
 9    Card card2 = stack2.peek();
10    System.out.println(card1 + " " + card2);
11    Queue<Card> winner = null;
12    if (card1.getRank() > card2.getRank()) {
13      winner = hand1;
14    }
15    if (card1.getRank() < card2.getRank()) {
16      winner = hand2;
17    }
18    if (winner != null) {
19      give(stack1, stack2, winner);
20      return;
21    }
22  } while (!settledByWar(stack1, stack2));
23 }
```

Figure 4-35: The playRound() method uses two Stacks. (Part 2 of 2)

The settledByWar() method (Figure 4–36) must take the two Stacks as arguments, so that it can play new cards onto them. The method tries to play four more cards from each player (removing them from the player's hand and pushing them onto the player's stack), but it may return early if one player runs out. If this happens, it must give the cards to the winner before returning.

```
 1 /**
 2  * Play a war over stack1 and stack2.  If this ends the game because
 3  * one player runs out of cards, give the cards to the winning
 4  * player and return true.  Otherwise, return false.
 5  */
 6 public boolean settledByWar(Stack stack1, Stack stack2) {
 7    System.out.println("War!");
 8    for (int i = 0; i < 4; i++) {
 9      if (hand1.isEmpty()) {
10        give(stack1, stack2, hand2);
11        return true;
12      }
13      stack1.push(hand1.remove());
14      if (hand2.isEmpty()) {
15        give(stack1, stack2, hand1);
16        return true;
17      }
18      stack2.push(hand2.remove());
19    }
20    return false;
21 }
```

Figure 4-36: The settledByWar() method.

All that remains is give() (Figure 4–37), which pops all of the cards off each Stack and adds them into the winner's hand.

```
 1 /** Give all of the Cards played to the winning player. */
 2 public void give(Stack<Card> stack1,
 3                  Stack<Card> stack2,
 4                  Queue<Card> winner) {
 5   if (winner == hand1) {
 6     System.out.println("Player 1 gets the cards");
 7   } else {
 8     System.out.println("Player 2 gets the cards");
 9   }
10   while (!(stack1.isEmpty())) {
11     winner.add(stack1.pop());
12   }
13   while (!(stack2.isEmpty())) {
14     winner.add(stack2.pop());
15   }
16 }
```

Figure 4-37: The give() method transfers all of the cards played in the last round to the winner of the round.

Figure 4–38 shows the first few rounds of a game.

```
 1 Welcome to War.
 2
 3 Hit return to play round:
 4 9d 2c
 5 Player 1 gets the cards
 6
 7 Hit return to play round:
 8 6h 6s
 9 War!
10 Kh 7s
11 Player 1 gets the cards
12
13 Hit return to play round:
14 Td Kd
15 Player 2 gets the cards
```

Figure 4-38: The first few of many rounds in a game of War.

Exercises

4.12   The following sequence of methods are to be invoked on an initially empty queue. Draw the state of the queue after each step. Indicate what is returned by any methods that return values.

```
add("a");
add("b");
add("c");
remove();
add("d");
add("e");
remove();
remove();
```

4.13   There is no method in our Queue interface which is equivalent to the `peek()` method in the Stack interface. Devise one and add it to the Queue interface. Be sure to specify whether it returns the front or the back element of the Queue.

4.14   How would the game of War differ if the piles of cards were stacks instead of queues? Do you think this makes the game more or less entertaining? Explain.

Summary

Stacks and queues are both collections of objects. A stack follows a last-in, first-out policy: objects are both pushed onto and popped off the top. A queue follows a first-in, first-out policy: objects are added to the back and removed from the front. Both of these abstract data types are formalized in interfaces, which we will implement in Chapters 5 and 6.

Java 1.5 introduces generic types and interfaces. These allow us to distinguish between, for example, a Stack of Integers and a Stack of Strings. This addition to the language greatly reduces the amount of casting we have to do when using general-purpose data structures. The only unpleasant feature is that generics do not play well with arrays.

One particularly important stack is the call stack. Whenever a method is invoked, a new call frame is pushed onto the stack. This keeps track of any variables in the method, as well as how far the method has progressed. When a method returns, the corresponding call frame is popped off the stack, and the next frame down becomes active.

Instead of returning, a method may throw an exception. The invoking method (corresponding to the next call frame) must either pass on the exception or catch it. If an exception is passed all the way back to the Java system, the program crashes and a stack trace is printed. An exception may be caught in a try/catch block.

If a method might conceivably throw an exception, this must be declared in the method's signature, unless the exception class is a descendant of the RuntimeException class. These exceptions correspond to preventable events, such as dividing by zero or popping an empty stack.

Vocabulary

call frame. System-controlled object indicating the current state (variable values, line number, etc.) of a method invocation.

call stack. System-controlled stack holding a call frame for each method invocation currently in progress.

catch. Intercept an exception so that it may be dealt with.

deque. Double-ended queue allowing insertion into or deletion from either end (Problem 4.18).

exception. Unusual situation caused by, for example, division by zero.

first-in, first-out (FIFO). Policy followed by a queue, in which the least-recently-inserted item is the first one removed.

generic. Class or interface with one or more type parameters. Generics allow us to write general-purpose code without awkward and dangerous casting from the Object class.

infix notation. Arithmetic notation in which the operator appears in between its operands, as $2 + 2$ (Project 4.20).

last-in, first-out (LIFO). Policy followed by a stack, in which the most-recently-inserted item is the first one removed.

peek. Return the topmost item on a stack without modifying the stack.

pop. Remove and return the topmost item on a stack.

postfix notation. Arithmetic notation in which the operator appears after its operands, as $2\ 2\ +$ (Project 4.20).

push. Add an item to the top of a stack.

queue. Collection of items stored in FIFO order. Supports the operations of adding and removing.

stack. Collection of items stored in LIFO order. Supports the operations of pushing, popping, and peeking.

stack trace. Printout of the state of the call stack. Useful for debugging.

throw. Cause an exception.

type parameter. Type which must be specified whenever a generic type is used. For example, the Stack type has a parameter indicating the type of the items on the Stack.

Problems

4.15   Write a program which reads numbers from the user until the user enters a 0. The program then prints out all of the numbers that were entered, in the order in which they were entered.

4.16   Write a program which reads numbers from the user until the user enters a 0. The program then prints out all of the numbers that were entered, in *the reverse of* the order in which they were entered.

4.17   Choose a previously implemented game and use exceptions to prevent users from making illegal moves. Explain why the game of Beetle is not a reasonable choice.

4.18   A *deque* (pronounced "deck"), or double-ended queue, is like a queue but it allows insertion into or deletion from either end. Write a Deque interface.

4.19   Write a class DoubleStackQueue which implements the Queue interface. Its only fields are two Stacks, `front` and `back`. Insertion is implemented by pushing onto `back`, while deletion is implemented by popping `front`. The challenge is to deal with the situation where `front` is empty, `back` is not, and we have to pop.

Projects

4.20   Java uses **infix notation** for arithmetic. In infix notation, the operator (+, –, *, or /) appears in between the operands. For example:

```
2 + 2
3 / 5
```

An alternative is **postfix notation**, where the operator appears at the end. The expressions above would be written as

```
2 2 +
3 5 /
```

The advantage of postfix notation is that complicated expressions do not require parentheses. For example, using infix notation, we need parentheses for the expression:

```
(5 - 2) * 4
```

The value of this expression is 12. If we leave out the parentheses, this becomes

```
5 - 2 * 4
```

which is –3.

Using postfix notation, the first expression is

```
5 2 - 4 *
```

but the second one is

```
5 2 4 * -
```

No parentheses, no ambiguity!

The behavior of a postfix calculator can be understood in terms of a stack. The stack is initially empty. Whenever a number is entered, it is pushed onto the stack. Whenever an operator is entered, the top two numbers on the stack are popped and combined with the appropriate operator. The result is pushed onto the stack.

Write a postfix calculator, in the form of a class Calc. Figure 4–39 shows the calculator at work.

```
 1 :  2
 2 2.0:  2
 3 2.0:  +
 4 4.0:  5
 5 5.0:  *
 6 20.0:  7
 7 7.0:  2
 8 2.0:  /
 9 3.5:  -
10 16.5:  quit
```

Figure 4-39: The postfix calculator (Project 4.20) at work.

Notice that the calculator prints the top item on the stack (if any) to the left of the prompt. Your calculator should support the operators +, *, -, and /, as well as the command quit. Use doubles, not ints. Make sure that, if the user enters 5, 3, and -, he gets 2, not –2.

Hint: Read in a String with `INPUT.nextLine()`. After you are sure that the String is not one of the commands mentioned, you can convert it into a double with the method `Double.parseDouble()`.

5

Array-Based Structures

This chapter discusses general-purpose array-based structures. Each of these classes has an array as a field. We present implementations of the Stack and Queue interfaces from Chapter 4, as well as a new interface List and one implementation of it.

An array has a fixed length—it can't get any longer or shorter. Section 5.1 presents techniques for getting around this problem, in the context of developing a class to represent a deck of playing cards.

Section 5.2 shows how to implement the Stack and Queue interfaces. Section 5.3 presents the List interface and the ArrayList class which implements it. The Iterator interface, explained in Section 5.4, is a general-purpose technique for traversing a List—that is, doing something with or to each element of the List.

These structures are so commonly used that standard implementations are built into Java. Section 5.5 introduces the Java collections framework, which provides many useful general-purpose data structures.

5.1 Shrinking and Stretching Arrays

The size of an array is determined when it is allocated. We can overwrite individual elements, but we can't make the array longer or shorter. In this section, we will see some ways around this

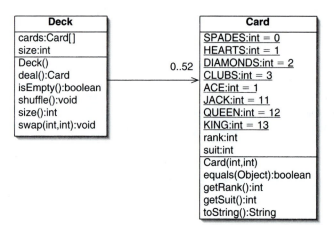

Figure 5-1: UML class diagram of the Deck and Card classes.

problem. As a running example, we will write the Deck class, which we mentioned in Chapter 4. A Deck holds a varying number of Cards—originally 52, fewer as Cards are dealt from the Deck. These two classes are illustrated in Figure 5–1.

The Card Class

Before writing Deck, let's take a moment to write Card. A Card has two fields, `rank` and `suit`. Since, once a Card is created, these things never change, we don't provide mutators for them, only accessors (Figure 5–2).

```
 1 /** A playing card. */
 2 public class Card {
 3
 4   /** Number or face on this Card. */
 5   private int rank;
 6
 7   /** Suit of this Card. */
 8   private int suit;
 9
10   /** Initialize the rank and suit. */
11   public Card(int rank, int suit) {
12     this.rank = rank;
13     this.suit = suit;
14   }
15
```

Figure 5-2: Fields, constructor, and accessors for the Card class. (Part 1 of 2)

```
16   /** Return the rank of this Card. */
17   public int getRank() {
18      return rank;
19   }
20
21   /** Return the suit of this Card. */
22   public int getSuit() {
23      return suit;
24   }
25
26 }
```

Figure 5-2: Fields, constructor, and accessors for the Card class. (Part 2 of 2)

The rank is either a number or one of ace, jack, king, or queen. We assign the values 1, 11, 12, and 13, respectively, to these other values. Rather than have these magic numbers scattered all over our code, we define a constant for each one. Similarly, we define a constant for each suit (Figure 5-3).

```
 1 /** Suit of spades. */
 2 public static final int SPADES = 0;
 3
 4 /** Suit of hearts. */
 5 public static final int HEARTS = 1;
 6
 7 /** Suit of diamonds. */
 8 public static final int DIAMONDS = 2;
 9
10 /** Suit of clubs. */
11 public static final int CLUBS = 3;
12
13 /** Rank of ace, equivalent to 1. */
14 public static final int ACE = 1;
15
16 /** Rank of jack. */
17 public static final int JACK = 11;
18
19 /** Rank of queen. */
20 public static final int QUEEN = 12;
21
22 /** Rank of king. */
23 public static final int KING = 13;
```

Figure 5-3: Constants from the Card class.

All that remain are the standard methods `equals()` and `toString()` (Figure 5-4). Note that suit is ignored in `equals()`. The `charAt()` method from the String class is used to good effect in the `toString()` method.

```
 1 /**
 2  * Return true if and only if that Card has the same rank as
 3  * this one.  Suit is ignored.
 4  */
 5 public boolean equals(Object that) {
 6   if (this == that) {
 7     return true;
 8   }
 9   if (that == null) {
10     return false;
11   }
12   if (getClass() != that.getClass()) {
13     return false;
14   }
15   Card thatCard = (Card)that;
16   return rank == thatCard.rank;
17 }
18
19 public String toString() {
20   return "" + "-A23456789TJQK".charAt(rank) + "shdc".charAt(suit);
21 }
```

Figure 5-4: Remaining methods from the Card class. An extra character is included at the beginning of the String of rank names because 'A' corresponds to 1, not 0.

Shrinking Arrays

It is clear that the Deck class will need an array of Cards. Specifically, since a Deck can never hold more than 52 cards, this array should have a length of 52 (Figure 5–5).

```
 1 /** Standard deck of 52 playing cards. */
 2 public class Deck {
 3
 4   /** The Cards in this Deck. */
 5   private Card[] cards;
 6
 7   /** Create all 52 Cards, in order. */
 8   public Deck() {
 9     cards = new Card[52];
10   }
11
12 }
```

Figure 5-5: A first draft of the Deck class. The constructor does not yet create the Cards as the comment promises.

When we create an instance of this class, we have room for 52 cards (Figure 5–6). The problem, of course, is that we don't always need this much room. How can we change the size of the array?

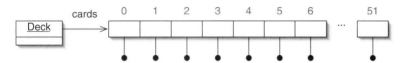

Figure 5-6: A Deck contains an array of Cards. The array has length 52.

The secret is to include an extra field in Deck: an int `size` telling us how many Cards are currently in the Deck. Only the first `size` elements in the array are considered part of the Deck. For example, if size is 3, then only elements 0, 1, and 2 are considered part of the Deck. While elements 3 and later have values, we don't know or care what they are. This is shown in Figure 5–7.

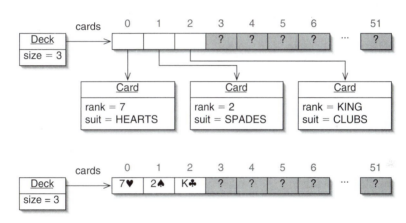

Figure 5-7: The field `size` indicates that only the first three positions in the array `cards` are considered "in use." This figure shows two instance diagrams of the same structure. The version above makes it explicit that each of the first three elements of `cards` is a reference to a Card instance. The version below simply shows each Card's rank and suit in the corresponding array position.

It is important to distinguish between the *size* of the Deck (how many Cards it currently contains) and the *capacity* of the Deck (the maximum number of Cards it can contain—52).

With this idea in mind, we can rewrite the Deck class so that the constructor fills the Deck with 52 Cards (Figure 5–8). This version of the constructor also creates all of the Cards by looping through the suits and the ranks.

The field `size` makes certain methods extremely easy to write (Figure 5–9).

```
1 /** Standard deck of 52 playing cards. */
2 public class Deck {
3
4   /** The Cards in this Deck. */
5   private Card[] cards;
6
7   /** Number of Cards currently in this Deck. */
8   private int size;
9
10  /** Create all 52 Cards, in order. */
11  public Deck() {
12    cards = new Card[52];
13    size = 0;
14    for (int suit = Card.SPADES; suit <= Card.CLUBS; suit++) {
15      for (int rank = Card.ACE; rank <= Card.KING; rank++) {
16        cards[size] = new Card(rank, suit);
17        size += 1;
18      }
19    }
20  }
21
22 }
```

Figure 5-8: By the end of the constructor for the revised Deck class, `size` is 52.

```
1 /** Return true if the Deck contains no Cards. */
2 public boolean isEmpty() {
3   return size == 0;
4 }
5
6 /** Return the number of Cards currently in the Deck. */
7 public int size() {
8   return size;
9 }
```

Figure 5-9: Methods indicating the fullness of a Deck are trivial.

The only method (besides the constructor) that modifies `size` is `deal()`, which removes and returns the top card on the Deck (Figure 5–10).

```
1 /** Remove one Card from the Deck and return it. */
2 public Card deal() {
3   size--;
4   return cards[size];
5 }
```

Figure 5-10: The `deal()` method modifies the field `size`.

Although `deal()` is a very short method, its behavior is interesting. It begins by reducing the size of the Deck on line 3. The Card we want to return is now at index `size`. This is in the "not in use" part of the Deck, but the Card is still there, so we can return it in line 4. This is illustrated in Figure 5–11.

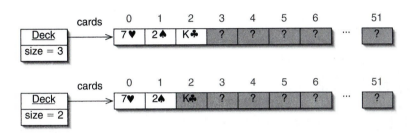

Figure 5–11: Dealing from a Deck. The Deck before dealing, with the king of clubs on top, is shown above. When `size` is reduced (below), element 2 ceases to be part of the Deck, but the value at that position does not change, so we can still return it.

All that remains to complete the Deck class is the `shuffle()` method. This could get quite complicated if we attempted to model the "riffle shuffle" that most Americans use when shuffling physical cards. Fortunately, there is a simpler algorithm. We must separate the *problem specification* (rearrange the Cards in a random order) from the *algorithm* we happen to know.

Rearranging the Cards in a random order means that any Card is equally likely to end up in position 51, any of the remaining Cards is equally likely to end up in position 50, and so on down. A simple algorithm falls out of this definition. We pick one index at random and swap the Card at that position with the one at position 51. There is a small probability (1 in 52) that we will pick index 51, but this is not a problem: we just swap the Card at position 51 with itself, which has no effect. There is a 1 in 52 chance that the Card that was on top of the Deck will remain there, which is exactly what we want.

We then pick one of the 51 remaining indices (0 through 50) and swap the Card there with the one at position 50. This continues down through position 1. We don't have to choose a random Card to swap into position 0, because there's only one Card left to choose from at that point.

The `shuffle()` method is shown in Figure 5–12. The swapping of Cards is handled by the method `swap()`. Since we don't want users of the Deck class to be swapping Cards at arbitrary indices (especially indices which are greater than or equal to `size`), we declare `swap()` protected.

Stretching Arrays

The field `size` allows us to change the size of a Deck at will, as long as `size` never exceeds the actual length of the array. What if a structure needs to grow beyond its original capacity? While this isn't necessary in a Deck, it is certainly an issue for stacks and queues, which can become arbitrarily large.

```
1 /** Randomly rearrange the Cards in the Deck. */
2 public void shuffle() {
3   for (int i = size - 1; i > 0; i--) {
4     swap(i, (int)(Math.random() * (i + 1)));
5   }
6 }
7
8 /** Swap the Cards at indices i and j. */
9 protected void swap(int i, int j) {
10   Card temp = cards[i];
11   cards[i] = cards[j];
12   cards[j] = temp;
13 }
```

Figure 5–12: The methods `shuffle()` and `swap()`.

The solution to this problem is somewhat shocking: we copy the entire contents of the array into a new, larger array (Figure 5–13). This operation can be time consuming, although we will see in Chapter 7 that it is not quite as bad as it appears.

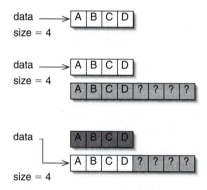

Figure 5–13: Stretching an array. The array `data` is full (top), so we can't add more elements. Instead, we copy the elements into a new, larger array (middle). Finally, `data` becomes a reference to the new array (bottom).

Exercises

5.1   Explain how to modify the Card class so that aces rank above kings, rather than below twos.

5.2   What would be the effect of swapping lines 14 and 15 in Figure 5–8?

5.3   Modify the `deal()` method (Figure 5–10) so that it throws an EmptyStructureException (Figure 4–27) if the Deck is empty.

5.4   Is it okay to invoke `shuffle()` on a non-full Deck? Explain.

5.5 Write a `main()` method to test the Deck class.

5.6 Does the stretching operation shown in Figure 5–13 alter the data structure's *size* or its *capacity*?

5.2 Implementing Stacks and Queues

We now have all the tools we need to implement the Stack and Queue interfaces from Chapter 4.

The ArrayStack Class

The ArrayStack class, which implements the Stack interface, is very similar to Deck. It contains an array `data` and an int `size`. When we create a new ArrayStack, `data` has room for one element and `size` is 0 (Figure 5–14). The Java wart involving generics and arrays comes up again on line 12. We can't allocate `new E[1]`, so we have to allocate `new Object[1]` and cast it to `E[]`. This causes a warning, but there's no way around it.

```
1 /** An array-based Stack. */
2 public class ArrayStack<E> implements Stack<E> {
3
4   /** Array of items in this Stack. */
5   private E[] data;
6
7   /** Number of items currently in this Stack. */
8   private int size;
9
10  /** The Stack is initially empty. */
11  public ArrayStack() {
12    data = (E[])(new Object[1]); // This causes a compiler warning
13    size = 0;
14  }
15
16 }
```

Figure 5–14: The generic ArrayStack class is similar to Deck.

The `isEmpty()` method (Figure 5–15) is identical to the one from Deck.

```
1 public boolean isEmpty() {
2   return size == 0;
3 }
```

Figure 5–15: It's easy to determine if an ArrayStack is empty.

The pop() method (Figure 5–16) is similar to deal(), although we throw an exception if the Stack is empty.

```
1 public Object pop() {
2   if (isEmpty()) {
3     throw new EmptyStructureException();
4   }
5   size--;
6   return data[size];
7 }
```

Figure 5-16: The pop() method can throw an EmptyStructureException.

The peek() method (Figure 5–17) is even easier because it doesn't change the Stack. We do have to be careful to return the element at position size - 1, which is the top item on the Stack, rather than at position size, which is the next available position in data.

```
1 public Object peek() {
2   if (isEmpty()) {
3     throw new EmptyStructureException();
4   }
5   return data[size - 1];
6 }
```

Figure 5-17: The peek() method returns the top element on the Stack.

All that remains is push(). If we try to push something onto a full Stack, the array is stretched, as described in Section 5.1. The code is given in Figure 5–18.

```
1 /** Return true if data is full. */
2 protected boolean isFull() {
3   return size == data.length;
4 }
5
6 public void push(Object target) {
7   if (isFull()) {
8     stretch();
9   }
10  data[size] = target;
11  size++;
12 }
13
```

Figure 5-18: The push() method and associated protected methods. The reason for doubling the length of **data**, rather than merely increasing it by 1, is explained in Chapter 7. (Part 1 of 2)

```
14 /** Double the length of data. */
15 protected void stretch() {
16   E[] newData = (E[])(new Object[data.length * 2]); // Warning
17   for (int i = 0; i < data.length; i++) {
18     newData[i] = data[i];
19   }
20   data = newData;
21 }
```

Figure 5-18: The push() method and associated protected methods. The reason for doubling the length of **data**, rather than merely increasing it by 1, is explained in Chapter 7. (Part 2 of 2)

Figure 5–19 shows the effects of push() and pop() operations on an ArrayStack.

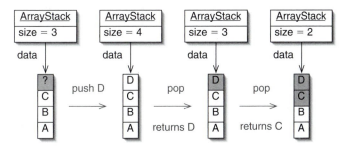

Figure 5-19: Instance diagram showing operations on an ArrayStack. These are the same operations shown in Figure 4–1. The shaded portions of **data** are not in use.

The ArrayQueue Class

The ArrayQueue class, which implements the Queue interface, makes further use of the idea of using only part of an array. There are, of course, complications.

We choose to make higher array indices correspond to elements closer to the back of the Queue. Thus, adding something to an ArrayQueue is exactly like pushing it onto an Array-Stack (Figure 5–20).

The problem comes when we remove an element from the queue. The first time we do this, the front of the queue is clearly at position 0. Afterward, the front of the queue is at index 1 (Figure 5–21).

We solve this problem with another field, an int front, which specifies where the queue starts. Whenever we remove, front is incremented, so we know where to find the first element the next time we remove. The next available position for adding is front + size.

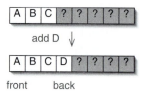

add D

Figure 5–20: Adding something into an ArrayQueue is exactly like pushing it onto an ArrayStack. For brevity, we leave out the ArrayStack object and show only the array.

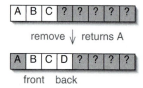

remove returns A

Figure 5–21: Removing an element causes the front of the queue to move along the array.

There is one more issue. After a series of insertions and deletions, the "in use" portion of the array runs up against the right end of the array. Once this happens, we can't add anything else to the queue, even though there are unused positions.

The solution is for the queue to wrap around, so that the next element added goes at position 0. This is illustrated in Figure 5–22.

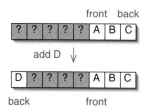

add D

Figure 5–22: After hitting the right end of the array, the queue wraps around to the beginning.

When we add an element, it should normally be placed at position

`front + size`

but it should instead be placed at position

`front + size - data.length`

if the first expression would produce an index beyond the end of the array. We could compute the position with an `if` statement:

```
int index = front + size;
if (index >= data.length) {
  index -= data.length;
}
```

A more elegant solution uses the % operator. Recall that this operator gives the remainder of a division. If we divide `front + size` by the capacity of the queue, the quotient is either 0 or 1. If it is 0, the % operator has no effect. If it is 1, the % operator subtracts the capacity one time. The single expression

```
(front + size) % data.length
```

therefore always produces the right index.

The code for the ArrayQueue class is given in Figure 5–23.

```
1  /** An array-based Queue. */
2  public class ArrayQueue<E> implements Queue<E> {
3
4    /** Array of items in this Queue. */
5    private E[] data;
6
7    /** Index of the frontmost element in this Queue. */
8    private int front;
9
10   /** Number of items currently in this Queue. */
11   private int size;
12
13   /** The Queue is initially empty. */
14   public ArrayQueue() {
15     data = (E[])(new Object[1]); // This causes a compiler warning
16     size = 0;
17     front = 0;
18   }
19
20   public void add(E target) {
21     if (isFull()) {
22       stretch();
23     }
24     data[(front + size) % data.length] = target;
25     size++;
26   }
27
28   public boolean isEmpty() {
29     return size == 0;
30   }
31
```

Figure 5-23: The ArrayQueue class. (Part 1 of 2)

```
32   /** Return true if data is full. */
33   protected boolean isFull() {
34     return size == data.length;
35   }
36
37   public E remove() {
38     if (isEmpty()) {
39       throw new EmptyStructureException();
40     }
41     E result = data[front];
42     front = (front + 1) % data.length;
43     size--;
44     return result;
45   }
46
47   /** Double the length of data. */
48   protected void stretch() {
49     E[] newData = (E[])(new Object[data.length * 2]); // Warning
50     for (int i = 0; i < data.length; i++) {
51       newData[i] = data[(front + i) % data.length];
52     }
53     data = newData;
54     front = 0;
55   }
56
57 }
```

Figure 5–23: The ArrayQueue class. (Part 2 of 2)

The operation of an ArrayQueue is illustrated in Figure 5–24.

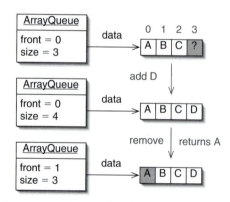

Figure 5–24: Operations on an ArrayQueue. These are the same operations shown in Figure 4–29.

Exercises

5.7 Suppose we modified line 12 of Figure 5–14 so that, in a new ArrayStack, **data** was an array of length 0. What problem would this cause?

5.8 Show that, when playing Idiot's Delight, there will never be more than 13 cards in any one stack. We can avoid stretching the stacks if we allocate an array this large when each ArrayStack is first constructed. Write a second, overloaded constructor for the ArrayStack class which takes one argument **capacity** and initializes data to be an array of length **capacity**. Modify the IdiotsDelight class to take advantage of this new constructor.

5.9 Can Deck be written as a subclass of ArrayStack? If so, is it a good idea? If not, why not?

5.10 Draw an instance diagram of an ArrayStack as it would look if, immediately after pushing D in Figure 5–19, we pushed E.

5.11 Write a **toString()** method for the ArrayStack class. Discuss whether it is preferable for the top of the Stack to appear on the left or the right end of the returned String.

5.12 What would happen if we were to add something to a full ArrayQueue without stretching the array?

5.13 Why is the **stretch()** method from ArrayQueue (Figure 5–23) more complicated than the one from ArrayStack (Figure 5–18)?

5.14 Write a **toString()** method for the ArrayQueue class. Discuss whether it is preferable for the front of the queue to appear on the left or the right end of the returned String.

5.3 The List Interface

The Stack and Queue interfaces, while useful, are somewhat limited. We can only get at the ends of such data structures. We cannot, for example, easily search through a Stack for some element. In this section, we present and implement the List interface, which describes a more general-purpose linear sequence.

The Interface

A List is a sequence of elements. The first element is element 0, the next is element 1, and so on. It is similar to an array, but it does not have a fixed size. Several methods are required of any List implementation. The List interface is given in Figure 5–25.

The behavior of most of the methods is explained in the comments.

We will implement the List interface with a class ArrayList. The constructor for ArrayList produces an initially empty List. Thus, if we declare

```
List<String> list = new ArrayList<String>();
```

```
 1 /** A list of elements. */
 2 public interface List<E> extends Iterable<E> {
 3
 4    /** Add target to the back of this List. */
 5    public void add(E target);
 6
 7    /** Return true if some item in this List equals() target. */
 8    public boolean contains(E target);
 9
10    /** Return the indexth element of this List. */
11    public E get(int index);
12
13    /** Return true if this List is empty. */
14    public boolean isEmpty();
15
16    /**
17     * Remove and return the indexth element from this List, shifting
18     * all later items one place left.
19     */
20    public E remove(int index);
21
22    /**
23     * Remove the first occurrence of target from this List, shifting
24     * all later items one place left.  Return true if this List
25     * contained the specified element.
26     */
27    public boolean remove(E target);
28
29    /** Replace the indexth element of this List with target. */
30    public void set(int index, E target);
31
32    /** Return the number of element in this List. */
33    public int size();
34
35 }
```

Figure 5-25: The List interface. The Iterable interface is discussed in Section 5.4.

and then

```
list.add("eggs");
list.add("bread");
list.add("tea");
```

then list is the ArrayList that is printed as [eggs bread tea].

At this point, list.contains("eggs") is true, but list.contains("rutabagas") is false.

The expression `list.get(1)` returns `"bread"` because, as with arrays, list indices start at 0.

Not surprisingly, `list.isEmpty()` returns false.

The expression `list.remove(0)` both modifies `list` to be [bread tea] and returns `"eggs"`.

If we perform the invocation `list.remove("llamachow")` on the resulting List, no change is made and `false` is returned. On the other hand, `list.remove("tea")` reduces `list` to [bread] and returns `true`.

Since there is only one element left, `list.size()` returns 1.

The ArrayList Class

We now implement the List interface with the ArrayList class. Like an ArrayStack, an ArrayList has two fields, `data` and `size` (Figure 5–26).

```
1 /** An array-based List. */
2 public class ArrayList<E> implements List<E> {
3
4   /** Array of elements in this List. */
5   private E[] data;
6
7   /** Number of elements currently in this List. */
8   private int size;
9
10   /** The List is initially empty. */
11   public ArrayList() {
12     data = (E[])(new Object[1]); // This causes a compiler warning
13     size = 0;
14   }
15
16 }
```

Figure 5-26: Fields and constructor for the ArrayList class.

Several of the ArrayList methods (Figure 5–27) are either trivial or identical to methods from ArrayStack.

The first interesting method is `contains()` (Figure 5–28). To determine whether an ArrayList contains some item, we work our way down `data`, comparing each element to the target. If we find it, we return `true`. If we get to the end of the "in use" portion of `data`, we return `false`.

The `toString()` method uses a similar `for` loop (Figure 5–29).

As specified by the List interface, there are two overloaded `remove()` methods (Figure 5–30). The first one removes and returns the item at a particular location. The second one removes the first occurrence of a particular item, if any.

```
 1 public void add(E target) {
 2   if (isFull()) {
 3     stretch();
 4   }
 5   data[size] = target;
 6   size++;
 7 }
 8
 9 public boolean isEmpty() {
10   return size == 0;
11 }
12
13 /** Return true if data is full. */
14 protected boolean isFull() {
15   return size == data.length;
16 }
17
18 public E get(int index) {
19   return data[index];
20 }
21
22 public void set(int index, E target) {
23   data[index] = target;
24 }
25
26 public int size() {
27   return size;
28 }
29
30 /** Double the length of data. */
31 protected void stretch() {
32   E[] newData = (E[])(new Object[data.length * 2]); // Warning
33   for (int i = 0; i < data.length; i++) {
34     newData[i] = data[i];
35   }
36   data = newData;
37 }
```

Figure 5-27: These methods from ArrayList are either trivial or identical to methods from ArrayStack.

In both cases, all subsequent elements are shifted one place to the left. This shifting is illustrated in Figure 5–31.

The remaining method, iterator(), is explained in Section 5.4.

```
1 public boolean contains(E target) {
2   for (int i = 0; i < size; i++) {
3     if (data[i].equals(target)) {
4       return true;
5     }
6   }
7   return false;
8 }
```

Figure 5-28: In contains(), each element is compared with target.

```
1 public String toString() {
2   String result = "[ ";
3   for (int i = 0; i < size; i++) {
4     result += data[i] + " ";
5   }
6   return result + "]";
7 }
```

Figure 5-29: The toString() method.

```
1 public E remove(int index) {
2   E result = data[index];
3   for (int i = index + 1; i < size; i++) {
4     data[i - 1] = data[i];
5   }
6   size--;
7   return result;
8 }
9
10 public boolean remove(E target) {
11   for (int i = 0; i < size; i++) {
12     if (data[i].equals(target)) {
13       for (int j = i; j < size - 1; j++) {
14         data[j] = data[j + 1];
15       }
16       size--;
17       return true;
18     }
19   }
20   return false;
21 }
```

Figure 5-30: ArrayList has two overloaded remove() methods. On a successful removal, both require that later Objects be shifted left.

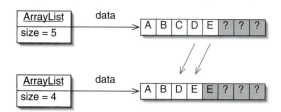

Figure 5–31: In the ArrayList above, the element C (at position 2) is to be removed. This requires each subsequent element to be shifted left one position.

Exercises

5.15   Explain what's wrong with the version of contains() in Figure 5–32.

```
1 public boolean contains(E target) {
2   for (E e : data) {
3     if (e.equals(target)) {
4       return true;
5     }
6   }
7   return false;
8 }
```

Figure 5–32: Broken version of contains() for Exercise 5.15.

5.16   The List interface specifies two overloaded remove() methods. Through experimentation, determine which one Java uses if we invoke remove(3) on a List<Integer>. How can we force Java to use the other one?

5.17   Modify the get() and set() methods (Figure 5–27) so that they throw an IndexOutOfBoundsException if the argument index is either too low (less than 0) or too high (greater than or equal to size). (IndexOutOfBoundsException is the direct superclass of ArrayIndexOutOfBoundsException.)

5.18   Explain why the loop in the first version of remove() (Figure 5–30) starts at index + 1 instead of index.

5.19   Write an equals() method for the ArrayList class. This method should compare only elements in the "in use" region of data.

5.20   Write a method indexOf() that takes one argument, an element target, and returns the index of the first occurrence of target in this ArrayList, or –1 if target does not appear.

5.21   Write a method `removeAll()` that takes one argument, an element `target`. It removes all elements which are `equals()` to `target` from this ArrayList.

5.22   Write a method `count()` that takes one argument, an element `target`. It returns the number of elements in this ArrayList which are `equals()` to `target`.

5.23   Write a `main()` method to test the ArrayList class.

5.4 Iterators

On many occasions we want to *traverse* a List—that is, *visit* (do something with or to) each element. To give just a few examples, we might want to:

- Traverse a List of Integers and add each one to a running tally.

- Traverse a List of Doubles to find the maximum of the elements.

- Print each element of a List.

- Compare each element of a List with the corresponding element of another List.

- Traverse a List of URLs to verify that each one leads to a web page that still exists.

A method to accomplish any of these things has the same basic structure as the `contains()` and `toString()` methods from ArrayList (Figure 5–28 and Figure 5–29):

```
for (int i = 0; i < size; i++) {
  // Do something with data[i]
}
```

Such a method would have to appear in the ArrayList class, because it directly accesses the fields `data` and `size`. We *could* write a method for each traversal we want to perform, but the ArrayList class is supposed to be general-purpose. Code for such specific tasks doesn't belong in this class.

A better approach is to produce an object called an *iterator* which allows us to traverse the List. An iterator has methods for three requests:

- "Are there more elements in the List?"

- "What is the next element?"

- "You know that last element you returned? Remove it from the List."

This abstract data type is formalized in the Iterator interface, which is in the java.util package.

The Iterator Interface

The Iterator interface in the java.util class specifies three methods: `hasNext()`, `next()`, and `remove()`. As shown in Figure 5–33, none of them take any arguments.

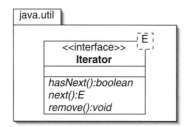

Figure 5-33: The Iterator interface is in the java.util package.

The `hasNext()` method returns true if there is a next element to be visited. The `next()` method returns the next element. These two methods are usually used in a loop like this:

```
java.util.Iterator iter = list.iterator();
while (iter.hasNext()) {
  // Do something with iter.next()
}
```

We must be careful to invoke `next()` only once on each pass through the loop, because it both returns an element and advances the Iterator. If we say something like

```
if ((iter.next() != null) || (iter.next().equals(target))) {
  ...
}
```

we will advance *two* elements at a time—almost certainly not what we want.

The `remove()` method removes the last item visited from the data structure associated with the Iterator. We should invoke this only after invoking `next()`.

The documentation for the Iterator mentions that these methods can throw certain exceptions. (These will be left as exercises in our implementation.) The `next()` method throws a java.util.NoSuchElementException if there are no more elements to visit. This can be avoided by always checking `hasNext()` before invoking `next()`.

The `remove()` method can throw a java.util.IllegalStateException if `next()` has never been invoked, or has not been invoked since the last invocation of `remove()`. (Only the last element returned by `next()` can be removed.) It is also legal to write an implementation of Iterator which does not support removal. In such a class, the `remove()` method does nothing but throw a java.util.UnsupportedOperationException.

The Iterable Interface

The Iterable interface requires one method, which returns an Iterator. The signature of this method is:

```
public Iterator<E> iterator();
```

Our List interface extends Iterable, so any class implementing List (such as ArrayList) must provide this method. We will do so momentarily.

If a class implements Iterable, we can traverse an instance of that class using an enhanced for loop (Appendix A). For example, if numbers is an ArrayList<Integer>, then we can compute its sum with this short code:

```
int sum = 0;
for (int n : numbers) {
  sum += n;
}
```

The ArrayIterator Class

The iterator() method in ArrayList has to return an instance of some class which implements Iterator. We will return an instance of the class ArrayIterator. An ArrayIterator knows about the ArrayList with which it is associated. In other words, an ArrayIterator is-a Iterator, but it has-a ArrayList (Figure 5–34).

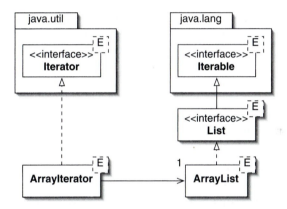

Figure 5–34: An ArrayIterator is-a java.util.Iterator, but it has-a ArrayList. Strangely, the Iterable interface is in the java.lang package, not the java.util package.

The iterator() method for ArrayList (Figure 5–35) simply creates an instance of ArrayIterator.

```
1 public java.util.Iterator<E> iterator() {
2   return new ArrayIterator<E>(this);
3 }
```

Figure 5–35: The iterator() method from ArrayList.

An ArrayIterator needs two fields: the ArrayList it is traversing and an int indicating how far down the ArrayList it is. It turns out to be convenient to keep track of the index of the *previously* visited element. We therefore call this int previous.

To find the next element to return, we increment `previous` and invoke `get(previous)` on the ArrayList. To determine if there are more elements to visit, we simply compare this number with the size of the ArrayList.

To remove the most recently returned element, we invoke `remove(previous)` on the Array-List. We also have to decrement `previous`, so that when we increment it in the next call to `next()`, it will be the index of the next unvisited element.

The code for the ArrayIterator class is given in Figure 5–36. Exceptions are left as exercises.

```java
1 /** Iterator associated with an ArrayList. */
2 public class ArrayIterator<E> implements java.util.Iterator<E> {
3
4   /** List being traversed. */
5   private ArrayList<E> list;
6
7   /** Index of the last element returned by next(). */
8   private int previous;
9
10  /** The Iterator begins ready to visit element 0. */
11  public ArrayIterator(ArrayList<E> list) {
12    this.list = list;
13    previous = -1;
14  }
15
16  public boolean hasNext() {
17    return (previous + 1) < list.size();
18  }
19
20  public E next() {
21    previous++;
22    return list.get(previous);
23  }
24
25  public void remove() {
26    list.remove(previous);
27    previous--;
28  }
29
30 }
```

Figure 5-36: The ArrayIterator class.

Example: Go Fish

To illustrate the use of Lists and Iterators, we now write a program for the game of Go Fish (Figure 5–37).

Go Fish

Players: 2–5

Object: To collect the most sets of four cards of the same rank.

Setup: Deal a hand of seven cards to each player.

Play: On your turn, first draw a card from the deck if your hand is empty. Ask any other player for cards of a particular rank. That player must give you all of the cards of that rank from his hand, which are added to your hand. If he doesn't have any cards of that rank, he tells you, "Go Fish," and you draw a card from the deck. If you complete a set of four cards of the same rank, remove all four cards from your hand and score one set. If you get a card of the rank you want (either from another player or by fishing from the deck), you get another turn. Otherwise, play passes to the next player.

Game End: The game ends when all thirteen sets have been scored. The player with the most sets wins.

Figure 5–37: Go Fish is a card game for children. Our implementation pits one player against the computer.

This program is fairly elaborate, but we've already written most of the components. The game itself is represented by the GoFish class. An instance of GoFish contains a Deck of Cards. It also contains two hands of cards, one for the computer and one for the user. A hand of cards is a special kind of List, so we'll extend the ArrayList class with the class GoFishHand. The UML class diagram is given in Figure 5–38.

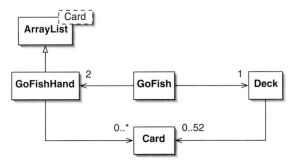

Figure 5–38: An instance of GoFish contains two GoFishHands and one Deck, both of which contain Cards. The GoFishHand class extends ArrayList<Card>.

The simple parts of the GoFish class are shown in Figure 5–39. On lines 33 and 34 of the constructor, we call the add() method which GoFishHand inherits from ArrayList.

```java
1 import java.util.Scanner;
2
3 /** The game of Go Fish. */
4 public class GoFish {
5
6    /** For reading from the console. */
7    public static final Scanner INPUT = new Scanner(System.in);
8
9    /** The computer's hand of Cards. */
10   private GoFishHand computerHand;
11
12   /** Number of sets of four the computer has laid down. */
13   private int computerScore;
14
15   /** The Deck. */
16   private Deck deck;
17
18   /** The player's hand of Cards. */
19   private GoFishHand playerHand;
20
21   /** Number of sets of four the player has laid down. */
22   private int playerScore;
23
24   /** Shuffle the Deck and deal seven Cards to each player. */
25   public GoFish() {
26      computerScore = 0;
27      playerScore = 0;
28      deck = new Deck();
29      deck.shuffle();
30      computerHand = new GoFishHand();
31      playerHand = new GoFishHand();
32      for (int i = 0; i < 7; i++) {
33         playerHand.add(deck.deal());
34         computerHand.add(deck.deal());
35      }
36   }
37
38   /** Create and play the game. */
39   public static void main(String[] args) {
40      System.out.println("Welcome to Go Fish.");
41      GoFish game = new GoFish();
42      game.play();
43   }
44
45 }
```

Figure 5-39: Beginning the GoFish class.

In the play() method (Figure 5–40), we want to keep going until the sum of the players' scores is 13. The complicated details of taking a turn for either the computer or the user are moved off into other methods. These methods return a boolean value which is true if the player in question earned a bonus turn. This is the reason for the unusual structure of lines 4–7. Lines 4–5 are a loop with no body which runs until either all 13 sets have been claimed or playerTurn() returns false. The actual work is done in playerTurn(), which is invoked only if the logical and expression's first operand

```
playerScore + computerScore < 13
```

is false. Line 6–7 do the same thing with computerTurn().

```
 1 /** Play until either the player or the computer wins. */
 2 public void play() {
 3   while (playerScore + computerScore < 13) {
 4     while ((playerScore + computerScore < 13)
 5            && (playerTurn())) {
 6     }
 7     while ((playerScore + computerScore < 13)
 8            && (computerTurn())) {
 9     }
10   }
11   System.out.println("The computer made " + computerScore
12                      + " sets");
13   System.out.println("You made " + playerScore + " sets");
14   if (playerScore > computerScore) {
15     System.out.println("You win!");
16   } else {
17     System.out.println("The computer wins");
18   }
19 }
```

Figure 5-40: The play() method invokes playerTurn() and computerTurn().

The lengthy playerTurn() method is given in Figure 5–41. Lines 6–8 have the player draw a card if the player's hand is empty. Line 9 prints the state of the game—we'll have to remember to write a toString() method. The bulk of the method, lines 10–25, deals with reading a rank from the user. Line 11 invokes the method toUpperCase() from the String class, making any lower-case letters in the input String uppercase. This allows the user to type either q or Q to indicate a queen.

Line 26 transfers the appropriate cards from the computer's hand to the player's hand. If no cards are transferred, lines 28 to 34 go fish, which might produce a bonus turn. The rest of the method deals with laying down sets.

The computerTurn() method (Figure 5–42) is similar, but the rank is chosen randomly. Lines 11–12 are a clever trick for converting from a numerical rank to a character (which might be A, T, J, Q, K, or a digit). We have already written code to do this in the Card class. Rather than do all that work again, we create a Card of the rank in question. (We arbitrarily specify HEARTS

```
 1 /**
 2  * Take a turn for the player.  Return true if the player has earned
 3  * a bonus turn.
 4  */
 5 public boolean playerTurn() {
 6   if (playerHand.isEmpty() && !(deck.isEmpty())) {
 7     playerHand.add(deck.deal());
 8   }
 9   System.out.println("\n" + this);
10   System.out.print("Which card will you ask for? ");
11   char cardName = INPUT.nextLine().toUpperCase().charAt(0);
12   int rank;
13   if (cardName == 'A') {
14     rank = Card.ACE;
15   } else if (cardName == 'T') {
16     rank = 10;
17   } else if (cardName == 'J') {
18     rank = Card.JACK;
19   } else if (cardName == 'Q') {
20     rank = Card.QUEEN;
21   } else if (cardName == 'K') {
22     rank = Card.KING;
23   } else {
24     rank = cardName - '0';
25   }
26   boolean bonusTurn = computerHand.give(rank, playerHand);
27   if (!bonusTurn) {
28     System.out.println("Go fish");
29     Card card = deck.deal();
30     System.out.println("You draw: " + card);
31     playerHand.add(card);
32     if (card.getRank() == rank) {
33       bonusTurn = true;
34     }
35   }
36   int sets = playerHand.meldSets();
37   playerScore += sets;
38   if (sets > 0) {
39     System.out.println("You lay down " + sets
40                        + " sets, bringing your total to "
41                        + playerScore);
42   }
43   return bonusTurn;
44 }
```

Figure 5–41: The playerTurn() method invokes give() and meldSets() on instances of GoFishHand.

because we don't care about the suit here.) We invoke the Card's `toString()` method to get a String representation of the Card. The character we want is character 0 in this String, which we get with the invocation `charAt(0)`.

```
 1 /**
 2  * Take a turn for the computer.  Return true if the computer has
 3  * earned a bonus turn.
 4  */
 5 public boolean computerTurn() {
 6   if (computerHand.isEmpty() && !(deck.isEmpty())) {
 7     computerHand.add(deck.deal());
 8   }
 9   System.out.println("\n" + this);
10   int rank = ((int)(Math.random() * 13)) + 1;
11   char rankCharacter = new Card(rank,
12                                 Card.HEARTS).toString().charAt(0);
13   System.out.println("The computer asks for " + rankCharacter);
14   boolean bonusTurn = playerHand.give(rank, computerHand);
15   if (!bonusTurn) {
16     System.out.println("Go fish");
17     Card card = deck.deal();
18     computerHand.add(card);
19     if (card.getRank() == rank) {
20       bonusTurn = true;
21     }
22   }
23   int sets = computerHand.meldSets();
24   computerScore += sets;
25   if (sets > 0) {
26     System.out.println("The computer lays down " + sets
27                        + " sets, bringing its total to "
28                        + computerScore);
29   }
30   return bonusTurn;
31 }
```

Figure 5-42: The computer asks for a random rank.

All that remains in the GoFish class is `toString()` (Figure 5–43). This method implicitly invokes the `toString()` method from GoFishHand, which was inherited from ArrayList.

We can summarize our work so far with a detailed UML class diagram (Figure 5–44).

Both of the methods in the GoFishHand class involve Iterators, so we go ahead and import java.util.Iterator (Figure 5–45).

```
1 public String toString() {
2    String result = "There are " + deck.size()
3                      + " cards in the deck\n";
4    result += "The computer has " + computerHand.size() + " cards\n";
5    return result + "Your hand: " + playerHand;
6 }
```

Figure 5-43: The `toString()` method for GoFish.

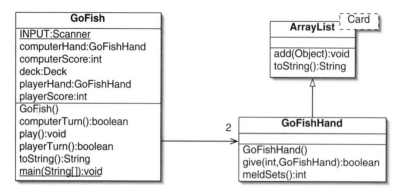

Figure 5-44: After writing GoFish, we know which methods we'll need in GoFishHand. The fields of the ArrayList class, and most of its methods, are not shown.

```
1 import java.util.Iterator;
2
3 /** Hand of cards for the game of Go Fish. */
4 public class GoFishHand extends ArrayList<Card> {
5 }
```

Figure 5-45: The GoFishHand class will make extensive use of Iterators.

The first method, `give()`, transfers all Cards of a given rank from one hand to another and returns a boolean indicating if any were transferred. Thus, `myHand.give(7,yourHand)` removes all of the 7s from `myHand`, adds them to `yourHand`, and returns `true` if there were any.

The cards to be given are found by iterating through the hand in question and examining the rank of each card (Figure 5–46).

The `meldSets()` method (Figure 5–47) traverses the current hand twice. In lines 7–10, it determines how many Cards there are of each rank. Thus, if this hand has two 6s, `rankCount[6]` is 2 at the end of line 10. This is an enhanced `for` loop. The second traversal, on lines 13–19, removes all those cards for which the rank count is 4.

Our program is now complete, as verified by a sample game (Figure 5–48).

```
1 /**
2  * Remove all Cards of the specified rank and add them to the hand
3  * taker. Return true if at least one Card was given.
4  */
5 public boolean give(int rank, GoFishHand taker) {
6   boolean foundAny = false;
7   Iterator<Card> iter = iterator();
8   while (iter.hasNext()) {
9     Card card = iter.next();
10    if (card.getRank() == rank) {
11      iter.remove();
12      taker.add(card);
13      foundAny = true;
14    }
15  }
16  return foundAny;
17 }
```

Figure 5-46: The give() method traverses the hand on which it is invoked.

```
1 /**
2  * Remove all sets of four same-rank Cards from this GoFishHand.
3  * Return the number of sets.
4  */
5 public int meldSets() {
6   // Count number of Cards of each rank
7   int[] rankCount = new int[14]; // Initialized to zeroes
8   for (Card c : this) {
9     rankCount[c.getRank()] += 1;
10  }
11  // Remove cards in complete sets
12  int cardsRemoved = 0;
13  Iterator<Card> iter = iterator();
14  while (iter.hasNext()) {
15    if (rankCount[iter.next().getRank()] == 4) {
16      cardsRemoved += 1;
17      iter.remove();
18    }
19  }
20  // Return number of complete sets
21  return cardsRemoved / 4;
22 }
```

Figure 5-47: The meldSets() method traverses the hand twice.

```
 1 Welcome to Go Fish.
 2
 3 There are 38 cards in the deck
 4 The computer has 7 cards
 5 Your hand: [ 5c 6s 6h 4d Js Qc 8d ]
 6 Which card will you ask for? 5
 7
 8 There are 38 cards in the deck
 9 The computer has 6 cards
10 Your hand: [ 5c 6s 6h 4d Js Qc 8d 5s ]
11 Which card will you ask for? 6
12 Go fish
13 You draw: 7h
14
15 There are 37 cards in the deck
16 The computer has 6 cards
17 Your hand: [ 5c 6s 6h 4d Js Qc 8d 5s 7h ]
18 The computer asks for 4
19
20 There are 37 cards in the deck
21 The computer has 7 cards
22 Your hand: [ 5c 6s 6h Js Qc 8d 5s 7h ]
23 The computer asks for Q
24
25 There are 37 cards in the deck
26 The computer has 8 cards
27 Your hand: [ 5c 6s 6h Js 8d 5s 7h ]
28 The computer asks for 4
29 Go fish
30
31 There are 36 cards in the deck
32 The computer has 9 cards
33 Your hand: [ 5c 6s 6h Js 8d 5s 7h ]
```

Figure 5-48: Beginning of a game of Go Fish.

Notice, incidentally, that we've stopped running into warnings about generic arrays. All of that ugliness is encapsulated inside the ArrayList class.

Exercises

5.24   Modify ArrayIterator so that `next()` throws a java.util.NoSuchElementException if the associated ArrayList has no more elements to visit.

5.25   Modify ArrayIterator so that `remove()` throws a java.util.IllegalStateException when appropriate. (Hint: Add a boolean field `removeAvailable` which is set to `true` by `next()` and to `false` by `remove()`. What is the initial value of this field?)

5.26   Rewrite the `toString()` method for ArrayList (Figure 5–29) so that it uses an Iterator rather than directly accessing the fields.

5.27   In `meldSets()` (Figure 5–47), why does the array `rankCount` have 14 elements instead of 13?

5.5 The Java Collections Framework: A First Look

The general-purpose linear structures we've constructed here are extremely common. Java therefore provides standard versions of them in the java.util package. These classes implement interfaces that descend from the Collection interface. Together, the classes and interfaces are known as the *Java collections framework*. Figure 5–49 gives us a first look at the framework.

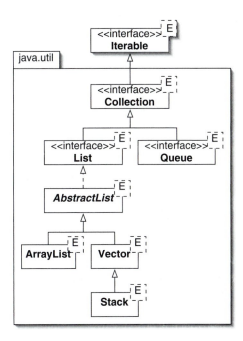

Figure 5-49: The Java collections framework consists of classes and interfaces in the java.util package.

The List interface is similar to the one we defined in Figure 5–25. Specifically, it contains all of the methods we mentioned, plus a few others, including those described in Exercises 5.19 through 5.21. List extends Collection, an interface about which we'll say more in Chapter 11.

The class ArrayList is similar to the one we wrote in this chapter. It is also similar to the somewhat out-of-date class Vector. As Java has evolved over time, new classes and interfaces have been added to the built-in library. To provide **backward compatibility**—that is, to allow old Java programs to run under new versions of Java—classes are rarely removed from the library. Thus, even though new programs should always use ArrayList, the Vector class is still present.

The framework does not include a Stack interface, but it does include a Stack class, which is similar to our ArrayStack class. The Stack class extends Vector. If an attempt is made to peek() at or pop() an empty Stack, a java.util.EmptyStackException is thrown.

Many object-oriented programmers feel that it is a bad idea for Stack to extend Vector. The reason is that Stack inherits some public methods like get(). These methods allow us to do unstackly things with a Stack, such as looking at the bottom element. Since the ability to do this depends on a particular implementation, it violates the encapsulation of the abstract data type. These issues aside, the java.util.Stack class is the one that comes with Java. We must either swallow our pride and use it or write our own.

Curiously, there is a Queue interface, but no array-based implementation. There is a non-array-based implementation, which we will see in Chapter 6.

Abstract Classes

List is implemented by the class AbstractList, which in turn is extended by ArrayList and Vector. AbstractList is an **abstract class**, meaning that we can't create an instance of it. An abstract class exists only to be extended by other classes. Conceptually, an abstract class is something like "vehicle" or "animal." It wouldn't make sense to have an instance of a category like this, but it would make sense to have an instance of "bicycle" or "lion."

An abstract class is similar to an interface. While it is a class—and therefore is extended rather than implemented—an abstract class can contain **abstract methods** which must be provided by any (nonabstract) subclass. All of the methods in an interface are implicitly abstract. (We could explicitly declare them to be abstract, but there would be no point.)

The key difference between an abstract class and an interface is that an abstract class can specify *both responsibilities and (partial) implementation*, while an interface can specify *only responsibilities*. In more technical terms, an abstract class can contain fields, abstract methods, and nonabstract methods, while an interface can contain only (implicitly) abstract methods.

For a more concrete example of an abstract class, we could have defined Stack as an abstract class (Figure 5–50). Any class extending this class would have to provide isEmpty(), pop(), and push(), but would inherit peek().

Exercises

5.28   Through experimentation, determine what happens if you try to extend an abstract class without providing one of the abstract methods specified.

5.29   Speculate on whether a class can extend more than one abstract class.

```
1 /** A last-in, first-out stack of Objects. */
2 public abstract class Stack {
3
4   /** Return true if the Stack is empty. */
5   public abstract boolean isEmpty();
6
7   /**
8    * Return the top Object on the Stack, but do not modify the
9   Stack.
10   * @throws EmptyStructureException if the Stack is empty.
11   */
12  public Object peek() {
13    Object result = pop();
14    push(result);
15    return result;
16  }
17
18  /**
19   * Remove and return the top Object on the Stack.
20   * @throws EmptyStructureException if the Stack is empty.
21   */
22  public abstract Object pop();
23
24  /** Add an Object to the top of the Stack. */
25  public abstract void push(Object target);
26
27 }
```

Figure 5–50: Stack as an abstract class. Most of the methods are abstract (and therefore must be provided by subclasses), but an implementation of **peek()** is provided.

5.30   The method **peek()** in Figure 5–50 could begin with the code:

```
if (isEmpty()) {
  throw new EmptyStructureException();
}
```

Explain why this is not necessary.

Summary

The size of an array cannot be changed, but the array-based structures discussed in this chapter are able to grow and shrink. They do this by maintaining a separate field indicating how many of the array positions are currently in use. This field also provides the index of the next available position. If all of the positions are in use, an array-based structure can be stretched by copying all of its elements into a new, larger array.

These techniques for stretching and shrinking are used in the ArrayStack class. The ArrayQueue class must do a little more work because, as elements are added to the back and removed from the front, the in-use portion of the array marches to the right. When it hits the right end of the array, it wraps around to the beginning. This is accomplished using the % operator.

The List interface describes a much more general data structure. It is implemented by the Array-List class. In addition to providing basic methods for accessing particular elements and so on, a List can return an Iterator. An Iterator allows us to traverse the List, visiting each element.

Java's collections framework, in the java.util package, includes a List interface, an ArrayList class, a Stack class, and a Queue interface. We will see more interfaces and classes from this framework in later chapters.

Vocabulary

abstract class. Class that cannot be instantiated but may contain abstract methods. Unlike an interface, an abstract class can also contain fields and nonabstract methods.

abstract method. Method signature with no body, to be provided by another class. Found in interfaces and abstract classes.

backward compatibility. Of a compiler or other system, ability to work with old software.

iterator. Object allowing us to traverse a data structure. In Java, an instance of the java.util.Iterator class.

Java collections framework. Set of classes in the java.util package descending from Collection. These are standard implementations of many common data structures.

traverse. Go through a data structure, visiting each element.

visit. Do something with or to an element of a data structure.

Problems

5.31   In the Card class, replace the constant ACE with two constants ACE_LOW=1 and ACE_HIGH=14. Make Deck abstract and provide two subclasses AceLowDeck (which has low aces) and AceHighDeck (which has high aces).

5.32   Rewrite the ArrayQueue class (Figure 5–23) so that, instead of a field `size` indicating the number of Objects in the queue, there is a field `back` indicating the next available position. How will you know when the queue is full?

5.33   Rewrite the ArrayQueue class (Figure 5–23) so that the `remove()` method shifts all of the data to the left, keeping the front of the queue at position 0. This allows the field front to be removed. Which methods become simpler as a result of this change? Which become more complicated?

5.34   Define a class ReverseArrayIterator, which implements java.util.Iterator but visits an ArrayList's elements in *reverse* order. Add a method `reverseIterator()` to the ArrayList class. The method returns an instance of ReverseArrayIterator.

5.35   Write a Deck class whose only field is of type ArrayList<Card>. Use the static `shuffle()` method in the API for the Collections class (which should not be confused with the Collection interface).

Projects

5.36   Write an abstract class ArrayBasedStructure which is extended by ArrayStack, ArrayQueue, and ArrayList. How much of the implementation can be moved up into this abstract superclass? Discuss whether this makes the overall code more or less clear.

5.37   Write an array-based implementation of the Deque interface from Problem 4.18.

6

Linked Structures

This chapter introduces linked structures. The structures in this chapter are made from chains of nodes, connected by references. These nodes are introduced in Section 6.1. The Stack and Queue interfaces are implemented in Section 6.2 and the List interface in Section 6.3. Finally, in Section 6.4, we examine the linked structures in the Java collections framework.

6.1 List Nodes

The structures in this chapter are composed of *list nodes*. A list node contains only one element, but it also contains (a reference to) another list node. A list node is represented by an instance of a class called, not surprisingly, ListNode (Figure 6–1).

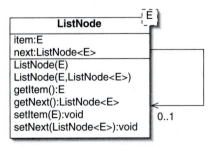

Figure 6–1: A ListNode contains another ListNode unless `next` is `null`.

157

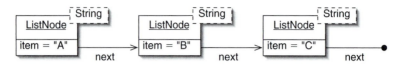

Figure 6-2: A chain of three ListNodes.

This arrangement allows us to make a chain of ListNodes, each containing a reference to the next one (Figure 6–2). The next field of the last node is null.

There are a number of ways to create the data structure in Figure 6–2. One is to create the nodes and then link them together:

```
ListNode<String> node1 = new ListNode<String>("A");
ListNode<String> node2 = new ListNode<String>("B");
ListNode<String> node3 = new ListNode<String>("C");
node1.setNext(node2);
node2.setNext(node3);
```

An alternate approach, taking advantage of the overloaded constructor, is to create the entire chain with one expression:

```
new ListNode<String>
  ("A", new ListNode<String>
    ("B", new ListNode<String>("C")))
```

As we'll see later in this chapter, these chains of nodes are usually constructed gradually, with nodes being added or removed as elements are pushed onto a Stack, removed from a Queue, and so on.

We can splice a node out of a chain if we can find the node's predecessor. For example, if the nodes in Figure 6–2 are named node1, node2, and node3, then the method invocation

```
node1.setNext(node2.getNext());
```

results in the situation shown in Figure 6–3.

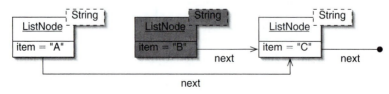

Figure 6-3: Splicing a node out of a chain.

The code for the ListNode class is simple (Figure 6–4).

```
1 /** Node in a linked list. */
2 public class ListNode<E> {
3
4   /** The item stored in this node. */
5   private E item;
6
7   /** The node following this one. */
8   private ListNode<E> next;
9
10  /** Put item in a node with no next node. */
11  public ListNode(E item) {
12    this.item = item;
13    next = null;
14  }
15
16  /** Put item in a node with the specified next node. */
17  public ListNode(E item, ListNode<E> next) {
18    this.item = item;
19    this.next = next;
20  }
21
22  /** Return the item stored in this node. */
23  public E getItem() {
24    return item;
25  }
26
27  /** Return the next node. */
28  public ListNode<E> getNext() {
29    return next;
30  }
31
32  /** Replace the item stored in this node. */
33  public void setItem(E item) {
34    this.item = item;
35  }
36
37  /** Set the next node. */
38  public void setNext(ListNode<E> next) {
39    this.next = next;
40  }
41
42 }
```

Figure 6-4: The ListNode class.

It is sometimes useful to have a *doubly linked* node, which knows about both the previous and the next node (Figure 6–5).

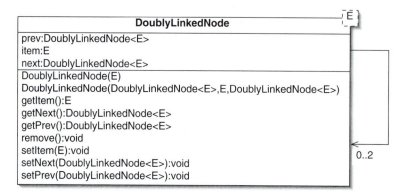

Figure 6-5: A DoublyLinkedNode knows about both its predecessor and its successor.

A chain of DoublyLinkedNodes is somewhat hairy looking, because there is one sequence of references leading forward and another leading backward (Figure 6–6).

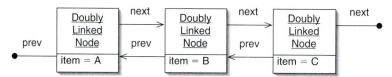

Figure 6-6: A chain of DoublyLinkedNodes. For clarity, type parameters have been omitted.

A chain of DoublyLinkedNodes is more difficult to maintain than a chain of singly linked nodes, but it has its uses. We can traverse the chain in either direction. Also, if we have a particular node, we can splice it out of the list without advance knowledge of its predecessor. This allows us to write a method `remove()` in the DoublyLinkedNode class (Figure 6–7).

```
1 /** Splice this node out of its chain. */
2 public void remove() {
3   if (prev != null) {
4     prev.next = next;
5   }
6   if (next != null) {
7     next.prev = prev;
8   }
9 }
```

Figure 6-7: The `remove()` method from the DoublyLinkedList class.

The rest of the code for the DoublyLinkedNode class is straightforward. It is left as Problem 6.25.

Exercises

6.1   Write code to produce the data structure shown in Figure 6–8.

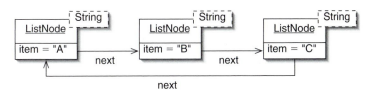

Figure 6-8: A circular chain of nodes, for Exercise 6.1.

6.2   Can the `item` field of a ListNode contain a ListNode? Can it be `null`?

6.3   Draw the data structure in Figure 6–6 as it would appear after invoking `remove()` on the middle node.

6.2 Stacks and Queues

We now present the LinkedStack and LinkedQueue classes, which respectively implement the Stack and Queue interfaces from Chapter 4.

The LinkedStack Class

A (nonempty) LinkedStack contains (a reference to) a ListNode, which in turn contains an element and perhaps another ListNode. In UML class diagrams, this relationship may be illustrated in any of several levels of detail, depending on what is being emphasized (Figure 6–9).

The activity of a LinkedStack is shown in Figure 6–10.

Like any linked structure, a LinkedStack always has just enough room for its elements. It is never necessary to stretch a linked structure by copying the elements.

The code for the LinkedStack class is very short (Figure 6–11).

In an empty LinkedStack, including a newly created one, `top` is `null`. The `isEmpty()` method only has to check for this.

The `push()` method splices a new node onto the beginning of the chain. As shown in Figure 6–12, each time we push something onto the Stack, a new node is created, but the old nodes don't change. The `next` field of the new ListNode gets the old value of `top`—that is, a reference to the rest of the chain. The other nodes aren't affected.

It is important to realize that the rightmost LinkedStack in Figure 6–12 is not in any sense "full." The positions of the nodes on paper or in memory are completely arbitrary. We could have drawn the top of the Stack at the bottom of the diagram. Whichever node is referred to by `top` is the top one, regardless of where it is drawn. All that matters is the chain of references. In fact, as

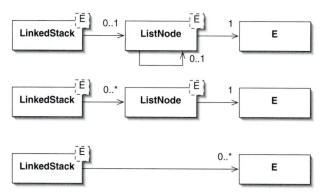

Figure 6-9: Three different UML class diagrams showing the relationship between the LinkedStack and ListNode classes and the class of the element type E. The most precise diagram (top) indicates that a LinkedStack may contain a ListNode, which contains an E and possibly another ListNode. The middle diagram indicates that a LinkedStack contains 0 or more ListNodes, each of which contains an E. The fact that some of these ListNodes are only indirectly contained in the LinkedStack is left out. The bottom diagram omits the ListNode class altogether, merely indicating that a LinkedStack contains 0 or more instance of E.

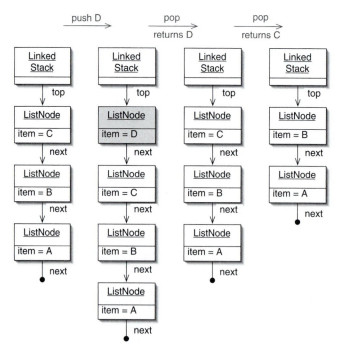

Figure 6-10: Activity of a LinkedStack. These are the same operations shown in Figure 4-1. Again, type parameters have been omitted for clarity.

```
 1 /** A linked Stack. */
 2 public class LinkedStack<E> implements Stack<E> {
 3
 4   /** The top ListNode in the Stack. */
 5   private ListNode<E> top;
 6
 7   /** The Stack is initially empty. */
 8   public LinkedStack() {
 9     top = null;
10   }
11
12   public boolean isEmpty() {
13     return top == null;
14   }
15
16   public E peek() {
17     if (isEmpty()) {
18       throw new EmptyStructureException();
19     }
20     return top.getItem();
21   }
22
23   public E pop() {
24     if (isEmpty()) {
25       throw new EmptyStructureException();
26     }
27     E result = top.getItem();
28     top = top.getNext();
29     return result;
30   }
31
32   public void push(E target) {
33     top = new ListNode<E>(target, top);
34   }
35
36 }
```

Figure 6-11: The LinkedStack class.

we'll see in Chapter 16, Java can sometimes move things around in memory without telling us. This doesn't cause a problem, because the reference chains (which node refers to which other node) are unaffected.

The pop() method is the complement of push(). It splices a node out, as described in Section 6.1. This method is longer for a couple of reasons. First, if the Stack is empty, we have to throw an

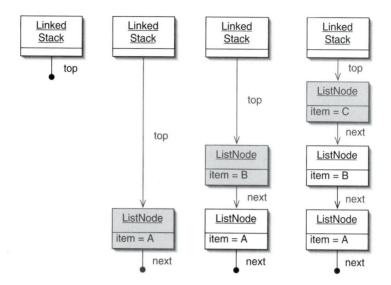

Figure 6-12: Pushing a series of elements onto a LinkedStack. At each step, modified references and newly created nodes are shown in grey. The value of next in the new node is always the same as the previous value of top.

exception. Second, we have to store the element from the node we are removing in a variable. We have to do this *before* we remove the node, because the node becomes unreachable once we change the value of top (Figure 6–13).

The reader with an eye to tidiness may wonder, "What happens to these unreachable nodes? Are they taking up memory?" In a language like C, the answer is yes. In Java, on the other hand, any object which can no longer be reached (because there are no references to it) magically disappears. This will be explained in Chapter 16.

The peek() method is easy, although we must be careful not to confuse top (the top node) and top.getItem() (the element contained in that node).

The LinkedQueue Class

The LinkedQueue class implements the Queue interface. Because we add elements to the back and remove them from the front, we have to keep track of both ends of the chain of nodes. This is illustrated in Figure 6–14.

The code for the LinkedQueue class is given in Figure 6–15.

The isEmpty() method looks just like the one from LinkedStack, with front standing in for top.

The add() method creates a new ListNode and adds it to the back of the Queue. An empty Queue needs special treatment, because the new node also becomes the front of the Queue. If the

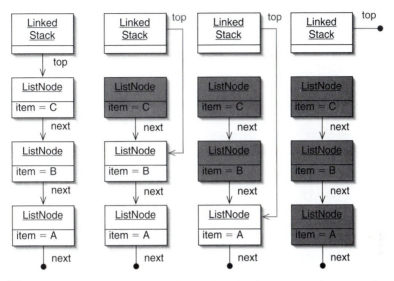

Figure 6-13: Repeated popping of a LinkedStack. Once **top** changes, the node to which it used to point becomes unreachable.

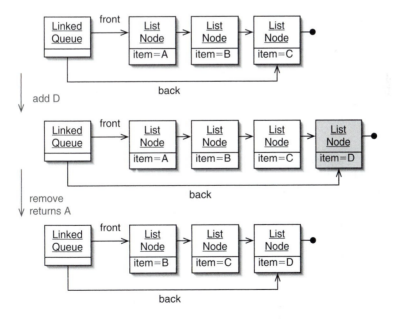

Figure 6-14: Activity of a LinkedQueue. These are the same operations shown in Figure 4–29. The references from the ListNodes are all the **next** fields.

```
 1 /** A linked Queue. */
 2 public class LinkedQueue<E> implements Queue<E> {
 3
 4    /** The front ListNode in the Queue. */
 5    private ListNode<E> front;
 6
 7    /** The back ListNode in the Queue. */
 8    private ListNode<E> back;
 9
10    /** The Queue is initially empty. */
11    public LinkedQueue() {
12      front = null;
13      back = null;
14    }
15
16    public void add(E target) {
17      ListNode<E> node = new ListNode<E>(target);
18      if (isEmpty()) {
19        front = node;
20        back = node;
21      } else {
22        back.setNext(node);
23        back = node;
24      }
25    }
26
27    public boolean isEmpty() {
28      return front == null;
29    }
30
31    public E remove() {
32      if (isEmpty()) {
33        throw new EmptyStructureException();
34      }
35      E result = front.getItem();
36      front = front.getNext();
37      return result;
38    }
39
40 }
```

Figure 6-15: The LinkedQueue class.

Queue is not empty, we simply splice the new node onto the back by setting the `next` field in the last node (Figure 6–16).

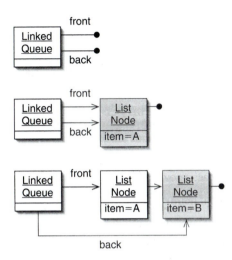

Figure 6–16: In a newly created LinkedQueue (top), both `front` and `back` are `null`. When the first element is added to the Queue (middle), the new node becomes both the front and the back of the Queue. Subsequent nodes are simply spliced onto the back of the Queue (bottom).

The `remove()` method is like `pop()` from LinkedStack. If we remove the last node, `front` becomes `null` (Figure 6–17). It does not matter that `back` still points to the node that was just removed. No method does anything with `back` without first checking whether `front` is `null`.

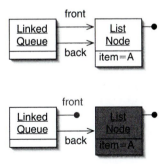

Figure 6–17: If there is only one element in a LinkedQueue, `front` and `back` are references to the same ListNode (top). The `remove()` method changes `front`, but leaves `back` pointing at this node (bottom).

Exercises

6.4 Draw a UML class diagram showing the relationship between Stack, ArrayStack, and LinkedStack.

6.5 The `pop()` method from the LinkedStack class (Figure 6–11) stores the element being popped in a temporary variable `result`. Why doesn't the `pop()` method from Array-Stack (Figure 5–16) need to do this?

6.6 Modify the Idiot's Delight program from Chapter 4 to use LinkedStacks instead of ArrayStacks.

6.7 Java automatically reclaims the memory used by objects and arrays which are no longer reachable. In Figure 6–17, the ListNode removed from the LinkedQueue is still reachable through the field `back`. Is there a danger that a great deal of memory could be taken up by such ListNodes? Explain.

6.3 The LinkedList Class

We now present a class LinkedList which implements the List interface from Chapter 5. A LinkedList has one field `front`, which is a ListNode. As in a LinkedStack, this node may in turn contain other ListNodes. The fields and trivial methods are shown in Figure 6–18.

```
 1 /** A linked list. */
 2 public class LinkedList<E> implements List<E> {
 3
 4   /** The first node in the List. */
 5   private ListNode<E> front;
 6
 7   /** A LinkedList is initially empty. */
 8   public LinkedList() {
 9     front = null;
10   }
11
12   public boolean isEmpty() {
13     return front == null;
14   }
15
16 }
```

Figure 6–18: A LinkedList contains a single chain of ListNodes.

Many of the LinkedList methods involve walking down the chain of references. The general form of this code is:

```
for (ListNode<E> node = front;
     node != null;
     node = node.getNext()) {
  // Do something with node.getItem()
}
```

The variable node refers to the node currently being processed. To advance to the next node, we set node to node.getNext().

This technique is used in the contains(), size(), and toString() methods (Figure 6–19).

```
 1 public boolean contains(E target) {
 2   for (ListNode<E> node = front;
 3        node != null;
 4        node = node.getNext()) {
 5     if (node.getItem().equals(target)) {
 6       return true;
 7     }
 8   }
 9   return false;
10 }
11
12 public int size() {
13   int tally = 0;
14   for (ListNode<E> node = front;
15        node != null;
16        node = node.getNext()) {
17     tally++;
18   }
19   return tally;
20 }
21
22 public String toString() {
23   String result = "( ";
24   for (ListNode<E> node = front;
25        node != null;
26        node = node.getNext()) {
27     result += node.getItem() + " ";
28   }
29   return result + ")";
30 }
```

Figure 6-19: Many LinkedList methods walk down the list using for loops.

Notice that these loops do not use an int to keep track of the current position in the list. We know when we've reached the end of the loop when node is null. In contrast, the get() and set() methods (Figure 6–20) *do* use an int, since they want to advance only a specific number of nodes.

```
 1 public E get(int index) {
 2   ListNode<E> node = front;
 3   for (int i = 0; i < index; i++) {
 4     node = node.getNext();
 5   }
 6   return node.getItem();
 7 }
 8
 9 public void set(int index, E target) {
10   ListNode<E> node = front;
11   for (int i = 0; i < index; i++) {
12     node = node.getNext();
13   }
14   node.setItem(target);
15 }
```

Figure 6-20: The get() and set() methods advance index nodes down the list.

It appears that the add() method can be written in a similar way. We advance down the List until we get to the last node, at which point we tack on a new one (Figure 6–21).

```
 1 public void add(E target) {
 2   ListNode last = front;
 3   while (last.getNext() != null) {
 4     last = last.getNext();
 5   }
 6   last.setNext(new ListNode(target));
 7 }
```

Figure 6-21: Broken first draft of the add() method.

Unfortunately, there is a catch. What if the List is empty? The method will throw a NullPointer-Exception when we try to invoke last.getNext() on line 4.

One solution is to add code to deal with this special case (Figure 6–22). There is, however, a more elegant way to handle the problem.

```
 1 public void add(E target) {
 2   if (isEmpty()) {
 3     front = new ListNode(target);
 4   } else {
 5     ListNode last = front;
 6     while (last.getNext() != null) {
 7       last = last.getNext();
 8     }
 9     last.setNext(new ListNode(target));
10   }
11 }
```

Figure 6-22: Special code is needed to handle the case where the LinkedList is empty.

The Predecessor Interface

Lines 3 and 9 of Figure 6–22 do almost exactly the same thing: create a new ListNode and set some reference to point to it. In line 3, this reference is the front field of a LinkedList. In line 9, it is the next field of a ListNode.

We can use polymorphism to write a single line of code which does whichever of these things is appropriate. If we have a variable which can refer to either a LinkedList or a ListNode, we can invoke a method on it which says, "Here is a new node. Make it the next one after you."

This variable must be of a polymorphic type. We have two choices: it can be some class which is a superclass of both LinkedList and ListNode, or it can be an interface which both of these classes implement. Since these classes have no fields or methods in common, a superclass doesn't really make sense; an interface is a better choice.

The Predecessor interface is given in Figure 6–23. It also describes a method getNext(), which returns the next node after the Predecessor.

```
 1 /**
 2  * Something that has a next ListNode.
 3  */
 4 public interface Predecessor<E> {
 5
 6   /** Get the next ListNode. */
 7   public ListNode<E> getNext();
 8
 9   /** Set the next ListNode. */
10   public void setNext(ListNode<E> next);
11
12 }
```

Figure 6-23: The Predecessor interface.

In order to use this interface, both ListNode and LinkedList will have to implement it. ListNode already provides these methods, so we just have to change the first noncomment line to:

```
public class ListNode<E> implements Predecessor<E> {
```

In the LinkedList class, we have to provide both of these methods and change the first noncomment line (Figure 6–24).

```
 1 /** A linked list. */
 2 public class LinkedList implements List<E>, Predecessor<E> {
 3
 4   public ListNode<E> getNext() {
 5     return front;
 6   }
 7
 8   public void setNext(ListNode<E> next) {
 9     front = next;
10   }
11
12 }
```

Figure 6-24: The LinkedList class must be modified to implement Predecessor.

The LinkedList class now implements two different interfaces. This is illustrated in Figure 6–25.

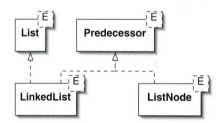

Figure 6-25: The Predecessor interface is implemented by two classes. The LinkedList class implements two interfaces.

Now we can write a more elegant version of the add() method for LinkedList (Figure 6–26).

```
1 public void add(E target) {
2   Predecessor<E> last = this;
3   while (last.getNext() != null) {
4     last = last.getNext();
5   }
6   last.setNext(new ListNode<E>(target));
7 }
```

Figure 6-26: The Predecessor interface allows us to write a shorter version of add() than the one in Figure 6–22.

Two-Finger Algorithms

We now consider the two remove() methods. One of these methods removes the element at a particular position; the other removes a particular Object. Both make use of the technique of splicing out a node. They also use the Predecessor interface to avoid special code for the case where the node being removed is the first one.

In each method, we walk down the list looking for either the ith node or the node containing target. Once we find the offending node, we have a problem: we've forgotten the previous node!

Our solution is to keep track of two nodes: the previous one and the current one (Figure 6–27). Since such an algorithm points at two consecutive nodes on each pass through its loop, it is known as a *two-finger algorithm*.

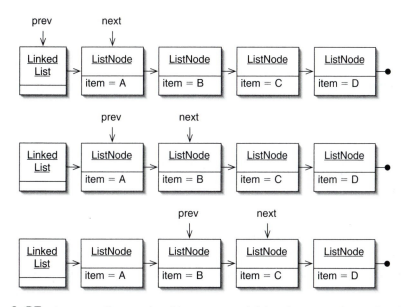

Figure 6–27: In a two-finger algorithm, two variables (prev and next) refer to two consecutive ListNodes. Labels on the references between objects are omitted for brevity.

The code for the remove() methods is given in Figure 6–28.

```
1 public E remove(int index) {
2    Predecessor<E> prev = this;
3    ListNode<E> node = front;
4    for (int i = 0; i < index; i++) {
```

Figure 6–28: Both of the remove() methods are two-finger algorithms. (Part 1 of 2)

```
 5      prev = node;
 6      node = node.getNext();
 7   }
 8   prev.setNext(node.getNext());
 9   return node.getItem();
10 }
11
12 public boolean remove(E target) {
13   Predecessor<E> prev = this;
14   ListNode<E> node = front;
15   while (node != null) {
16      if (node.getItem().equals(target)) {
17         prev.setNext(node.getNext());
18         return true;
19      }
20      prev = node;
21      node = node.getNext();
22   }
23   return false;
24 }
```

Figure 6-28: Both of the remove() methods are two-finger algorithms. (Part 2 of 2)

The ListIterator Class

All that remains is the iterator() method. As in ArrayList, it simply creates and returns an Iterator (Figure 6–29).

```
1 public java.util.Iterator<E> iterator() {
2   return new ListIterator<E>(this);
3 }
```

Figure 6-29: The iterator() method returns an instance of ListIterator.

Specifically, it returns an instance of the ListIterator class (Figure 6–30). A ListIterator keeps track of both the node containing the Object most recently returned by next() and the predecessor of that node.

```
1 /** Iterator used by the LinkedList class. */
2 public class ListIterator<E> implements java.util.Iterator<E> {
3
4    /** The Predecessor of node. */
5    private Predecessor<E> prev;
6
```

Figure 6-30: The ListIterator class. (Part 1 of 2)

```
 7   /**
 8    * The ListNode containing the last element returned, or the
 9    * LinkedList itself if no elements have yet been returned.
10    */
11   private Predecessor<E> node;
12
13   /** The ListIterator starts at the beginning of the List. */
14   public ListIterator(LinkedList<E> list) {
15     prev = null;
16     node = list;
17   }
18
19   public boolean hasNext() {
20     return node.getNext() != null;
21   }
22
23   public E next() {
24     prev = node;
25     node = node.getNext();
26     return ((ListNode<E>)node).getItem();
27   }
28
29   public void remove() {
30     prev.setNext(node.getNext());
31     node = prev;
32   }
33
34 }
```

Figure 6–30: The ListIterator class. (Part 2 of 2)

The remove() method of ListIterator leaves both prev and node referring to the same Predecessor. This is not a problem, because hasNext() does not look at prev, and next() begins by setting prev = node anyway.

Exercises

6.8   Modify the get() and set() methods (Figure 6–20) so that they throw an IndexOutOfBoundsException if the argument index is either too low (less than 0) or too high (greater than or equal to the length of the list).

6.9   Write an equals() method for the LinkedList class.

6.10   Write a method indexOf() that takes one argument, an element target, and returns the index of the first occurrence of target in this LinkedList, or −1 if target does not appear.

6.11   Write a method `removeAll()` that takes one argument, an element `target`. It removes all elements which are `equals()` to `target` from this LinkedList.

6.12   Write a method `count()` that takes one argument, an element `target`. It returns the number of elements in this LinkedList which are `equals()` to `target`.

6.13   Rewrite both versions of `remove()` so that only one variable is needed. (Hint: Replace `node` with `prev.getNext()`.)

6.14   Modify ListIterator so that `next()` throws a java.util.NoSuchElementException if there are no more elements to visit.

6.15   Modify ListIterator so that `remove()` throws a java.util.IllegalStateException when appropriate. Is it necessary to add an additional field as in Exercise 5.25?

6.16   Can the `toString()` method from Exercise 5.26 be used in the LinkedList class?

6.17   Draw a UML class diagram showing the relationship between the ListIterator, LinkedList, ListNode classes.

6.18   Draw a UML instance diagram showing the state of a ListIterator after an invocation of `remove()`.

6.19   If we made GoFishHand (Chapter 5) extend LinkedList instead of ArrayList, would we have to change anything else in the GoFishHand or GoFish classes? Explain.

6.20   Can line 24 in Figure 6–30 be replaced with `prev = prev.getNext()`? Explain.

6.21   Explain why a cast is needed on line 26 of Figure 6–30.

6.22   Write a LinkedList method `swap()` that takes two ints as arguments and swaps the elements at those two positions. Your method should not traverse the list twice to find the two elements, and it should not create or destroy any nodes.

6.4 The Java Collections Framework Revisited

The Java collections framework contains a class LinkedList which is similar to the one we've developed in this chapter. This class is actually a doubly linked list, which allows for efficient insertion into and removal from either end of the structure. (It provides methods `addFirst()`, `addLast()`, `removeFirst()`, and `removeLast()`.) A LinkedList can function as a stack, a queue, or even a deque (Problem 4.18).

LinkedList is a subclass of AbstractSequentialList, which is in turn a subclass of AbstractList (Figure 6–31). This arrangement emphasizes the fact that linked structures are *sequential access*, while array-based structures are *random access*. In a sequential access data structure, it

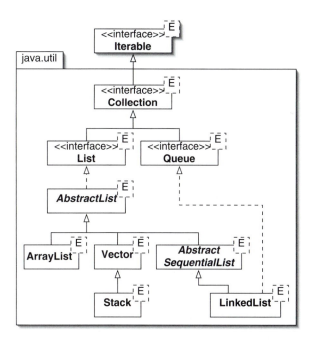

Figure 6-31: Java's own LinkedList class extends AbstractSequentialList, which extends AbstractList.

is necessary to go through the preceding elements (by following a chain of references) to get at an element in the middle. In a random access data structure, we can jump to any point instantaneously. VHS tapes are sequential access, for example, but DVDs are random access.

If ArrayLists and LinkedLists are built into Java, why have we bothered to write these classes ourselves? There are a number of reasons.

First, these are relatively easy data structures to build. Without understanding these, we would have little hope of understanding the more complex structures yet to come. These early data structures introduce standard techniques which will come in handy later on.

Second, some day we will likely have to write a data structure that is very similar to, but not identical to, a built-in structure. (See the projects for examples.) Also, we may end up working in a language where a standard library has not yet been established, so we will have to write these things ourselves.

Finally, knowing what's going on "under the hood" allows us to use the built-in structures more effectively. For example, if we're often going to have to access items out of the middle of a List, we should choose an ArrayList rather than a LinkedList. On the other hand, if we're only adding things to the ends and we want to make sure we never have to perform an expensive copying operation to stretch the List, we should choose a LinkedList.

Exercises

6.23   Suppose we need a List where we often have to remove the frontmost element. Using our own implementations, is an ArrayList or a LinkedList more efficient, or are they both about the same? What about using the versions from the Java collections framework? (Hint: An operation that may have to traverse the entire structure is less efficient than one that does not.)

6.24   Repeat Exercise 6.23 for the case where we often have to remove the *rearmost* element.

Summary

A ListNode contains one element and possibly a reference to another ListNode. We can build arbitrarily long chains of ListNodes. A DoublyLinkedNode also contains a reference to the previous node, if any.

The LinkedStack class splices nodes in and out of one end of a chain. The LinkedQueue class must keep track of both ends of the chain.

The LinkedList class is a general-purpose linked structure. The Predecessor interface allows us to avoid writing special code for adding an element to an empty List, removing the first element, and so on. Some algorithms, called two-finger algorithms, require that we keep track of two consecutive nodes so that, when we find what we're looking for, we can splice it out.

The Java collections framework provides a class LinkedList. It is doubly linked, so we can easily remove things from either end. Even though we usually use such built-in structures when they are available, it is worth knowing how they work and how to build them ourselves.

Vocabulary

doubly linked. Of a list node, having references to both the next and previous nodes in the chain. Of a linked structure, being composed of doubly linked nodes.

list node. Object containing an element and a reference to another list node. List nodes can be strung together in chains.

random access. Allowing access at any point, like an array or a DVD.

sequential access. Allowing access only by traversing intervening points, like a linked structure or a VHS tape.

two-finger algorithm. An algorithm that requires keeping track of two consecutive list nodes.

Problems

6.25   Complete the code for the DoublyLinkedNode class.

6.26   Write the DoublyLinkedNode class as a subclass of ListNode. Why does this make writing remove() awkward?

6.27   Write a LinkedList method reverse() which reverses the order of the elements in the List. No ListNodes should be created or destroyed in the process.

6.28   Rewrite the game of War from Chapter 4 using structures from the Java collections framework.

6.29   Many of the LinkedList methods, such as size(), would run forever if invoked on a LinkedList like the one in Figure 6–32. Write code to produce such a list. Devise and implement a method isCyclic() which returns true if the LinkedList on which it is invoked has this problem. (Hint: If two cross-country runners start off down a course at different speeds, will the faster runner eventually "lap" the slower one if the course is cyclic?)

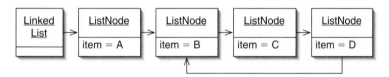

Figure 6–32: A cyclic LinkedList.

Projects

6.30   Rewrite the LinkedStack class from scratch so that it holds primitive ints. The ListNode class must also be altered. (This revised LinkedStack is more efficient than the general-purpose one, because it doesn't have to follow references or create instances of the Integer class.)

6.31   Implement the Deque interface from Problem 4.18. Write it from scratch—don't extend one of the classes from the Java collections framework. (Hint: Use a doubly linked list.)

6.32   Devise and write code for an efficient List implementation where elements are always inserted in groups of five and are never removed.

6.33   Write a DoublyLinkedList class which implements List but uses DoublyLinkedNodes. Use two interfaces, Predecessor and Successor. (Hint: The prev field of the first node and the next field of the last node should refer back to the DoublyLinkedList.)

III

Algorithms

7

Analysis of Algorithms

One of the programming goals we mentioned in Chapter 1 was efficiency. In this chapter, we look at techniques for measuring efficiency. Section 7.1 shows how to directly time programs and points out some problems with this approach. Section 7.2 introduces some powerful mathematical tools to simplify our reasoning about the efficiency of algorithms. The connection between this math and actual algorithms is made in Section 7.3. Several variations on analysis, such as considering the average or the worst-case running time, are explored in Sections 7.4 and 7.5.

If the thought of doing math makes you nervous, you may wish to review Appendix C.

7.1 Timing

If we want to know which of two methods is faster, the most obvious approach is to time them. The TimeTest program (Figure 7–1) compares the `get()` methods from the ArrayList and LinkedList classes in the Java collections framework.

Lines 14–16 of the method `test()` add many elements to `list`. We don't care what these elements are, so this is one of those rare occasions where it makes sense to create instances of the Object class.

To determine the time taken by line 18, we examine the clock before and after invoking `get()`. To get the current time, we invoke the static `currentTimeMillis()` method of the System

```
1 import java.util.*;
2
3 /** Time tests to compare performance of various algorithms. */
4 public class TimeTest {
5
6   /** Number of Objects to store in each data structure. */
7   public static final int LIST_LENGTH = 100;
8
9   /**
10   * Store LIST_LENGTH Objects in list.  Time list's get() method,
11   * printing the number of milliseconds taken.
12   */
13  public static void test(List<Object> list) {
14    for (int i = 0; i < LIST_LENGTH; i++) {
15      list.add(new Object());
16    }
17    long before = System.currentTimeMillis();
18    list.get(5);
19    long after = System.currentTimeMillis();
20    System.out.println((after - before) + " milliseconds");
21  }
22
23  /** Compare ArrayList with LinkedList. */
24  public static void main(String[] args) {
25    System.out.print("ArrayList: ");
26    test(new ArrayList<Object>());
27    System.out.print("LinkedList: ");
28    test(new LinkedList<Object>());
29  }
30
31 }
```

Figure 7-1: The TimeTest class compares the `get()` methods of the ArrayList and LinkedList classes.

class. For historical reasons involving the UNIX operating system, this is given as the number of milliseconds since midnight, January 1, 1970, Greenwich mean time. Because this is a very large number, the return type of `currentTimeMillis()` is long. A long is similar to an int, but its range is roughly $\pm 10^{19}$.

Unfortunately, running our program doesn't give us much information:

```
ArrayList: 0 milliseconds
LinkedList: 0 milliseconds
```

Any modern computer is so fast that, on either of these data structures, the `get()` method takes less than one millisecond to run. A reasonable solution is to look at the time required to perform each operation a million times (Figure 7–2).

```
1 /** Number of times to perform the operation being timed. */
2 public static final int TEST_RUNS = 1000000;
3
4 /**
5  * Store LIST_LENGTH Objects in list.  Time list's get() method,
6  * printing the number of milliseconds taken.
7  */
8 public static void test(List<Object> list) {
9    for (int i = 0; i < LIST_LENGTH; i++) {
10     list.add(new Object());
11   }
12   long before = System.currentTimeMillis();
13   for (int i = 0; i < TEST_RUNS; i++) {
14     list.get(5);
15   }
16   long after = System.currentTimeMillis();
17   System.out.println((after - before) + " milliseconds");
18 }
```

Figure 7-2: We can improve the resolution of our timing by performing the operation in question many times.

The exact result of running this program varies from one run to the next. For example, one run might give

```
ArrayList: 21 milliseconds
LinkedList: 39 milliseconds
```

while another might give

```
ArrayList: 22 milliseconds
LinkedList: 40 milliseconds
```

This variation is due to a number of factors beyond our control, such as how Java manages its memory (Chapter 16) and what other programs are running on our machine. We could try harder to control these conditions and apply various statistical techniques to determine which method is faster, but the short answer is that the method from ArrayList is roughly twice as fast as the method from LinkedList. They are both very fast, so this is not a big difference.

The story is different if we get element 50 instead of element 5. Now the method from LinkedList takes vastly longer:

```
ArrayList: 22 milliseconds
LinkedList: 226 milliseconds
```

In retrospect, this is not surprising. In an ArrayList, `get()` jumps right to the array element in question. In a LinkedList, it is necessary to traverse all of the previous list nodes to find the one we want. Our timing experiment provides empirical evidence that the time to get element i of a LinkedList increases with i, while the time to get element i of an ArrayList is independent of i. If we need a List and `get()` is going to be a very common operation, an ArrayList is a good choice.

We now have some evidence that LinkedList search time increases with i, but a couple of data points are not really a convincing case. Rather than perform a more extensive battery of tests, we can use some formal, mathematical tools to make statements about the efficiency of an algorithm. Section 7.2 introduces these tools.

The material that follows is important for designing general-purpose algorithms and data structures. Empirical timing is still important in optimization.

Exercises

7.1   The famous Y2K bug occurred because some old programs used two decimal digits to store years. This became a problem in the year 2000, because such programs had no way to tell whether "00" meant 1900 or 2000.

        A similar problem will occur for Java programs when the number of milliseconds since the beginning of 1970 exceeds the capacity of a long. In what year will this occur, given that the maximum value of a long is 9,223,372,036,854,775,807? What if `getTime()` returned an int, which has a maximum value of 2,147,483,647? What about those UNIX/C systems which use an int to store the number of *seconds* since the beginning of 1970?

7.2 Asymptotic Notation

Suppose we have two methods we wish to compare. We have determined that the running time for method A is $10n^2 - 5$ milliseconds to process n elements, while that for method B is $100n + 200$ milliseconds. (We will discus how to arrive at these expressions in Section 7.3.) Which method should we prefer?

The answer depends on the value of n. As seen in Figure 7–3, for $n = 6$ method A is faster, but for $n = 16$ method B is much faster.

We would prefer to say that one method is faster in general, rather than for some particular value of n. The time differences for small values of n are relatively insignificant. What really concerns us is the ***asymptotic*** behavior of the running-time functions: what happens as n becomes very large?

Figure 7–3 suggests that the running time for method A is larger than that for method B. If n is at least 12, B is faster.

Our intuition is correct in this example, but graphs can be deceiving. If we had plotted the graph only up to $n = 6$ (Figure 7 4), we might have concluded that method A is faster. To be confident in our statement about which method is faster for large values of n, we need a proof.

Theorem: $10n^2 - 5 > 100n + 200$ for any value of $n \geq 12$.

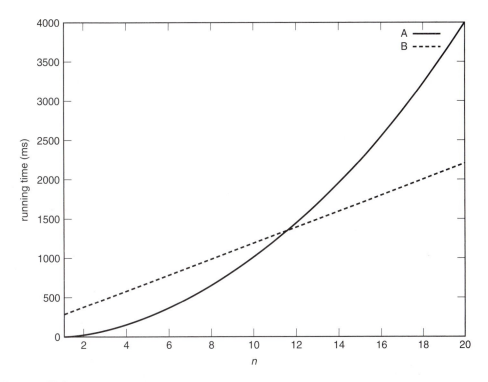

Figure 7-3: Method A is faster than method B for small values of n, but slower for large values.

Proof: For any $n \geq 12$:

$$
\begin{aligned}
10n^2 - 5 &\geq 120n - 5 \\
&= 100n + 20n - 5 \\
&\geq 100n + 240 - 5 \\
&> 100n + 200
\end{aligned}
$$

The first and third inequalities follow because of the assumption that $n \geq 12$. This completes the proof.

Actual running times will depend on a number of factors that don't really concern us, including the speed of the hardware, the quality of the compiler, and the skill of the programmer. We would prefer to make statements about the speed of an *algorithm* in general, rather than a particular implementation of it. This way, we don't have to redo our analysis if we change programming languages or buy a faster computer.

To keep our running-time expressions general, we allow them to contain unspecified constants. For example, we might find that the running time for algorithm A is $an^2 + b$, while that for

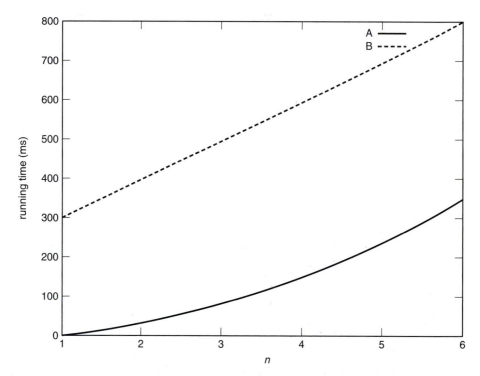

Figure 7-4: If the graph is plotted at a different scale, method A looks better.

algorithm B is $cn + d$, with a, b, c, and d being unspecified constants that depend on factors such as the speed of the hardware.

The thought of doing proofs with all these unspecified constants lying around may be unnerving. Fortunately, there is a huge shortcut. Functions can be classified into *orders*. (Whenever we talk about orders, we assume that all of the functions involved map nonnegative integers onto nonnegative real numbers and are *monotonically nondecreasing*—that is, $f(n + 1) \geq f(n)$. An algorithm for which the running-time function did not fit into this category would be fairly strange.)

Some common orders are shown in Figure 7–5. We will give a formal definition of an order later in this section.

For any function f, $\Theta(f)$ is pronounced "the order of f" or simply "order f." Each order is an infinitely large set of functions. The name of the order indicates one of the functions in that order. For example, n^2 is one of the functions in $\Theta(n^2)$.

Among the orders in Figure 7–5, $\Theta(2^n)$ is the largest and $\Theta(1)$ the smallest. This is what makes orders so useful: for sufficiently large n, a function is asymptotically larger than *any* function in a lower order. For example, for sufficiently large n, a function in $\Theta(n \log n)$ is asymptotically larger than any function in $\Theta(n)$ and asymptotically smaller than any function in $\Theta(n^2)$.

Order	Nickname
$\Theta(2^n)$	—
$\Theta(n^3)$	cubic
$\Theta(n^2)$	quadratic
$\Theta(n \log n)$	—
$\Theta(n)$	linear
$\Theta(\log n)$	logarithmic
$\Theta(1)$	constant

Figure 7-5: Some common orders of functions. Θ is the upper-case Greek letter theta. There are other orders (see page 191), but these are the most frequently encountered.

Two rules go a long way toward identifying the order of a function:

- Multiplying or dividing a function by a positive constant doesn't change its order. For example, $3n^2$ and $0.2n^2$ are both in $\Theta(n^2)$.

- A function's order is not changed by adding or subtracting a function in a lower order. For example, $2^n - n + \log n$ is in $\Theta(2^n)$.

Let's use these rules to find the order of $f(n) = 5n^3 + 3n^2 - 4n + 11$.

By the first rule, $5n^3$ is in $\Theta(n^3)$. Similarly, $3n^2$ is in $\Theta(n^2)$, $4n$ is in $\Theta(n)$, and 11 is in $\Theta(1)$. These are all lower orders, so we can ignore them by the second rule. Therefore, $f(n)$ is in $\Theta(n^3)$. This was hardly any work at all, and we now know a great deal about how $f(n)$ compares with other functions.

Let's look at some more examples. Given the running-time expressions in Figure 7–6, which algorithm should we use?

Algorithm	Running Time
Column frobbing	$an^2 - b \log n$
Row zorching	$cn + d$

Figure 7-6: Running-time expressions for two fictitious algorithms with silly names.

The running time for the column frobbing algorithm is in $\Theta(n^2)$. The running time for the row zorching algorithm is in $\Theta(n)$. $\Theta(n)$ is a lower order, so we should choose row zorching.

Figure 7–7 presents two more running times to compare. Dynamic inversion takes time in $\Theta(n^3)$, but what about synchronized absquatulation?

Algorithm	Running Time
Dynamic inversion	$an^3 + bn^2 + c$
Synchronized absquatulation	$\dfrac{n(n+1)}{2}$

Figure 7-7: More running-time expressions. The algorithm names don't mean anything.

Multiplying it out, we find that

$$\frac{n(n+1)}{2} = \frac{1}{2}n^2 + \frac{1}{2}n.$$

Now we are back in familiar territory: Synchronized absquatulation takes time in $\Theta(n^2)$, so it is faster than dynamic inversion (for sufficiently large n).

A final challenge is given in Figure 7–8.

Algorithm	Running Time
Cubic flensing	an^3
Factorial decortication	$n!$

Figure 7-8: Even yet still more running-time expressions. $n!$, pronounced "n factorial," is the product of the integers 1 through n.

Can we wrangle $n!$ into some form we recognize?

$$n! = 1 \cdot 2 \cdot \ldots \cdot n$$

Things don't look good. Notice, however, that this is *at least*

$$1 \cdot \underbrace{2 \cdot 2 \cdot \ldots \cdot 2}_{n-1 \text{ twos}}$$

or

$$2^{n-1} = \frac{1}{2}2^n.$$

Factorial decortication takes time which is *at least* in $\Theta(2^n)$. Since cubic flensing is in the lower order $\Theta(n^3)$, we should choose cubic flensing.

Rather than proving that $\Theta(n!) = \Theta(2^n)$, which is not true, we proved something like $\Theta(n!) \geq \Theta(2^n)$. This trick is so useful that there is special notation for it.

If $\Theta(f)$ is the set of functions which grow like f, then $\Omega(f)$ is the set of functions which grow like f or much more quickly. In set theory terms, it is the union of $\Theta(f)$ and all higher orders. We proved that $n!$ is in $\Omega(2^n)$. Various related notations are summarized in Figure 7–9.

Analogy	Notation	Set
$\Theta(f) \geq \Theta(g)$	$f \in \Omega(g)$	$\Theta(g)$ and all higher orders
$\Theta(f) = \Theta(g)$	$f \in \Theta(g)$	$\Theta(g)$
$\Theta(f) \leq \Theta(g)$	$f \in O(g)$	$\Theta(g)$ and all lower orders

Figure 7-9: Order relations between two functions f and g. The symbol $\in$ is read "is a member of (the set)." Ω is the upper-case Greek letter omega. O is the upper-case Greek letter omicron, but it is normally pronounced "big oh." Be careful not to read too much into the analogies; a function in $O(g)$ might actually be larger than g.

Remember that functions in the same order can differ by a constant factor. Consequently, a function in $O(g)$ might actually be larger than g. For example, $3n^2 \in O(n^2)$, but $3n^2$ is larger than n^2 (by a factor of 3).

We can define these notations more formally. First, $f \in O(g)$ if and only if, for some constant $c > 0$, there is some $n_0 \geq 0$ such that $f(n) < cg(n)$ for any $n \geq n_0$.

We've seen n_0 before; that's just a threshold so that only large values of n are considered. (In Figure 7–3, n_0 was 12.) The constant c is there so that multiplying either function by a constant won't have any effect. Put another way, the definition says that $f \in O(g)$ if and only if at least one function in $\Theta(g)$ is larger than f for sufficiently large n.

Similarly, $f \in \Omega(g)$ if and only if, for some constant $c > 0$, there is some $n_0 \geq 0$ such that $f(n) > cg(n)$ for any $n \geq n_0$.

Combining these, we get the formal definition of an order:

$f \in \Theta(g)$ if and only if $f \in O(g)$ and $f \in \Omega(g)$.

Showing that $f \in O(g)$ is called finding an *asymptotic upper bound* on f. Showing that $f \in \Omega(g)$ is called finding an *asymptotic lower bound*. Showing that $f \in \Theta(g)$ is called finding an *asymptotically tight bound*.

There are other orders besides those listed in Figure 7–5. For $k > 1$, the orders $\Theta(kn)$ are called *exponential* orders. For $k > 0$, the orders $\Theta(nk)$ are called *polynomial* orders. These fit into the order hierarchy right where we would expect. For example, $n^5 \in \Omega(n^4)$, $2^n \in O(3^n)$, and $in \in \Omega(nj)$ for any $i, j > 1$.

Exercises

7.2   What is the order of the expression $3n^2 + 5n + n \log n$?

7.3   What is the order of the expression $5n \log 5n$?

7.4   What is the order of the expression $(n + 3)(n - 2)$?

7.5   What is the order of the expression $2^n + \sqrt{\log n}$?

7.6   What is the order of the volume of an $n \times n \times n$ cube? What about the surface area? Answer the same questions for a cylinder of radius n and height n.

7.7   Use the identity

$$\log_a x = \frac{\log_b x}{\log_b a}$$

to prove that $\Theta(\log_2 n)$, $\Theta(\log_{10} n)$, and $\Theta(\log e \, n)$ are the same order.

7.8   Prove that $\Theta(\max(f, g)) = \Theta(f + g)$. (Hint: Since $\max(f, g) = \max(g, f)$ and $f + g = g + f$, you may assume without loss of generality that $f(n)$ is larger than $g(n)$ for sufficiently large values of n.)

7.3 Counting Steps

Now we know what we're aiming for when we analyze an algorithm: the order of the running time. We accomplish this through the following process:

1. Write the algorithm down in precise English or in any programming language, such as Java.

2. Determine how many *steps* are accomplished by each line and how many times the line is executed. The time used by the line is the product of these two expressions. We'll say more in a moment about what constitutes a step.

3. The total running time for the algorithm is the sum of the time required for each line. The order of this expression is the same as the order of the most time-consuming line.

For example, let's analyze the `size()` method from our LinkedList class. The method is reproduced in Figure 7–10, with extra line breaks added to keep each line simple. The time this takes depends on the size of the list, which we'll call n.

Each line here performs only a single step. We define a step as a constant amount of work. In other words, a step cannot depend on the size of the input or data structure in question. Any of the following constitutes a single step:

•   Accessing or setting a variable or field, including an element of an array.

•   Addition, subtraction, multiplication, division, and other basic arithmetic operators. (Strictly speaking, the time it takes to add two numbers depends on the sizes of the numbers. Since numbers in Java, as in most other programming languages, have a limited range, there is no potential for abuse by adding thousand-digit numbers.)

•   Finding the length of an array or String.

```
1 public int size() {
2   int tally = 0;
3   for (ListNode<E> node = front;
4        node != null;
5        node = node.getNext()) {
6     tally++;
7   }
8   return tally;
9 }
```

Figure 7-10: The size() method from our LinkedList class. The three parts of the for loop header have been placed on separate lines for clarity.

- Comparisons using ==, <, etc.

- Any fixed number of single steps, such as two additions and a variable assignment.

All of the *operators* which are built into the Java language, such as + and &&, count as single steps. This is not necessarily true of *methods* in the Java library, such as those in the collections framework. In general, if a method or operation is so trivial that you cannot imagine what simpler operations might be used to construct it, it can probably be considered a single step.

It is not a problem that some steps take longer than others, since they are all in $\Theta(1)$. Suppose the longest step takes 100 milliseconds and the shortest step takes 20 milliseconds. Assuming that every step takes 100 milliseconds gives us an upper bound on the total running time. Assuming that every step takes 20 milliseconds gives us a lower bound. These two running-time expressions are in the same order, so they are equivalent for our purposes.

Returning to size(), we see that each line performs a single step, except for lines 7 and 9, which don't do anything. How many times is each line executed?

Lines 1, 2, 3, and 8 are executed only once. The for loop test on line 4 is executed once each time we enter the loop, plus one more time when the test fails. Lines 5 and 6 are each executed once on each pass through the loop.

Since tally starts at 0 and ends up equal to n, there must be n passes through the loop. We now know how much total time is taken by each line, as summarized in Figure 7-11. Line 4 does the most work, taking total time in $\Theta(n + 1) = \Theta(n)$. We conclude that the running time for size() is linear.

Alternately, let c be the time taken by a single step. The total time taken by size() is:

$$c + c + c + c(n + 1) + cn + cn + c = 3cn + 5c \in \Theta(n)$$

Most algorithms are analyzed in terms of n, with n being the size of some data structure. Other analyses are possible. For example, the constructor for the Deck class from Chapter 5 is shown in Figure 7-12. This is analyzed in terms of r, the number of ranks, and s, the number of suits. The running time is dominated by line 9, which takes time in $\Theta((r + 1)s) = \Theta(rs)$.

It is not always possible to write an algorithm so that each line takes only one step each time it is run. For example, suppose we want to analyze the contructor for the GoFish class, again in terms

```
1 public int size() {              // 1 step, once
2   int tally = 0;                  // 1 step, once
3   for (ListNode<E> node = front;  // 1 step, once
4        node != null;              // 1 step, n + 1 times
5        node = node.getNext()) {   // 1 step, n times
6     tally++;                       // 1 step, n times
7   }
8   return tally;                    // 1 step, once
9 }
```

Figure 7-11: The size() method, with the time taken by each line.

```
1 /** Create all 52 Cards, in order. */
2 public Deck() {                                   // 1 step, once
3   cards = new Card[52];                            // 1 step, once
4   size = 0;                                        // 1 step, once
5   for (int suit = Card.SPADES;                     // 1 step, once
6        suit <= Card.CLUBS;                         // 1 step, s + 1 times
7        suit++) {                                   // 1 step, s times
8     for (int rank = Card.ACE;                      // 1 step, s times
9          rank <= Card.KING;                        // 1 step, (r + 1)s times
10         rank++) {                                 // 1 step, rs times
11       cards[size] = new Card(rank, suit);         // 1 step, rs times
12       size += 1;                                  // 1 step, rs times
13     }
14   }
15 }
```

Figure 7-12: The constructor for the Deck class can be analyzed in terms of s, the number of suits, and r, the number of ranks.

of r and s. The constructor is reproduced in Figure 7–13. Line 5 invokes the Deck constructor, which uses more than one step. Even though it is executed only once, this turns out to be the most expensive line in the algorithm. The analysis of shuffle() is left as Exercise 7.10. It is not precisely true that the add() method invoked in lines 12 and 13 takes constant time, but this can be remedied by a simple modification (Exercise 7.11).

Since we can ignore all lines except the one with the highest-order running time, it is often okay to collapse several lines together. Specifically, all three parts of a for loop header can be taken as a single step, which is run as many times as the loop test—that is, one more than the number of passes through the loop. An example, a method to add up the elements of a two-dimensional array (matrix), is given in Figure 7–14.

A trickier algorithm to analyze is one which adds up only the numbers for which $j \leq i$. (If we number the rows and columns from the upper left, this is the lower left half of the matrix, including the diagonal.) The code is almost identical, except for the test in the inner loop (Figure 7–15).

The dominant term in the running time of this algorithm is the number of times the inner loop (lines 7–9) runs. This number is not immediately obvious, because it is different in each pass

```
1 /** Shuffle the Deck and deal seven Cards to each player. */
2 public GoFish() {                       // 1 step, once
3    computerScore = 0;                    // 1 step, once
4    playerScore = 0;                      // 1 step, once
5    deck = new Deck();                    // (r + 1)s steps, once
6    deck.shuffle();                       // rs + 1 steps, once
7    computerHand = new GoFishHand();      // 1 step, once
8    playerHand = new GoFishHand();        // 1 step, once
9    for (int i = 0;                       // 1 step, once
10       i < 7;                            // 1 step, 8 times
11       i++) {                            // 1 step, 7 times
12    playerHand.add(deck.deal());         // 1 step, 7 times
13    computerHand.add(deck.deal());       // 1 step, 7 times
14   }
15 }
```

Figure 7-13: Some lines in the constructor from the GoFish class take more than one step.

```
1 /** Return the sum of the elements of matrix. */
2 public static double sum(double[][] matrix) {      // once
3    double result = 0;                               // once
4    for (int i = 0; i < matrix.length; i++) {        // n + 1 times
5      for (int j = 0; j < matrix[i].length; j++) {   // n(n + 1) times
6        result += matrix[i][j];                       // n * n times
7      }
8    }
9    return result;                                    // once
10 }
```

Figure 7-14: This method accepts an $n \times n$ array as input and runs in $\Theta(n^2)$ time. Each line counts as a single step, so only the number of times each line is executed is shown.

through the outer loop. When i is 0, the inner loop runs once. When i is 1, the inner loop runs twice. This continues until i is $n - 1$, when the inner loop runs n times. The total number of passes through the inner loop, then, is:

$$1 + 2 + \ldots + n$$

This can be rewritten as:

$$\sum_{i=1}^{n} i$$

```
 1 /**
 2  * Return sum of matrix elements on or below the diagonal.
 3  */
 4 public static double sumLowerTriangle(double[][] matrix) {
 5    double result = 0;
 6    for (int i = 0; i < matrix.length; i++) {
 7       for (int j = 0; j <= i; j++) {
 8          result += matrix[i][j];
 9       }
10    }
11    return result;
12 }
```

Figure 7–15: In this method, the number of times the inner loop runs depends on the value of i.

Using the theorem from Section C.3 of Appendix C, we determine that this is:

$$\frac{n(n+1)}{2} \in \Theta(n^2)$$

A slightly easier approach is to reason that, on each pass through the outer loop, the inner loop runs at most n times. Using the theorem from Section C.5, we have:

$$\sum_{i=1}^{n} i \le n \cdot n \in O(n^2)$$

Because of the $\le$, this allows us to make only a O statement, not a Θ statement. A O statement is often sufficient.

A single `for` loop typically takes time in $\Theta(n)$, while a doubly nested `for` loop typically takes time in $\Theta(n^2)$. Figure 7–16 shows a method with a quadruply nested `for` loop.

It is very easy to find an asymptotic upper bound on the running time of `sum4d()`. The first loop, starting on line 4, runs n times. The second loop runs at most n times for each pass through the first loop, for a total in $O(n^2)$. Similarly, the third loop takes time in $O(n^3)$. The fourth loop (and hence the entire method) takes time in $O(n^4)$.

We must be careful not to overgeneralize the result about nested loops. It is safe to use only for loops of the common form

```
for (int i = 0; i < n; i++) {
   ...
}
```

which run at most n times.

```
 1 /** Return the sum of the elements of arr. */
 2 public static double sum4d(double[][][][] arr) { // once
 3   double result = 0;                             // once
 4   for (int i = 0; i < arr.length; i++) {         // O(n) times
 5     for (int j = 0; j < i; j++) {                // O(n2) times
 6       for (int k = 0; k < j; k++) {              // O(n3) times
 7         for (int m = 0; m < k; m++) {            // O(n4) times
 8           result += arr[i][j][k][m];             // O(n4) times
 9         }
10       }
11     }
12   }
13   return result;                                 // once
14 }
```

Figure 7-16: This method, which sums the elements of a four-dimensional array, contains a quadruply nested `for` loop.

An enhanced `for` loop also runs at most n times, where n is the number of elements in the data structure being traversed.

A loop may run less than n times if it is stopped early by a return or break statement, or if it deals with more than one element on each pass.

Exercises

7.9   An instance of the built-in class java.lang.BigInteger represents an integer, which can be arbitrarily large. Is it safe to assume that the `add()` method from this class takes constant time? Explain.

7.10   Analyze the running time of the `shuffle()` method from the Deck class (**Figure 5–12**) in terms of r and s.

7.11   Modify the Go Fish program so that the `add()` method of the GoFishHand class takes constant time. (Hint: See Exercise 5.8.)

7.12   Show that the running time of `sum4d()` (**Figure 7–16**) is in $\Theta(n^4)$.

7.4 Best, Worst, and Average Case

Figure 7–17 shows the `contains()` method from our ArrayList class. It is difficult to analyze because of the `if` statement on line 3. The method clearly takes time linear in `size` if we have to search through all of the elements in the ArrayList, but it might take much less if the element at position 0 happens to be `equals()` to `target`. The running time depends not only on the *size* of the data structure, but also on its *contents*.

```
1 public boolean contains(E target) {
2   for (int i = 0; i < size; i++) {
3     if (data[i].equals(target)) {
4       return true;
5     }
6   }
7   return false;
8 }
```

Figure 7-17: The running time for the `contains()` method from our ArrayList class depends on the contents of the ArrayList.

At this point, we have to decide which kind of analysis we're doing. The easiest, but least useful, is ***best-case*** analysis. This tells us how fast the program runs if we get really lucky about the data. For `contains()`, the best case occurs when the first item in the list is `target`. The best-case running time is $\Theta(1)$.

Best-case analysis is not very reassuring. An algorithm might shine in some incredibly rare circumstance but have lousy performance in general.

More useful is ***worst-case*** analysis: at any `if` statement, take the more expensive branch. For `contains()`, this means assuming that `target` is not in the ArrayList, giving a running time of $\Theta(n)$. It is only a slight abuse of the notation to simply say that `contains()` takes time in $O(n)$—it might be in $\Theta(n)$ or it might be in a lower order.

We can also perform ***average-case*** analysis. This is tricky, as it requires that we make some assumption about what the "average" data set looks like.

Given a set of different ***events*** which might occur, the average running time is:

$$\sum_{events} \langle \text{probability of event occuring} \rangle \cdot \langle \text{running time if event occurs} \rangle$$

We must always be careful to choose our events so that they are ***exhaustive*** (at least one of them will occur) and ***mutually exclusive*** (no more than one of them will occur).

To analyze the average performance of `contains()`, let's assume that `target` is present exactly once, but is equally likely to be at any index in the ArrayList. The appearance of `target` at any particular index is an event. There are n different possible events, and we assume that they are equally likely. Thus, the probability of each event occurring is $1/n$.

If `target` is at index 0, there is one pass through the loop. If `target` is at index 1, there are two passes, and so on. The average running time for `contains()` is therefore:

$$\sum_{i=0}^{n-1}\frac{1}{n}(i+1) = \frac{1}{n}\sum_{i=1}^{n}i$$

$$= \frac{n+1}{2}$$

$$\in \Theta(n)$$

Notice that this is the same order as the worst-case running time, but not as good as the best case. It is always true that:

best case ≤ average case ≤ worst case

Consequently, if the best and worst cases are in the same order, the average case must also be in that order.

Exercises

7.13   What is the average result of rolling a 6-sided die?

7.14   We want to know the average *output* (not running time) of the method in Figure 7–18. We might try to do this by determining the average result of rolling a die and then squaring that. What's wrong with this reasoning?

```
1 /** Roll a die, square the result, and return it. */
2 public static int dieSquared() {
3   Die die = new Die();
4   die.roll();
5   return die.getTopFace() * die.getTopFace();
6 }
```

Figure 7–18: Code for Exercise 7.14. The average output of this method is not simply the square of the average die roll.

7.5 Amortized Analysis

A fourth kind of analysis, somewhere between average and worst case, is ***amortized*** analysis. The subtle differences between these three are in the questions they answer.

Average-case analysis answers the question, "How much time does this algorithm take on a *typical run?*"

Worst-case analysis answers the question, "How much time does this algorithm take on the *worst possible run?*"

Amortized analysis answers the question, "If this algorithm is run several times, what is the average time *per run*, given the worst possible *sequence* of runs?"

Unlike average-case analysis, amortized analysis does not have to make any assumptions about what a "typical" run looks like. Often, the amortized running time is the same as the worst-case running time, because the worst possible sequence of runs is just the worst possible individual run, over and over again. For some algorithms, though, it is not possible for the worst run to occur many times in a row.

As an example, consider the `add()` method from our ArrayList class, which is reproduced in Figure 7–19. This method takes constant time in the best case, but linear time in the worst case.

```
1 public void add(E target) {  // 1 step, once
2   if (isFull()) {            // 1 step, once
3     stretch();               // n steps, 0 or 1 times
4   }
5   data[size] = target;       // 1 step, once
6   size++;                    // 1 step once
7 }
```

Figure 7-19: The `add()` method from our ArrayList class takes constant time unless the ArrayList is full. In that worst case, it takes time linear in the size of the ArrayList.

To find the amortized time, we imagine the worst possible *sequence* of runs. This occurs when we start with a new, empty ArrayList (capacity 1) and invoke `add()` n times. What is the total time for all of these invocations? The time for operations other than stretching adds up to something in $\Theta(n)$. How much time do we spend stretching the ArrayList?

We can find the pattern by writing down a few examples (Figure 7–20). If we start at capacity 1 and double every time the ArrayList fills up, we need to stretch the ArrayList every time its size exceeds a power of 2.

Invocation	1	2	3	4	5	6	7	8	9	...	n
Time		1	2		4				8		$n-1$

Figure 7-20: Amount of time spent copying over a sequence of invocations of `add()`. For simplicity, we assume that n is one more than a power of 2, a move we will justify in Chapter 8.

The total time for this sequence of runs is therefore:

$$1 + 2 + 4 + \ldots + (n-1)$$

It's not immediately clear what this adds up to, or even how many terms it has. As luck would have it, we don't need to know how many terms there are. If we simply assume there are t terms, numbered 0 through $t - 1$, we find that this sum is:

$$(n-1) + \ldots + 4 + 2 + 1 = \sum_{i=0}^{t-1} \frac{n-1}{2^i}$$

$$= (n-1) \cdot 2^0 + (n-1) \sum_{i=1}^{t-1} \left(\frac{1}{2}\right)^i$$

$$< 2(n-1)$$

The worst possible sequence of add() invocations requires that we copy less than $2(n-1)$ elements. The amortized time *per operation* is:

$$\frac{2(n-1)}{n} \in O(1)$$

Since we need $\Omega(1)$ time per operation just to add the new element, we conclude that the amortized running time of add() is in $\Theta(1)$. Since the average-case time is always at least as good as the amortized time, it follows that add() takes constant time on average.

Now suppose we rewrite the stretch() method so that, instead of doubling the capacity of the ArrayList, it merely increases the capacity by 1. This seems like a reasonable idea—why allocate a bunch of extra memory that we might never use?

What effect does this change have on the amortized running time of add()? Again, we consider when and how much we have to copy (Figure 7–21).

Invocation	1	2	3	4	5	6	7	8	9	...	n
Time		1	2	3	4	5	6	7	8		$n-1$

Figure 7–21: Amount of time spent copying over a sequence of invocations of add(), when stretch() is modified to increase the ArrayList's capacity by only 1.

The total time spent copying is now:

$$1 + 2 + 3 + \ldots + (n-1) = \sum_{i=1}^{n-1} i$$

$$= \frac{(n-1)n}{2}$$

Dividing this by n operations, we find that the amortized time per operation is now linear, rather than constant. Amortized analysis tells us that we should prefer the version of `stretch()` that doubles the capacity of the ArrayList.

Exercise

7.15   All of the Stack and Queue operations, under both array-based and linked implementations, take amortized time in the same order. Which order is it?

Summary

Analysis of algorithms gives us mathematical tools for comparing the efficiency of different algorithms. While empirically timing programs is important in optimization, it depends on factors such as hardware speed and compiler quality. In designing general-purpose data structures and algorithms, we are interested in asymptotic behavior: what happens to the running time as the size of the data becomes arbitrarily large?

The running time of a method can be expressed as a function, and functions can be classified into orders. A function's order is unchanged if it is multiplied by a constant factor or if a lower-order function is added. Thus, things like faster hardware do not affect the order of an algorithm's running-time function. There are a number of special notations (O, Θ, Ω), for dealing with orders.

To find the running time of an algorithm, we determine the running time for each line. This is the number of simple (constant-time) steps the line accomplishes, multiplied by the number of times the line is run. The algorithm's running time has the same order as the running time of the most expensive line in the algorithm. The algebra of sums comes in handy when analyzing algorithms with nested loops.

There are four kinds of analysis we can perform. They produce running times which are ordered as follows:

$$\text{best case} \leq \text{average case} \leq \text{amortized} \leq \text{worst case}$$

Worst-case analysis is the most common. Average-case analysis is also useful, but requires some assumption about what "average" data looks like. Amortized analysis is appropriate when the worst case (such as stretching an array) cannot happen on every run.

Vocabulary

amortized. Analysis of the time per operation over the worst possible sequence of inputs.

asymptotic. Pertaining to the behavior of a function $f(n)$ in the limit, as n becomes very large.

asymptotic lower bound. Lower bound on the order of a function f, expressed as $f \in \Omega(g)$ for some g.

asymptotic upper bound. Upper bound on the order of a function f, expressed as $f \in O(g)$ for some g.

asymptotically tight bound. Precise statement of the order of a function f, expressed as $f \in \Theta(g)$ for some g.

average case. Analysis of expected behavior, given some assumption about average input.

best case. Analysis assuming the best possible input.

exponential. Any order of the form $\Theta(k^n)$, for some $k > 1$.

monotonically nondecreasing. Of a function f over the integers, $f(n + 1) \geq f(n)$.

order. Set of functions growing at the same rate, within a constant factor.

polynomial. Any order of the form $\Theta(n^k)$, for some $k > 0$.

step. Series of operations taking time in $\Theta(1)$.

worst case. Analysis assuming the worst possible input.

Problems

7.16   Add a method `addFirst()` to our List interface from Section 5.3. Unlike `add()`, `addFirst()` should put the new element at the *front* of the List. Provide this method in both our ArrayList class (Section 5.3) and our LinkedList class (Section 6.3). What is the order of the running time of each version?

7.17   Since method invocation uses time to push and pop the call stack, there may be an efficiency cost in using accessors and mutators rather than accessing fields directly. Some compilers are smart enough to skip the method invocation, preserving encapsulation while not incurring a speed cost. Run an experiment to determine whether your compiler does this.

7.18   Modify the LinkedList class from Section 6.3 so that `size()` takes constant time.

Projects

7.19   Complete Figure 7–22.

7.20   Complete Figure 7–23. Drop any fractions and approximate very large values using scientific notation as shown. You will probably have to use both a calculator/computer and some algebra to accomplish this.

	ArrayList				LinkedList			
	Best	**Avg**	**Amort**	**Worst**	**Best**	**Avg**	**Amort**	**Worst**
add()			$\Theta(1)$	$\Theta(n)$				
contains()	$\Theta(1)$	$\Theta(n)$		$\Theta(n)$				
get()				$\Theta(1)$				$\Theta(n)$
isEmpty()								
iterator()								
remove()								
size()					$\Theta(n)$	$\Theta(n)$	$\Theta(n)$	$\Theta(n)$

Figure 7–22: Comparison of algorithms from our ArrayList and LinkedList classes, for Project 7.19. (Analyze the version of **remove()** which takes an index as an argument.)

Time to process *n* elements (milliseconds)	1 second	1 minute	1 hour	1 day	1 year
$\log_2 n$		$10^{18,061}$			
n	1,000	60,000			3.1×10^{10}
$n \log_2 n$					
n^2			1,897		
n^3					
2^n	9				

Figure 7–23: Number of elements that can be processed in a given amount of time for various running-time functions. For Project 7.20.

8

Searching and Sorting

This chapter introduces the simplest algorithms for searching and sorting arrays. We will see more sophisticated algorithms for these tasks in Chapters 9, 12, and 14.

Searching is the task of determining whether a collection contains some particular element. The `contains()` method from the List interface (Chapter 5) performs searching. In this chapter, we will see a couple of ways to do this more efficiently if the collection is already in order from smallest to largest. Linear search is covered in Section 8.1, binary search in Section 8.2.

Sorting is the task of putting a collection in increasing order. We will not bother to write a game involving sorting, but it should be clear that this is a useful operation to perform in many situations. In many card games, for example, sorting one's hand makes it easier to decide which play to make. We might also wish to print a list of mailing addresses or book titles in sorted order. Section 8.3 presents the insertion sort algorithm.

For simplicity, we introduce the searching and sorting algorithms as static methods operating on arrays of ints. In Section 8.4, we introduce an interface that allows us to search and sort arrays of other things. Section 8.5 closes out the chapter with some thoughts on sorting linked lists.

8.1 Linear Search

Suppose we want to determine whether an array of ints contains some target number. The obvious approach is the one used in the contains() method of the ArrayList class (Section 5.3): start at the beginning and examine each element in turn. This algorithm is called *linear search*. Not surprisingly, it takes linear time in both the worst and average cases.

We can make the algorithm slightly more efficient if we know in advance that the array is sorted. The numbers we encounter during a search increase as we move from left to right across the array. If we ever encounter a number which is larger than the target, we can stop searching. Since all of the remaining numbers must be even larger, the target can't possibly appear later in the array.

The code for this improved linear search is given in Figure 8–1.

```
1 /** Return true if target appears in the sorted array data. */
2 public static boolean linearSearch(int[] data, int target) {
3   for (int i = 0; (i < data.length) && (data[i] <= target); i++) {
4     if (data[i] == target) {
5       return true;
6     }
7   }
8   return false;
9 }
```

Figure 8-1: If the array data is already sorted, a linear search can sometimes be stopped early.

In the worst case, this is no faster than the old version. On average, although the running time is still in $\Theta(n)$, the number of elements we have to examine in a successful search is reduced by a factor of 2. A formal proof of this is left as Exercise 8.2.

To analyze the average number of passes through the loop on an unsuccessful search, we define an exhaustive set of mutually exclusive events. Let event i be the event that the target, if it were present, would belong right before element i. There is one event for each of the n numbers (events 0 through $n-1$), plus event n, where the target is larger than anything in the array.

In event n, we have to examine n elements to determine that the target is not present. In events 0 through $n-1$, we have to examine $i+1$ elements. If we assume that the $n+1$ events are equally likely, the average number of elements examined is:

$$\frac{1}{n+1}n + \sum_{i=0}^{n-1}\frac{1}{n+1}(i+1) = \frac{n}{n+1} + \frac{1}{n+1}\sum_{i=1}^{n}i$$

$$= \frac{n}{n+1} + \frac{1}{n+1}\frac{n(n+1)}{2}$$

$$= \frac{n}{n+1} + \frac{n}{2}$$

Thus, on average, we only have to look at between $n/2$ and $(n/2) + 1$ elements.

Exercises

8.1 There are $n!$ permutations of a set of n elements. For example, the set $\{A, B, C\}$ has $3! = 6$ permutations: ABC, ACB, BAC, BCA, CAB, and CBA. There are $(n + 1)!$ permutations of the set after we add a new target. Argue that, if each of these permutations is equally likely, each of the $n + 1$ places where the target might belong is equally likely.

8.2 Analyze the average time for a *successful* linear search.

8.2 Binary Search

We can take further advantage of the fact that an array is sorted by starting our search in the middle of the array. If we happen to find the target, we can return `true` immediately. If not, comparing the middle element to the target reveals whether the target belongs in the left or right half of the array. In other words, a constant amount of work allows us to divide the data in half. We then repeat this procedure until either we find the target or we run out of data. This algorithm, called *binary search*, is illustrated in Figure 8–2.

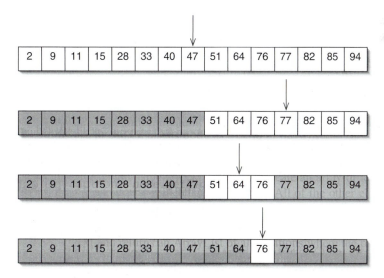

Figure 8–2: Binary search for 76 in a sorted array. Every time a number is compared to the target, half of the remaining array (shaded) is ruled out as a potential location.

The code is given in Figure 8–3. The indices `bottom` and `top` specify the region of the array still under consideration. The loop shrinks this region until either the target is found or the region becomes empty.

```
1 /** Return true if target appears in the sorted array data. */
2 public static boolean binarySearch(int[] data, int target) {
3   int bottom = 0;
4   int top = data.length - 1;
5   while (bottom <= top) {
6     int midpoint = (top + bottom) / 2;
7     if (target < data[midpoint]) {
8       top = midpoint - 1;
9     } else if (target == data[midpoint]) {
10      return true;
11    } else {
12      bottom = midpoint + 1;
13    }
14  }
15  return false;
16 }
```

Figure 8-3: In the `binarySearch()` method, each pass through the `while` loop on lines 5–14 rules out half of the array as a potential location for `target`.

Analysis of Binary Search

The running time of binary search is proportional to the number of times the loop runs. This is the number of times we have to divide the data in half before we run out of data.

We assume that n, the length of the array, is an exact power of 2. We will justify this shortcut in a moment. When we examine the middle element (or as close as we can get, given that n is even), one side of the array has $n/2$ elements and the other side has $(n/2) - 1$ elements. In the worst case, we always have to look in the larger piece.

For example, if $n = 8$, we have one pass where there are 8 candidate elements, one where there are 4, one where there are 2, and one where there is 1. This is four passes. Notice that $2^3 = 8$. If n were $2^4 = 16$, we would need 5 passes.

The number of passes through the loop is $p + 1$, where $2^p = n$. The number p is, by definition, the base 2 logarithm of n. It is helpful to think of a base 2 logarithm as the number of times a number has to be divided in half before it gets down to 1 (Figure 8–4). We need $p + 1$ passes here because, after we get the search region down to a single element, we have to compare that last element to the target.

In the worst-case, then, the number of passes through the loop is $1 + \log_2 n \in \Theta(\log n)$. This is an improvement over the linear running time of linear search.

The average-case running time for a successful binary search also turns out to be logarithmic. The proof is left as a problem.

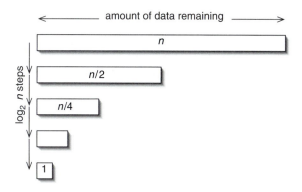

Figure 8–4: The base 2 logarithm of n is the number of times we have to divide n in half to get down to 1.

Assuming n Is a Power of Two

We do not generally expect n to be a power of two, but for most running-time functions this shortcut will not change the order of our result.

Theorem: Let $f(n)$ and $g(n)$ be two monotonically nondecreasing functions. If $f(n) = g(n)$ for exact powers of two, and $cg(n) > g(2n)$ for some constant c, then $f(n) \in \Theta(g(n))$ in general.

The condition that $cg(n) > g(2n)$ indicates that this theorem does not work for very quickly growing functions like 2^n. We will rarely encounter running-time functions like this. The theorem does work for any function in a polynomial or lower order.

Proof: We will show that $f(n) \in O(g(n))$ and $f(n) \in \Omega(g(n))$. The theorem follows from this.

To understand the proof, consider Figure 8–5.

The functions are known to be equal at the marked points. Between these points, $f(n)$ must stay within the dashed boundary. If it did not, it would have to decrease at some point. Since both functions are monotonically nondecreasing, this cannot happen.

To see that $f(n) \in O(g(n))$, consider the function $cg(n)$. We know that $cg(2) > g(4)$, $cg(4) > g(8)$, and so on. In terms of the graph, $cg(n)$ is always above the boundary boxes, and therefore greater than $f(n)$. In other words, $f(n) \in O(cg(n)) = O(g(n))$.

By a similar argument, $f(n) \in \Omega(g(n))$. Therefore, $f(n) \in \Theta(g(n))$.

This completes the proof.

Returning to the analysis of binary search, consider the case where n is *not* a power of 2. For example, suppose n is 15. We then need four passes, considering 15, 7, 3, and 1 elements, respectively. In fact, we need four passes for any n from 8 through 15. These are the values of n for which $3 \le \log_2 n < 4$.

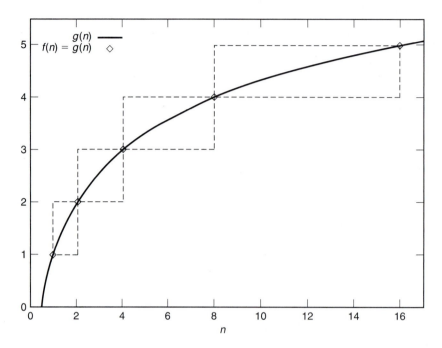

Figure 8-5: Intuition for proof that it's safe to assume *n* is a power of 2. The functions *f(n)* and *g(n)* coincide at exact powers of 2, and *f(n)* stays within the marked boundary.

In general, the number of passes is $1 + \lfloor \log_2 n \rfloor$. The notation $\lfloor x \rfloor$, read "*floor x*," means "*x* rounded down to the nearest integer." Analogously, $\lceil x \rceil$, read "*ceiling x*," means "*x* rounded up to the nearest integer." Since $\log_2 n$ is an integer for exact powers of 2, assuming that *n* is a power of 2 allows us to ignore floors and ceilings.

Exercises

8.3   In the analysis of binary search, we assumed that *n* is a power of 2. This means that *n* is even (unless it is 1), so there is no middle element. Which element does `binary-Search()` examine first?

8.4   The analysis of binary search given in this section is for a worst-case *successful* search, where we find the target just before we run out of places to look. What is the order of the running time for an *unsuccessful* search?

8.5   Instead of assuming that *n* is a power of 2, it is sometimes useful to assume that *n* is even. Prove that this is a safe thing to do.

8.3 Insertion Sort

The search algorithms in the previous two sections require that the array to be searched is already in sorted order. There are many algorithms for getting an array into this sorted state. This section discusses one of the simplest sorting algorithms, *insertion sort*.

Insertion sort is the algorithm many people use when sorting a hand of cards. Begin with all of the cards on the table. Pick up one card and place it in the left hand. Pick up a second card and add it to the left hand, either to the left or right of the first card depending on whether it is smaller or larger. Insert a third card into its proper place in this sequence, and so on, until all of the cards have been inserted.

To implement insertion sort on an array of ints, we use an idea from the ArrayList class: we divide the output array into "in use" and "not in use" regions (Figure 8–6). The numbers in the "in use" region are already sorted. When the algorithm finishes, the entire array is in the "in use" region, so all of the numbers are sorted.

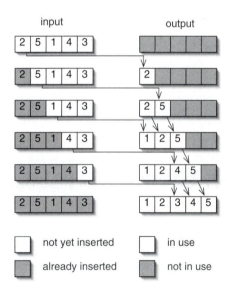

Figure 8-6: A first version of insertion sort uses two arrays: one to hold the data still to be inserted (left) and another to hold the result (right). When a number is inserted in the output, any larger numbers have to be shifted over one position.

The observant reader will notice that the "in use" portion of the input array is always exactly the same size as the "not in use" portion of the output array. We can use the same array for both purposes. In fact, instead of producing a new output array, we can simply rearrange the elements of the input array.

Given this improvement, the first number we actually have to insert is element 1. Element 0 would always be inserted at position 0, and it's already there. It will be moved if any smaller numbers are later inserted. This improved version is illustrated in Figure 8–7.

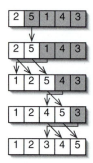

Figure 8-7: An improved version of insertion sort uses the input array to hold both the sorted portion (unshaded) and the numbers still to be inserted (shaded). In each step, the next available unsorted number is inserted into the sorted region of the array.

The code for `insertionSort()` is given in Figure 8–8. The main loop inserts each element in turn (except element 0). The loop on lines 6–8 works through the sorted region from right to left, moving each element one position to the right as it goes. This both finds the correct place for `target` and makes sure there is room to put it there when it arrives.

```
1 /** Arrange the numbers in data from smallest to largest. */
2 public static void insertionSort(int[] data) {
3   for (int i = 1; i < data.length; i++) {
4     int target = data[i];
5     int j;
6     for (j = i - 1; (j >= 0) && (data[j] > target); j--) {
7       data[j + 1] = data[j];
8     }
9     data[j + 1] = target;
10  }
11 }
```

Figure 8-8: Code for `insertionSort()`.

The running time of insertion sort depends on the running time of this inner loop. This is effectively a linear search through the i numbers which have already been sorted. In the best case, `data` was already in order, so the inner loop takes a single step for each insertion. The best-case running time for insertion sort is:

$$\sum_{i=1}^{n-1} 1 = n - 1$$

$$\in \Theta(n)$$

In the worst case, data was in *reverse* order, so each number must be moved all the way to the beginning of the array as it is inserted. The total time required for this is:

$$\sum_{i=1}^{n-1} i = \frac{(n-1)n}{2}$$

$$\in \Theta(n^2)$$

In the average case, we can assume that when we insert element i it is equally likely to end up in any of the positions 0 through i. (This is effectively the same assumption we made in analyzing the average-case performance of linear search.) Each insertion is into a sequence of $i - 1$ already sorted numbers, so it takes at least $(i - 1)/2$ comparisons on average. The total average case running time for insertion sort is therefore at least:

$$\sum_{i=1}^{n-1} \frac{i-1}{2} = \sum_{i=1}^{n-1} \frac{i}{2} - \sum_{i=1}^{n-1} \frac{1}{2}$$

$$= \frac{1}{2}\sum_{i=1}^{n-1} i - \frac{n-1}{2}$$

$$= \frac{1}{2}\frac{(n-1)n}{2} - \frac{n-1}{2}$$

$$\in \Omega(n^2)$$

Since the average-case time can't be worse-than the worst-case time (which is quadratic), the average-case time must also be in $O(n^2)$, and therefore in $\Theta(n^2)$.

We will see some more efficient sorting algorithms in Chapters 9, 12, and 14, but we now have a benchmark. Any sorting algorithm that takes time in an order higher than $\Theta(n^2)$ is less efficient than insertion sort and not worth considering.

Remember that asymptotic notation roughly indicates the rate at which a function grows, but obscures constant factors. For example, a method that takes $10n^2$ milliseconds to run is in a higher order than one that takes $200n$ milliseconds, but is actually faster for very *small* values of n. Because it is so simple, insertion sort has a low constant factor within its order. It is therefore a good algorithm to use when the number of elements being sorted is very small.

Exercises

8.6   On line 4 of the code for `insertionSort()` (Figure 8–8) we store `data[i]` in a separate variable `target`. The version in Figure 8–9 omits this "redundant" variable. Explain why it doesn't work.

```
 1 /** Arrange the numbers in data from smallest to largest. */
 2 public static void insertionSort(int[] data) {
 3   for (int i = 1; i < data.length; i++) {
 4     int j;
 5     for (j = i - 1; (j >= 0) && (data[j] > data[i]); j--) {
 6       data[j + 1] = data[j];
 7     }
 8     data[j + 1] = data[i];
 9   }
10 }
```

Figure 8-9: Broken version of `insertionSort()` for Exercise 8.6.

8.7   What is the amortized running time of insertion sort? (Hint: You should be able to answer this almost instantly, without doing any algebra.)

8.8   Assume that all $n!$ permutations of the elements of `data` are equally likely (see Exercise 8.1). Argue that, after element i is inserted, it is equally likely to appear in any of the positions 0 through i.

8.4 The Comparable Interface

Our implementations of searching and sorting algorithms have dealt only with ints. It would be trivial to write similar versions for doubles.

Can we use polymorphism to write methods which will work on Objects? If so, we could use the same methods to search and sort structures containing Integers, Cards, or anything else.

This is not quite possible, because the notions of "greater than" and "less than" don't make sense for all classes. For example, what would it mean for one LinkedStack to be greater than another? What about graphic windows, customers, or sound clips?

It only makes sense to sort things which are comparable. Java provides a built-in interface Comparable. All of the wrapper classes, as well as String, implement Comparable (Figure 8–10).

Comparable is generic because we can't compare instances of different subclasses. The type parameter specifies the class in question. Thus, Boolean implements Comparable<Boolean>, Character implements Comparable<Character>, and so on.

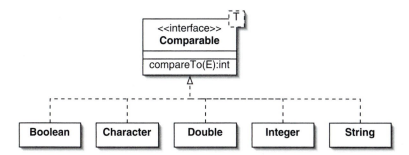

Figure 8-10: Many classes implement the Comparable interface. The type parameter T simply stands for type. This name is somewhat arbitrary, but it doesn't make sense to talk about the "element" of a Comparable the same way we would talk about the elements of a List.

If we want a generic class to hold only instances of comparable classes, we must specify its type parameter as:

```
<E extends Comparable<E>>
```

This means, "some class E that implements Comparable<E>." In this context, Java does not distinguish between implementing an interface and extending a class; the keyword **extends** covers both cases.

For example, suppose we want an ArrayList that can only hold Comparables. We can create SortableArrayList, a subclass of ArrayList (Figure 8–11).

```
1 /** An array-based List of Comparables. */
2 public class SortableArrayList<E extends Comparable<E>>
3   extends ArrayList<E> {
4 }
```

Figure 8-11: The class SortableArrayList is like ArrayList, but it can hold only Comparable objects.

The Comparable interface specifies one method, `compareTo()`. This compares the current element to some other element and returns an int. Given two objects `a` and `b`, `a.compareTo(b)` returns a negative number if `a` is less than `b`, zero if `a` equals `b`, and a positive number if `a` is greater than `b`.

At first glance, this seems excessively complicated. Wouldn't it be clearer to supply three methods, `isLessThan()`, `equals()`, and `isGreaterThan()`?

It might be clearer, but it would be less efficient. There are many algorithms, such as binary search, where we need to do a different thing in each of these three cases. If we simply provided boolean methods, we would need to compare `target` with each array element *twice* (Figure 8–12). If the elements were large data structures (say, very long Strings corresponding to DNA sequences), this would be a lot of redundant computation.

```
1 public boolean contains(E target) {
2    insertionSort();
3    int bottom = 0;
4    int top = size() - 1;
5    while (bottom <= top) {
6      int midpoint = (top + bottom) / 2;
7      if (target.isLessThan(get(midpoint))) {     // Illegal!
8        top = midpoint - 1;
9      } else if (target.equals(get(midpoint))) { // Illegal!
10       return true;
11     } else {
12       bottom = midpoint + 1;
13     }
14   }
15   return false;
16 }
```

Figure 8-12: A `contains()` method for the SortableArrayList class using binary search. If the Comparable interface specified separate methods `isLessThan()`, `equals()`, and `isGreaterThan()`, we would have to perform two comparisons in each pass through the loop. Comparable doesn't work this way, so this code is incorrect.

With the single `compareTo()` method, we perform the comparison once, then examine the simple result of the comparison twice (Figure 8–13).

```
1 public boolean contains(E target) {
2    insertionSort();
3    int bottom = 0;
4    int top = size() - 1;
5    while (bottom <= top) {
6      int midpoint = (top + bottom) / 2;
7      int comparison = target.compareTo(get(midpoint));
8      if (comparison < 0) {
9        top = midpoint - 1;
10     } else if (comparison == 0) {
11       return true;
12     } else {
13       bottom = midpoint + 1;
14     }
15   }
16   return false;
17 }
```

Figure 8-13: With the `compareTo()` method, we have to perform the potentially expensive comparison only once in each pass through the loop.

Incidentally, the compareTo() method in the String class uses *lexicographical order* to compare Strings. This is similar to alphabetical order, but it considers all upper-case letters to be earlier than all lower-case ones. It also handles nonalphabetic characters such as digits and punctuation marks, with the order specified by Unicode (which is identical to ASCII for common characters).

The contains() method in Figure 8–13 begins by insertion sorting the SortableArrayList. Code for this method is given in Figure 8–14.

```
1 /** Arrange the elements in this List from smallest to largest. */
2 public void insertionSort() {
3   for (int i = 1; i < size(); i++) {
4     E target = get(i);
5     int j;
6     for (j = i - 1;
7            (j >= 0) && (get(j).compareTo(target) > 0);
8            j--) {
9       set(j + 1, get(j));
10    }
11    set(j + 1, target);
12  }
13 }
```

Figure 8-14: The insertionSort() method for the SortableArrayList class.

If we want to make one of our own classes Comparable, we have to declare that it implements Comparable and provide the compareTo() method. In some classes, this amounts to a simple subtraction. For example, Figure 8–15 shows a compareTo() method for the Die class from Chapter 1.

```
1 public int compareTo(Die that) {
2   return topFace - that.topFace;
3 }
```

Figure 8-15: The compareTo() method for the Die class is a simple subtraction.

When a class implements Comparable, the compareTo() method should be consistent with the equals() method. In other words, a.equals(b) should be true for exactly those values of a and b for which a.compareTo(b) returns 0.

Exercises

8.9   What is the value of "Z".compareTo("a")? (Note that the "Z" is upper case.)

8.10   Modify the Card class (Section 5.1) so that it implements Comparable.

8.5 Sorting Linked Lists

The binary search algorithm depends on random access, so it is not suitable for use with linked structures. Most sorting algorithms also depend on random access, but some of them can be adapted to work with linked lists. In this section, we look at insertion sort for a linked list.

In order for our insertion sort to run efficiently, we must be careful to avoid the methods `get()`, `set()`, and `size()`, which all take linear time on linked lists. Instead of trying to directly convert the code from SortableArrayList, we return to the original idea of the insertion sort algorithm: insert each item in order into a new list.

Our plan is illustrated in Figure 8–16. We will create a new, empty list. Going through the original list, we'll insert each one in order into this new list. When we're done, we change the `front` reference in the old list to point to the front of the new one.

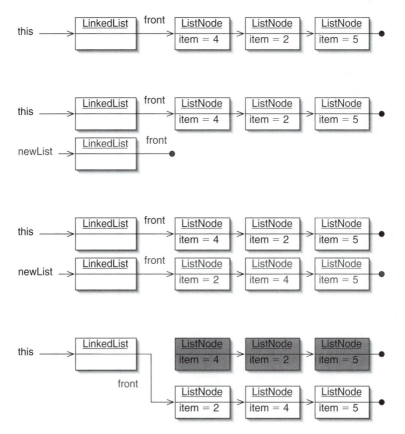

Figure 8-16: Plan for insertion sorting a list. We first create a new, empty List. We then insert the elements of the old list into the new one in order. Finally, we change the `front` reference to point to the new chain of nodes.

The code is given in Figure 8–17.

```
1  /** A linked List of Comparables. */
2  public class SortableLinkedList<E extends Comparable<E>>
3      extends LinkedList<E> {
4
5    /** Add target in order, assuming this List is sorted. */
6    protected void addInOrder(E target) {
7      Predecessor<E> prev = this;
8      ListNode<E> node = getNext();
9      while ((node != null)
10             && (node.getItem().compareTo(target) < 0)) {
11       prev = node;
12       node = node.getNext();
13     }
14     prev.setNext(new ListNode<E>(target, node));
15   }
16
17   /** Arrange the elements in this List from smallest to largest. */
18   public void insertionSort() {
19     SortableLinkedList<E> newList = new SortableLinkedList<E>();
20     for (E e : this) {
21       newList.addInOrder(e);
22     }
23     setNext(newList.getNext());
24   }
25
26 }
```

Figure 8–17: The SortableLinkedList class.

Exercises

8.11   Define an interface SortableList that is implemented by both SortableArrayList and SortableLinkedList. Draw a UML class diagram showing the relationship between your interface, these two classes, List, ArrayList, and LinkedList.

Summary

Two useful searching algorithms are linear search and binary search. Linear search works through an array from left to right, taking linear time in the worst case. Binary search starts in the middle and rules out half of the array on each pass through the loop, taking logarithmic time. In analyzing binary search, we assume that n is an exact power of 2. This is usually an acceptable shortcut.

The insertion sort algorithm inserts each element in turn into a sequence of already sorted elements. In the worst case, where the array was in reverse order to start with, insertion sort takes quadratic time.

The running times of searching algorithms are summarized in Figure 8–18.

Algorithm	Best Case	Average Case	Worst Case	Notes
linear search	$\Theta(1)$	$\Theta(n)$	$\Theta(n)$	
binary search	$\Theta(1)$	$\Theta(\log n)$	$\Theta(\log n)$	
interpolation search	$\Theta(1)$	$\Theta(\log (\log n))$	$\Theta(n)$	Section 12.4. Worst case unlikely if data are uniformly distributed.

Figure 8–18: Running times of searching algorithms. Some terminology in this table will be introduced in later chapters.

The running times of sorting algorithms are summarized in Figure 8–19.

Algorithm	Best Case	Average Case	Worst Case	Notes
insertion sort	$\Theta(n)$	$\Theta(n^2)$	$\Theta(n^2)$	Small constant factor. In place.
merge sort	$\Theta(n \log n)$	$\Theta(n \log n)$	$\Theta(n \log n)$	Section 9.3.
Quicksort	$\Theta(n \log n)$	$\Theta(n \log n)$	$\Theta(n^2)$	Section 9.4. Small constant factor. In place. Worst case can be made unlikely.
bucket sort	$\Theta(n)$	$\Theta(n)$	$\Theta(n^2)$	Section 12.4. Average case depends on uniform distribution of data.
heapsort	$\Theta(n \log n)$	$\Theta(n \log n)$	$\Theta(n \log n)$	Section 14.1. In place.

Figure 8–19: Some terminology in this table will be introduced in later chapters. By convention, some algorithm names are written as single words, and Quicksort is capitalized.

The Comparable interface allows us to compare instances of classes that implement it, including Integers, Doubles, and Strings. We can make our own classes Comparable by providing the compareTo() method.

Most sorting algorithms depend on random access, so they do not work efficiently on linked lists.

Vocabulary

binary search. Search that starts in the middle of a structure, ruling out half of the elements on each step.

ceiling. Mathematical operation rounding a number x up to the nearest integer. Written $\lceil x \rceil$.

floor. Mathematical operation rounding a number x down to the nearest integer. Written $\lfloor x \rfloor$.

insertion sort. Sort that traverses a structure, inserting each element into its proper place among the already sorted elements.

lexicographical order. Generalization of alphabetic order on Strings, in which each character is compared in turn until a difference is found or one String runs out of characters.

linear search. Search that traverses a structure from left to right.

search. Determine whether some element is present in a structure. Also any algorithm for searching.

selection sort. Sort that traverses a structure, repeatedly finding the smallest element and adding it to the sequence of already sorted elements (Project 8.14).

sort. Arrange a collection in increasing order. Also any algorithm for sorting.

Problems

8.12   Prove that a successful binary search takes logarithmic time on average. (Hint: Assume that the target is equally likely to be at any of the n positions in the array. For how many of these positions is the target discovered in one pass through the loop? Two? Three?)

8.13   The contains() method in Figure 8–13 sorts the list every time it is invoked. What is the worst-case running time of this method? Modify the SortableArrayList class so that the list keeps track of whether it is sorted and does so only when necessary. (Hint: You'll have to override any method that might cause the list to become unsorted, such as add(). Rather than replicate the bulk of the method from the superclass ArrayList in your own code, you can invoke it as super.add().)

Projects

8.14   In the insertion sort algorithm, we repeatedly find the next element and insert it into the already sorted region of the array. The *selection sort* algorithm instead begins by finding the smallest element in the array and swapping it with the element at position 0. The second smallest element (that is, the smallest element besides the one now at position 0) is then found and swapped with element 1. The third smallest element is placed at position 2, and so on. Implement selection sort and analyze its best-, average-, and worst-case running time.

8.15   Modify SortableArrayList so that it implements Comparable<SortableArrayList>. The order should be similar to the lexicographical order for Strings. Specifically, compare the elements at each position, starting with element 0. The first SortableArrayList to have a smaller element at some position is the smaller one. If one of them runs out of elements before a difference is found, the one that ran out is the smaller one, just as the String `"gar"` is less than `"gargoyle"`.

8.16   Do Project 8.15, but with SortableLinkedList instead.

Recursion

9

The chapter discusses recursion, a powerful technique for designing algorithms. Section 9.1 uses a puzzle to introduce the recursive way of thinking. The analysis of recursive algorithms requires new techniques, which are explained in Section 9.2. Two recursive sorting algorithms are introduced in Sections 9.3 and 9.4. While recursive algorithms are often very concise and elegant, their efficiency can sometimes be improved by converting them into a nonrecursive form, as explained in Section 9.5.

9.1 Thinking Recursively

We begin with a classic puzzle, the Towers of Hanoi (Figure 9–1).

The Towers of Hanoi

Players: 1

Object: To move a stack of disks from one of three pegs to a specified destination peg.

Setup: There are three pegs. The first peg contains a number of disks, each smaller than the one beneath it. The other two pegs are initially empty.

Play: On a turn, you can move the topmost disk from one peg to any other peg, with the restriction that a disk can never be on top of a smaller disk.

Figure 9–1: The Towers of Hanoi puzzle.

As an example, the sequence of moves necessary to solve the three-disk version of the puzzle is shown in Figure 9–2.

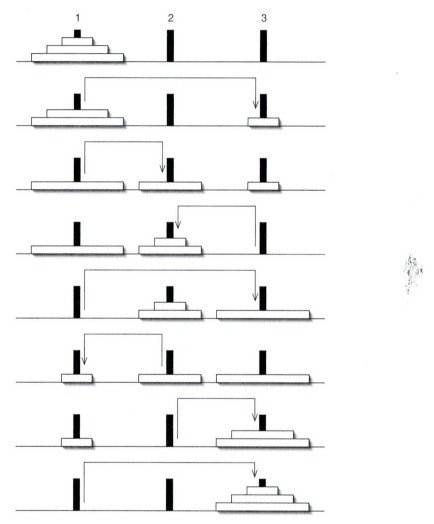

Figure 9-2: There are seven moves in the solution to the three-disk Towers of Hanoi puzzle.

We want to write a program to solve the puzzle. Specifically, it should print out the sequence of moves needed to get all of the disks onto the destination peg. To move three disks from peg 1 to peg 3 (using peg 2 as a spare), our program should print:

```
1 => 3
1 => 2
3 => 2
1 => 3
2 => 1
2 => 3
1 => 3
```

Solving the one-disk puzzle is trivial: just move the disk directly from the source peg to the destination peg. We write a simple method (Figure 9–3), which we invoke as hanoi1(1, 3).

```
1 /** Move a single disk from source to dest. */
2 public static void hanoi1(int source, int dest) {
3   System.out.println(source + " => " + dest);
4 }
```

Figure 9–3: A method to solve the one-disk Towers of Hanoi puzzle.

To solve the puzzle for two disks, we have to move the small disk to the spare peg to get it out of the way. We can then move the large disk to the destination, and then finally move the small disk back on top of it (Figure 9–4). We need to specify the spare disk as a third argument, so this method is invoked as hanoi2(1, 3, 2).

```
1 /** Move two disks from source to dest, using a spare peg. */
2 public static void hanoi2(int source, int dest, int spare) {
3   System.out.println(source + " => " + spare);
4   System.out.println(source + " => " + dest);
5   System.out.println(spare + " => " + dest);
6 }
```

Figure 9–4: The method for the two-disk puzzle requires an extra argument to identify the spare peg.

The method for the three-disk puzzle (Figure 9–5) is somewhat longer.

The spacing in Figure 9–5 is there to suggest a key insight. The solution can be broken down into three parts. In lines 4–6, we move two disks from the source to the spare. In line 8, we move the largest disk from the source to the destination. In lines 10–12, we move two disks from the spare to the destination.

```
1 /** Move three disks from source to dest, using a spare peg. */
2 public static void hanoi3(int source, int dest, int spare) {
3
4     System.out.println(source + " => " + dest);
5     System.out.println(source + " => " + spare);
6     System.out.println(dest + " => " + spare);
7
8     System.out.println(source + " => " + dest);
9
10    System.out.println(spare + " => " + source);
11    System.out.println(spare + " => " + dest);
12    System.out.println(source + " => " + dest);
13
14 }
```

Figure 9–5: The method hanoi3() is longer, but a pattern begins to emerge.

In lines 4–6, we are moving the two smallest disks. The location of the larger disk is irrelevant to this task. It is as if we were simply moving the two disks by themselves, and *we already know how to do this*. We can do this by invoking hanoi2(). The same is true of lines 10–12. We can therefore write a shorter version of hanoi3() (Figure 9–6).

```
1 /** Move three disks from source to dest, using a spare peg. */
2 public static void hanoi3(int source, int dest, int spare) {
3     hanoi2(source, spare, dest);
4     System.out.println(source + " => " + dest);
5     hanoi2(spare, dest, source);
6 }
```

Figure 9–6: An improved version of hanoi3() invokes hanoi2(). Line 3 moves two disks from **source** to **spare**. Line 5 moves two disks from **spare** to **dest**.

Similarly, we can rewrite hanoi2() using hanoi1() (Figure 9–7).

```
1 /** Move two disks from source to dest, using a spare peg. */
2 public static void hanoi2(int source, int dest, int spare) {
3     hanoi1(source, spare);
4     System.out.println(source + " => " + dest);
5     hanoi1(spare, dest);
6 }
```

Figure 9–7: The method hanoi2() can be rewritten using hanoi1().

We now have a pattern that will allow us to write a method to solve the puzzle for any number of disks, provided that we've written all of the previous methods. For example, once we've written hanoi1() through hanoi16(), we can write hanoi17() (Figure 9–8).

```
 1 /** Move 17 disks from source to dest, making use of a spare peg. */
 2 public static void hanoi17(int source, int dest, int spare) {
 3   hanoi16(source, spare, dest);
 4   System.out.println(source + " => " + dest);
 5   hanoi16(spare, dest, source);
 6 }
```

Figure 9-8: The pattern can be extended to any number of disks.

This is fine, but we still have to do the tedious work of writing all these methods. It would be much better if we could write *a single method* which would work for *any number of disks*. This method has to accept the number of disks as an argument. A first attempt is shown in Figure 9–9. A method which invokes itself like this is called *recursive*.

```
 1 /**
 2  * Move the specified number of disks from source to dest, making
 3  * use of a spare peg.
 4  */
 5 public static void hanoi(int disks, int source, int dest,
 6                          int spare) {
 7   hanoi(disks - 1, source, spare, dest);
 8   System.out.println(source + " => " + dest);
 9   hanoi(disks - 1, spare, dest, source);
10 }
```

Figure 9-9: First attempt at a method to solve the puzzle for any number of disks.

Unfortunately, this method is slightly broken. If we ask for

hanoi(1, 1, 3, 2);

the program crashes, giving an error message like:

java.lang.StackOverflowError

We'll explain this message in more detail in Section 9.5. For now, let's step through the execution and see if we can figure out what happened.

The method begins by invoking

hanoi(0, 1, 2, 3);

which invokes

hanoi(-1, 1, 3, 2);

which invokes

hanoi(-2, 1, 2, 3);

and so on, until the computer runs out of memory. To prevent this, we have to provide a *base case*—that is, some situation where the problem is so simple that the method does not have to recursively invoke itself. For the Towers of Hanoi puzzle, the base case is the situation where there is only one disk. Once we check for the base case (Figure 9–10), our method works correctly.

```
 1 /**
 2  * Move the specified number of disks from source to dest, making
 3  * use of a spare peg.
 4  */
 5 public static void hanoi(int disks, int source, int dest,
 6                         int spare) {
 7   if (disks == 1) {
 8     System.out.println(source + " => " + dest);
 9   } else {
10     hanoi(disks - 1, source, spare, dest);
11     System.out.println(source + " => " + dest);
12     hanoi(disks - 1, spare, dest, source);
13   }
14 }
```

Figure 9–10: A correct recursive program must check for the base case.

In general, to solve a problem recursively, we must deal with two cases:

1.   The base case, where we can solve the problem directly, and

2.   The recursive case, where we solve the problem in terms of easier subproblems.

When we say that subproblems must be "easier," we mean that they must be closer to the base case. In the Towers of Hanoi, we solve the problem of moving n disks in terms of the easier problem of moving $n - 1$ disks.

For a second example of recursion, consider the task of printing a LinkedList backward. An *iterative* approach (that is, one using loops instead of recursion) would be to find the last item, then the second-to-last item, and so on (Figure 9–11).

```
1 /** Return a String representing this list in reverse order. */
2 public String toStringReversed() {
3   String result = "( ";
4   for (int i = size() - 1; i >= 0; i--) {
5     result += get(i) + " ";
6   }
7   return result + ")";
8 }
```

Figure 9–11: An iterative `toStringReversed()` method for our LinkedList class.

This method works, but it is not very efficient. Each invocation of `get()` requires us to walk down the list from the beginning to find the item at position i, which takes time linear in i. The total time for this version of `toStringReversed()` is:

$$1 + 2 + 3 + \dots + n = \sum_{i=1}^{n} i \in \Theta(n^2)$$

(We are pretending here that String concatenation takes constant time, which is not exactly true. More on this in Chapter 13.)

A better recursive solution is to divide the problem into two cases:

1. If there are no nodes, return the empty String.

2. Otherwise, generate a String for the *rest* of the list (the part after the first item). Add the first item to the end of this String and return it.

We would like to add parentheses at the beginning and end of the list. We could deal with the left parenthesis in the base case, but there's no good time to add the right parenthesis. To avoid this complication, we move the recursive part of the problem into a separate ***helper method*** (Figure 9–12).

```
 1 /** Return a String representing this list in reverse order. */
 2 public String toStringReversed() {
 3   return "( " + toStringReversedHelper(front) + ")";
 4 }
 5
 6 /**
 7  * Return a String representing the portion of a LinkedList starting
 8  * at node, in reverse order.
 9  */
10 protected String toStringReversedHelper(ListNode node) {
11   if (node == null) {
12     return "";
13   } else {
14     return toStringReversedHelper(node.getNext()) + node.getItem()
15            + " ";
16   }
17 }
```

Figure 9-12: An alternate version of `toStringReversed()` invokes a recursive helper method.

Notice that `toStringReversedHelper()` does not deal with the entire list, but merely the chain of nodes starting at `node`.

To show that a recursive algorithm works correctly, we must demonstrate that:

1.   The base case works correctly, and

2.   If the recursive method works for a problem of size $n - 1$, then it works for a problem of size n.

In this case, `toStringReversedHelper()` certainly works correctly for the base case, where `node` is `null`. It returns the empty String, so `toStringReversed()` returns `"( )"`.

Now suppose `node` is *not* `null`, but instead is a reference to the first of a chain of n nodes (Figure 9–13).

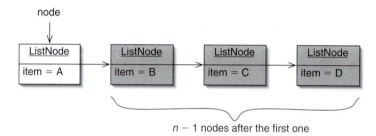

Figure 9-13: A chain of n nodes consists of a first node followed by $n - 1$ more nodes.

If we assume that the recursive invocation

`toStringReversedHelper(node.getNext())`

correctly returns the String `"D C B "`, then clearly the expression

`toStringReversedHelper(node.getNext()) + node.getItem() + " "`

evaluates to `"D C B A "`, which is what we want. In general, if the method works for a chain of $n - 1$ nodes, it works for a chain of n nodes.

Since we know that the method works properly for an empty chain (`null`), we can now conclude that it works for a chain of one node. From this, we can conclude that it works for a chain of two nodes. Indeed, we can conclude that it works for *any number* of nodes.

Let's write `toStringReversed()` for our ArrayList class as a third and final example of recursion. It would be easy—and indeed, more natural—to do this one using a `for` loop, but it can also be done using recursion. In fact, *any* recursive procedure can be written iteratively, and vice versa.

Again we need a helper method, and the design of the algorithm is similar:

1.   If there are no elements being considered, return the empty String.

2.   Otherwise, generate a String for *all of the elements after the current one*. Add the current element to the end of this String and return it.

The code is shown in Figure 9–14, emphasizing the parts which are different from the LinkedList versions.

```
1 /** Return a String representing this List in reverse order. */
2 public String toStringReversed() {
3   return "( " + toStringReversedHelper(0) + ")";
4 }
5
6 /**
7  * Return a String representing the portion of this List starting
8  * at position i, in reverse order.
9  */
10 protected String toStringReversedHelper(int i) {
11   if (i == size) {
12     return "";
13   } else {
14     return toStringReversedHelper(i + 1) + data[i] + " ";
15   }
16 }
```

Figure 9–14: The method `toStringReversed()` and the recursive method `toStringReversedHelper()` for our ArrayList class.

Exercises

9.1   Write a recursive method to compute *n*! (*n* factorial).

9.2   Write a recursive method to compute the sum of the first *n* positive integers.

9.3   Write a recursive method to determine whether a String is a palindrome—that is, reads the same forward and backward. The Strings `"amanaplanacanalpanama"` and `"deified"` are palindromes, as is any String of length 0 or 1. (Hint: For the recursive case, examine the region of the String which does not include the first or last characters. You will find the `substring()` method of the String class helpful.)

9.4   Write a recursive version of `binarySearch()` (Figure 8–3). You will need *two* base cases: one for when the target is found and another for when there are no data left to examine.

9.2 Analyzing Recursive Algorithms

Recursive algorithms can be difficult to analyze, because it is not clear how many times they will be invoked. Some new techniques are needed.

Let's start with the LinkedList version of `toStringReversedHelper()` (Figure 9–12). The corresponding method `toStringReversed()` will have a running time in the same order, because it only does a constant amount of additional work.

Our standard method of dealing with the if statement doesn't work. If we take the "best-case" branch, we conclude that the algorithm takes constant time. If we take the "worst-case" branch, we conclude that the algorithm never stops! The problem is that our selection of branch depends on n. We always take the first branch for $n = 0$ and the second for larger values of n. To analyze a recursive algorithm, we must think recursively, in terms of a base case and a recursive case.

The method takes a constant amount of time in the base case—let's call it one step. In the recursive case, it takes one step plus the time for the recursive invocation. We formalize this in an equation called a ***recurrence***. Let $T(n)$ be the time taken to process a chain of n nodes. Then we can write the following recurrence:

$$T(n) = \begin{cases} 1 & \text{if } n = 0 \\ 1 + T(n-1) & \text{otherwise} \end{cases}$$

Solving a recurrence means transforming it into an equation with $T(n)$ on the left and no mention of T on the right. In general, solving recurrences can be extremely difficult. However, if we are able to guess the right answer, it is easy to use the recurrence to verify our answer.

In this case, it seems reasonable that `toStringReversedHelper()` takes time in $\Theta(n)$. Let's guess that $T(n) = n$. Substituting this into the bottom half of the recurrence, we find:

$$\begin{aligned} T(n) &= 1 + T(n-1) \\ &= 1 + n - 1 \\ &= n \end{aligned}$$

So far, so good. Unfortunately, our guess implies that $T(0) = 0$, while the recurrence says that $T(0) = 1$. We got close, but our guess does not work for the base case. It must work *exactly* to constitute a solution.

Let's try guessing $T(n) = n + 1$. For the base case:

$$T(0) = 1 = 0 + 1$$

That works. How about the recursive case?

$$\begin{aligned} T(n) &= 1 + T(n-1) \\ &= 1 + (n-1) + 1 \\ &= n + 1 \end{aligned}$$

Success! We conclude that `toStringReversed()` runs in linear time. The ArrayList version has the same recurrence, so it also runs in linear time.

Here is the recurrence for hanoi():

$$T(n) = \begin{cases} 1 & \text{if } n = 1 \\ 1 + 2T(n-1) & \text{otherwise} \end{cases}$$

This is more difficult to solve, because there are *two* recursive calls. We therefore begin by repeatedly expanding the recursive case:

$$\begin{aligned} T(n) &= 1 + 2T(n-1) \\ &= 1 + 2(1 + 2T(n-2)) \\ &= 1 + 2(1 + 2(1 + 2T(n-3))) \end{aligned}$$

We can draw this expansion out as a **recursion tree** (Figure 9–15). We start by writing down $T(n)$. We replace this with the time taken in addition to the recursive calls (for this recurrence, 1), and add two copies of $T(n-1)$. We then replace each of these with a 1 and two copies of $T(n-2)$, and so on.

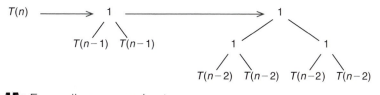

Figure 9–15: Expanding a recursion tree.

This expansion continues until we have many copies of $T(1)$, which can be replaced with 1. The total running time, then, is the number of 1s in the tree. We can't actually expand the tree all the way without specifying a particular value of n. Instead, we take the sum of the totals on each level of the tree (Figure 9–16). There is 1 step at the top level, 2 at the next level, 4 at the next level, and so on. If we count the top level as level 0, there are $2i$ steps on level i. There are n levels, corresponding to $T(n)$ down through $T(1)$. The bottommost level is therefore level $n-1$, consisting of 2^{n-1} steps.

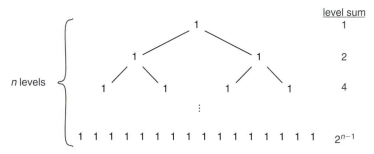

Figure 9–16: To find the sum of a recursion tree, determine how many steps there are at each level.

The total number of steps in the entire tree is:

$$1 + 2 + 4 + \ldots + 2^{n-1} = \sum_{i=0}^{n-1} 2^i$$
$$= 2^n - 1$$

Let's verify $2^n - 1$ as a solution to the recurrence.

For the base case, $2^1 - 1 = 1$, which is correct.

For the recursive case:

$$
\begin{aligned}
T(n) &= 1 + 2T(n-1) \\
&= 1 + 2(1(2^{n-1} - 1)) \\
&= 1 + 2^n - 2 \\
&= 2^n - 1
\end{aligned}
$$

Solved! We conclude that `hanoi()` takes time in $\Theta(2n)$.

The recursion tree method can be used to analyze algorithms with only one recursive call. For example, consider the recurrence:

$$
T(n) = \begin{cases} 1 & \text{if } n = 0 \\ 1 + T(n-2) & \text{otherwise} \end{cases}
$$

The recursion tree is shown in Figure 9–17. Assuming n is even (Exercise 8.5), we get the solution:

$$T(n) = n/2 + 1.$$

Figure 9–17: When there is only one recursive call, the recursion tree has only one branch.

Exercises

9.5   Solve the recurrence below, assuming n is odd.

$$
T(n) = \begin{cases} 1 & \text{if } n = 1 \\ 1 + T(n-2) & \text{otherwise} \end{cases}
$$

9.6   Solve the recurrence below, assuming n is a power of 2.

$$T(n) = \begin{cases} 1 & \text{if } n = 1 \\ 1 + T(n/2) & \text{otherwise} \end{cases}$$

9.7   Solve the recurrence below.

$$T(n) = \begin{cases} 1 & \text{if } n = 1 \\ n + T(n-1) & \text{otherwise} \end{cases}$$

9.8   According to the ancient legend of the Towers of Hanoi, there is a temple where priests
       are laboring to solve the puzzle with 64 golden disks. When they complete their task,
       the world will end. Assuming the priests make one move per second, how much time
       will this take?

9.3 Merge Sort

We can use recursion to design sorting algorithms that are more efficient than insertion sort. This
section describes one such algorithm, *merge sort*.

The recursive idea behind merge sort is:

1.   If there is only one number to sort, do nothing.

2.   Otherwise, divide the numbers into two groups. Recursively sort each group, then
       merge the two sorted groups into a single sorted array.

This process is illustrated in Figure 9–18.

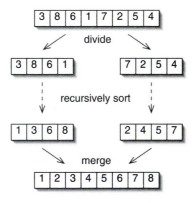

Figure 9–18: In merge sort, the data to be sorted (top) are divided into two groups.
Each group is recursively sorted. The results are then merged into the final result.

Merge sort is an example of a ***divide-and-conquer*** algorithm. In such an algorithm, we divide the data into smaller pieces, recursively conquer each piece, and then combine the results into a final result.

A sorting algorithm that modifies an existing array, such as insertion sort, is called an ***in-place*** sort. Merge sort is *not* an in-place sort. Instead, it returns a new array containing the numbers from the original array in sorted order. In the code for the main `mergeSort()` method (Figure 9–19), notice that the return type is `int[]`.

```
1 /**
2  * Return an array containing the numbers from data, in order from
3  * smallest to largest.
4  */
5 public static int[] mergeSort(int[] data) {
6    return mergeSortHelper(data, 0, data.length - 1);
7 }
```

Figure 9–19: The `mergeSort()` method returns a new array, rather than modifying data.

Suppose we have a variable `numbers` that currently refers to some array of ints. If we want it to refer to a sorted version of that array, we have to invoke this method as:

```
numbers = mergeSort(numbers);
```

If we merely

```
mergeSort(numbers);
```

then `numbers` will not change; the sorted array is returned, but it hasn't been saved anywhere.

The method `mergeSort()` uses a recursive helper method (Figure 9–20). The arguments `bottom` and `top` indicate the region of the array to be sorted.

```
1 /**
2  * Return an array containing the numbers in data between indices
3  * bottom and top, inclusive, in order from smallest to largest.
4  */
5 protected static int[] mergeSortHelper(int[] data, int bottom,
6                                        int top) {
7    if (bottom == top) {
8       return new int[] { data[bottom] };
9    } else {
```

Figure 9–20: The recursive helper method `mergeSortHelper()`. (Part 1 of 2)

```
10        int midpoint = (top + bottom) / 2;
11        return merge(mergeSortHelper(data, bottom, midpoint),
12                     mergeSortHelper(data, midpoint + 1, top));
13   }
14 }
```

Figure 9-20: The recursive helper method `mergeSortHelper()`. (Part 2 of 2)

This code captures the algorithm with remarkable simplicity. The base case returns an array containing a single number. The recursive case merges the results of two recursive calls, each dealing with half of the region currently being sorted.

One more helper method, `merge()`, is needed. The job of this method is to combine two sorted arrays into one longer, sorted array (Figure 9–21).

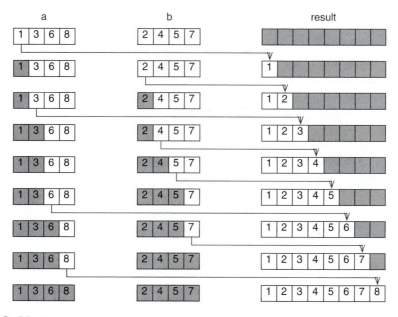

Figure 9-21: The merging process combines two short sorted arrays into a longer one. At each step, the smallest element of either array is added to the end of the output array.

The `merge()` method (Figure 9–22) is not recursive, but is longer than either `mergeSort()` or `mergeSortHelper()`. It is not as complicated as it appears. The main loop on lines 8–16 fills up the array `result` by repeatedly taking the smallest element from the beginning of `a` or `b`. The indices `i` and `j` are indices into these arrays, telling where the next available element is. (This is the same trick we used with ArrayLists, but with the "not in use" portion at the left end of the array.) The complicated test on line 9 deals with the cases in which we've reached the end of one of the arrays. If array `b` is empty, we have to take the next element from `a`, and vice versa.

```
 1 /**
 2  * Combine the two sorted arrays a and b into one sorted array.
 3  */
 4 protected static int[] merge(int[] a, int[] b) {
 5    int[] result = new int[a.length + b.length];
 6    int i = 0;
 7    int j = 0;
 8    for (int k = 0; k < result.length; k++) {
 9      if ((j == b.length) || ((i < a.length) && (a[i] <= b[j]))) {
10        result[k] = a[i];
11        i++;
12      } else {
13        result[k] = b[j];
14        j++;
15      }
16    }
17    return result;
18 }
```

Figure 9-22: Once two arrays are sorted, this method merges them together.

Analysis of Merge Sort

Merge sort is more complicated than insertion sort. Is it worth the effort?

An invocation of merge() takes time linear in the total length of the resulting array. (The main loop always runs exactly n times.) The recurrence for mergeSortHelper(), assuming n is a power of 2, is:

$$T(n) = \begin{cases} 1 & \text{if } n = 1 \\ n + 2T(n/2) & \text{otherwise} \end{cases}$$

The solution is not obvious, so we expand a recurrence tree (Figure 9-23). It is clear that each level of the tree adds up to n. We need $1 + \log_2 n$ levels before we can convert the n copies of $T(1)$ at the bottom into ones.

This gives a total running time of:

$$n(1 + \log_2 n) \in \Theta(n \log n)$$

This is a strictly lower order than the quadratic running time of insertion sort, so merge sort is faster for sorting large arrays.

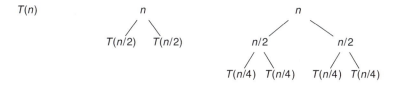

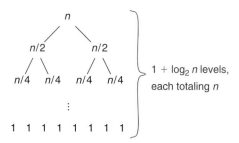

1 + log₂ n levels, each totaling n

Figure 9–23: As the recursion tree for merge sort is expanded, each level adds up to n steps. The total number of levels is $1 + \log_2 n$, so the entire tree adds up to $n(1 + \log_2 n)$.

Exercises

9.9 Explain the three arguments passed to `mergeSortHelper()` in line 6 of Figure 9–19.

9.10 Write a `mergeSort()` method for the SortableArrayList class from Section 8.4. Your method should invoke some kind of `mergeSortHelper()` to get a new, sorted list, but it should not simply return this result. Instead, it should copy the elements in this new list back into the original SortableArrayList. How does this affect the running time of `mergeSort()`?

9.11 Is the analysis of merge sort for the best, worst, or average case? Explain.

9.12 Write a recurrence for the total size of all the arrays created during an invocation of `mergeSortHelper()`. What is the solution to this recurrence?

9.4 Quicksort

Quicksort (by convention, the name is all one word, capitalized) is another divide-and-conquer sorting algorithm. In merge sort, the dividing was trivial. We simply took the left and right halves of the region being sorted. All of the hard work was done in recombining the sorted pieces by merging. In Quicksort, the hard work is in the dividing and the recombining is trivial.

Here's the plan:

1.   If there are one or fewer numbers to sort, do nothing.

2.   Otherwise, partition the region into "small" and "large" numbers, moving the small numbers to the left end and the large numbers to the right. Recursively sort each section. The entire array is now sorted.

The process is illustrated in Figure 9–24.

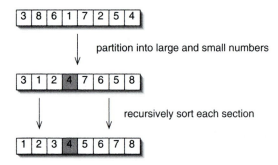

Figure 9-24: Quicksort works by dividing the array into "small" and "large" numbers—in this case, numbers less than or equal to 4 and numbers greater than 4. Each section is then recursively sorted.

As in merge sort, the primary methods are very short and elegant (Figure 9–25).

```
 1 /** Arrange the numbers in data from smallest to largest. */
 2 public static void quicksort(int[] data) {
 3   quicksortHelper(data, 0, data.length - 1);
 4 }
 5
 6 /**
 7  * Arrange the numbers in data between indices bottom and top,
 8  * inclusive, from smallest to largest.
 9  */
10 protected static void quicksortHelper(int[] data, int bottom,
11                                       int top) {
12   if (bottom < top) {
13     int midpoint = partition(data, bottom, top);
14     quicksortHelper(data, bottom, midpoint - 1);
15     quicksortHelper(data, midpoint + 1, top);
16   }
17 }
```

Figure 9-25: The methods `quicksort()` and `quicksortHelper()`.

All of the hard work is done in the helper method `partition()`. The partitioning algorithm begins by choosing some array element as the **pivot**. We arbitrarily choose the last number in the region being partitioned as the pivot (Figure 9–26). Numbers less than or equal to the pivot are considered small, while numbers greater than the pivot are considered large. As it runs, the algorithm maintains four regions: those numbers known to be small, those known to be large, those which haven't been examined yet, and the pivot itself.

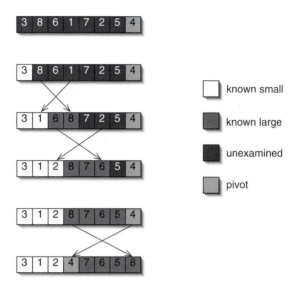

known small

known large

unexamined

pivot

Figure 9–26: The partitioning algorithm chooses one number as the pivot. Four regions are maintained: small numbers, large numbers, unexamined numbers, and the region containing the pivot. The algorithm's last action is to swap the pivot into place between the small and large numbers.

Working from left to right, each unexamined number is compared to the pivot. If it is large, the region of large numbers is simply extended. Otherwise, the newly discovered small number is swapped with the first known large number (if there are any) to keep all of the small numbers together. This continues until there are no unexamined numbers left. Finally, the pivot is swapped with the first large number (if any), so that it is between the small and large numbers.

The `partition()` method and its helper `swap()` are shown in Figure 9–27.

The number of variables in `partition()` make it appear complicated, but they are only there to maintain the four regions. Specifically:

- `data[bottom]` through `data[firstAfterSmall - 1]` are known to be small.

- `data[firstAfterSmall]` through `data[i - 1]` are known to be large.

- `data[i]` through `data[top - 1]` have not yet been examined.

- The pivot is at `data[top]`.

```
1  /**
2   * Choose one element of data in the region between bottom and top,
3   * inclusive, as the pivot. Arrange the numbers so that those less
4   * than or equal to the pivot are to the left of it and those
5   * greater than the pivot are to the right of it. Return the final
6   * position of the pivot.
7   */
8  protected static int partition(int[] data, int bottom, int top) {
9    int pivot = data[top];
10   int firstAfterSmall = bottom;
11   for (int i = bottom; i < top; i++) {
12     if (data[i] <= pivot) {
13       swap(data, firstAfterSmall, i);
14       firstAfterSmall++;
15     }
16   }
17   swap(data, firstAfterSmall, top);
18   return firstAfterSmall;
19 }
20
21 /** Swap the elements of data at indices i and j. */
22 protected static void swap(int[] data, int i, int j) {
23   int temp = data[i];
24   data[i] = data[j];
25   data[j] = temp;
26 }
```

Figure 9-27: The methods `partition()` and `swap()`.

The index `firstAfterSmall` is the index of the first element that is not known to be small. When we swap element `firstAfterSmall` with element i on line 13, we are usually swapping element i with the first known large number. If there are no known large numbers yet, `firstAfterSmall` equals i, so we simply swap the element with itself; as desired, this has no effect.

Similarly, on line 17, `firstAfterSmall` is the index of either the first large number or (if there are no large numbers) the pivot. In either case, swapping the pivot into this position is correct.

Analysis of Quicksort

An invocation of `partition()` takes time linear in the length of the array being sorted, because there are n passes through the loop. What about `quicksortHelper()`? Partitioning a region of size n as evenly as possible, we might end up with $\lceil n/2 \rceil$ small numbers and $\lfloor n/2 \rfloor$ large numbers. We ignore the floor and ceiling by assuming that n is an exact power of 2. Since one of the small numbers (the pivot) is not considered in either of the recursive invocations, this gives the recurrence:

$$T(n) = \begin{cases} 1 & \text{if } n = 1 \\ n + T(n/2) + T((n/2) - 1) & \text{otherwise} \end{cases}$$

Since this is strictly less than the recurrence for merge sort, it is tempting to conclude that quicksort takes time in O(n log n). While this is true in the best case, partition() *might not divide the region evenly in half*. In the worst case, there might be *no* large numbers. For example, if the array is already sorted, the number we choose as the pivot is the largest element. There are then $n - 1$ numbers to the left of the pivot and none to the right. In this case, the recurrence is:

$$T(n) = \begin{cases} 1 & \text{if } n = 1 \\ n + T(n - 1) & \text{otherwise} \end{cases}$$

The solution to this recurrence is:

$$\sum_{i=1}^{n} i = \frac{n(n + 1)}{2} \in \Theta(n^2)$$

Quicksort takes quadratic time in the worst case.

While the analysis is beyond the scope of this book, it turns out that Quicksort takes time in $\Theta(n$ log $n)$ in the average case. Quicksort is therefore better than insertion sort, but not as good as merge sort.

Since it has a low constant factor associated with its running time, and operates in place, Quicksort is sometimes used instead of merge sort when n is not expected to be very large. There are also a number of minor changes (see the Exercises) which can be made to the algorithm to greatly decrease the likelihood of the worst-case running time.

The class java.util.Arrays has several overloaded versions of the static method sort(). The ones for arrays of primitive types use an optimized version of Quicksort that makes the worst-case behavior unlikely. The version for arrays of objects uses merge sort. The difference has to do with the fact that two objects that are equals() may not be identical. For example, two Cards with the same rank but different suits are equals(). If a sort keeps such elements in the same order as in the original array, the sort is said to be *stable*. Merge sort is stable, but Quicksort is not. Since equal primitives must be absolutely identical, stability is not an issue when sorting primitives.

Exercises

9.13   What is the order of the running time of Quicksort if data is originally in *reverse* sorted order? What if all the elements are identical?

9.14   Add a quicksort() method to the SortableArrayList class from Section 8.4.

9.15   Modify `quicksortHelper()` so that, before invoking `partition()`, it swaps a random element in the region being sorted with the last element. With this change, no particular input can consistently produce the worst-case behavior.

9.16   Suppose the variable `numbers`, of type List<Integer>, contains many numbers in no particular order. How can it be sorted in one line of code? (Hint: See the java.util.Collections class in the API.)

9.5 Avoiding Recursion

Any iterative program can be written recursively, and vice versa. Some algorithms, such as merge sort and Quicksort, are naturally recursive—it would be very awkward to specify them iteratively. Others, such as the methods for printing a List in reverse order, can reasonably be done either iteratively or recursively.

All other things being equal, it is better to avoid recursion. The reason has to do with the call stack, which was explained in Chapter 4. Every time we invoke a method, we have to push a frame onto the call stack. This uses both time and memory, so we would prefer to avoid it. This section shows how to convert a recursive method into an iterative one. It should be emphasized that these are optimizations which may improve efficiency at the expense of program clarity; this tradeoff is not always worthwhile.

The relationship between recursion and the call stack also explains the error message we get if we fail to include a base case in a recursive method:

`java.lang.StackOverflowError`

This happens because we keep pushing new frames onto the call stack until we run out of memory—in other words, the stack overflows. In contrast, an iterative program which fails to include a proper stopping condition will simply run forever (Figure 9–28).

```
1 public static void iterateForever() {
2   while (true) {
3   }
4 }
5
6 public static void recurForever() {
7   recurForever();
8 }
```

Figure 9-28: The method `iterateForever()` never stops, but `recurForever()` eventually causes a stack overflow.

Tail Recursion

The conversion from recursion to iteration is easy for algorithms which are ***tail recursive***. A tail-recursive algorithm is one in which the recursive invocation is the *very last thing* we do. For example, consider the recursive version of get() for our LinkedList class shown in Figure 9–29.

```
1 public Object get(int index) {
2   return getHelper(index, front);
3 }
4
5 /**
6  * Return the item stored in the indexth Node of the chain
7  * starting at node.
8  */
9 public E getHelper(int index, ListNode <E> node) {
10   if (index == 0) {
11     return node.getItem();
12   } else {
13     return getHelper(index - 1, node.getNext());
14   }
15 }
```

Figure 9-29: The method getHelper() is tail recursive.

The recursive invocation on line 13 is the last thing we do in getHelper(). It would therefore be somewhat wasteful to maintain a call frame for the current invocation, which has no work left to do. Some languages, such as Scheme, automatically take advantage of this fact when presented with a tail-recursive program. Java does not, so we'll have to handle it ourselves.

To convert this into an iterative algorithm, we don't recur with new arguments. Instead, we simply change the values of the existing arguments and go back to the beginning (Figure 9–30).

```
1 /**
2  * Return the item stored in the indexth Node of the chain
3  * starting at node.
4  */
5 public E getHelper(int index, ListNode <E> node) {
6   while (true) {
7     if (index == 0) {
8       return node.getItem();
9     } else {
10       index--;
11       node = node.getNext();
12     }
13   }
14 }
```

Figure 9-30: Instead of recurring, this iterative version of getHelper() changes the values of the arguments index and **node** and returns to the beginning of the method.

This behaves exactly like the recursive version, but it does not cause the call stack to grow. Of course, we could clean it up further, getting rid of the helper method and using the loop test to check whether index is zero (Figure 9–31).

```
1 public E get(int index) {
2   ListNode <E> node = front;
3   while (index > 0) {
4     index--;
5     node = node.getNext();
6   }
7   return node.getItem();
8 }
```

Figure 9–31: A cleaner iterative version of get() doesn't need the helper method.

When first learning about recursion, many students develop the misconception that a recursive invocation simply means, "Change the arguments and go back to the beginning of the method." This is true for tail-recursive algorithms, but most interesting recursive algorithms are not tail recursive.

If a recursive algorithm is not tail recursive, the only way to convert it into iterative form may be to manage our own version of the call stack. This is complicated and, since it does not eliminate stack manipulation, rarely worth the effort. As we shall see momentarily, however, certain non-tail-recursive algorithms can be made far more efficient by converting them into iterative form.

Dynamic Programming

In the thirteenth century, Leonardo Fibonacci was challenged to solve the following problem:

Begin with a pair of newborn rabbits, one male and one female. Beginning in its second month of life, each pair produces another pair every month. Assuming the rabbits never die, how many pairs will there be after n months?

The answer involves recursive thinking. In months 0 and 1, there is only one pair of rabbits. This is the base case. After that, the number of pairs each month is the sum of the number of pairs present last month (who are still alive) and the number of pairs present two months ago (who are now old enough to produce another pair). We can express this as a recurrence:

$$F(n) = \begin{cases} 1 & \text{if } n < 2 \\ F(n-1) + F(n-2) & \text{otherwise} \end{cases}$$

The beginning of the Fibonacci sequence is shown in Figure 9–32. This sequence appears in many contexts throughout science and mathematics.

n	0	1	2	3	4	5	6	7	8	9	10
$F(n)$	1	1	2	3	5	8	13	21	34	55	89

Figure 9–32: Beginning of the Fibonacci sequence.

A method for computing $F(n)$ falls naturally out of the recurrence (Figure 9–33).

```
1 /** Return the nth Fibonacci number. */
2 public static int fibo(int n) {
3   if (n < 2) {
4     return 1;
5   } else {
6     return fibo(n - 1) + fibo(n - 2);
7   }
8 }
```

Figure 9-33: Natural recursive algorithm for computing $F(n)$.

This method works, but it is woefully inefficient. Its running time is given by the recurrence:

$$T(n) = \begin{cases} 1 & \text{if } n < 2 \\ 1 + T(n-1) + T(n-2) & \text{otherwise} \end{cases}$$

Since $T(n) \geq F(n)$ in both the base case and the recursive case, we conclude that $T(n) \in \Omega(F(n))$. While the proof is beyond the scope of this book, it is known that $F(n)$ grows exponentially. Specifically, $F(n) \in \Theta(\phi^n)$, where ϕ (the lower-case Greek letter phi) is the golden ratio, roughly 1.618.

Our method is not tail recursive. After returning from the first recursive invocation, we have two more things to do: another recursive invocation and an addition. We cannot just change the value of n and go back to the beginning of the method. There is, however, another approach.

Notice that fibo() does a lot of redundant work. For example, in the course of computing fibo(5), we have to compute fibo(3) twice (Figure 9–34).

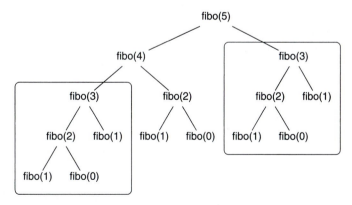

Figure 9-34: Invoking fibo(5) recursively invokes fibo(4) and fibo(3), and so on. This is redundant, because fibo(3) is computed twice.

To avoid this redundant work, we can maintain a table of previously computed values. As we compute $F(n)$ for each value of n, we can look up the value for any smaller n (Figure 9–35). This technique is called ***dynamic programming***.

```
 1 /** Return the nth Fibonacci number. */
 2 public static int fibo(int n) {
 3   int[] f = new int[n + 1];
 4   f[0] = 1;
 5   f[1] = 1;
 6   for (int i = 2; i <= n; i++) {
 7     f[i] = f[i - 1] + f[i - 2];
 8   }
 9   return f[n];
10 }
```

Figure 9–35: The dynamic programming version of `fibo()` stores previously-computed values in the array `f` to avoid redundancy.

This method takes time linear in n—a vast improvement!

Dynamic programming is applicable only to algorithms that do redundant work. Neither merge sort nor Quicksort falls into this category.

Exercises

9.17   Modify the `hanoi()` method (Figure 9–10) so that it returns a String rather than printing. Convert the resulting method into iterative form using dynamic programming.

9.18   The method `quicksortHelper()` (Figure 9–25) is not tail recursive, but the second recursive invocation *is* the last thing we do. Modify the algorithm to eliminate this recursion, leaving the other recursive invocation intact.

9.19   A StackOverflowError is similar to an Exception. Experiment to find out whether you can throw a StackOverflowError. Can you catch one?

Summary

A recursive algorithm is one which invokes itself. To solve a problem recursively, we define a simple base case and a recursive case. In the recursive case, we solve the problem in terms of subproblems which are closer to the base case.

Recursive algorithms are analyzed using recurrences. To solve a recurrence, we generally expand it into a recursion tree, then determine the number of steps at each level and the number of levels. We plug our solution back into the recurrence to verify that it is correct.

Two useful recursive algorithms are merge sort and Quicksort. Both of these are divide-and-conquer algorithms which divide the data into parts, recursively sort the parts, and then recombine the solutions.

In merge sort, the hard work is in the recombining. Merge sort takes time in $\Theta(n \log n)$. It requires the allocation of additional arrays, so it is not an in-place sort.

In Quicksort, the hard work is in the dividing, partitioning the array into small and large numbers. While Quicksort takes time in $\Theta(n \log n)$ on average, its worst-case running time is quadratic. The worst case occurs if the array was already sorted, but simple improvements can make the worst case unlikely. Because Quicksort is an in-place sort with a low constant factor in its running time, some programmers nonetheless prefer it to merge sort.

Recursion allows for the design of powerful, elegant algorithms, but it uses up time and space for the call stack. While it is not always possible, efficiency can sometimes be improved by eliminating recursion. A tail-recursive algorithm, in which the recursive invocation is the last step, can easily be converted into a loop. If the algorithm is only returning a value (as opposed to modifying an existing data structure), redundant computation can be avoided by storing the results of previous invocations in a table. This latter technique is called dynamic programming.

Vocabulary

base case. In a recursive algorithm, the simple case that does not require a recusive call.

divide and conquer. Of an algorithm, working by dividing the data into pieces, recursively solving the pieces, and recombining the solutions. Merge sort and Quicksort are both divide-and-conquer algorithms.

dynamic programming. Technique for improving the efficiency of recursive algorithms that do redundant work. Solutions to subproblems are stored so that they can be looked up rather than recomputed.

helper method. A method, usually protected, used in a recursive algorithm. Often the recursive helper method requires some extra arguments specifying the subproblem in question.

in place. Of a sort, moving elements around inside the original array rather than creating new data structures.

iterative. Of an algorithm, using loops instead of recursion.

merge sort. Sort that divides the data into two halves, recursively sorts each half, and then merges the two sorted halves.

pivot. In partitioning Quicksort, the element used to divide the data. Elements less than or equal to the pivot are considered small. Elements greater than the pivot are considered large.

Quicksort. Sort that partitions the data into small and large elements and then recursively sorts each half.

recurrence. Equation defining a function in terms of itself. Used to analyze the running time of a recursive algorithm.

recursion tree. Technique for solving recurrences by repeatedly replacing the function with the components of its recursive definition.

recursive. Of an algorithm, invoking itself on simpler subproblems.

solve. For a recurrence, reduce to a nonrecursive form.

stable. Of a sort, leaving `equals()` elements in the same order they were in originally.

tail recursive. Of a recursive algorithm, having the recursive call be the very last step before returning.

Problems

9.20 Illustrate the history of the call stack, as in Section 4.2, for the invocation:

```
hanoi(3, 1, 3, 2)
```

9.21 Modify `fibo()` (Figure 9–33) so that it prints out a message at the beginning and end of each invocation. These messages show the history of the call stack. For example, if `fibo(4)` is invoked, the text in Figure 9–36 should be printed. (Hint: For the indentation, pass a String of spaces as an argument. On a recursive invocation, pass a slightly longer String.)

```
 1 fibo(4)
 2   fibo(3)
 3     fibo(2)
 4       fibo(1)
 5       1
 6       fibo(0)
 7       1
 8     2
 9     fibo(1)
10     1
11   3
12   fibo(2)
13     fibo(1)
14     1
15     fibo(0)
16     1
17   2
18 5
```

Figure 9-36: Desired output for Problem 9.21, showing the history of the call stack.

9.22 Determine whether insertion sort (Section 8.3) is stable.

9.23 Merge sort can be modified to use less memory. Instead of allocating new arrays with every recursive invocation, a single new array is allocated when the sorting begins. The two halves of `data` are copied into regions of this new array. Since the numbers in `data` are no longer needed, `data` can serve as the "working space" when these halves are themselves subdivided. This continues, back and forth, until the base case is reached (Figure 9–37).

Implement this improved version of merge sort. Compare the space used by this algorithm with the result of Exercise 9.12.

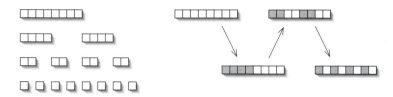

Figure 9–37: In the normal merge sort algorithm, each recursive invocation allocates new arrays (left). The version described in Problem 9.23 uses only two arrays, each one serving as working space for the other (right).

9.24 Write a `mergeSort()` method for the SortableLinkedList class from Section 8.5. As in Exercise 9.10, the original SortableLinkedList should be sorted when you are done. Your method must take time in $\Theta(n \log n)$. (Hint: Look at the constructor from GoFish (Figure 5–39) for an idea about dividing any list into two even halves. Make sure you deal with the case where the list being divided is of odd length.)

9.25 Write a `quicksort()` method for the SortableLinkedList class from Section 8.5. Your method must take time in $\Theta(n \log n)$ on average and in $\Theta(n^2)$ in the worst case. (Hint: Keep track of nodes rather than indices. When you need to swap two values, use `getItem()` and `setItem()` to change the *contents* of the nodes rather than moving the nodes. Think about how you might specify a region of a linked list.)

Projects

9.26 Simpler algorithms often have smaller constant factors associated with their running-time than more sophisticated algorithms. For sufficiently small arrays, for example, insertion sort may actually be faster than Quicksort. Modify the Quicksort algorithm so that, if the region to be sorted is below a certain length, insertion sort is used instead. Using the timing techniques from Chapter 7, find an appropriate length at which to make this change.

9.27   Modify the recursive `fibo()` method (Figure 9–33) to simulate the call stack manually. Begin by rearranging the method so that only one step or recursive invocation
occurs on each line. Define a class Frame which simulates a call frame. Finally, modify
the `fibo()` method so that it begins by pushing a single Frame onto a fresh stack. The
method then repeatedly pops the stack and handles the resulting Frame. This may result
in pushing other Frames onto the stack. This loop continues until the stack is empty—
that is, until there is no more work to do.

This project should leave you with a page or two of code—and a greater appreciation of
recursion!

IV

Trees and Sets

10

Trees

All of the data structures we have seen so far, such as arrays and linked lists, are linear. In a linear structure, there is a first item and a last item. Every item (except the last) has a successor and every item (except the first) has a predecessor.

This chapter introduces trees, which are more general structures for representing branching or hierarchical data. For example, biological classification diagrams, many organizational charts in businesses, and sports playoff brackets are trees. We have seen a few trees already in this book, including class inheritance diagrams like Figure 3–10 and recursion trees like Figure 9–16.

We begin with a discussion of the simplest kind of trees, binary trees. Using the game of Questions as a running example, Section 10.1 introduces tree terminology and discusses the implementation of binary trees. The issue of traversing trees is addressed in Section 10.2. More general trees are covered in Section 10.3, where we use trees to design an intelligent Tic Tac Toe player.

10.1 Binary Trees

There is a considerable amount of terminology regarding trees. We will introduce it in the context of the game of Questions (Figure 10–1).

255

Questions

Players: 2, the knower and the guesser.

Object: The knower thinks of something and the guesser attempts to determine what it is.

Play: The knower thinks of a person, place, or thing. The guesser asks yes-or-no questions of the knower, who must answer truthfully. Play continues until the guesser wins or gives up.

The variation in which the number of questions is limited (usually to 20) is left as a problem.

Figure 10-1: The game of Questions. In our implementation, the computer is the guesser.

In our implementation, several games are played. The program loses at first, but increases its knowledge after each game. A transcript is given in Figure 10–2.

```
 1 Welcome to Questions.
 2
 3 Is it ... a giraffe? no
 4 I give up.
 5 What is it? a helicopter
 6 I need a question to distinguish that from a giraffe.
 7 The answer for a helicopter should be yes.
 8 Enter the question: Can it fly?
 9 Play again (yes or no)? yes
10
11 Can it fly? no
12 Is it ... a giraffe? no
13 I give up.
14 What is it? an apple pie
15 I need a question to distinguish that from a giraffe.
16 The answer for an apple pie should be yes.
17 Enter the question: Have you eaten one?
18 Play again (yes or no)? yes
19
20 Can it fly? no
21 Have you eaten one? yes
22 Is it ... an apple pie? yes
23 I win!
```

Figure 10-2: Our Questions program gets smarter with every game. We assume that the vast majority of readers have eaten an apple pie, but not a giraffe.

After a few hundred games, the program gets pretty good at playing Questions. The program's knowledge is stored in a tree (Figure 10–3).

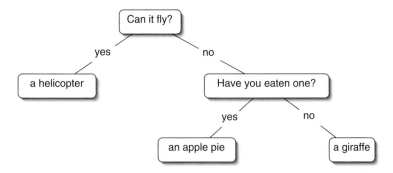

Figure 10–3: The program's binary decision tree at the end of the session in Figure 10–2.

Tree Terminology

The tree in Figure 10–3 is a *binary tree*. Formally, a binary tree is either:

1.   empty, or

2.   a node with a left subtree and a right subtree. Each of these subtrees is itself a binary tree.

Each rounded rectangle in Figure 10–3 is a node. The entire tree consists of the node labeled "Can it fly?" and two subtrees. The left subtree consists of (the node labeled) "a helicopter," an empty left subtree, and an empty right subtree.

The nodes directly below a node are its *children*. For example, the two children of "Have you eaten one?" are "an apple pie" and "a giraffe." The most important feature distinguishing binary trees from more general trees (Section 10.3) is that, in a binary tree, no node can have more than two children.

Other family relations follow in the way we would expect. For example, "Can it fly?" is the *parent* of "a helicopter." Every node in a binary tree has exactly one parent, except for the one at the top, which has no parent. Nodes with the same parent are *siblings*.

The node at the top of a tree is called the *root*. While a botanical tree has its root at the bottom, a computer science tree has its root at the top. Nodes with no children are called *leaves*. Nodes that are not leaves are *internal nodes*.

The *depth* of a node is the number of lines (not nodes!) along the path back to the root. Thus, the root is at depth 0, its children are at depth 1, and so on. A *level* of the tree is the set of nodes at a particular depth. The *height* of a tree is the depth of the deepest node.

Let's review these terms using the binary tree in Figure 10–4. This tree has height 4, because node J is at depth 4. Node A is the root. The leaves are K, L, F, J, and D. The internal nodes are A, G, H, E, B, I, and C. More information about some of the nodes is given in Figure 10–5.

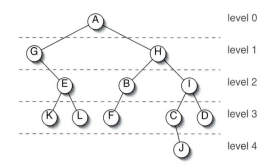

Figure 10-4: A binary tree with the nodes divided into levels.

Node	Parent	Children	Sibling	Depth
A	—	G, H	—	0
B	H	F	I	2
C	I	J	D	3
D	I	—	C	3
E	G	K, L	—	2

Figure 10-5: Information about some of the nodes in Figure 10–4.

A node's **descendants** are itself, its children, their children, and so on. Thus, every node in a tree is a descendant of the root. In Figure 10–4, the descendants of H are H, B, I, F, C, D, and J. A node's **proper descendants** are all of its descendants *except itself.*

A node's **ancestors** are itself, its parent, its grandparent, and so on. In Figure 10–4, the ancestors of L are L, E, G, and A. A node's **proper ancestors** are all of its ancestors except itself.

The number of nodes in a binary tree depends on the height of the tree and on how "skinny" or "bushy" the tree is (Figure 10–6). At one extreme is a **linear tree**, where every internal node has only one child. At the other extreme is a **perfect** binary tree, where all of the leaves are at the same depth and every internal node has exactly two children. (Some texts use the word 'complete' rather than 'perfect.')

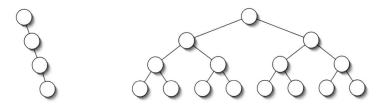

Figure 10-6: A linear tree (left) and a perfect binary tree (right). Both of these trees are of height 3.

The number of nodes in a binary tree of height h can be anywhere between $h + 1$ (for a linear tree) and

$$\sum_{d=0}^{h} 2^d = 2^{h+1} - 1$$

(for a perfect binary tree).

Conversely, a binary tree with n nodes has height between $\log_2(n + 1) - 1$ (for a perfect binary tree) and $n - 1$ (for a linear tree).

These precise formulae are easy to derive from a few examples. The most important thing to remember is that $h \in \Theta(\log n)$ for perfect binary trees.

Implementing Binary Trees

The recursive definition of a binary tree on page 257 is very similar to the following definition of a list. A list is either

1. empty, or

2. an item followed by a list.

This definition was implemented in the ListNode class in Section 6.1. Recursively defined structures often lend themselves to linked implementations. We define a class BinaryNode that is similar to ListNode. The difference is that, instead of having a single field `next` referring to the rest of the list, we have two fields `left` and `right` referring to the left and right subtrees.

Since we might have trees of different kinds of things, we again create a generic class. The Questions game needs a tree of Strings. Figure 10–7 shows the linked representation of the decision tree in Figure 10–3.

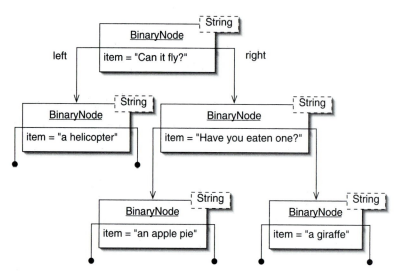

Figure 10-7: UML instance diagram showing the linked representation of the binary tree in Figure 10–3.

The code for the BinaryNode class is given in Figure 10–8.

```
1 /** Node in a binary tree. */
2 public class BinaryNode<E> {
3
4   /** The item associated with this node. */
5   private E item;
6
7   /** The node at the root of the left subtree. */
8   private BinaryNode<E> left;
9
10  /** The node at the root of the right subtree. */
11  private BinaryNode<E> right;
12
13  /** Put item in a leaf node. */
14  public BinaryNode(E item) {
15    this.item = item;
16    // left and right are set to null by default
17  }
18
```

Figure 10-8: The BinaryNode class. More methods will be added in Section 10.2. (Part 1 of 2)

```
19   /** Put item in a node with the specified subtrees. */
20   public BinaryNode(E item,
21                       BinaryNode<E> left,
22                       BinaryNode<E> right) {
23     this.item = item;
24     this.left = left;
25     this.right = right;
26   }
27
28   /** Return the item associated with this node. */
29   public E getItem() {
30     return item;
31   }
32
33   /** Return the root of the left subtree. */
34   public BinaryNode<E> getLeft() {
35     return left;
36   }
37
38   /** Return the root of the right subtree. */
39   public BinaryNode<E> getRight() {
40     return right;
41   }
42
43   /** Return true if this is a leaf. */
44   public boolean isLeaf() {
45     return (left == null) && (right == null);
46   }
47
48   /** Replace the item associated with this node. */
49   public void setItem(E item) {
50     this.item = item;
51   }
52
53   /** Replace the left subtree with the one rooted at left. */
54   public void setLeft(BinaryNode<E> left) {
55     this.left = left;
56   }
57
58   /** Replace the right subtree with the one rooted at right. */
59   public void setRight(BinaryNode<E> right) {
60     this.right = right;
61   }
62
63 }
```

Figure 10-8: The BinaryNode class. More methods will be added in Section 10.2. (Part 2 of 2)

With this structure in hand, we can now write the Questions game. An instance of the Questions class contains a BinaryNode (the root), which may refer in turn to additional BinaryNodes (Figure 10–9).

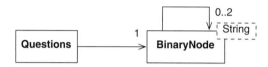

Figure 10-9: An instance of Questions contains an instance of BinaryNode, which refers to its children, and so on.

The easy parts of the program are shown in Figure 10–10.

```
 1 import java.util.Scanner;
 2
 3 /** The game of Questions. */
 4 public class Questions {
 5
 6   /** For reading from the console. */
 7   public static final Scanner INPUT = new Scanner(System.in);
 8
 9   /** Root of the decision tree. */
10   private BinaryNode<String> root;
11
12   /**
13    * Initially, the program guesses that the player is thinking of
14    * a giraffe.
15    */
16   public Questions() {
17     root = new BinaryNode<String>("a giraffe");
18   }
19
20   /** Create and repeatedly play the game. */
21   public static void main(String[] args) {
22     Questions game = new Questions();
23     System.out.println("Welcome to Questions.");
24     do {
25       System.out.println();
26       game.play();
27       System.out.print("Play again (yes or no)? ");
28     } while (INPUT.nextLine().equals("yes"));
29   }
30
31 }
```

Figure 10-10: Easy parts of the Questions program.

Initially, the program's decision tree consists of a single node, containing the String "a giraffe". The tree expands through learning—more on that in the moment. For now, let's imagine that the tree is more elaborate, as in Figure 10–3.

Every internal node in the tree contains a question and every leaf contains a guess as to what the knower has in mind. The play() method starts at the root of the tree, asking the question (or making the guess) stored there. For now, suppose it's a question. If the player answers "yes," the program repeats the process on the left subtree. Otherwise, it goes to the right.

This continues until the program hits a leaf, when it makes a guess. If the guess is correct, the program has won. Otherwise, the program has lost. The play() method is shown in Figure 10–11.

```
1 /** Play until the program wins or gives up. */
2 public void play() {
3   BinaryNode<String> node = root;
4   while (!(node.isLeaf())) {
5     System.out.print(node.getItem() + " ");
6     if (INPUT.nextLine().equals("yes")) {
7       node = node.getLeft();
8     } else {
9       node = node.getRight();
10    }
11  }
12  System.out.print("Is it ... " + node.getItem() + "? ");
13  if (INPUT.nextLine().equals("yes")) {
14    System.out.println("I win!");
15  } else {
16    System.out.println("I give up.");
17    learn(node);
18  }
19 }
```

Figure 10-11: The play() method.

When the program loses, it learns from experience. This is handled by the learn() method, which replaces all three fields in the leaf node that was an incorrect guess. The field item is replaced by the new question, left is replaced by a new leaf node containing the correct answer, and right is replaced by a new leaf node containing the incorrect guess. No other nodes in the tree are affected. This process is illustrated in Figure 10–12 and the code is in Figure 10–13.

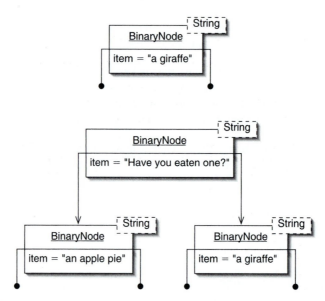

Figure 10-12: A node before (top) and after (bottom) learning. This corresponds to lines 13–15 in Figure 10–13.

```
 1 /**
 2  * Node is a leaf corresponding to an incorrect guess.  Gather
 3  * information from the user and add two children to node.
 4  */
 5 protected void learn(BinaryNode<String> node) {
 6    System.out.print("What is it? ");
 7    String correct = INPUT.nextLine();
 8    System.out.println("I need a question to distinguish that from "
 9                       + node.getItem() + ".");
10    System.out.println("The answer for " + correct
11                       + " should be yes.");
12    System.out.print("Enter the question: ");
13    String question = INPUT.nextLine();
14    node.setLeft(new BinaryNode<String>(correct));
15    node.setRight(new BinaryNode<String>(node.getItem()));
16    node.setItem(question);
17 }
```

Figure 10-13: The `learn()` method adds two children to a leaf.

Exercises

10.1   Is the root of a (nonempty) binary tree always, sometimes, or never a leaf? Explain.

10.2   What are the minimum and maximum number of siblings a node in a binary tree can have? What if the node is the root?

10.3   A ternary tree is just like a binary tree, but each node has *three* subtrees. What are the maximum and minimum number of nodes in a ternary tree of height h?

10.4   It would be nice to have a method isRoot() for the BinaryNode class which returns true if the node is the root of its tree. Explain why it is not possible to write such a method using the current representation. How might the BinaryNode class be modified to allow such a method to be written?

10.5   Can an internal node in the Questions program's decision tree have only one child? If so, is it the left or right child? If not, why not?

10.2 Tree Traversal

In Section 5.4, we discussed traversing linear structures—that is, visiting each item in turn. We have traversed linear structures using Iterators and in methods such as toString().

A linear structure is normally traversed from front to back. Occasionally it is useful to traverse one from back to front. With trees, the order of traversal is less obvious. The root should probably be either first or last, but what about the other nodes?

It turns out that there are four meaningful orders in which to traverse a binary tree: *preorder*, *inorder*, *postorder*, and *level order*. For reference, the four traversals of the tree in Figure 10–4 are shown in Figure 10–14.

Traversal Order	Order in which Nodes are Visited
Preorder	AGEKLHBFICJD
Inorder	GKELAFBHCJID
Postorder	KLEGFBJCDIHA
Level order	AGHEBIKLFCDJ

Figure 10–14: Traversing the binary tree in Figure 10–4.

The first three orders have very elegant algorithms based on the recursive structure of a tree. Indeed, these algorithms are generally given as definitions of the traversal orders. For example, the algorithm for preorder traversal is:

1. Visit the root.

2. Recursively traverse the left subtree preorder.

3. Recursively traverse the right subtree preorder.

This algorithm is easily translated into a method for the BinaryNode class (Figure 10–15). Note that the base case is handled in an unusual way here. Rather than checking for the base case (an empty tree) at the beginning of the method, we check before each recursive invocation. This is necessary because the empty tree is represented by null, and we can't invoke methods on null.

```
 1 /**
 2  * Return a String representation of the tree rooted at this node,
 3  * traversed preorder.
 4  */
 5 public String toStringPreorder() {
 6    String result = "";
 7    result += item;
 8    if (left != null) {
 9       result += left.toStringPreorder();
10    }
11    if (right != null) {
12       result += right.toStringPreorder();
13    }
14    return result;
15 }
```

Figure 10–15: This method for the BinaryNode class traverses a tree preorder.

The inorder traversal algorithm is almost identical, except that we traverse the left subtree *before* visiting the root (Figure 10–16).

```
 1 /**
 2  * Return a String representation of the tree rooted at this node,
 3  * traversed inorder.
 4  */
 5 public String toStringInorder() {
 6    String result = "";
 7    if (left != null) {
 8       result += left.toStringInorder();
 9    }
```

Figure 10–16: The only difference between preorder traversal (Figure 10–15) and inorder traversal is the order of lines 7–13. (Part 1 of 2)

```
10    result += item;
11    if (right != null) {
12      result += right.toStringInorder();
13    }
14    return result;
15 }
```

Figure 10–16: The only difference between preorder traversal (Figure 10–15) and inorder traversal is the order of lines 7–13. (Part 2 of 2)

Visiting the root *after* both subtrees results in a postorder traversal (Figure 10–17).

```
1 /**
2  * Return a String representation of the tree rooted at this node,
3  * traversed postorder.
4  */
5 public String toStringPostorder() {
6    String result = "";
7    if (left != null) {
8      result += left.toStringPostorder();
9    }
10   if (right != null) {
11     result += right.toStringPostorder();
12   }
13   result += item;
14   return result;
15 }
```

Figure 10–17: In a postorder traversal, the root is visited after both subtrees.

As we mentioned in Section 9.5, any recursive algorithm can be converted into an iterative one by explicitly simulating the call stack. While this is generally not worth the effort, it is instructive to look at an iterative version of `toStringPreorder()`. It turns out that, for this particular algorithm, we don't have to store complete call frames on the stack—just the root of each subtree to be traversed (Figure 10–18).

```
1 /**
2  * Return a String representation of the tree rooted at this node,
3  * traversed preorder.
4  */
5 public String toStringPreorder() {
6    String result = "";
7    Stack<BinaryNode<E>> stack = new ArrayStack<BinaryNode<E>>();
8    stack.push(this);
```

Figure 10–18: An iterative version of `toStringPreorder()` using an explicit stack. It is necessary to push the right child before the left child because of the last-in, first-out policy of a stack. (Part 1 of 2)

```
 9   while (!(stack.isEmpty())) {
10     BinaryNode<E> node = stack.pop();
11     result += node.item;
12     if (node.right != null) {
13       stack.push(node.right);
14     }
15     if (node.left != null) {
16       stack.push(node.left);
17     }
18   }
19   return result;
20 }
```

Figure 10-18: An iterative version of `toStringPreorder()` using an explicit stack. It is necessary to push the right child before the left child because of the last-in, first-out policy of a stack. (Part 2 of 2)

The stack holds the roots of the subtrees we have yet to traverse. In the example of Figure 10–4, while we are traversing the subtree rooted at G, G's sibling H is at the bottom of the stack, waiting its turn. As we find proper descendants of G, they are pushed onto the top of the stack, so they are handled before H.

A curious thing happens if we replace the stack with a queue. Now G's proper descendants are handled *after* H. If we add the left child to the queue before the right child, we get the algorithm for the level order traversal (Figure 10–19). The root is visited first, then all of the nodes at depth 1, then depth 2, and so on.

```
 1 /**
 2  * Return a String representation of the tree rooted at this node,
 3  * traversed level order.
 4  */
 5 public String toStringLevelOrder() {
 6   String result = "";
 7   Queue<BinaryNode<E>> q = new ArrayQueue<BinaryNode<E>>();
 8   q.add(this);
 9   while (!(q.isEmpty())) {
10     BinaryNode<E> node = q.remove();
11     result += node.item;
12     if (node.left != null) {
13       q.add(node.left);
14     }
15     if (node.right != null) {
16       q.add(node.right);
17     }
18   }
19   return result;
20 }
```

Figure 10-19: Changing the stack to a queue and swapping the order of child insertion results in the algorithm for level order traversal.

Level order traversal is sometimes called **breadth-first** because it traverses all the way across each level before going deeper (Figure 10–20). The other traversals are called **depth-first** because they go all the way down to a leaf before "backing up" and trying a different path.

Any traversal takes time in $\Theta(n)$ because it does a constant amount of work visiting each node. If the order isn't important and the tree is perfect or close to perfect, depth-first traversals are more efficient. The issue is not time but space. A depth-first traversal uses space for the call stack. The number of call frames is proportional to the height of the tree, which is in $\Theta(\log n)$ in a perfect tree. A breadth-first traversal, on the other hand, uses space for a queue. This can be as large as an entire level of the tree, which is in $\Theta(n)$ in a perfect tree.

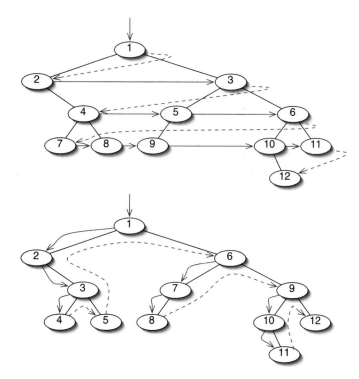

Figure 10–20: A breadth-first traversal (top) visits every node in each level before going on to the next level. A depth-first traversal (bottom) goes all the way down to a leaf before "backing up" and traversing a different subtree.

Exercises

10.6   In the preorder tree traversal, the base case is an empty tree. Would a leaf be a legitimate base case? Explain.

10.7   Is the order in which nodes are visited in a postorder traversal the reverse of the order produced by a preorder traversal? Explain.

10.8   Does a depth-first or a breadth-first traversal use more memory when traversing a linear tree?

10.9   Project 4.20 defined infix and postfix notation. Draw a binary tree which produces the infix expression 3 + 2 * 4 when traversed inorder and the postfix expression 3 2 4 * + when traversed postorder. What expression is produced if this tree is traversed preorder?

10.3 General Trees

While binary trees are quite common in computer science, many trees are not binary trees. We define a ***general tree*** recursively as a node and zero or more subtrees, which are themselves general trees. General trees differ from binary trees in three ways:

- A node in a general tree may have more than two children.

- A node in a general tree has a (possibly empty) sequence of children, rather than a certain number of "slots" to fill. Among binary trees, there is a difference between a tree with a left subtree but no right subtree and a tree with a right subtree but no left subtree. No such distinction is made for general trees (Figure 10–21).

- General trees cannot be empty. This restriction is made to avoid having to distinguish between a node with no subtrees and a node with several empty subtrees, which would be drawn identically.

Figure 10–21: The two binary trees at left are considered different: one has an empty right subtree, while the other has an empty left subtree. Among general trees like the one at right, no such distinction is drawn.

We have seen a number of general trees already. For example, inheritance diagrams showing the relationships between classes, such as Figure 3–10, are general trees. Another general tree is shown in Figure 10–22.

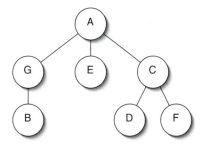

Figure 10-22: A general tree.

Representing General Trees

There are a couple of ways to represent general trees. The simplest is to represent each node as an item plus a linear structure (a simple array or some kind of List) containing references to its children (Figure 10–23). This is called the ***array of children*** or ***list of children*** representation.

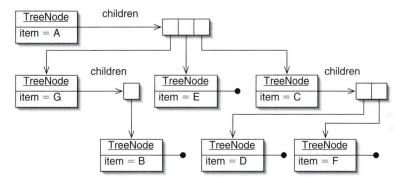

Figure 10-23: Array of children representation of the general tree in Figure 10–22. TreeNode is a generic type, but the type parameters have been omitted here for clarity.

A less intuitive but more space-efficient representation has each node keeping track of its first child and its next sibling (Figure 10–24). This is called the ***first-child, next-sibling*** representation.

The code for each of these representations is left as a problem.

Example: An Intelligent Tic Tac Toe Player

Many important data structures involve trees, as we shall see in Chapters 11, 14, and 17. Trees are also useful when discussing a variety of computer science concepts, such as inheritance and recursion. We now examine one particular application of trees: writing a program to play the game of Tic Tac Toe (Figure 10–25).

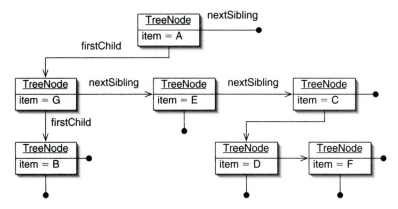

Figure 10-24: First-child, next-sibling representation of the general tree in Figure 10–22.

Tic Tac Toe (Noughts and Crosses)

Players: 2, X and O.

Object: To be the first player to get three of her marks in a row, horizontally, vertically, or diagonally.

Board: The board is a 3×3 grid of squares. Each square is either vacant or contains an X or an O. Initially, all squares are vacant.

Play: X moves first. On a turn, a player writes her mark in any vacant square.

Game End: The game ends when one player wins by getting three marks in a row or all nine squares are filled (a tie).

Figure 10-25: The game of Tic Tac Toe is so simple that even a computer can play it well. In our implementation, the computer plays as X, the user as O.

As with Questions, this program has the computer playing against the user. This is an elementary exercise in artificial intelligence. For a game as simple as Tic Tac Toe, we can write a program which *never loses* (although a good opponent can always force a tie). A transcript of the program at work is shown in Figure 10–26.

```
 1 Welcome to Tic Tac Toe.
 2
 3 X..
 4 ...
 5 ...
 6
 7 Enter row: 0
 8 Enter column: 2
 9 X.0
10 X..
11 ...
12
13 Enter row: 2
14 Enter column: 0
15 X.0
16 XX.
17 0..
18
19 Enter row: 1
20 Enter column: 2
21 X.0
22 XX0
23 0.X
24
25 Game over.
```

Figure 10-26: The Tic Tac Toe program cannot be defeated.

The easy parts of the program, which deal with managing the board, are shown in Figure 10–27.

```
 1 import java.util.Scanner;
 2
 3 /** The game of Tic Tac Toe. */
 4 public class TicTacToe {
 5
 6   /** For reading from the console. */
 7   public static final Scanner INPUT = new Scanner(System.in);
 8
 9   /** Squares on the board, each of which is '.', 'X', or '0'. */
10   private char[][] squares;
11
12   /** The board is initially empty. */
13   public TicTacToe() {
14     squares = new char[][] {{'.', '.', '.'},
15                             {'.', '.', '.'},
16                             {'.', '.', '.'}};
17   }
```

Figure 10-27: Easy parts of the Tic Tac Toe program. (Part 1 of 2)

```
18
19   public String toString() {
20     String result = "";
21     for (int row = 0; row < 3; row++) {
22       for (int column = 0; column < 3; column++) {
23         result += squares[row][column];
24       }
25       result += "\n";
26     }
27     return result;
28   }
29
30   /** Create and play the game. */
31   public static void main(String[] args) {
32     TicTacToe game = new TicTacToe();
33     System.out.println("Welcome to Tic Tac Toe.\n");
34     game.play();
35     System.out.println(game);
36     System.out.println("Game over.");
37   }
38
39 }
```

Figure 10-27: Easy parts of the Tic Tac Toe program. (Part 2 of 2)

The program also needs methods for determining when the game is over and who, if anyone, won (Figure 10–28). The method score() has to check each of the eight possible victory lines (three vertical, three horizontal, and two diagonal); this work is moved into the protected method scoreLine() for clarity.

```
1 /** Return true if the game is over. */
2 public boolean gameOver() {
3   if (score() != 0) {
4     return true;
5   }
6   for (int row = 0; row < 3; row++) {
7     for (int column = 0; column < 3; column++) {
8       if (squares[row][column] == '.') {
9         return false;
10      }
11    }
12  }
```

Figure 10-28: Additional methods are needed to detect the end of the game and the winner. (Part 1 of 2)

```
13   return true;
14 }
15
16 /** Return 1 if X has won, -1 if O has won, and 0 otherwise. */
17 public int score() {
18   int lineScore;
19   for (int i = 0; i < 3; i++) {
20     lineScore = scoreLine(squares[i][0],
21                           squares[i][1],
22                           squares[i][2]);
23     if (lineScore != 0) {
24       return lineScore;
25     }
26     lineScore = scoreLine(squares[0][i],
27                           squares[1][i],
28                           squares[2][i]);
29     if (lineScore != 0) {
30       return lineScore;
31     }
32   }
33   lineScore = scoreLine(squares[0][0],
34                         squares[1][1],
35                         squares[2][2]);
36   if (lineScore != 0) {
37     return lineScore;
38   }
39   return scoreLine(squares[0][2], squares[1][1], squares[2][0]);
40 }
41
42 /**
43  * Return 1 if all three characters are 'X', -1 if they are all 'O',
44  * and 0 otherwise.
45  */
46 protected int scoreLine(char a, char b, char c) {
47   if ((a == 'X') && (b == 'X') && (c == 'X')) { return 1; }
48   if ((a == 'O') && (b == 'O') && (c == 'O')) { return -1; }
49   return 0;
50 }
```

Figure 10-28: Additional methods are needed to detect the end of the game and the winner. (Part 2 of 2)

With those details out of the way, we are ready to tackle the hard part. How do we decide which is the best move to make? This decision is easiest near the end of the game. We consider each possible move for X, taking the one with the highest score. In Figure 10–29, one of the moves leads to a win for X, so we should choose that one.

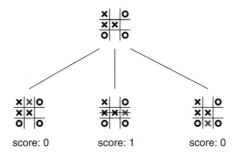

Figure 10-29: Three possible moves near the end of a game of Tic Tac Toe. X chooses the move which maximizes the score.

This is the approach used by playBestMove(), which is invoked by play() (Figure 10–30). This method works through each square on the board and, if the square is vacant, tries playing there (line 32). The value of the resulting board position is determined by score() (line 33). This value is then compared with the best move so far (lines 34–38). Before trying the next option, it is necessary to undo the move that was just considered (line 39). Finally, after all moves have been considered, the best move is made and left in place (line 43).

```
 1 /** Play one game. */
 2 public void play() {
 3   char player = 'X';
 4   for (int move = 0; move < 9; move++) {
 5     if (gameOver()) {
 6       return;
 7     }
 8     if (player == 'X') {
 9       playBestMove();
10       player = 'O';
11     } else {
12       System.out.println(this);
13       System.out.print("Enter row: ");
14       int row = INPUT.nextInt();
15       System.out.print("Enter column: ");
16       int column = INPUT.nextInt();
17       squares[row][column] = 'O';
18       player = 'X';
19     }
20   }
21 }
22
```

Figure 10-30: The play() method invokes playBestMove(). Line 33 will be modified later to make the program smarter. (Part 1 of 2)

```
23 /** Find the best move for X and play it on the board. */
24 protected void playBestMove() {
25    int score;
26    int bestScore = -2;
27    int bestRow = -1;
28    int bestColumn = -1;
29    for (int row = 0; row < 3; row++) {
30      for (int column = 0; column < 3; column++) {
31        if (squares[row][column] == '.') {
32          squares[row][column] = 'X';
33          score = score();
34          if (score > bestScore) {
35            bestScore = score;
36            bestRow = row;
37            bestColumn = column;
38          }
39          squares[row][column] = '.';
40        }
41      }
42    }
43    squares[bestRow][bestColumn] = 'X';
44 }
```

Figure 10-30: The play() method invokes playBestMove(). Line 33 will be modified later to make the program smarter. (Part 2 of 2)

If it is not possible to win in a single move, we must consider how the opponent might reply (Figure 10–31). The opponent, playing O, is trying to *minimize* the score. The value of each leaf is determined by invoking score(). The value of an internal node is determined by taking either the minimum (if the node represents a board with O to play) or the maximum (X to play) of the node's children. This approach to game playing is therefore called the ***minimax*** algorithm. By considering all possible moves out to the end of the game, we can determine the best move.

We could build the game tree as a data structure, but this would be a waste of space. Once we determine the value of a child, we *no longer need* the subtree rooted at that child. Thus, instead of creating the subtree and then examining the value of child, we invoke a method which determines the value of the root by determining the value of its descendants. When the child's value is returned, all of the frames used in computing this value have been popped off the call stack. The game tree therefore corresponds to a tree of method invocations, with one node per invocation.

We modify line 33 of Figure 10–30 to invoke a new method minimaxForO(), which determines the value of the current board position, given that it is O's turn. The structure of minimaxForO() is almost identical to that of playBestMove(). The differences are:

- It *returns the value* of the board on which it is invoked, rather than *making the best move*.

- It looks for the move leading to the *minimum* score, rather than the *maximum*.

- It invokes minimaxForX() instead of score().

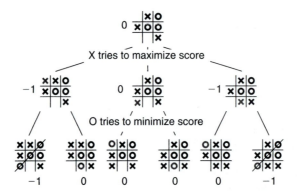

Figure 10-31: The minimax algorithm at work. Scores are calculated directly at leaves. At internal nodes, the score is that of the "best" child, from the point of view of the player about to move. For example, the leftmost node in the middle level has two children with values –1 and 0. Since O is trying to minimize the score at this point, the value of this node is –1.

The method minimaxForX() is similar to minimaxForO(), but it looks for the *maximum* of scores found by invoking minimaxForO(). The code for both methods is given in Figure 10–32. Since these two methods invoke each other, they are said to be ***mutually recursive***.

```
 1 /** Return the value of the current position if it is O's turn. */
 2 protected int minimaxForO() {
 3   int score = score();
 4   if (gameOver()) {
 5     return score;
 6   }
 7   int bestScore = 2;
 8   for (int row = 0; row < 3; row++) {
 9     for (int column = 0; column < 3; column++) {
10       if (squares[row][column] == '.') {
11         squares[row][column] = 'O';
12         score = minimaxForX();
13         if (score < bestScore) {
14           bestScore = score;
15         }
16         squares[row][column] = '.';
17       }
18     }
19   }
20   return bestScore;
21 }
22
```

Figure 10-32: The mutually recursive methods minimaxForO() and minimaxForX() are almost identical. (Part 1 of 2)

```
23 /** Return the value of the current position if it is X's turn. */
24 protected int minimaxForX() {
25   int score = score();
26   if (gameOver()) {
27     return score;
28   }
29   int bestScore = -2;
30   for (int row = 0; row < 3; row++) {
31     for (int column = 0; column < 3; column++) {
32       if (squares[row][column] == '.') {
33         squares[row][column] = 'X';
34         score = minimaxForO();
35         if (score > bestScore) {
36           bestScore = score;
37         }
38         squares[row][column] = '.';
39       }
40     }
41   }
42   return bestScore;
43 }
```

Figure 10–32: The mutually recursive methods `minimaxForO()` and `minimaxForX()` are almost identical. (Part 2 of 2)

Exercises

10.10   Explain why Figure 6–25 is *not* a tree.

10.11   Which of the four traversal orders discussed in Section 10.2 is *not* well defined for general trees? Explain.

10.12   Ignoring the fact that the game may end before the entire board is filled, exactly how many nodes are there in the complete game tree for Tic Tac Toe? (This is a simple game. The trees for more complicated games like Chess and Go have more nodes than there are electrons in the universe!)

10.13   Explain lines 7 and 29 of Figure 10–32.

10.14   We can define evenness and oddness of nonnegative integers as follows:

A number *n* is even if it is 0 or *n* – 1 is odd.

A number *n* is odd if it is not 0 and *n* – 1 is even.

Express these algorithms as two mutually recursive methods `isEven()` and `isOdd()`, each of which takes an int as an argument and returns a boolean.

Summary

A tree is a branching, hierarchical structure. We have defined both binary trees and general trees. A binary tree either is empty or consists of a node, a left subtree, and a right subtree. A general tree (which cannot be empty) consists of a node and zero or more subtrees. There is a lot of terminology surrounding trees, most of it drawn from either genealogy or botany.

The number of nodes in a binary tree depends on both the height of the tree and on how "bushy" it is. In the widest possible binary tree, called a perfect tree, the number of nodes is exponential in the height of the tree. Conversely, the height of such a tree is logarithmic in the number of nodes.

Binary trees can be traversed in four orders: preorder, inorder, postorder, and level order. The first three have very elegant recursive algorithms, but level order traversal requires a queue. Most of these orders are also defined for general trees.

A binary tree is usually represented by a linked structure similar to a linked list. For more general trees, representations include the array of children representation and the first-child, next-sibling representation. In some applications, such as our Tic Tac Toe player, trees are not explicitly constructed as data structures, but are implicit in the way the program runs.

Vocabulary

ancestor. Any of a node, its parent, its grandparent, and so on. All of these except for the node itself are proper ancestors.

array of children. General tree representation in which each node has an array of references to child nodes.

binary tree. Tree that either is empty or consists of a node and a left and right subtree, each of which is a binary tree.

breadth-first. Any tree traversal, such as level order, in which all of the nodes at a given depth are visited before deeper nodes.

child. Node directly below another node in a tree.

depth. Number of lines on a path from a tree node back to the root.

depth-first. Any tree traversal, such as preorder, which goes all the way to a leaf before "backing up" and trying a different branch.

descendant. Any of a node, its children, their children, and so on. All of these except for the node itself are proper descendants.

first child, next sibling. General tree representation in which each node has references to its first (leftmost) child and next sibling.

general tree. Tree consisting of a node and zero or more subtrees, each of which is a general tree.

height. Of a tree, the depth of the deepest node.

inorder. Traversal in which the left subtree is traversed, the root is visited, and then the right subtree is traversed.

internal node. Tree node that is not a leaf.

leaf. Tree node that has no children.

level. Set of nodes at the same depth within a tree.

level order. Tree traversal in which the root is visited, then the nodes on level 1, then the nodes on level 2, and so on.

linear tree. Tree in which each internal node has one child.

list of children. General tree representation in which each node has a list of references to child nodes.

minimax. Algorithm for playing games in which one player tries to maximize the score while the opponent tries to minimize it. The value of a node (board configuration) is either the score (if it is an end-of-game node), the maximum of its children's values (if it is the maximizing player's turn), or the minimum of its children's values (if it is the minimizing player's turn). The move leading to the highest-valued node should be chosen.

mutually recursive. Of two or more algorithms, invoking each other.

parent. Node directly above another node in a tree. Every node has exactly one parent, except for the root, which has no parent.

perfect binary tree. Binary tree in which all of the leaves are at the same depth and every internal node has two children.

postorder. Tree traversal in which the subtrees are traversed and then the root is visited.

preorder. Tree traversal in which the root is visited and then the subtrees are traversed.

root. Node at the top of a tree.

sibling. Tree node with the same parent as another node.

Problems

10.15 Write a class for a node in a ternary tree, as defined in Exercise 10.3.

10.16 Modify the traversal methods from Section 10.2 to include parentheses. For example, an invocation of `toStringInorder()` on (the root of) the tree in Figure 10–4 should return the String `"((G((K)E(L)))A(((F)B)H((C(J))I(D))))"`.

10.17 Modify the Questions game so that it prints out its decision tree at the end of each game. The output should look like that shown in Figure 10–33. (Hint: Write a recursive method to print the tree. This method takes the amount of indentation as one of its arguments.)

10.18 Modify the Questions program so that the guesser loses if it hasn't guessed successfully after twenty questions.

```
1 Can it fly?
2   Does it lay eggs?
3      a robin
4      a helicopter
5   Have you eaten one?
6      an apple pie
7      a giraffe
```

Figure 10-33: Sample output for Problem 10.17.

10.19   Write the TreeNode class as depicted in Figure 10–23. Include a method `toString-Preorder()`, equivalent to the one in Figure 10–15.

10.20   Write the TreeNode class as depicted in Figure 10–24. Include a method `toString-Postorder()`, equivalent to the one in Figure 10–17.

10.21   Using the code from one of the previous two problems, modify the Questions game so that it can handle multiple choice questions.

10.22   Modify the Tic Tac Toe program so that the user gets to choose whether to go first or second.

10.23   Replace the methods `minimaxForO()` and `minimaxForX()` (Figure 10–32) with a single recursive method `minimax()`, which takes the player whose turn it is as an additional argument.

Projects

10.24   Add methods `preorderIterator()` and `levelOrderIterator()` to the Binary-Node class. Each should return an Iterator which traverses the tree in the specified order. (Hint: Define two new classes, each implementing the Iterator interface. Each class needs a field of type Stack or Queue.)

10.25   Modify the Tic Tac Toe program so that it looks ahead only a certain number of moves. This number should be passed in to the constructor as an argument `maxDepth`. Run a tournament between players with max depths of 1, 3, 5, 7, and 9. Explain whether searching deeper produces a better player.

10.26   Write a minimax player for the Mancala game from Project 2.33. For the program to take its turn in a reasonable amount of time, you will need to implement limited depth as in Project 10.25. Notice that in Mancala a move by one player is sometimes followed by another move by the same player.

11

Sets

A *set* is a collection of elements in which the same element does not appear more than once. For example, {A, B, C} is a set, but {A, B, C, A} is not. Unlike a list (Section 5.3), a set does not have any particular ordering: a given element either is or is not a member of the set. Thus, {A, B, C} and {C, B, A} are the same set.

Almost every large program makes use of sets. In this chapter, we present a Set interface (Section 11.1) and three implementations: ordered lists (Section 11.2), binary search trees (Section 11.3), and hash tables (Section 11.4). In Section 11.5, we revisit the Java collections framework, discussing Java's own Set interface, some built-in implementations, and the related Map interface.

11.1 The Set Interface

The game of Anagrams (Figure 11–1) involves three sets of Strings: the sets of words in front of each player and the set of legal words. There are also two collections of letters (the bag and the pool), but these are *not* sets, because the same letter may appear more than once in a given collection.

Anagrams

Players: 2–6.

Object: To be the first player with five words.

Setup: The game involves a large set of letter tiles. Each tile has a letter written on it. At the beginning of the game, all of the tiles are placed in a bag.

Play: On a turn, a player draws a tile from the bag and places it in a pool in the middle of the table. If the player can form a word of four or more letters from those in the pool, he takes those letters and forms the word in front of himself.

Alternately, a player may steal a word from another player. He must combine all of the letters in the stolen word with at least one letter from the pool to make a new word. The letters may be rearranged in the new word.

If a player cannot make or steal a word after drawing a tile, he must pass.

Figure 11–1: The game of Anagrams. Our implementation handles only two players.

A transcript of the game in action is given in Figure 11–2.

```
 1 Welcome to Anagrams.
 2
 3 To make a word from the pool, enter it.
 4 To steal a word, enter the new word, a space, and the word being
 5 stolen.
 6 To pass, just hit return.
 7
 8 PLAYER 1 TO PLAY
 9 Letters in pool:
10 r
11 Player 1's words: ( )
12 Player 2's words: ( )
13 Your play:
14
15 PLAYER 2 TO PLAY
16 Letters in pool:
17 ir
18 Player 1's words: ( )
19 Player 2's words: ( )
20 Your play:
21
```

Figure 11–2: Beginning of a game of Anagrams. On the last move, Player 1 steals the word 'ripe' by adding a 'z' to make 'prize.' (Part 1 of 2)

```
22 PLAYER 1 TO PLAY
23 Letters in pool:
24 eir
25 Player 1's words: ( )
26 Player 2's words: ( )
27 Your play:
28
29 PLAYER 2 TO PLAY
30 Letters in pool:
31 eipr
32 Player 1's words: ( )
33 Player 2's words: ( )
34 Your play: ripe
35
36 PLAYER 1 TO PLAY
37 Letters in pool:
38 z
39 Player 1's words: ( )
40 Player 2's words: ( ripe )
41 Your play: prize ripe
42
43 PLAYER 2 TO PLAY
44 Letters in pool:
45 n
46 Player 1's words: ( prize )
47 Player 2's words: ( )
```

Figure 11–2: Beginning of a game of Anagrams. On the last move, Player 1 steals the word 'ripe' by adding a 'z' to make 'prize.' (Part 2 of 2)

An instance of the Anagrams class contains three instances of Set<String> and two of Letter-Collection (Figure 11–3). We will write the Set interface and the main Anagrams class in this

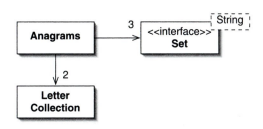

Figure 11–3: An instance of the Anagrams class contains three instances of implementations of the Set interface and two of LetterCollection.

section. The LetterCollection class is discussed in Section 11.4, as it foreshadows one of the Set implementations. Most of the rest of this chapter deals with implementing the Set interface. An efficient Set implementation is crucial for this game, because one of the Sets (the set of legal words) may contain hundreds of thousands of elements.

A simple Set interface is shown in Figure 11–4. The Set interface in the Java collections framework specifies many additional methods, but this version will suffice for now.

```
 1 /** A set of Objects. */
 2 public interface Set<E> {
 3
 4    /** Add target to this Set. */
 5    public void add(E target);
 6
 7    /** Return true if this Set contains target. */
 8    public boolean contains(E target);
 9
10    /** Remove target from this Set. */
11    public void remove(E target);
12
13    /** Return the number of elements in this Set. */
14    public int size();
15
16 }
```

Figure 11–4: A simple Set interface. Like the List interface in Section 5.3, it involves a generic type.

We now write the Anagrams class to illustrate the use of Sets. The easy parts are shown in Figure 11–5.

```
 1 import java.util.*;
 2
 3 /** The game of Anagrams. */
 4 public class Anagrams {
 5
 6    /** For reading from the console. */
 7    public static final Scanner INPUT = new Scanner(System.in);
 8
 9    /** Letters in the bag. */
10    private LetterCollection bag;
11
12    /** Letters in the pool. */
13    private LetterCollection pool;
14
```

Figure 11–5: Easy parts of the Anagrams class. (Part 1 of 2)

```
15   /** Large set of legal words. */
16   private Set<String> words;
17
18   /** Words scored by player 1. */
19   private Set<String> words1;
20
21   /** Words scored by player 2. */
22   private Set<String> words2;
23
24   /** Create and play the game. */
25   public static void main(String[] args) {
26     Anagrams game = new Anagrams();
27     System.out.println("Welcome to Anagrams.");
28     System.out.println();
29     System.out.println("To make a word from the pool, enter it.");
30     System.out.println("To steal a word, enter the new word, a"
31                        + "space, and the word being stolen.");
32     System.out.println("To pass, just hit return.");
33     System.out.println();
34     game.play();
35   }
36
37 }
```

Figure 11–5: Easy parts of the Anagrams class. (Part 2 of 2)

Next we write the play() and playTurn() methods (Figure 11–6).

```
1  /** Play until someone gets five words. */
2  public void play() {
3    while (true) {
4      System.out.println("PLAYER 1 TO PLAY");
5      playTurn(words1, words2);
6      if (words1.size() == 5) {
7        System.out.println("Player 1 wins!");
8        return;
9      }
10     System.out.println("PLAYER 2 TO PLAY");
11     playTurn(words2, words1);
```

Figure 11–6: The play() and playTurn() methods make extensive use of methods from the Set interface. (Part 1 of 2)

```
12    if (words2.size() == 5) {
13      System.out.println("Player 2 wins!");
14      return;
15    }
16  }
17 }
18
19 /** Play one turn for the specified player. */
20 public void playTurn(Set<String> player, Set<String> opponent) {
21    pool.add(bag.draw());
22    System.out.println("Letters in pool:\n" + pool);
23    System.out.println("Player 1's words: " + words1);
24    System.out.println("Player 2's words: " + words2);
25    System.out.print("Your play: ");
26    String play = INPUT.nextLine();
27    int spaceIndex = play.indexOf(' ');
28    if (spaceIndex != -1) {        // Stolen word
29      String word = play.substring(0, spaceIndex);
30      if (!(words.contains(word))) {
31        System.out.println("Sorry, " + word + " is not a word.");
32      } else {
33        String stolen = play.substring(spaceIndex + 1, play.length());
34        player.add(word);
35        opponent.remove(stolen);
36        pool.add(stolen);
37        pool.remove(word);
38      }
39    } else if (!(play.equals(""))) { // Regular play
40      if (!(words.contains(play))) {
41        System.out.println("Sorry, " + play + " is not a word.");
42      } else {
43        player.add(play);
44        pool.remove(play);
45      }
46    }
47    System.out.println();
48 }
```

Figure 11-6: The play() and playTurn() methods make extensive use of methods from the Set interface. (Part 2 of 2)

The play() method is a fairly simple loop that runs until one player has five words. This is detected by invoking the size() method from the Set interface.

The playTurn() method is more complicated. It begins by taking a letter out of the bag and adding it to the pool (line 21). After reading a line from the user (line 26), the method invokes the indexOf() method of the resulting String (line 27). This method returns the index of the first appearance of the specified character (a space), or −1 if that character does not appear.

If the line contains a space, it can be recognized as a command to steal a word (line 28). The line is separated into two words on lines 29 and 33 using the substring() method of the String class. For example, if play is "prize ripe" then play.indexOf(' ') returns 5, play.substring(0, 5) returns "prize", and play.substring(6, 10) returns "ripe".

The playTurn() method next verifies that the word is legal (line 30). If it is, the word is added to the player's set (line 34) and the stolen word is removed from the opponent's set (line 35). Finally, all the letters in the stolen word are added to the pool (line 36) and all the letters in the new word are removed from the pool (line 37). The net effect of these last two method invocations is to remove from the pool those letters which are in the new word but *not* in the stolen word.

Lines 39–46 handle the simpler case of a regular play. Here, the method only has to verify that the word is legal, add it to the player's set, and remove the letters from the pool.

All that remains is the constructor (Figure 11–7). Lines 9–19 deal with reading words from a text file. (We'll discuss file handling in much more detail in Chapter 17.) The file must be called words.txt and must be in the directory from which the program is run. A good list of words can be found in the file /usr/share/dict/words on most Unix systems, including Mac OS X.

```
 1 /**
 2  * Read in the dictionary from the file "anagram-words" and create
 3  * the letters.
 4  */
 5 public Anagrams() {
 6   bag = new LetterCollection(true);
 7   pool = new LetterCollection(false);
 8   words = new HashTable<String>("");
 9   try {
10     Scanner input = new Scanner(new java.io.File("words.txt"));
11     while (input.hasNextLine()) {
12       words.add(input.nextLine());
13     }
14   } catch (java.io.IOException e) {
15     e.printStackTrace();
16     System.exit(1);
17   }
18   words1 = new OrderedList<String>();
19   words2 = new OrderedList<String>();
20 }
```

Figure 11-7: The constructor for the Anagrams class creates three Sets.

Varying which class we use for words provides a striking example of the importance of an efficient Set implementation. Given a large words.txt file with tens or hundreds of thousands of words, the program as written takes at most a few seconds to start up. On the other hand, if we change line 8 to

```
words = new OrderedList<String>();
```

(note that this constructor takes no argument), the program seems to hang. It would eventually finish, but only after an unacceptable amount of time. The program is *unusable* because it is so inefficient.

Changing line 8 to

```
words = new BinarySearchTree<String>();
```

is just as bad in the likely event that words.txt is in alphabetical order. (We'll explain this behavior in Section 11.3.)

The impatient reader may think, "Why bother with these other, inefficient data structures? Let's cut to the chase and learn about hash tables!" The author offers the following reasons:

1.   Working through ordered lists and binary search trees provides a vivid demonstration of how data structures may be correct but still not sufficiently efficient.

2.   While the simple versions of these data structures are not efficient, more complicated variations are. For example, red-black trees (Chapter 14) are based on binary search trees.

3.   There are some jobs for which hash tables are not the data structure of choice; a programmer must have a diverse toolkit.

4.   As in a good film, the final revelation is more satisfying if suspense has been built up beforehand.

Exercises

11.1   Line 28 of Figure 11–6 seems a bit awkward. In general, it is clearer to say

```
if (x == 1) {
  // do one thing
} else {
  // do another thing
}
```

than

```
if (x != 1) {
  // do another thing
} else {
  // do one thing
}
```

which is equivalent. We might therefore be tempted to change the line to

```
if (spaceIndex == -1) {
```

and to swap lines 29–38 with lines 40–45. Why does this not work?

11.2 Modify the Anagrams program to enforce the constraint that words must be at least four letters long. (This is not necessary if all shorter words are removed from the file `words.txt`.)

11.3 Modify the Anagrams program to prevent a player from "stealing" a word that the opponent doesn't actually have.

11.2 Ordered Lists

The most obvious approach to implementing the Set interface is to use one of the linear structures introduced in Part II. Since a Set changes size as items are added and removed, a linked structure seems in order. In this section, we look at an ***ordered list***, a data structure based on a linked list.

Many efficient Set implementations depend on the elements being Comparable (Section 8.4). We will therefore develop a class OrderedList for sets of such elements. An OrderedList is just like a LinkedList, except that:

1. The elements of an OrderedList must implement the Comparable interface.

2. The elements of an OrderedList are kept in order.

3. The OrderedList class implements the Set interface. It provides the methods `add()`, `contains()`, `remove()`, and `size()`. No duplicate elements are allowed.

The words "just like ... except" suggest that OrderedList might extend LinkedList (Figure 11–8). The problem with this approach is that the LinkedList class implements the List interface, which conflicts with the Set interface. Specifically, the `add()` method from the List interface should add the argument `target` to the *end* of the list, even if it *is* already present, while the `add()` method from the Set interface may add `target` at *any position*, but *not* if it is already present. Since the `add()` method in OrderedList would override the one in LinkedList, an OrderedList would behave like a Set. As far as the Java compiler could tell, however, it would be a legitimate value for a variable of type List, because it would be a descendant of LinkedList.

To see why this is a problem, suppose OrderedList extended LinkedList. If someone executed the code

```
List<String> livestock = new OrderedList<String>();
livestock.add("llama");
livestock.add("llama");
```

then they might expect `list.size()` to return 2—but it would return 1. A variable may be set to a reference to an object created very far away in the code (even in a different class), so this

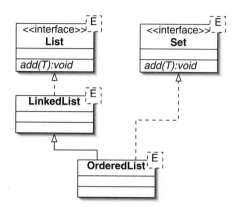

Figure 11-8: It would be a bad idea for OrderedList to extend LinkedList, because it would then have to provide two conflicting **add()** methods.

could lead to some extremely tricky bugs. We should extend a class only when an instance of the subclass works in place of an instance of the superclass.

Although we won't have OrderedList extend LinkedList, there's no reason not to cut and paste like crazy. Figure 11–9 shows the trivial parts of the OrderedList class. On line 2, the generic type E is constrained to be a Comparable type.

We now discuss the other three methods from the Set interface: contains(), add(), and remove(). This sequence will be followed for all three Set implementations in this chapter. Within each implementation, all three methods have very similar structures. This happens because, to add something to a Set, we must first find where it belongs, then (if it is not present) put it there. To remove something, we must first find where it belongs, then (if it is present) remove it. Since the final "put it there" and "remove it" operations take constant time, all three methods have the same order of running time for a given implementation.

```
1 /** A linked list of Comparable items, in increasing order. */
2 public class OrderedList<E extends Comparable<E>>
3   implements Set<E>, Predecessor<E> {
4
5   /** The first node in the list. */
6   private ListNode<E> front;
7
```

Figure 11-9: Trivial parts of the OrderedList class. The type specified by the type parameter E must be a Comparable type. (Part 1 of 2)

```
 8   /** An OrderedList is initially empty. */
 9   public OrderedList() {
10     front = null;
11   }
12
13   public ListNode<E> getNext() {
14     return front;
15   }
16
17   public void setNext(ListNode<E> next) {
18     front = next;
19   }
20
21   public int size() {
22     int tally = 0;
23     for (ListNode<E> node = front;
24          node != null;
25          node = node.getNext()) {
26       tally++;
27     }
28     return tally;
29   }
30
31   public String toString() {
32     String result = "( ";
33     for (ListNode<E> node = front;
34          node != null;
35          node = node.getNext()) {
36       result += node.getItem() + " ";
37     }
38     return result + ")";
39   }
40
41 }
```

Figure 11-9: Trivial parts of the OrderedList class. The type specified by the type parameter E must be a Comparable type. (Part 2 of 2)

A comment on terminology: some texts say things like, "An ordered list is a linear-time implementation of the set interface." This is a slight abuse of the terminology, because data structures don't have running times; algorithms do. A more precise statement would be, "In the ordered list implementation of the Set interface, the methods contains(), add(), and remove() all run in linear time."

Search

The contains() method for the OrderedList class (Figure 11–10) is a linear search. As in the linear search of a sorted array (Section 8.1), we can take advantage of the fact that the list elements are in order. If we find an element which is larger than target, we've gone too far and can immediately conclude that target is not in the list.

```
1 public boolean contains(E target) {
2   ListNode<E> node = front;
3   while (node != null) {
4     int comparison = target.compareTo(node.getItem());
5     if (comparison < 0) {
6       return false;
7     }
8     if (comparison == 0) {
9       return true;
10    }
11    node = node.getNext();
12  }
13  return false;
14 }
```

Figure 11-10: The main loop of the contains() method for the OrderedList class has three branches (lines 5–11), depending on the result of the comparison.

As with the linear search algorithm for arrays, this method runs in linear time in the worst case. In an average unsuccessful search, the number of comparisons made is roughly $n/2$, which is also linear.

Insertion

Insertion is slightly more complicated than search. Once we find an item which is larger than target, we have to splice in a new node containing target (Figure 11–11).

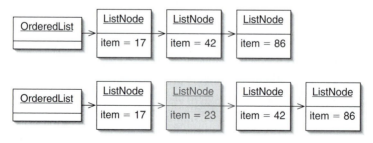

Figure 11-11: An OrderedList before (top) and after (bottom) inserting the element 23.

Since splicing in a new node requires knowledge of the previous node, this is a two-finger algorithm (Figure 11–12).

```
 1 public void add(E target) {
 2   Predecessor<E> prev = this;
 3   ListNode<E> node = front;
 4   while (node != null) {
 5     int comparison = target.compareTo(node.getItem());
 6     if (comparison < 0) {
 7       prev.setNext(new ListNode<E>(target, node));
 8       return;
 9     }
10     if (comparison == 0) {
11       return;
12     }
13     prev = node;
14     node = node.getNext();
15   }
16   prev.setNext(new ListNode<E>(target));
17 }
```

Figure 11-12: With the exception of the emphasized code, `add()` is identical to `contains()`.

Deletion

Deletion has the same structure (Figure 11–13), the only difference being that we remove `target` if we find it and do nothing if we don't.

```
 1 public void remove(E target) {
 2   Predecessor<E> prev = this;
 3   ListNode<E> node = front;
 4   while (node != null) {
 5     int comparison = target.compareTo(node.getItem());
 6     if (comparison < 0) {
 7       return;
 8     }
 9     if (comparison == 0) {
10       prev.setNext(node.getNext());
11       return;
12     }
13     prev = node;
14     node = node.getNext();
15   }
16 }
```

Figure 11-13: The `remove()` method.

The OrderedList data structure is easy to implement, but it requires linear time for search, insertion, and deletion. We will see more efficient data structures in the next two sections. OrderedLists should be used only for very small sets.

Exercises

11.4   In the constructor for the Anagrams class (Figure 11–7, line 14), the add() method is invoked many times on the Set words. If words is an OrderedList, under what circumstances will this take the largest possible amount of time (for a given number of words *n*)? Is this likely to occur?

11.5   Is it acceptable to swap lines 5–7 and 8–10 in Figure 11–10? Explain.

11.3 Binary Search Trees

We now turn to a second implementation of the Set interface, which is more efficient under some circumstances. A *binary search tree* is a binary tree in which all of the items in the left subtree are less than the root and all of the items in the right subtree are greater than the root. The subtrees are themselves binary search trees. An example is shown in Figure 11–14.

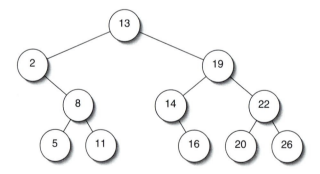

Figure 11–14: In a binary search tree, numbers less than the root are in the left subtree, while numbers greater than the root are in the right subtree. The subtrees are themselves binary search trees.

We use the linked representation of binary trees from Section 10.1. Like an instance of the Questions class from Chapter 10, a (non-empty) BinarySearchTree object contains (a reference to) a BinaryNode (Figure 11–15). This may in turn contain additional BinaryNodes—the roots of its subtrees.

The easy parts of the BinarySearchTree class are given in Figure 11–16. Like the OrderedList class, this is suitable only for Sets of Comparable objects.

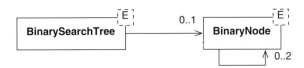

Figure 11–15: A BinarySearchTree instance usually contains a BinaryNode, which can contain further BinaryNodes.

```
 1 /** A binary search tree of Comparables. */
 2 public class BinarySearchTree<E extends Comparable<E>>
 3   implements Set<E> {
 4
 5   /** Root node. */
 6   private BinaryNode<E> root;
 7
 8   /** A BinarySearchTree is initially empty. */
 9   public BinarySearchTree() {
10     root = null;
11   }
12
13   public int size() {
14     return size(root);
15   }
16
17   /** Return the size of the subtree rooted at node. */
18   protected int size(BinaryNode<E> node) {
19     if (node == null) {
20       return 0;
21     } else {
22       return 1 + size(node.getLeft()) + size(node.getRight());
23     }
24   }
25
26 }
```

Figure 11–16: Easy parts of the BinarySearchTree class. Like many tree-related methods, the `size()` method is recursive.

Search

The advantage of a binary search tree is that we may have to look at very few of the items in the tree to determine whether some target is present (Figure 11–17). We start by comparing the target to the root. Depending on the result of this comparison, we either descend to the left child, declare success, or descend to the right child. The search fails only if we try to descend to a non-existent child—for example, we try to go right when there is no right child.

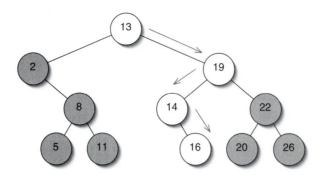

Figure 11-17: Successful search for 16 in a binary search tree. The shaded nodes are never examined.

The code for the `contains()` method (Figure 11–18) is similar to the version from the OrderedList class. As we examine each node, we decide what to do next based on the result of comparing `target` with the item in the current node.

```
1 public boolean contains(E target) {
2    BinaryNode<E> node = root;
3    while (node != null) {
4       int comparison = target.compareTo(node.getItem());
5       if (comparison < 0) {      // Go left
6          node = node.getLeft();
7       } else if (comparison == 0) { // Found it
8          return true;
9       } else {                   // Go right
10         node = node.getRight();
11      }
12   }
13   return false;
14 }
```

Figure 11-18: On each pass through the main loop, the `contains()` method checks whether `target` is less than, equal to, or greater than the item in `node`.

Searching a binary search tree is often much faster than searching an ordered list, because the number of comparisons we have to make is not proportional to the number of nodes in the tree, but merely to the *height of the tree*. In a perfect tree, this is $\Theta(\log n)$.

Unfortunately, binary search trees are generally not perfect. In the worst case, each internal node has only one child. This happens in the Anagrams program when the word file is in alphabetical order: every new node is a right child. When this happens, search takes linear time.

While the analysis is beyond the scope of this book, it turns out that *on average* (assuming items are inserted in random order and there are no deletions), the running times of `contains()`, `add()`, and `remove()` for binary search trees are all in $\Theta(\log n)$.

Insertion

When we insert something into a binary search tree, we must first search for it. We have to make a change only if the search fails. This means that we have just tried to descend into a null child. All we have to do is add a new leaf node at that position (Figure 11–19).

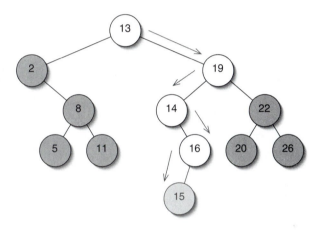

Figure 11–19: Inserting 15 into a binary search tree. The search fails when 16 has no left child, so we add a new leaf there.

There are two complications to the code:

- Once we reach a null node, we have forgotten how we got there. Since we need to modify either the `left` or `right` field in the parent of the new leaf, we'll need this information.

- We need to deal with the situation in which the binary search tree is empty.

These are the same problems we had when adding an element to the end of a LinkedList (Section 6.3). The solution is also the same. We define an interface Parent (Figure 11–20), which is implemented by both the BinaryNode and BinarySearchTree classes. Where the Predecessor interface had a `setNext()` method, the Parent interface has a `setChild()` method. The first argument to `setChild()` is an int specifying which child to set. The comment defines the meaning of this int in such a way that we can use the result of an invocation of `compareTo()` to determine which child to set.

The implementations of these methods for the BinaryNode class are trivial (Figure 11–21).

```
 1 /**
 2  * Something which has children, such as a BinarySearchTree or a
 3  * BinaryNode.
 4  */
 5 public interface Parent<E> {
 6
 7   /**
 8    * Return the left child if direction < 0, or the right child
 9    * otherwise.
10    */
11   public BinaryNode<E> getChild(int direction);
12
13   /**
14    * Replace the specified child of this parent with the new child.
15    * If direction < 0, replace the left child.  Otherwise, replace
16    * the right child.
17    */
18   public void setChild(int direction, BinaryNode<E> child);
19
20 }
```

Figure 11-20: Both the BinaryNode and BinarySearchTree classes must be modified to implement the Parent interface.

```
 1 public BinaryNode<E> getChild(int direction) {
 2   if (direction < 0) {
 3     return left;
 4   } else {
 5     return right;
 6   }
 7 }
 8
 9 public void setChild(int direction, BinaryNode<E> child) {
10   if (direction < 0) {
11     left = child;
12   } else {
13     right = child;
14   }
15 }
```

Figure 11-21: The getChild() and setChild() methods for the BinaryNode class.

The versions for the BinarySearchTree class are even simpler (Figure 11–22). Since there is only one "child" (the root of the tree), the argument direction is ignored.

With the Parent interface in place, we can write the two-finger method add() (Figure 11–23). If we reach line 17 and have to create a new node, comparison is the direction we last moved.

```
1 public BinaryNode<E> getChild(int direction) {
2   return root;
3 }
4
5 public void setChild(int direction, BinaryNode<E> child) {
6   root = child;
7 }
```

Figure 11-22: The getChild() and setChild() methods for the BinarySearchTree class.

```
1 public void add(E target) {
2   Parent<E> parent = this;
3   BinaryNode<E> node = root;
4   int comparison = 0;
5   while (node != null) {
6     comparison = target.compareTo(node.getItem());
7     if (comparison < 0) {        // Go left
8       parent = node;
9       node = node.getLeft();
10    } else if (comparison == 0) { // It's already here
11      return;
12    } else {                      // Go right
13      parent = node;
14      node = node.getRight();
15    }
16  }
17  parent.setChild(comparison, new BinaryNode<E>(target));
18 }
```

Figure 11-23: As with the OrderedList class, the add() method for the Binary-SearchTree class is a two-finger algorithm.

Deletion

As is usual for Set implementations, the remove() method is the most complicated. The challenge is to make sure the tree is still a binary search tree when we're done with the deletion.

We begin with a search. If it succeeds, we need to get rid of the node containing target.

If the offending node is a leaf, this is easy—we just replace the appropriate reference in the parent with null.

If the node has only one child, we just splice it out much as we would a node in a linked list (Figure 11-24). The one child of the node being removed takes its place. Since all nodes in this subtree are less than the parent of the removed node, the binary search tree is still valid.

The complicated case is when the node we want to delete has *two* children. We can't just splice it out, because then we would be trying to plug in two children where there is room for only one.

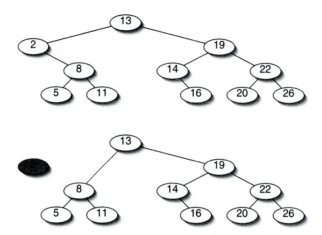

Figure 11-24: Before (top) and after (bottom) deleting 2 from a binary search tree. The deleted node's child 8 becomes a child of the deleted node's parent 13.

Instead, we find some other node which does not have two children, copy the item at that node into this one, and delete the other node (Figure 11–25).

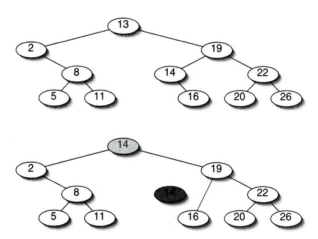

Figure 11-25: Before (top) and after (bottom) deleting 13 from a binary search tree. The node to be deleted has two children, so we can't just splice it out. Instead, we replace its item with the item from another node (14) and delete *that* node.

We must be very careful about which node we choose to delete so that the tree will still be a binary search tree. It is always safe to choose the *inorder successor* of the node we originally wanted to delete. This is the node that would appear next in an inorder traversal of the tree. We can always find a node's inorder successor by going to the right child, then going left until we hit a node with no left child. The inorder successor is not necessarily a leaf—it can have a right child, it just can't have a left child.

It is safe to replace the node we want to delete with its inorder successor because the inorder successor is the leftmost element in the right subtree. It is therefore larger than anything in the left subtree and smaller than anything else in the right subtree.

The `remove()` method (Figure 11–26) is another two-finger algorithm. If we find `target`, we need to modify `parent`, rather than `node`. We therefore need to remember the direction we moved when we left `parent`.

```
1 public void remove(E target) {
2   Parent<E> parent = this;
3   BinaryNode<E> node = root;
4   int direction = 0;
5   while (node != null) {
6     int comparison = target.compareTo(node.getItem());
7     if (comparison < 0) {      // Go left
8       parent = node;
9       node = node.getLeft();
10    } else if (comparison == 0) { // Found it
11      spliceOut(node, parent, direction);
12      return;
13    } else {                   // Go right
14      parent = node;
15      node = node.getRight();
16    }
17    direction = comparison;
18  }
19 }
```

Figure 11–26: The `remove()` method for the BinarySearchTree class.

If target is discovered, `remove()` invokes `spliceOut()` (Figure 11–27). The first two cases (lines 9–12) deal with nodes that do not have two children. For example, if `node` has no left child (lines 9–10), `node`'s right child replaces `node` as a child of `parent`.

We don't need special code for the case where node is a leaf, because in this situation

`parent.setChild(direction, node.getRight());`

is equivalent to:

`parent.setChild(direction, null);`

When `node` has two children (lines 13–15), `spliceOut()` invokes `removeLeftmost()` (Figure 11–28). This both removes the leftmost node in the right subtree (the inorder successor) and returns the item from that node, which `spliceOut()` then installs in the node which was originally to be deleted.

```
 1 /**
 2  * Remove node, which is a child of parent.  Direction is positive
 3  * if node is the right child of parent, negative if it is the
 4  * left child.
 5  */
 6 protected void spliceOut(BinaryNode<E> node,
 7                          Parent<E> parent,
 8                          int direction) {
 9   if (node.getLeft() == null) {
10     parent.setChild(direction, node.getRight());
11   } else if (node.getRight() == null) {
12     parent.setChild(direction, node.getLeft());
13   } else {
14     node.setItem(removeLeftmost(node.getRight(), node));
15   }
16 }
```

Figure 11-27: The method `spliceOut()` removes an individual node. If the node has two children, it invokes `removeLeftmost()`.

```
 1 /**
 2  * Remove the leftmost descendant of node and return the
 3  * item contained in the removed node.
 4  */
 5 protected E removeLeftmost(BinaryNode<E> node, Parent<E> parent) {
 6   int direction = 1;
 7   while (node.getLeft() != null) {
 8     parent = node;
 9     direction = -1;
10     node = node.getLeft();
11   }
12   E result = node.getItem();
13   spliceOut(node, parent, direction);
14   return result;
15 }
```

Figure 11-28: The method `removeLeftmost()` both modifies the BinarySearchTree (removing a node) and returns a value (the item in that node).

BinarySearchTrees should not be used in the plain form explained here. While the average running time for search, insertion, and deletion is logarithmic, the worst-case running time is linear. This worst case occurs if the data are already in order (or in reverse order), causing the tree to be linear. Such data sets are not uncommon. Specifically, the file of legal words for the Anagrams game is probably in alphabetical order, so a BinarySearchTree is no better than an OrderedList.

In Chapters 14 and 17, we will see variations on binary search trees that guarantee logarithmic performance in the worst case.

Exercises

11.6   Expand the definition of a binary search tree to include the possibility of duplicate items.

11.7   Why is it necessary to declare the variable `comparison` outside the `while` loop in `add()` (Figure 11–23), but not in `contains()` (Figure 11–18) or `remove()` (Figure 11–26)?

11.8   When an element is added to a binary search tree, a new node is added as a child of an existing node. Before the addition, was this existing node always, sometimes, or never a leaf? Explain.

11.9   In the worst case, searching a binary search tree takes linear time. Can this happen when performing a binary search (Section 8.2) on a sorted array? Explain.

11.10   Suppose a binary search tree is balanced in the sense that the left and right subtrees have the same height. Could deleting the root cause the tree to become imbalanced with the left side taller than the right side? With the right side taller? How would search time for the tree be affected if there were many deletions?

11.11   In `remove()`, would it be acceptable to replace a node with its inorder *predecessor* instead of its inorder *successor*? Explain.

11.4 Hash Tables

The third and final implementation of the Set interface presented in this chapter is the hash table. Before explaining hash tables proper, we take a brief detour to write the LetterCollection class for the Anagrams game.

Direct Addressing

A LetterCollection is, not surprisingly, a collection of letters. Put another way, it requires that we know how many of each letter are in the collection. Since there are only 26 different letters, this does not require a data structure as complicated as an ordered list or a binary search tree. All we need is an array of 26 ints, one for each letter (Figure 11–29). It is also handy to keep track of the total number of letters in the collection.

If we want to know, for example, how many 'd's are in a LetterCollection, we look at the appropriate element of the array `tiles`. To find the index, we take advantage of the fact that, in Java, we can do arithmetic on chars. If we have a char `letter`, the index we want is `letter - 'a'`. This expression gives 0 if `letter` is `'a'`, 1 if it is `'b'`, and so on.

The code is given in Figure 11–30. When invoked with the argument `true`, the constructor creates a LetterCollection containing letters in proportion to their frequency in English text. For example, there are 50 'e's, but only 3 'q's.

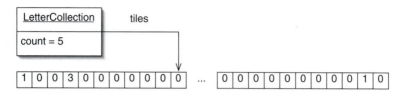

Figure 11-29: UML instance diagram of a LetterCollection containing one `'a'`, three `'d'`s, and one `'y'`. While there isn't room to show it, the array has 26 elements.

```
1 /** Collection of letters for use in Anagrams. */
2 public class LetterCollection {
3
4   /** Total number of letters. */
5   private int count;
6
7   /**
8    * Number of each letter.  For example, tiles[0] is the number of
9    * 'a's.
10   */
11  private int[] tiles;
12
13  /**
14   * If full is true, there are 416 letters, with more copies of
15   * more common letters like 'e'.  Otherwise, the new
16   * LetterCollection is empty.
17   */
18  public LetterCollection(boolean full) {
19    if (full) {
20      tiles = new int[] {29, 5, 12, 16, 50, 9, 8, 20, 28,
21                         4, 5, 16, 9, 30, 28, 8, 3, 30,
22                         24, 36, 14, 8, 8, 4, 9, 3};
23      count = 416;
24    } else {
25      tiles = new int[26];      // All zeroes
26      count = 0;
27    }
28  }
29
```

Figure 11-30: The LetterCollection class. (Part 1 of 2)

```
30    /** Add a single letter to this LetterCollection. */
31    public void add(char letter) {
32      tiles[letter - 'a']++;
33      count++;
34    }
35
36    /** Add each letter in word to this LetterCollection. */
37    public void add(String word) {
38      for (char c : word.toCharArray()) {
39        tiles[c - 'a']++;
40      }
41      count += word.length();
42    }
43
44    /** Remove and return a random letter. */
45    public char draw() {
46      int rand = (int)(Math.random() * count);
47      for (int i = 0; i < 26; i++) {
48        if (rand < tiles[i]) {
49          tiles[i]--;
50          count--;
51          return (char)('a' + i);
52        } else {
53          rand -= tiles[i];
54        }
55      }
56      return '?';                      // This should never happen
57    }
58
59    /** Remove each letter in word from this LetterCollection. */
60    public void remove(String word) {
61      for (char c : word.toCharArray()) {
62        tiles[c - 'a']--;
63      }
64      count -= word.length();
65    }
66
67    public String toString() {
68      String result = "";
69      for (int i = 0; i < 26; i++) {
70        for (int j = 0; j < tiles[i]; j++) {
71          result += (char)('a' + i);
72        }
73      }
74      return result;
75    }
76
77 }
```

Figure 11-30: The LetterCollection class. (Part 2 of 2)

On lines 38–40 and 60–62, we use enhanced `for` loops to traverse Strings. Strings do not support enhanced `for` loops (an apparent oversight in Java 1.5), but arrays of chars do, so we use the `toCharArray()` method in the String class.

We could use a similar data structure to represent a *set* of chars. Remember that the difference between a set and a collection is that the same item cannot appear more than once in the same set. Instead of an array of ints, then, we would need only an array of booleans.

In either case, this approach is called **direct addressing**. When we want to look up some element, we go directly to the appropriate place in the array. Direct addressing should be used wherever it is applicable, because it is incredibly fast: looking up an element takes constant time.

Hash Functions and Hash Codes

Unfortunately, direct addressing cannot be used for every set. The first problem is that the set of possible elements might be vastly larger than the set of elements actually stored. For example, suppose an employer is storing a set of employee Social Security numbers. There are a billion possible nine-digit Social Security numbers, but no company has anywhere near this many employees. A direct addressing table would be a huge waste of space.

This problem is solved using a **hash function**. This is a function which takes an int as input and returns an array index. For example, we might use the function $f(x) = x$ mod 10. Figure 11–31 shows several three-digit numbers stored in an array of length 10. If we want to store 526 in the array, we put it at position 526 mod 10 = 6. We store the number there, rather than merely a boolean value of `true`, because more than one number "hashes to" this position.

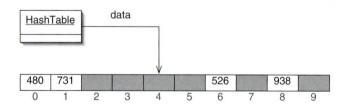

Figure 11–31: In a hash table, a hash function maps each potential element to an array index. The shaded positions do not contain set elements; in practice, some invalid value such as –1 or `null` is stored there.

This design, called a **hash table**, appears to have all of the advantages of direct addressing, even though it works when the number of possible elements is much larger than the number of elements actually stored. There are, of course, some complications.

First, the elements to be stored might not be integers. Most of the built-in classes of which we are likely to store Sets (String, Integer, Double, etc.) have a method `hashCode()` which takes no arguments and returns an int which can be passed to a hash function. This int is called the **hash code**.

The hashCode() method must return the same value for two objects which are equals(). The converse is not true, though: if a.hashCode() == b.hashCode(), it does not follow that a.equals(b). Sometimes two different, nonidentical objects have the same hash code.

If we want to store instances of one of our own classes in a hash table, we must define both equals() and hashCode(). This is necessary because the hash table Set methods use hash-Code() to find the right position in the table, then use equals() to verify that the item at that position is the one we're looking for. If these methods don't provide consistent results, the hash table might give an incorrect result when asked if some object is in the Set.

Different objects sometimes produce the same hash code. Furthermore, even if they didn't, the hash function might occasionally map two different hash codes to the same index. For example, 37 mod 10 = 87 mod 10. This is called a *collision*.

We try to choose a hash function which makes collisions rare. If our hash codes tend to be even numbers, then $f(x) = x$ mod 10 is a bad hash function, because more elements will be put at the even positions than at the odd positions. A better choice is $f(x) = x$ mod s, where s is some prime number. This tends to disrupt any patterns in the data. This is where the data structure gets its name: "to hash" means "to chop up and mix around."

No matter how good our hash function is, collisions cannot be completely avoided. Since there are more potential elements than positions in the table, some elements *must* hash to the same location. This is the *pigeonhole principle*: if there are n pigeonholes and more than n pigeons, at least one hole will have more than one pigeon. We now discuss a number of techniques for dealing with collisions.

Collision Resolution

The first approach, called *chaining*, is to keep a sequence of ListNodes (effectively an ordered list) at each position in the table (Figure 11–32). To search, insert, or delete, we simply use the hash function to find the right list and then perform the appropriate ordered list operation there.

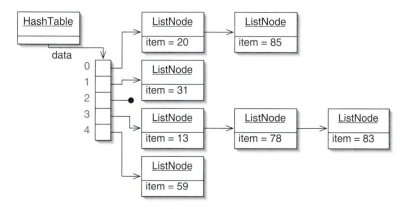

Figure 11–32: In a hash table with chaining, each position in the array contains an ordered list of elements that hash to that index.

If we know in advance how many elements the Set contains (n), we can choose the array length to be proportional to this—say, $2n$. This limits the average number of elements per list to a constant, in this case 1/2. While all of the data could end up in the same list if we were very unlucky with our hash function, the *average* time for search, insertion, and deletion is $\Theta(1)$. This is an astounding result: the time to perform a search is *independent of the size of the set*!

Chaining works, but all of the references involved in such a linked structure take up considerable space. The two remaining collision resolution techniques avoid this by storing all of the elements directly in the array. This is called **open addressing**. While the analysis is beyond the scope of this book, hash tables using open addressing have performance in the same order as hash tables using chaining.

The first open addressing technique is **linear probing** (Figure 11–33). If there is a collision during insertion, we simply move on to the next unoccupied position. If this would move us past the end of the array, we wrap around to the beginning.

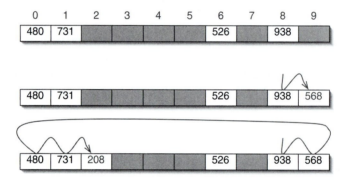

Figure 11-33: Linear probing. For simplicity, only the array is shown here. The original array is at the top. When 568 is inserted (middle), it hashes to position 8, which is occupied, so the next position is used. When 208 is inserted (bottom), positions 8, 9, 0, and 1 must be tried before the empty position 2 is found.

There are three problems with linear probing:

- The table can fill up. With chaining, if we underestimate the number of elements in the set, the lists get longer and search is slower. With linear probing, the hash table fails catastrophically: when there's no more room, we simply can't insert any more elements.

  We can solve this problem by **rehashing** when the table gets too full. Rehashing is copying all of the elements into a fresh table. If we make the new table larger, as we did with our ArrayList class, the new table is not full.

- We can't simply remove an item to delete it. In Figure 11–33, suppose we removed 480 and then searched for 208. We would hit an unoccupied position and incorrectly conclude that 208 is not in the table.

We get around this problem by replacing a deleted item with a special value `deleted`. This is neither `null` nor is it `equals()` to any target, so searches continue past it. This in turn creates another problem: the table may become full of `deleted`s, with very few actual data elements. This, too, can be solved by occasionally rehashing.

- *Clusters* of contiguous occupied positions tend to occur and grow (Figure 11–34). Once a cluster appears, an element which hashes to a position in the cluster may result in a linear search to the end of the cluster. Worse, an insertion into any position in a cluster expands the cluster.

Figure 11–34: Linear probing can result in clusters. In this table, the shaded positions are unoccupied. Any new element is 25% likely to end up in the large cluster near the right end, which both slows down search and expands the cluster.

The problem of clustering is reduced by a second open addressing technique, ***double hashing***. In double hashing, we use *two* hash functions. The first function tells us where to look first, while the second one tells us how many positions to skip each time we find an occupied one (Figure 11–35). If we choose our two hash functions well, two elements which originally hash to the same position are unlikely to follow the same *sequence* of positions through the table. This reduces the risk of clustering. Note that linear probing is a special case of double hashing, where the second hash function always returns 1.

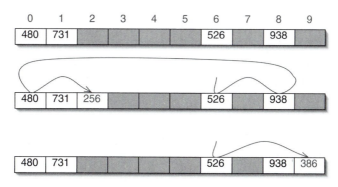

Figure 11–35: Double hashing reduces clustering. In this table, the first hash function is $f(x) = x \bmod 10$ and the second hash function is $g(x) = \lfloor x/100 \rfloor$. When 256 is inserted, we first look in position 6 and then every 2 positions thereafter. When 386 is inserted, we again start at position 6, but then proceed 3 positions at a time.

It is crucial that the size of the table and the number returned by the second hash function be ***relatively prime***—that is, have no factors in common other than 1. To see why, suppose we have an array of length 10 and the second hash function returns 5. A search that begins at position 7 will go to position 2, then back to 7. Only two positions are checked before the algorithm gives up and incorrectly concludes that the table is full!

The easiest way to ensure relative primality is to make the table size a power of two, then require that the second hash function always returns an odd number.

We now present an implementation of hash tables using double hashing. The basics are shown in (Figure 11–36). The constructor requires some instance of the generic type E to use for `deleted`. In the hash functions, we have to use the absolute value function `Math.abs()` because `hashCode()` is not guaranteed to return a nonnegative number and % does not work as modulo if its first argument is negative.

```
1 /** A hash table of Comparables, using double hashing. */
2 public class HashTable<E> implements Set<E> {
3
4   /**
5    * Special object to indicate a slot previously occupied by a
6    * Comparable.
7    */
8   private E deleted;
9
10  /** Comparables stored in this table. */
11  private E[] data;
12
13  /** Number of occupied slots (including deleteds). */
14  private int fullness;
15
16  /**
17   * A HashTable is initially empty, but an initial capacity may
18   * be specified.
19   */
20  public HashTable(E deleted) {
21    data = (E[])(new Object[1]); // All null; compiler warning
22    fullness = 0;
23    this.deleted = deleted;
24  }
25
26  /** First hash function. */
27  protected int hash1(E target) {
28    return Math.abs(target.hashCode()) % data.length;
29  }
30
```

Figure 11–36: Easy parts of the HashTable class. (Part 1 of 2)

```
31   /** Second hash function. */
32   protected int hash2(E target) {
33     int result = Math.abs(target.hashCode()) % (data.length - 1);
34     if (result % 2 == 0) { return result + 1; }
35     return result;
36   }
37
38   public int size() {
39     int tally = 0;
40     for (E item : data) {
41       if ((item != null) && (item != deleted)) {
42         tally++;
43       }
44     }
45     return tally;
46   }
47
48 }
```

Figure 11-36: Easy parts of the HashTable class. (Part 2 of 2)

Search

To search (Figure 11–37), we use hash1() to decide where to start. If this position is occupied by something other than `target`, we use hash2() to decide how many positions to skip ahead. This continues until we get back to the beginning, find a null slot, or find `target`.

```
 1 public boolean contains(E target) {
 2   int start = hash1(target);
 3   int i = start;
 4   while (data[i] != null) {
 5     if (target.equals(data[i])) {
 6       return true;
 7     }
 8     i = (i + hash2(target)) % data.length;
 9     if (i == start) {
10       return false;
11     }
12   }
13   return false;
14 }
```

Figure 11-37: The contains() method.

Insertion

Insertion (Figure 11–38) is almost identical to search, followed if necessary by installing `target`. It may also be necessary to rehash. In our implementation, if the table is at least half full (including `deleted`s), we rehash into a larger table before inserting. As in our ArrayList class, we double the capacity of the table when we stretch it, so the amortized time for rehashing is still constant.

```
1 public void add(E target) {
2   if (fullness >= data.length / 2) {
3     rehash();
4   }
5   int start = hash1(target);
6   int i = start;
7   while (data[i] != null) {
8     if (target.equals(data[i])) {
9       return;
10    }
11    i = (i + hash2(target)) % data.length;
12    if (i == start) {
13      return;
14    }
15  }
16  data[i] = target;
17  fullness++;
18 }
19
20 /**
21  * Copy all of the elements into a new array twice as large.
22  */
23 public void rehash() {
24   HashTable<E> newTable = new HashTable<E>(deleted);
25   newTable.data = (E[])(new Object[data.length * 2]);
26   for (int i = 0; i < data.length; i++) {
27     if ((data[i] != null) && (data[i] != deleted)) {
28       newTable.add((E)(data[i]));
29     }
30   }
31   data = newTable.data;
32   fullness = newTable.fullness;
33 }
```

Figure 11–38: The add() and rehash() methods.

Deletion

In `remove()` (Figure 11–39), we replace `target` with `deleted` if we find it.

Where applicable, hash tables are far and away the best Set implementation. The average running times for search, insertion, and deletion are constant. The worst case is linear, but this is not nearly as likely to occur with hash tables as it is with binary search trees.

```
 1 public void remove(E target) {
 2   int start = hash1(target);
 3   int i = start;
 4   while (data[i] != null) {
 5     if (target.equals(data[i])) {
 6       data[i] = deleted;
 7       return;
 8     }
 9     i = (i + hash2(target)) % data.length;
10     if (i == start) {
11       return;
12     }
13   }
14 }
```

Figure 11-39: The remove() method.

There are only two drawbacks to hash tables. First, traversal is not efficient. Visiting all of the elements requires a search through the entire table, which is presumably mostly empty. This takes time proportional to the capacity of the table, not to the number of elements. Second, with open addressing, deletion is a bit awkward; we have to leave behind a special value deleted and occasionally rehash. A hash table may not be the best Set implementation to use in an application where many deletions are expected.

Exercises

11.12   Analyze the worst-case running times of the methods in the LetterCollection class. Give your results in terms of n, the size of the set, and (where appropriate) w, the length of the word involved.

11.13   Consider two instances a and b of some class. If a.hashCode() == b.hashCode(), does it follow that a.compareTo(b) == 0? What about vice versa? Explain.

11.14   Why can't we simply use

```
public int size() {
   return fullness;
}
```

for the size() method in the HashTable class?

11.15   What would happen if someone invoked add(null) on a HashTable as defined in this section? Write an assertion to prevent this.

11.16   We need to use the special values null and deleted to keep track of unoccupied positions in the table. Devise and explain another way to keep track of these things, so that we could store `null` as a member of the Set and we wouldn't need to specify a value for `deleted` when invoking the constructor.

11.17   Which approach would have better cache performance: chaining or open addressing? Explain.

11.18   Modify the code in Figure 11–36 so that the HashTable uses linear probing instead of double hashing. (Hint: Only one method has to be modified.)

11.19   Assuming a good `hashCode()` method and a good hash function, an element chosen at random is equally like to hash to any position in the table. What is the probability that two elements chosen at random hash to the same location?

11.20   Suppose we perform 1,000 insertions followed by 900 deletions in a HashTable as defined in this section, then rehash. In what sense is the resulting data structure inefficient?

11.21   The HashTable class defined in this section can store only Comparable objects, because it implements the Set interface. What would we have to change to allow a HashTable to store objects of any class? Would this same idea work for the OrderedList and Binary-Search classes? Explain.

11.5 The Java Collections Framework Again

We now return to the Java collections framework, which has been discussed in Section 5.5 and 6.4. In the java.util package, the interface Collection is extended by an interface Set (Figure 11–40), which is similar to the one we defined in Section 11.1. An implementation of either of these interfaces holds a number of elements. The difference between a collection and a set is that the same element may appear more than once in a collection, but not in a set. ("The same" is defined in terms of the `equals()` method.)

The Set interface is extended by SortedSet. This interface is intended for sets where the elements have some ordering. Usually this means that the elements implement Comparable. (It is possible to store non-Comparable elements by defining a "Comparator," but this is beyond the scope of this book.)

Two nonabstract classes implement the Set interface: HashSet and TreeSet. A HashSet is very much like the HashTable we defined in Section 11.4. A TreeSet is similar to the Binary-SearchTree we defined in Section 11.3, but it uses some advanced techniques (to be discussed in Chapter 14) to guarantee that search, insertion, and deletion take time in O(log n) even in the worst case.

Maps

It is often necessary to associate members of one class with members of another. For example, in a dictionary, words are associated with definitions. In the Java collections framework, the Map interface defines this functionality. In a Map, each of a set of *keys* is associated with a

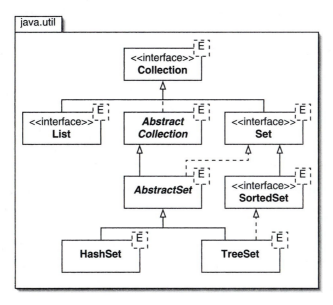

Figure 11-40: More of the Java collections framework, with emphasis on descendants of the Set interface.

value. In the dictionary example, the words are keys and their definitions are values. Each key may appear only once in a Map, although it is possible for several keys to be associated with the same value.

The Map interface requires the methods `put()` and `get()` for installing key-value pairs and for looking up the value associated with a key. For example, if we execute the code

```
Map<String, Integer> numbers = new TreeMap<String, Integer>();
numbers.put("five", 5);
numbers.put("twelve", 12);
numbers.put("a dozen", 12);
```

then `numbers.get("twelve")` returns the Integer 12, as does `numbers.get("a dozen")`.

The data structures for Maps are the same as those used for Sets, with a small amount of extra work needed to keep track of the values in addition to the keys. The inheritance hierarchy for descendants of the Map interface is almost identical to that for descendants of Set (Figure 11–41). It is necessary for each class to have *two* generic types: one for the type of the keys and another for the type of the values.

The API description of the Map class mentions the class Map.Entry. (The name is strange because this is an "inner class" of Map. Inner classes are beyond the scope of this book.) A Map.Entry holds one key and one value. We can get the Set of Map.Entry instances from a Map by invoking the method `entrySet()` on the Map.

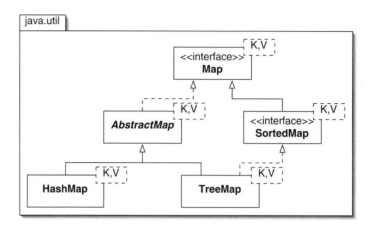

Figure 11-41: The Map interface and its descendants.

Exercises

11.22   Read the API documentation for the HashMap class. Speculate on whether HashMap uses chaining or open addressing.

11.23   Suppose we have a program that uses square roots, but often takes the square roots of the same numbers over and over again. We can speed it up by storing a Map associating values with their square roots. Every time the square root of some number is taken, we first consult the Map. If the number is present, we return the stored result rather than recomputing it. If not, we compute the square root (using Math.sqrt()), store the association in the Map, and return the result. This technique is called *memoization*. Write a method memoizedSqrt() that behaves as described. The Map must be a field in the class containing the method, not a variable within the method.

Summary

A set is a collection of objects containing no duplicates. We have discussed three implementations of our Set interface: OrderedList, BinarySearchTree, and HashTable. The performance of various Set implementations is summarized in Figure 11–42.

An ordered list is a linked list in which the elements are in order. It should be used only for very small sets.

A binary search tree is a binary tree where all of the elements in the left subtree are less than the root and all of the elements in the right subtree are greater than the root. While its average performance is good, it performs very poorly when the data are already sorted—a common situation.

Set Implementation	Average	Worst Case	Notes
ordered list	$\Theta(n)$	$\Theta(n)$	
binary search tree	$\Theta(\log n)$	$\Theta(n)$	
hash table	$\Theta(1)$	$\Theta(n)$	Worst case unlikely.
red-black tree	$O(\log n)$	$O(\log n)$	Section 14.4.
B-tree	$O(\log n)$ disk accesses	$O(\log n)$ disk accesses	Section 17.4. Used only for extremely large sets.

Figure 11–42: Running times for search, insertion, and deletion using various Set implementations.

A hash table stores elements in an array, using a hash function to determine where in the array to place each element. Since there are more potential elements than positions in the array, collisions can occur. Three approaches to collision resolution are chaining, linear probing, and double hashing. Hash tables have extremely good performance on average, and the worst case is not likely to occur. Hash tables are the best Set implementation except where traversal or deletion is a common operation.

The Java collections framework defines a Set interface, implemented by TreeSet and HashSet. There is also a Map interface for associating keys with values, implemented by TreeMap and HashMap.

Vocabulary

binary search tree. Binary tree in which all of the items in the left subtree are less than the root and all of the items in the right subtree are greater than the root. The subtrees are themselves binary search trees.

chaining. Collision resolution technique in which a linked list is kept for each position in the hash table.

clustering. In a hash table, phenomenon where many consecutive positions are occupied.

collision. Event of two elements mapping to the same position in a hash table.

direct addressing. Technique of maintaining an array indexed by the elements in a set or collection.

double hashing. Open addressing technique in which a second hash function indicates how many positions to skip ahead each time an occupied position is found.

hash code. Integer passed to a hash function. Usually generated by an object's `hashCode()` method.

hash function. Function mapping hash codes to table indices.

hash table. Set implementation similar to a direct addressing table. To find the proper position for an element, the element's hash code is passed to a hash function.

inorder successor. Next node in the inorder traversal of a tree. A node's inorder successor is the leftmost (and hence smallest) element in its right subtree.

key. Item associated with a value in a Map. Each key may appear only once, but more than one key may be associated with the same value.

linear probing. Open addressing technique in which, if a position is occupied, search continues to the following position.

memoization. Technique of storing previously-computed values so that they may be looked up later (Exercise 11.23).

open addressing. Any collision resolution technique, such as linear probing or double hashing, in which all of the elements are stored directly in the hash table.

ordered list. Set implemented as a linked list with the elements in increasing order.

pigeonhole principle. Principle that, if more than *n* elements are being distributed into *n* sets, at least one set must contain more than one element.

rehash. In a hash table, store all of the elements in a new table.

relatively prime. Of two integers, having no factors other than 1 in common.

set. Collection in which the same element does not appear more than once.

value. Item associated with a key in a Map.

Problems

11.24   Modify the Anagrams program so that anywhere from 2 to 6 people can play.

11.25   Implement the Set interface using an ordered version of an ArrayList.

11.26   Add a method `addAll()` to our Set interface (Figure 11–4). This should accept another Set as an argument and add all of the elements of that Set to this one. (For the mathematically minded, `addAll()` turns this Set into the union of the two Sets.) Implement this method for all three Set implementations in this chapter.

11.27   Add a method `retainAll()` to our Set interface (Figure 11–4). This should accept another Set as an argument and remove all elements of this Set which are not in that one. (For the mathematically minded, this turns this Set into the intersection of the two Sets.) Implement this method for all three Set implementations in this chapter.

Projects

11.28   Write an UnorderedList class which implements our Set interface but does not require that its generic type is Comparable.

11.29   Implement hash tables using chaining.

11.30   Implement the game of Geography (Figure 11–43). Your implementation should allow any number of people to play against the computer. You should be able to find a good list of city names by searching the web for files called `cities.txt`.

Geography

Players: 2 or more.

Object: To be the last player eliminated.

Play: The first player names a city. The next player then names another city which starts with the letter at the end of the previous city name. For example, the first player might say, 'Portland,' the next player 'Denver,' the next 'Raleigh,' and so on.

Elimination: A player is eliminated if she can't think of a suitable city or if she names a city that has already been used in the current game.

Figure 11–43: The game of Geography is a good way to pass the time on long voyages.

Advanced Topics

V

12

Advanced Linear Structures

This chapter covers some advanced techniques for using linear structures. Section 12.1 introduces bit vectors, an extension of the idea of direct addressing from Section 11.4. Bit vectors are used in an application to help us choose a game to play. Section 12.2 discusses techniques for representing sparse arrays, where almost all of the elements have the same value. Section 12.3 introduces the idea of representing a multidimensional array using a single one-dimensional array. That section concludes with a new implementation of Tic Tac Toe using the ideas from this chapter. Section 12.4 covers some advanced algorithms for searching and sorting.

12.1 Bit Vectors

It should come as no surprise that the author has a fairly large collection of games. A small sampling of games, with some of their properties, is listed in Figure 12–1.

When the author gets together with friends, he often has to answer the question, "Which game shall we play?" Sometimes people want something quick and light that can be played while waiting for others to arrive. Other times, people are ready to settle down for an evening-long brain-burner. If, for example, there are five people and they want to play a strategy game taking 1–2 hours, the options are Formula Dé, El Grande, and Puerto Rico. Let's write a program to list the appropriate games for any situation.

Game	Players	Time	Difficulty	Type
Apples to Apples	4–8	<1 hour	low	diplomacy
Bamboleo	2–7	<1 hour	low	dexterity
Bohnanza	3–7	<1 hour	medium	diplomacy/luck
Carcassonne	2–5	<1 hour	medium	luck/strategy
Cosmic Wimpout	2–10	<1 hour	low	luck
Formula Dé	2–10	1–2 hours	medium	luck/strategy
Give Me the Brain	3–8	<1 hour	low	luck
El Grande	2–5	1–2 hours	high	strategy
Lord of the Fries	3–8	<1 hour	medium	luck
Pitchcar	2–8	<1 hour	low	dexterity
Puerto Rico	3–5	1–2 hours	high	strategy
Samurai Swords	2–5	>2 hours	high	strategy
Settlers of Catan	3–4	1–2 hours	medium	diplomacy/luck/strategy
Starmada	2–8	>2 hours	high	strategy
Twister	2–4	<1 hour	low	dexterity

Figure 12-1: A few games from the author's collection.

We could maintain a set of Game objects, each of which has a field for each of the various attributes. A more space-efficient option is to maintain, for each game, a *single integer* encoding all of the game's attributes (except the title). This representation is called a ***bit vector*** (Figure 12–2).

If we think of each game as having a *set of features*, we recognize this as a variation of direct addressing (Section 11.4). For example, the bit vector for Bohnanza represent the set of features:

{3-player, 4-player, 5-player, 6-player, 7-player, less-than-1-hour, medium-difficulty, diplomacy, luck}

Bit vectors make it easy to efficiently perform certain set operations, such as intersection and union. For example, if we want to know what Bohnanza and El Grande have in common, we take the intersection of their feature sets (Figure 12–3).

If we want to know if a game is suitable for a particular situation, we can make up a bit vector for the situation (Figure 12–4). The intersection of a game's bit vector with the situation bit

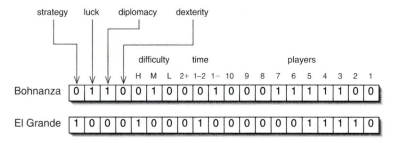

Figure 12-2: In a bit vector, each bit represents a single feature of the game. For example, El Grande can take 2, 3, 4, or 5, players, plays in 1–2 hours, is of high difficulty, and involves strategy.

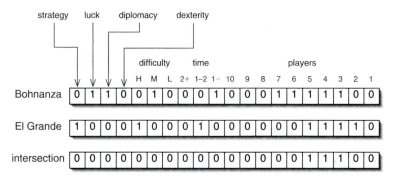

Figure 12-3: The bitwise intersection of two bit vectors tells what elements two sets have in common. In the resulting bit vector, the bits that are on in *both* of the others are on. Here, Bohnanza and El Grande can both handle 3–5 players.

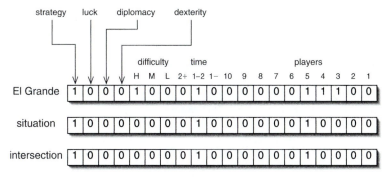

Figure 12-4: If a game's intersection with the situation equals the situation, the game is suitable. It does not matter that this situation does not specify a desired difficulty level.

vector tells what they have in common. If this is equal to the situation bit vector, the game has all of the required features.

In Java, we can represent a bit vector with up to 32 features using an int. The bit vector

$$00000000000000000000000000000100$$

represents the number 4 in binary. In our example, this bit vector also represents a 3-player game, with the extra bits at the left being ignored.

In binary, the number 2^i is represented by a bit vector with only the ith bit from the right turned on. Put another way, it is a 1 with i zeroes after it.

Java has an operator << for shifting a pattern of bits to the left a given number of spaces. If we want a bit vector with only the fifth bit turned on, we use the Java expression:

```
1 << 5
```

If we want several bits turned on, we simply take the union of the bit vectors for the individual bits. The bitwise or operator | allows us to find the union of two bit vectors. For example, to produce the bit vector

$$00000000000000000000001000100001$$

we use the Java expression:

```
(1 << 0) | (1 << 5) | (1 << 9)
```

Manipulating individual bits like this manually would be incredibly tedious and error prone. Instead, we define constants (Figure 12–5). The static method `playerRange()` is provided because many games can accept a range of player numbers.

```
 1 /** A game with this feature takes less than an hour to play. */
 2 public static final int LESS_THAN_ONE_HOUR = 1 << 10;
 3
 4 /** A game with this feature takes an hour or two to play. */
 5 public static final int ONE_TO_TWO_HOURS = 1 << 11;
 6
 7 /** A game with this feature takes over two hours to play. */
 8 public static final int OVER_TWO_HOURS = 1 << 12;
 9
10 /** A game with this feature is easy to pick up. */
11 public static final int LOW_DIFFICULTY = 1 << 13;
12
```

Figure 12–5: Constants and the `playerRange()` function make specifying bit vectors for games much easier. (Part 1 of 2)

```
13 /** A game with this feature is of moderate difficulty. */
14 public static final int MEDIUM_DIFFICULTY = 1 << 14;
15
16 /** A game with this feature take considerable study to play. */
17 public static final int HIGH_DIFFICULTY = 1 << 15;
18
19 /** A game with this feature involves agility or a steady hand. */
20 public static final int DEXTERITY = 1 << 16;
21
22 /** A game with this feature involves talking people into things. */
23 public static final int DIPLOMACY = 1 << 17;
24
25 /** A game with this feature involves significant randomness. */
26 public static final int LUCK = 1 << 18;
27
28 /** A game with this feature involves careful planning. */
29 public static final int STRATEGY = 1 << 19;
30
31 /**
32  * Return a bit vector with a feature for each number of players
33  * from minPlayers through maxPlayers.
34  */
35 public static int playerRange(int minPlayers, int maxPlayers) {
36   int result = 0;
37   for (int i = minPlayers; i <= maxPlayers; i++) {
38     result |= 1 << (i - 1);
39   }
40   return result;
41 }
```

Figure 12-5: Constants and the `playerRange()` function make specifying bit vectors for games much easier. (Part 2 of 2)

Now we can specify the bit vector for Lord of the Fries simply as:

```
playerRange(3, 8) | LESS_THAN_AN_HOUR | MEDIUM_DIFFICULTY | LUCK
```

Java's bitwise operators are listed in Figure 12–6. Almost all modern processors have built-in instructions for these operations, so they are extremely fast.

Figure 12–7 provides some examples of these operations.

A couple of things to watch out for:

- Be careful not to confuse the *logical and* operator && with the *bitwise and* operator &. The former is used with boolean values, the latter with numerical primitive types. For added confusion, if you use & on two boolean values, *you'll get their logical and—but not short-circuited!* A similar warning applies to || vs |.

Operator	Description	Notes
&	bitwise and	result is on where *both* operands are on for taking intersections
|	bitwise or	result is on where *at least one* operand is on for taking unions
^	bitwise exclusive or (xor)	result is on where *exactly one* operand is on
~	bitwise not	unary result is on where operand is off
<<	shift left	shifts in zero from right
>>	shift right	copies leftmost bit use with numbers
>>>	shift right	shifts in zero from left use with bit vectors

Figure 12-6: Bitwise operators. Assignment operators such as & = and << = are also available.

Expression	Bit Vector
a	10000000010101010101010101000000000
b	00000000011001100110011000000000000
a & b	00000000010001000100010000000000000
a | b	10000000011101110111011100000000000
a ^ b	10000000001100110011001100000000000
~a	01111111101010101010101011111111
a << 3	00000101010101010101010000000000000
a >> 3	11110000000010101010101010101000000
a >>> 3	00010000000010101010101010101000000

Figure 12-7: Examples of bitwise operations. The values of **a** and **b** are arbitrary.

- There are two different shift right operators, which differ in the way they handle the leftmost bit. Suppose we have the bit vector:

  10000000010000000000001000000000

  Shifting it two places to the right with >>> does what we would expect:

  00100000000100000000000010000000

  In contrast, shifting it two places to the right with >> copies the leftmost bit:

  *11*100000000100000000000010000000

  This option is included because bitwise operators are also sometimes used to multiply and divide ints by powers of two. In decimal notation, we can multiply a number by 10^3 = 1,000 by shifting it three places left. Similarly, in binary, we can multiply a number by 2^3 = 8 by shifting it three places left. To *divide* by a power of two, we shift to the right.

  Computers represent negative integers using a special binary notation which is beyond the scope of this book. The important detail here is that the leftmost bit is a 1 in a negative number, so shifting a negative number to the right with >>> would incorrectly produce a positive result. The >> works correctly for division.

  We should use >> for numerical division by powers of two, but >>> for shifting bit vectors to the right.

We now know more than enough to write the GameCollection class (Figure 12–8). The only nonconstant field is games, which maps Strings (game titles) to Integers (bit vectors).

```
1 import java.util.Map;
2 import java.util.TreeMap;
3
4 /** A bunch of games and their associated attributes. */
5 public class GameCollection {
6
7    // See Figure 12-5 for constants
8
9    /** Map associating game titles with attribute bit vectors. */
10   private Map<String, Integer> games;
11
12   /** A GameCollection is initially empty. */
13   public GameCollection() {
14      games = new TreeMap<String, Integer>();
15   }
16
```

Figure 12–8: The GameCollection class. (Part 1 of 2)

```
17   /** Add a new game to this collection. */
18   public void addGame(String title, int attributes) {
19     games.put(title, attributes);
20   }
21
22   /**
23    * Print the names of games which have all of the features in the
24    * constraints bit vector.
25    */
26   public void findGames(int constraints) {
27     for (Map.Entry<String, Integer> game : games.entrySet()) {
28       if ((constraints & game.getValue()) == constraints) {
29         System.out.println(game.getKey());
30       }
31     }
32   }
33
34   // See Figure 12-5 for the playerRange() method
35
36 }
```

Figure 12-8: The GameCollection class. (Part 2 of 2)

The loop on lines 27–31 iterates through the entries in this map. Each value of game is of type Map.Entry, so we can extract the key (title) or value (attribute bit vector) of the entry as needed.

A main() method which adds all of the games in Figure 12–1 and then invokes findGames() is shown in Figure 12–9.

```
1 /** Create a GameCollection, fill it, and find some for today. */
2 public static void main(String[] args) {
3   GameCollection collection = new GameCollection();
4   collection.addGame("Apples to Apples",
5                       playerRange(4, 8) | LESS_THAN_ONE_HOUR
6                       | LOW_DIFFICULTY | DIPLOMACY);
7   collection.addGame("Bamboleo",
8                       playerRange(2, 7) | LESS_THAN_ONE_HOUR
9                       | LOW_DIFFICULTY | DEXTERITY);
10  collection.addGame("Bohnanza",
11                      playerRange(3, 7) | LESS_THAN_ONE_HOUR
12                      | MEDIUM_DIFFICULTY | DIPLOMACY | LUCK);
13  collection.addGame("Carcassonne",
14                      playerRange(2, 5) | LESS_THAN_ONE_HOUR
15                      | MEDIUM_DIFFICULTY | LUCK | STRATEGY);
```

Figure 12-9: After adding a bunch of games to the database, we can ask for one fitting certain constraints. (Part 1 of 2)

```
16   collection.addGame("Cosmic Wimpout",
17                      playerRange(2, 10) | LESS_THAN_ONE_HOUR
18                      | LOW_DIFFICULTY | LUCK);
19   collection.addGame("Formula De",
20                      playerRange(2, 10) | ONE_TO_TWO_HOURS
21                      | MEDIUM_DIFFICULTY | LUCK | STRATEGY);
22   collection.addGame("Give Me the Brain",
23                      playerRange(3, 8) | LESS_THAN_ONE_HOUR
24                      | LOW_DIFFICULTY | LUCK);
25   collection.addGame("El Grande",
26                      playerRange(2, 5) | ONE_TO_TWO_HOURS
27                      | HIGH_DIFFICULTY | STRATEGY);
28   collection.addGame("Lord of the Fries",
29                      playerRange(3, 8) | LESS_THAN_ONE_HOUR
30                      | MEDIUM_DIFFICULTY | LUCK);
31   collection.addGame("Pitchcar",
32                      playerRange(2, 8) | LESS_THAN_ONE_HOUR
33                      | LOW_DIFFICULTY | DEXTERITY);
34   collection.addGame("Puerto Rico",
35                      playerRange(3, 5) | ONE_TO_TWO_HOURS
36                      | HIGH_DIFFICULTY | STRATEGY);
37   collection.addGame("Samurai Swords",
38                      playerRange(2, 5) | OVER_TWO_HOURS
39                      | HIGH_DIFFICULTY | STRATEGY);
40   collection.addGame("Settlers of Catan",
41                      playerRange(3, 4) | ONE_TO_TWO_HOURS
42                      | MEDIUM_DIFFICULTY | DIPLOMACY | LUCK
43                      | STRATEGY);
44   collection.addGame("Starmada",
45                      playerRange(2, 8) | OVER_TWO_HOURS
46                      | HIGH_DIFFICULTY | STRATEGY);
47   collection.addGame("Twister",
48                      playerRange(2, 4) | LESS_THAN_ONE_HOUR
49                      | LOW_DIFFICULTY | DEXTERITY);
50   collection.findGames(playerRange(5, 5) | ONE_TO_TWO_HOURS
51                      | STRATEGY);
52
```

Figure 12-9: After adding a bunch of games to the database, we can ask for one fitting certain constraints. (Part 2 of 2)

BitSets

If we want to keep track of a set with more than 32 potential elements, we can use the BitSet class in the java.util package (Figure 12–10). A BitSet represents a long bit vector as a series of binary numbers. It performs arithmetic (similar to that we'll do in Section 12.3) to find the right bit in the right number. Like an ArrayList, a BitSet can also grow as necessary. Of course, since

BitSet is an encapsulated class, we don't have to think about the details; we can simply treat it as an arbitrarily long bit vector.

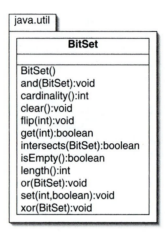

Figure 12-10: UML class diagram showing some of the methods in the java.util.BitSet class.

The and(), or(), and xor() methods have return types of void. Rather than returning a new BitSet, each of these modifies the existing BitSet. For example, if a is the BitSet 101100 and b is the BitSet 1010, then invoking a.or(b) changes a to 101110.

The cardinality() method returns the number of bits in a BitSet which are on. In contrast, length() returns the number of bits which are "in use," ignoring any leading zeroes. Continuing the example above, b.cardinality() returns 2, but b.length() returns 4.

The other methods are self-explanatory, given that int arguments specify indices in the BitSet. See the API for additional details and a few other methods.

Exercises

12.1   What is the value of 23 & 17?

12.2   What is the value of 23 | 17?

12.3   What is the value of 23 ^ 17?

12.4   What is the value of 23 << 5?

12.5   What is the value of 23 >> 2?

12.6   Give an expression that returns true if and only if the int n represents an empty bit vector.

12.7   Give an expression that returns true if and only if bit i of int n is on.

12.8   Given an int representation of a game, write an expression that returns true if and only if the game does *not* involve luck.

12.9   Speculate on why the player numbers in Figure 12–2 increase from right to left rather than left to right.

12.10 The GameCollection class uses a TreeMap. A HashMap would also work. Why would a HashMap be less efficient?

12.11 There are &= and |= operators, but there is no ~= operator. Why? (Hint: Try using ~= in a meaningful expression.)

12.12 Discuss whether the bitwise operators, such as &, are short-circuited.

12.13 Given two values *a* and *b*, *a* xor *b* is true when exactly one of *a* or *b* is true. The bitwise xor operator is ^. How would you find the logical xor of two boolean values?

12.2 Sparse Arrays

Suppose a city express bus runs down Main Street every ten minutes. To stay on schedule, it is supposed to stop at certain cross streets at certain times (Figure 12–11).

Cross Street	Time
2nd	:00
9th	:03
14th	:05
17th	:06
23rd	:09

Figure 12–11: Schedule for the city express bus running down Main Street.

We could represent this information using direct addressing: create an array of length 24, with the time for each stop at the appropriate index (Figure 12–12). All of the other elements of the array would be set to some other value, such as –1.

Figure 12–12: The bus schedule represented as a simple array. The shaded elements, where there are no stops, hold the value –1.

This works, but it wastes a lot of space. The problem is that the array is *sparse*—almost all of the elements have the same value. A better representation for a sparse array is to keep track of the exceptions to this default value using a Map (Figure 12–13). In our example this uses space linear in the number of stops, rather than in the number of cross streets.

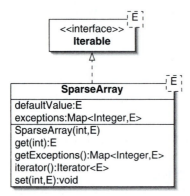

Figure 12–13: UML class diagram of a proposed SparseArray class. The two arguments to the constructor are the size of the array and the default value.

This improved representation of sparse arrays can also increase speed. If we want to iterate through the stops, we don't have to waste time on the intervening streets. This idea of saving time by skipping over irrelevant data is worth remembering. We will see it again in Chapter 16.

Now suppose we have buses running up and down various streets and avenues of the city. We need to keep track of the locations of the stops within a two-dimensional grid. We could use the same idea as before, mapping two-dimensional coordinates to times. (More realistically, the value at each stop would be a Map itself, associating times with bus numbers.) This saves space over a simple array representation, but it does not allow us to easily traverse a single row or column.

The solution to this problem is sketched in Figure 12–14. If we want to, for example, traverse column 2, we go to position 2 in the column header array across the top, then follow the chain of references down to the column footer array at the bottom. This visits only the exceptional elements in this column.

The individual exceptional elements are represented by quadruply linked list nodes (Figure 12–15). Each one knows its location as well as its neighbors above, below, to the left, and to the right. As in a doubly linked list, once we find such a node, we can remove it without having to know its predecessor. This is especially important here, because if we find a node by going down through a column, we don't want to have to search through the row to find its neighbor to the left.

Another advantage of this representation is that we can traverse a row or column in either direction.

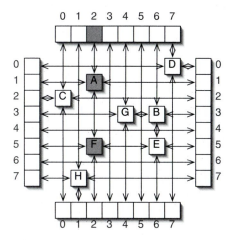

Figure 12–14: Conceptual drawing of a sparse, two-dimensional array. The arrays around the edges are headers and footers for the rows and columns. Only the shaded elements are examined in a top-down traversal of column 2.

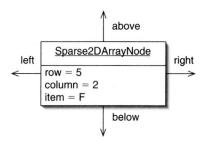

Figure 12–15: A node in a sparse two-dimensional array is quadruply linked. It contains references to its neighbors in four directions. The neighbors themselves are not shown here.

Exercises

12.14   If the field `exceptions` in Figure 12–13 is a TreeMap, what is the order of the running time of the `get()` and `set()` methods?

12.3 Contiguous Representation of Multidimensional Arrays

Recall from Figure 2–7 that a multidimensional array in Java is normally represented as an array of arrays. It is also possible to represent such an array as a single one-dimensional array

(Figure 12–16). The rows are placed one right after another in memory, so this is called a *con-tiguous representation*.

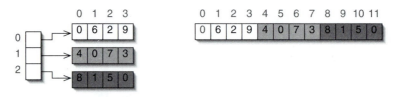

Figure 12–16: A multidimensional array can be represented as an array of arrays (left) or as a single one-dimensional array (right).

The only challenge here is determining which elements correspond in the two arrays. This is resolved with a simple formula. The element at position $<r, c>$ in the array of arrays is at position $r \cdot w + c$ in the contiguous array, where w is the width of the array (number of columns). The term $r \cdot w$ gets us to the beginning of the right row. Adding c then gets us to the right position within that row.

This formula can be generalized to higher dimensions. Suppose we have an n-dimensional array with dimensions $d_0, d_1, ..., d_{n-1}$. The element at position $<i_0, i_1, ..., i_{n-1}>$ is found at index:

$$\sum_{j=0}^{n-1} \left(i_j \cdot \prod_{k=j+1}^{n-1} d_k \right)$$

The second large symbol above is an upper-case Greek letter pi. It indicates the product of many factors in the same way that an upper-case sigma indicates the sum of many terms. Pi stands for "product," sigma for "sum."

For example, in a $8 \times 10 \times 6$ array, the element at position $<2, 4, 1>$ is at index:

$$2 \cdot (10 \cdot 6) + 4 \cdot 6 + 1 \cdot 1 = 145$$

This conversion seems like a lot of work. Is it worth the effort? Yes and no.

There are some advantages to this representation. It saves some space and time by eliminating references. By ensuring that all of the data are in one contiguous block of memory, it also ensures good cache performance. Finally, traversing every element of the array becomes slightly simpler—it's a single `for` loop, rather than one nested loop for each dimension.

On the other hand, none of these advantages is huge. The number of references followed to reach a particular element in an array of arrays representation is the same as the number of dimensions. High-dimensional arrays are rare. If we allocate an array of arrays all at once (as we usually do), it is likely to all be placed in the same area of memory, so cache performance is not an issue. Finally, a few nested `for` loops may be less complicated than the conversion between coordinate systems.

It is usually just as well to use the array-of-arrays representation and let the compiler handle the coordinates. Still, the idea of contiguous representation can be useful, as we'll see in the next example and again in Section 14.1.

Example: Tic Tac Toe Revisited

Recall the game of Tic Tac Toe from Figure 10–25. Our implementation in Section 10.3 used an array of arrays of characters to represent the board. We will now write a different version, using the ideas of bit vectors and contiguous representation from this chapter.

We interpret the board as a set of nine squares, numbered 0 through 8. It can therefore be represented contiguously by an array of length 9. We could use a contiguous array of chars, but we go one step farther: we use bit vectors of length 9.

There is one bit vector for the squares occupied by X and another for the squares occupied by O. If we want to know which squares are occupied by either player (to determine whether a move is legal), we take the union (bitwise or) of these two bit vectors.

The code for the new program is given in Figure 12–17

```
1 import java.util.Scanner;
2
3 /** The game of Tic Tac Toe. */
4 public class TicTacToe {
5
6    /** For reading from the console. */
7    public static final Scanner INPUT = new Scanner(System.in);
8
9    /** Bit vector of squares occupied by X. */
10   private int xSquares;
11
12   /** Bit vector of squares occupied by O. */
13   private int oSquares;
14
15   /** Bit vector of all nine squares. */
16   private int allSquares;
17
18   /** Bit vectors of winning triples of squares. */
19   private int[] winningLines;
20
21   /** The board is initially empty. */
22   public TicTacToe() {
23      xSquares = 0;
24      oSquares = 0;
25      allSquares = (1 << 9) - 1;
26      winningLines = new int[8];
```

Figure 12–17: The Tic Tac Toe program using bit vectors. (Part 1 of 4)

```
27    winningLines[0] = 1 | (1 << 1) | (1 << 2); // Top row
28    winningLines[1] = winningLines[0] << 3; // Middle row
29    winningLines[2] = winningLines[1] << 3; // Bottom row
30    winningLines[3] = 1 | (1 << 3) | (1 << 6); // Left column
31    winningLines[4] = winningLines[3] << 1; // Middle column
32    winningLines[5] = winningLines[4] << 1; // Right column
33    winningLines[6] = 1 | (1 << 4) | (1 << 8); // Diagonal
34    winningLines[7] = (1 << 2) | (1 << 4) | (1 << 6); // Diagonal
35  }
36
37  /** Return true if the game is over. */
38  public boolean gameOver() {
39    if (score() != 0) {
40      return true;
41    }
42    return (xSquares | oSquares) == allSquares;
43  }
44
45  /** Return the value of the current position if it is O's turn. */
46  protected int minimaxForO() {
47    int score = score();
48    if (gameOver()) {
49      return score;
50    }
51    int bestScore = 2;
52    int occupied = xSquares | oSquares;
53    for (int move = 1; move < allSquares; move <<= 1) {
54      if ((occupied & move) == 0) {
55        oSquares |= move;          // Play the move
56        score = minimaxForX();
57        if (score < bestScore) {
58          bestScore = score;
59        }
60        oSquares ^= move;          // Unplay the move
61      }
62    }
63    return bestScore;
64  }
65
66  /** Return the value of the current position if it is X's turn. */
67  protected int minimaxForX() {
68    int score = score();
69    if (gameOver()) {
70      return score;
71    }
```

Figure 12–17: The Tic Tac Toe program using bit vectors. (Part 2 of 4)

```
72      int bestScore = -2;
73      int occupied = xSquares | oSquares;
74       for (int move = 1; move < allSquares; move <<= 1) {
75         if ((occupied & move) == 0) {
76           xSquares |= move;          // Play the move
77           score = minimaxForO();
78           if (score > bestScore) {
79             bestScore = score;
80           }
81           xSquares ^= move;          // Unplay the move
82         }
83       }
84      return bestScore;
85    }
86
87    /** Play one game. */
88    public void play() {
89      char player = 'X';
90      for (int move = 0; move < 9; move++) {
91        if (gameOver()) {
92          return;
93        }
94        if (player == 'X') {
95          playBestMove();
96          player = 'O';
97        } else {
98          System.out.println(this);
99          System.out.print("Enter move (0-8): ");
100          int index = INPUT.nextInt();
101          oSquares |= 1 << index;
102          player = 'X';
103        }
104      }
105    }
106
107    /** Find the best move for X and play it on the board. */
108    protected void playBestMove() {
109      int score;
110      int bestScore = -2;
111      int bestMove = -1;
112      int occupied = xSquares | oSquares;
113      for (int move = 1; move < allSquares; move <<= 1) {
114        if ((occupied & move) == 0) {
115          xSquares |= move;          // Play the move
116          score = minimaxForO();
```

Figure 12-17: The Tic Tac Toe program using bit vectors. (Part 3 of 4)

```
117            if (score > bestScore) {
118                bestScore = score;
119                bestMove = move;
120            }
121            xSquares ^= move;          // Unplay the move
122        }
123     }
124     xSquares |= bestMove;          // Play the move
125  }
126
127  /** Return 1 if X has won, -1 if O has won, and 0 otherwise. */
128  public int score() {
129     for (int line : winningLines) {
130        if ((xSquares & line) == line) {
131           return 1;
132        }
133        if ((oSquares & line) == line) {
134           return -1;
135        }
136     }
137     return 0;
138  }
139
140  public String toString() {
141     String result = "";
142     int column = 0;
143     for (int square = 1; square < allSquares; square <<= 1) {
144        if ((xSquares & square) != 0) {
145           result += 'X';
146        } else if ((oSquares & square) != 0) {
147           result += 'O';
148        } else {
149           result += '.';
150        }
151        column++;
152        if (column % 3 == 0) { result += "\n"; }
153     }
154     return result;
155  }
156
157  // See Figure 10-27 for the main() method
158 }
```

Figure 12-17: The Tic Tac Toe program using bit vectors. (Part 4 of 4)

When we need to iterate through the squares on the board, we use a `for` loop of the form:

`for (int move = 1; move < allSquares; move <<= 1) { ... }`

Within the body of such a loop, `move` is the bit vector ending in 000000001 on the first pass, 000000010 on the second pass, and so on.

Exercises

12.15   A contiguous array of length $r \cdot c$ is used to represent a two-dimensional array with r rows and c columns. Give formulae for finding the row and column of element i in the contiguous array.

12.16   In a triangular array of width w, the first row has w columns, the second row $w - 1$ columns, and so on down to the last row, which has one column. This can be represented as one contiguous array. Devise a formula for finding the index of the element in row r, column c.

12.17   Would a contiguous representation work well in general for ragged arrays? Explain.

12.18   Explain lines 25 and 120 of the Tic Tac Toe program in Figure 12–17.

12.4 Advanced Searching and Sorting

This section presents additional algorithms for the searching and sorting problems introduced in Chapter 8. These algorithms rely on making an additional assumption about the data. Specifically, they assume that the data are uniformly distributed across a known range. For example, the data might all be real numbers which are greater than or equal to zero and less than one, with any number within this range equally likely to occur.

Interpolation Search

Suppose we want to look up a name in a phone book. We would not open the book to the first page and start reading names (linear search). We would do something more akin to binary search: open the book in the middle, then move left or right.

We would probably be even more sophisticated than this. If the name we are looking for starts with 'T,' we would open the book about three quarters of the way through. In other words, we would use the position of the letter in the alphabet to make an educated guess about the location of the name in the book.

In doing this, we are implicitly assuming that all first letters are equally likely—that names are *uniformly distributed* within the alphabet. This is not precisely true (there are more names starting with 'S' than with 'I'), but it's close enough to make this trick useful.

This improvement on the binary search algorithm is called *interpolation search*. It differs from binary search in that, instead of choosing the position in the middle of the range being searched, we estimate where the target is likely to fall within that range.

The code is given in Figure 12–18. The key computation is on lines 14–15. On line 13, we determine the fraction of the array region in question which is likely to be less than or equal to target. For example, if lo is 0, hi is 50, and target is 35, we expect to find target about 35/50 of the way along the region, so fraction is 0.7. Line 14 translates this back into an index.

```
1 public static boolean interpolationSearch(double[] data,
2                                            double target) {
3    int bottom = 0;
4    int top = data.length - 1;
5    while (bottom <= top) {
6      double lo = data[bottom];
7      double hi = data[top];
8      if (lo == hi) {
9        return target == lo;
10     }
11     if ((target < lo) || (target > hi)) {
12       return false;
13     }
14     double fraction = (target - lo) / (hi - lo);
15     int midpoint = bottom + (int)((top - bottom) * fraction);
16     if (target < data[midpoint]) {
17         top = midpoint - 1;
18     } else if (target == data[midpoint]) {
19         return true;
20     } else {
21         bottom = midpoint + 1;
22     }
23   }
24   return false;
25 }
```

Figure 12-18: Interpolation search.

In the worst case, interpolation search takes linear time. This worst case occurs only if the assumption of uniform distribution is deeply wrong. On average, interpolation search takes time in O(log (log n)), which is extremely small. The proof is beyond the scope of this book.

A Lower Bound on Comparison Sorting

A sorting algorithm in which we examine the data only by comparing them to each other is called a ***comparison sort***. All of the sorting algorithms we have seen so far (insertion sort, merge sort, and Quicksort) are comparison sorts. Merge sort has a worst-case running time in $\Theta(n \log n)$. Can a comparison sort do better than this? Surprisingly, we can prove that the answer is "No."

Suppose we have three numbers to sort: a, b, and c. There are six possibilities for the correct order: *abc*, *acb*, *bac*, *bca*, *cab*, or *cba*. (For simplicity, we assume there are no duplicate numbers.) For example, if $a < b$, $b > c$, and $a > c$, the correct order is *cab*.

In general, if there are n items to be sorted, there are $n!$ possibilities for the correct order. Every time we make a comparison, we rule out some of the possible orders. In the example above, once we see that $a < b$, we know that the only remaining possible orders are abc, acb, and cab.

In the worst case, we rule out at most half of the remaining orders with each comparison. (If we rule out, say, two-thirds of them, this isn't the worst-case—the worst case is when the comparison turns out the other way and we rule out only one-third.) The number of comparisons we have to make, and therefore the running time of the algorithm, is at least the number of times we have to halve $n!$ before it gets down to 1. In other words, it is in $\Omega(\log_2 (n!))$.

At this point it is necessary to invoke a ridiculously obscure mathematical fact that the reader could not possibly be expected to know. **Stirling's approximation** tells us that:

$$\log(n!) \in \Theta(n \log n).$$

It follows that the worst-case running time of *any* comparison sort is in $\Omega(n \log n)$. We can't hope to do better than merge sort.

While the proof is beyond the scope of this book, it can also be shown that the *average*-case running time of any comparison sort is also in $\Omega(n \log n)$.

Bucket Sort

We can beat the $\Omega(n \log n)$ lower bound on average sorting time with a sorting algorithm which is *not* a comparison sort. We do this by making an additional assumption about the data. The assumption we make is the same one we made for interpolation search: the data are numbers uniformly distributed across some range.

The algorithm, **bucket sort**, accepts an array of n numbers (Figure 12–19). For simplicity, assume that they are doubles, each greater than or equal to zero and less than one. We first create

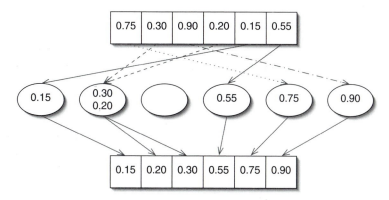

Figure 12–19: Bucket sort. The numbers in the data array (top) are copied into various buckets (middle), approximately one per bucket. The contents of the buckets are then sorted and copied back into the original array (bottom). Dashes and dots are merely to make the arrows easier to distinguish.

a list of *n* buckets. Traversing the data, we place each number into a bucket, with lower numbers near one end, higher numbers near the other end. Some buckets may contain more than one number, while others may be empty. Finally, we go through the buckets. Each bucket is sorted and its contents copied in order back into the original array.

The assumption comes into play in placing the numbers into the buckets. A number x is placed in bucket $\lfloor xn \rfloor$. We expect the number 0.75, for example, to end up about three-quarters of the way down the array, so we place it in a bucket at that position. Because we are performing arithmetic (multiplication) on the data, rather than merely comparing them to each other, bucket sort is not a comparison sort.

Like positions in a hash table, the buckets are not expected to contain many elements each. Specifically, placing *n* numbers in *n* buckets, we expect to get about one number per bucket. It therefore does not matter much which algorithm we use to sort the buckets. Insertion sort is a good choice, because it works quickly on very short lists.

Code for the algorithm is given in Figure 12–20.

```
1 /**
2  * Arrange the numbers in data from smallest to largest.
3  * Assume each is 0.0 <= x < 1.0.
4  */
5 public static void bucketSort(double[] data) {
6    int n = data.length;
7    List<SortableLinkedList<Double>> buckets
8      = new ArrayList<SortableLinkedList<Double>>();
9    for (int i = 0; i < n; i++) {
10     buckets.add(new SortableLinkedList<Double>());
11   }
12   for (int i = 0; i < n; i++) {
13     buckets.get((int)(data[i] * n)).add(data[i]);
14   }
15   int i = 0;
16   for (SortableLinkedList<Double> bucket : buckets) {
17     bucket.insertionSort();
18     for (Double d : bucket) {
19       data[i] = d;
20       i++;
21     }
22   }
23 }
```

Figure 12–20: Code for the bucket sort algorithm.

We represent the buckets as an ArrayList of SortableLinkedLists. Lines 7–11 create the buckets. Lines 12–14 copy the numbers into the buckets. Each bucket is sorted on line 17. The elements of the sorted bucket are then copied back into `data`.

What is the running time of bucket sort? Creating the buckets and placing the numbers in the buckets take time in $\Theta(n)$. Copying the numbers back into the array also takes linear time. The only tricky part is sorting the buckets. In the worst case, all of the numbers end up in the same bucket, which takes time in $\Theta(n^2)$ to sort using insertion sort. This is unlikely if our assumption of uniform distribution is correct. Using some statistics beyond the scope of this book, it is possible to prove that the average total time to sort all of the buckets is in $\Theta(n)$, so the average running time for bucket sort is linear.

Exercises

12.19   Why are lines 7–9 necessary in Figure 12–18?

12.20   Describe an input (an array of length 3 and a target) for which interpolation search must examine every element of the array.

12.21   Find a number n such that $\log_2 (\log_2 n)$ is 1. Do the same for 2 through 5.

12.22   Can interpolation search be modified to search any array of Comparables? Explain.

12.23   Does the proof about the worst-case time of comparison sorts hold if the data may contain duplicate elements? Explain.

12.24   Explain why a LinkedList is a better choice than an ArrayList for representing each bucket in bucket sort.

12.25   What is the order of the worst-case running time for bucket sort if the buckets are sorted using merge sort instead of insertion sort?

12.26   Can bucket sort be used to sort an array of any Comparable type? Explain.

Summary

A bit vector is a good data structure for representing a set of boolean features. Set operations such as union and intersection can be performed easily and efficiently. Like many other languages, Java provides a variety of bitwise operators for manipulating bits within an int. The java.util.BitSet class is useful for bit vectors too long to fit in a single int.

If an array is sparse, representing every element explicitly wastes space. A better option is to store the default value along with a list of exceptions. For two-dimensional sparse arrays, a representation involving quadruply linked nodes allows easy traversal along any row or column.

A multidimensional array can be represented as a single contiguous array. While this is usually not worth the extra code complexity for simple rectangular arrays, the idea can come in handy. We will see this again in Section 14.1.

Interpolation search is a refinement of binary search. Making the assumption that the data are evenly distributed across some range, it makes an educated guess as to where the target is located in the array. Interpolation search starts with this guess; in contrast, binary search starts in the middle of the array. Like binary search, interpolation search takes linear time in the unlikely worst case, but its average-case performance is in O(log (log n)).

A comparison sort is a sorting algorithm which examines the data only by comparing them to each other. All sorting algorithms in previous chapters are comparison sorts. The average-case and worst-case running time of any comparison sort must be in $\Omega(n \log n)$.

Bucket sort is not a comparison sort. It works by distributing the data into a number of buckets, sorting the buckets, and then copying the bucket contents back into the array. On average, there is only one item per bucket, so sorting them does not take much time. The average-case running time of bucket sort is in $\Theta(n)$. In the worst case, all of the data may end up in the same bucket, giving a running time of $\Theta(n^2)$, but this is unlikely if the assumption of uniform distribution is anywhere close to correct.

Vocabulary

bit vector. Condensed direct addressing table in which a single bit is allocated for each element.

bucket sort. Sorting algorithm that distributes elements into buckets, sorts the buckets, and then copies them back into the original array.

comparison sort. Any sorting algorithm in which the elements are examined only by comparing them to each other (as opposed to doing arithmetic on them). Insertion sort, merge sort, and Quicksort are comparison sorts, but bucket sort is not.

contiguous representation. Representation of a complicated data structure in a single array. Arithmetic is used, rather than references, to locate elements.

interpolation search. Search algorithm similar to binary search, in which arithmetic is used to estimate the position of the target within the region being searched.

sparse. Of an array, having the same value at almost all positions.

Stirling's approximation. $\log(n!) \in \Theta(n \log n)$

uniformly distributed. Having any member of a set (or a range of numbers) equally likely to occur. For example, rolling a fair die many times should produce a uniform distribution over the set {1, 2, 3, 4, 5, 6}. In contrast, in many sums of two die rolls, 7 would occur much more frequently than 11.

Problems

12.27 Modify the GameCollection program so that it uses BitSets instead of ints for the bit vectors. The `clone()` method of the BitSet class returns an identical copy of the BitSet; the return type of this method is Object, so you'll have to cast the result to a BitSet.

12.28 Implement the SparseArray class illustrated in Figure 12–13. Take care that, after `set()` is used to set some element to the default value, there is no longer an entry in `exceptions` for that element.

12.29 Write a comparison sort that works on arrays of exactly four elements without using any kind of loop or recursion.

12.30 Write a version of `bucketSort()` using classes from java.util, rather than our own classes. Do this in a separate directory so that, when you refer to a class like ArrayList, Java uses the version from java.util rather than our version. It will help to import java.util.*. Since you know the length of `buckets` in advance, you can prevent any stretching by using the ArrayList constructor that allows you to specify the capacity. The API for the Collections class may be useful.

Projects

12.31 Implement the two-dimensional sparse array representation outlined in Section 12.2. Include a UML class diagram of your classes.

12.32 Modify the `bucketSort()` method (Figure 12–20) so that the data can be distributed across any range. Take the minimum and maximum values in the array as the boundaries of the range. Your method should handle the possibility that some or all of the data are negative. How does this affect the running time of the algorithm?

13

Strings

This chapter covers special topics related to the widely used String class. Section 13.1 discusses this class and the related StringBuilder class. Section 13.2 presents three algorithms for string matching, which is the problem of determining where (if anywhere) a given pattern string appears in a longer text string.

13.1 Strings and StringBuilders

As described in Appendix A, there is some special syntax for using the String class. The double-quote syntax allows us to create an instance of the String class without using the keyword new. The + operator allows us to easily concatenate Strings. Thus, we can say

```
String sport = "foot" + "ball";
```

instead of the much more cumbersome:

```
String sport = new String(new char[] {'f', 'o', 'o', 't'});
sport = sport.concat(new String(new char[] {'b', 'a', 'l', 'l'}));
```

We saw in Section 2.1 that Strings are immutable. Once a String is created, it cannot be modified. This makes it dangerous to use == to compare Strings, but allows Java to sometimes save space by not storing redundant copies of identical Strings.

The immutability of Strings sometimes has a cost in efficiency. Consider the `toString()` method from our ArrayList class in Section 5.3, reproduced in Figure 13–1.

```
1 public String toString() {
2    String result = "[ ";
3    for (int i = 0; i < size; i++) {
4       result += data[i] + " ";
5    }
6    return result + "]";
7 }
```

Figure 13–1: The `toString()` method from the ArrayList class uses Strings.

Every time we use the + operator, a new String must be created and the contents of the old String copied into it. It would be better if we could avoid some of this copying (Figure 13–2). The built-in StringBuilder class allows us to do just this.

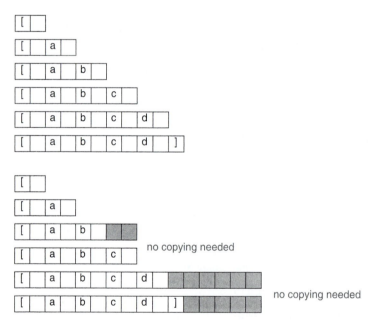

Figure 13–2: The `toString()` method of an instance of our ArrayList class returns a String such as "[a b c d]". Using Strings (top), it is necessary to create a new String instance every time new characters are added. A StringBuilder (bottom) stretches like an ArrayList, so it is not necessary to copy the array every time we add new characters.

If a String is like an array of characters, a StringBuilder is like an ArrayList of characters. We can optionally specify the capacity of a StringBuilder as an argument to the constructor, but it can stretch when necessary. Because the capacity of a StringBuilder doubles when it runs out of room, appending a new character takes constant amortized time. Creating a new String with an extra character, on the other hand, takes time linear in the number of characters previously in the String.

An improved version of the `toString()` method using a StringBuilder is given in Figure 13–3. We should generally write our `toString()` methods this way.

```
1 public String toString() {
2    StringBuilder result = new StringBuilder("[ ");
3    for (int i = 0; i < size; i++) {
4        result.append(data[i] + " ");
5    }
6    result.append("]");
7    return result.toString();
8 }
```

Figure 13–3: The `toString()` method using a StringBuilder.

Some of the methods from the String and StringBuilder classes are given in Figure 13–4. There are more methods not listed here; we'll leave the details for the API. The discussion that follows highlights some information that should let us use these classes more effectively.

Because instances of the String class are immutable, none of the listed methods of the String class have a return type of void. There would generally be no point in a method which neither returns a value nor modifies the object on which it is invoked. Instead, many of these methods return new Strings.

The `contains()` method returns `true` if its argument is a *substring* of `this`. A substring is a consecutive sequence of 0 or more characters within a String. For example, the invocation

`"bookkeeper".contains("ookkee")`

returns `true`.

The `substring()` method, given two arguments `start` and `end`, returns the substring from index `start` up to *but not including* index `end`. Thus,

`"sesquipedalian".substring(3, 7)`

returns characters 3 through 6—that is, `"quip"`.

A substring starting at index 0 is called a *prefix*. The method `startsWith()` determines whether its argument is a prefix. A substring running up against the other end of a String is called a *suffix*. The method `endsWith()` determines whether its argument is a suffix.

To avoid keeping redundant copies of identical Strings, the String class maintains a pool of instances. If *a String expression involving no variables* is identical to some instance in this pool, the value of the expression is a reference to the existing instance instead of a new String. If it is not, a new instance is added to the pool. To cause any other String instance to be treated this way, we can invoke its `intern()` method. Thus, if two Strings a and b are `equals()`, then

`a.intern() == b.intern();`

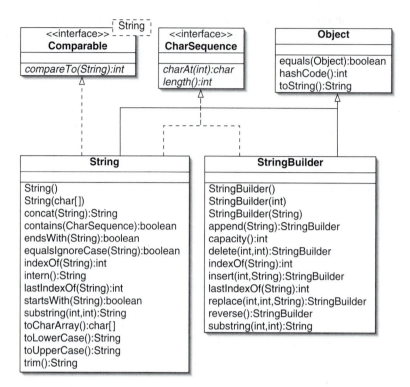

Figure 13-4: UML class diagram of the String and StringBuilder classes, the Object class, and some associated interfaces.

The `trim()` method returns a new String with any spaces, tabs, or newline characters removed from the ends. For example,

```
"     dramatic pause     ".trim()
```

is `"dramatic pause"`.

Many of the methods in the StringBuilder class have the return type StringBuilder. These methods actually modify the instance on which they are invoked. They could have the return type void, but for lack of anything else useful to return, they return the object on which they are invoked.

Exercises

13.1   We can't say

```
String state = "stressed".reverse();
```

because the String class has no `reverse()` method. Show how to accomplish the same thing using the StringBuilder class.

13.2   Create an immutable version of the Die class from Chapter 1. The roll() method, instead of modifying the current instance, should return a new one. What methods need to be removed?

13.3   Look up the getChars() method of the String class in the API. This method has a return type of void. What is the point of this, when Strings are immutable?

13.2 String Matching

The *string matching* problem is to find where, if anywhere, a certain *pattern* appears within a certain *text*. For example, the pattern

and

appears in the text

Am**and**a_**and**_Ferdin**and**

at positions 2, 7, and 17.

A common example is the "find and replace" feature of any word processor or text editor. String matching is also used by the UNIX utility grep, and in research involving DNA. (DNA strands are, for computational purposes, Strings made of the letters 'A,' 'T,' 'C,' and 'G.')

This section deals with several algorithms for string matching. For simplicity, our algorithms find only the *first* match within the text. We define a class for each algorithm (Figure 13–5).

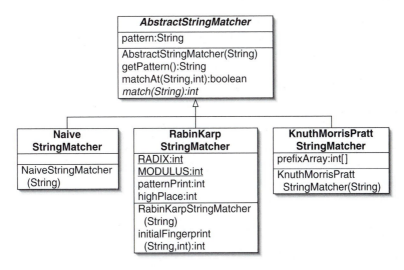

Figure 13-5: The classes discussed in this section. The match() method in AbstractStringMatcher is abstract, so each of the other three classes must provide it.

To use one of these classes, we create an instance with the pattern as an argument to the constructor. We then invoke the instance's `match()` method, with the text as an argument. For example:

```
AbstractStringMatcher matcher = new NaiveStringMatcher("and");
int result = matcher.match("Amanda_and_Ferdinand");
```

The code for the AbstractStringMatcher class is given in Figure 13–6. The only nontrivial method is `matchAt()`, which determines whether the pattern matches the text at one specified position. Two of the subclasses make use of this method, so it makes sense to put it here.

```
 1 /** Searches for a pattern String in various text Strings. */
 2 public abstract class AbstractStringMatcher {
 3
 4   /** The pattern being sought. */
 5   private String pattern;
 6
 7   /** Pattern is the pattern being sought. */
 8   public AbstractStringMatcher(String pattern) {
 9     this.pattern = pattern;
10   }
11
12   /** Return the pattern this StringMatcher seeks. */
13   protected String getPattern() {
14     return pattern;
15   }
16
17   /** Return true if the pattern appears in text at position. */
18   protected boolean matchAt(String text, int position) {
19     for (int i = 0; i < pattern.length(); i++) {
20       if (pattern.charAt(i) != text.charAt(i + position)) {
21         return false;
22       }
23     }
24     return true;
25   }
26
27   /**
28    * Return the index of the first appearance of the pattern in
29    * text, or -1 if it does not appear.
30    */
31   public abstract int match(String text);
32
33 }
```

Figure 13–6: The AbstractStringMatcher class. The `match()` method, being abstract, has no body here.

Naive String Matching

The most obvious approach to string matching is to simply check each position for a match (Figure 13–7). This is called the *naive string matching* algorithm.

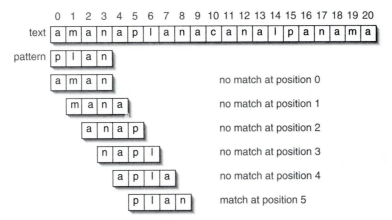

Figure 13-7: Naive string matching simply compares the pattern against each position in the text until a match is found or the end of the text is reached.

The code for the NaiveStringMatcher class is given in Figure 13–8.

```
1 /** Simply checks each position in the text for the pattern. */
2 public class NaiveStringMatcher extends AbstractStringMatcher {
3
4   /** Pattern is the pattern being sought. */
5   public NaiveStringMatcher(String pattern) {
6     super(pattern);
7   }
8
9   public int match(String text) {
10    for (int position = 0;
11         position + getPattern().length() < text.length();
12         position++) {
13      if (matchAt(text, position)) {
14        return position;
15      }
16    }
17    return -1;
18  }
19
20 }
```

Figure 13-8: The NaiveStringMatcher simply checks each position in the pattern.

In the worst case, the naive algorithm checks every character in the pattern at each position. This would happen if, for example, the pattern were "eeeeeek" and the text consisted entirely of es.

Checking for a match takes time in $\Theta(p)$, where p is the length of the pattern. If t is the length of the text, and we assume $t > p$, the number of possible positions is:

$$t - p + 1 \in O(t)$$

The total running time for the algorithm is therefore in $O(p \cdot t)$. The next two algorithms employ clever shortcuts to improve performance.

The Rabin–Karp Fingerprinting Algorithm

Our next algorithm uses an idea from hash tables (Section 11.4) to reduce the number of character comparisons we have to do. Imagine, for the moment, that our pattern and text consist entirely of decimal digits (Figure 13–9).

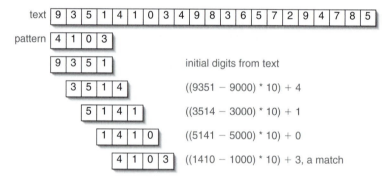

Figure 13-9: Idea for the Rabin–Karp fingerprinting algorithm when the pattern and text contain only decimal digits. The arithmetic operations are explained later in the text.

This appears very similar to the naive algorithm: we compare the pattern against each successive region of the text. There are two advantages in this situation. First, it appears that we can treat each region of text as an int; comparing two ints is much faster than comparing the Strings representing those ints. Second, we can easily advance to the next region.

In each step of the naive algorithm, we had to compare each character in the pattern with a character in the text. Here, we can get the next int by subtracting off the leftmost digit, multiplying by 10, and adding on the new digit. We don't have to look at the intervening digits, so this saves time.

In general, if the section of the text currently being examined starts at position i, the next section is:

$$(((\text{old section}) - (\langle\text{character } i\rangle \cdot 10^{p-1})) \cdot 10) + \langle\text{character } (i+p)\rangle$$

It's beginning to look as if we can check each position (except the first) in constant time, for a total running time in $\Theta(p + t)$. Unfortunately, there is a catch. The statement that comparing two integers takes constant time is true only if there is a limit to the size of an integer. If the pattern is a hundred digits long, we can't fit it into an int.

The solution is to do all of this arithmetic modulo some number m. The section of text we are currently examining, modulo m, is called a ***fingerprint***. We compare the fingerprint of the pattern with the fingerprint of each successive section of the text. Since they are both ints, this really does take constant time. To avoid overflow, we must choose m such that $10m$ is no more than $2^{31} - 1$, the largest value that an int can hold.

We now have the same problem that we had with hash tables: two different stretches of text might have the same fingerprint. Therefore, if we find a fingerprint match, we have to verify that the pattern really appears by using the `matchAt()` method from StringMatcher.

On the other hand, if the fingerprint of some section of the text does *not* match the fingerprint from the pattern, we know there's no match at this point. With a good choice of m (a prime number is good), our "hash function" should produce each possible positive int value with roughly equal frequency. In this case, we rarely have to check for actual matches.

This algorithm, the ***Rabin–Karp fingerprinting algorithm***, does not actually require that the pattern and text be made of decimal digits. A decimal number is said to have ***radix*** 10. The radix is the "base" of the number system. In radix 10, there are ten different characters that might appear at each position. In radix 2 (binary), there are only 2. 16-bit Unicode characters, which Java uses, can be treated as radix 65536 digits. We therefore need to choose m such that $65536m \leq 2^{31} - 1$. A suitable prime choice is 65521.

Figure 13–10 shows the algorithm at work on normal text.

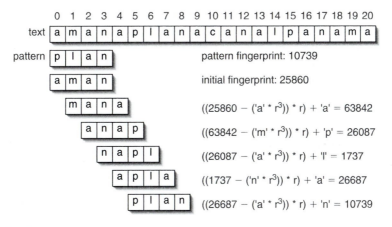

Figure 13–10: The Rabin–Karp fingerprinting algorithm. All arithmetic is done modulo 65521. The radix *r* is 65536.

The code for the RabinKarpStringMatcher is given in Figure 13–11.

```
 1 /** String matcher using the Rabin-Karp fingerprinting algorithm. */
 2 public class RabinKarpStringMatcher extends AbstractStringMatcher {
 3
 4   /** Arithmetic is done modulo this number to avoid overflow. */
 5   public static final int MODULUS = 65521;
 6
 7   /** Strings are treated as numbers in this base. */
 8   public static final int RADIX
 9     = (Character.MAX_VALUE + 1) % MODULUS;
10
11   /** Fingerprint of the pattern. */
12   private int patternPrint;
13
14   /** Value of a 1 in the highest place in the pattern. */
15   private int highPlace;
16
17   /** Pattern is the pattern being sought. */
18   public RabinKarpStringMatcher(String pattern) {
19     super(pattern);
20     patternPrint = initialFingerprint(pattern, pattern.length());
21     highPlace = 1;
22     for (int i = 1; i < pattern.length(); i++) {
23       highPlace = (highPlace * RADIX) % MODULUS;
24     }
25   }
26
27   /** Return fingerprint for the first length characters of str. */
28   protected int initialFingerprint(String str, int length) {
29     int result = 0;
30     for (int i = 0; i < length; i++) {
31       result = (result * RADIX) % MODULUS;
32       result = (result + str.charAt(i)) % MODULUS;
33     }
34     return result;
35   }
36   public int match(String text) {
37     int textPrint = initialFingerprint(text, getPattern().length());
38     for (int position = 0;
39          position + getPattern().length() < text.length();
40          position++) {
41       if ((textPrint == patternPrint)
42            && (matchAt(text, position))) {
43         return position;
44       }
45       // Remove left character
46       textPrint -= (highPlace * text.charAt(position)) % MODULUS;
```

Figure 13-11: The Rabin–Karp fingerprinting algorithm. (Part 1 of 2)

```
47          if (textPrint < 0) {
48            textPrint += MODULUS * (1 + (-textPrint / MODULUS));
49          }
50          // Shift over
51          textPrint = (textPrint * RADIX) % MODULUS;
52          // Add right character
53          textPrint += text.charAt(position + getPattern().length());
54          textPrint %= MODULUS;
55        }
56      return -1;
57    }
58
59 }
```

Figure 13-11: The Rabin–Karp fingerprinting algorithm. (Part 2 of 2)

Throughout the class, we have to be very careful about modular arithmetic. Whenever we add or multiply numbers, we must take them % MODULUS after the operation to avoid any danger of overflow. This operation should be performed in advance on any number, such as RADIX on line 8, that might be greater than MODULUS. If we subtract, as on line 44, we may have to add a multiple of MODULUS back in so that we don't end up with a negative number.

In line 8, we use the constant Character.MAX_VALUE to get the largest legal value for a character. One more than this is the radix. The field highPlace is the multiplier for the leftmost character. In Figure 13–9, for example, this would be 1000.

In the worst case, the Rabin–Karp fingerprinting algorithm has to check for an exact match at every position, so it does no better than the naive algorithm. Since most positions are checked in constant time, the average running time is in $\Theta(p + t)$. A formal proof is beyond the scope of this book.

The Knuth–Morris–Pratt Skipping Algorithm

A third string matching algorithm is the ***Knuth–Morris–Pratt skipping algorithm***. This improves on the naive algorithm by avoiding redundant comparisons. The idea is illustrated in Figure 13–12.

In the Knuth–Morris–Pratt skipping algorithm, we begin by searching for matches at various positions. If a mismatch is found at the first character, we move on to the next position, just as in the naive algorithm. The difference arises when several characters are matched and then a mismatch is found. In the naive algorithm, we would simply shift over one position and try again. In the Knuth–Morris–Pratt skipping algorithm, we shift over several places, avoiding redundant comparisons.

How many places can we shift over? We want to shift over as far as possible without any risk of missing a match. When we have already seen "retre" in Figure 13–12, there might be a match if we shift the pattern over so that the pattern prefix "re" lines up under the same characters.

(The observant reader will note that we *could* shift over even farther, because we already know that the 'n' and the 't' won't match. While the algorithm can be modified to take this information

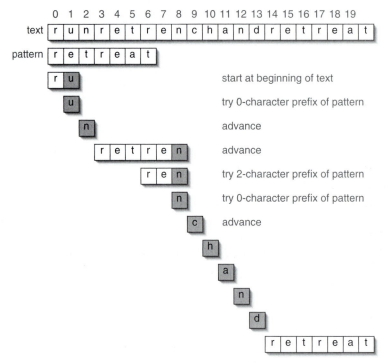

Figure 13–12: The Knuth–Morris–Pratt skipping algorithm. If a mismatch (shaded) is found on the first character of an attempt, the matcher advances to the next position. If a mismatch is found after matching one or more characters, the matcher tries again on a prefix of the pattern. The already-matched characters don't have to be compared again.

into account, it significantly increases complexity without improving the order of the running time. We therefore pay attention only to text characters to the left of the mismatch.)

If we can skip ahead like this often, we can save considerable time. The Knuth–Morris–Pratt algorithm uses information about the pattern to do exactly this.

The algorithm begins by computing a ***prefix array*** for the pattern. Element i of the prefix array is the answer to the question:

How long is the longest prefix of the pattern that can be shifted to the right to match the part of the pattern *ending* at position i?

The prefix array for `"retreat"` is shown in Figure 13–13.

There are several things to notice about the prefix array:

- Most of the elements are zero. This is usually true unless the pattern contains many repetitions.

```
            0  1  2  3  4  5  6
  pattern  | r | e | t | r | e | a | t |
prefix array | 0 | 0 | 0 | 1 | 2 | 0 | 0 |
```

Figure 13-13: Prefix array for the pattern `"retreat"`. Element 3 is 1 because the one-character prefix `"r"` matches the part of the pattern ending at position 3. Element 4 is 2 because the two-character prefix `"re"` matches the part of the pattern ending at position 4.

- The first element is *always* zero, because no prefix can ever be shifted right to match the part of the pattern ending here.

- No element exceeds the previous number by more than one. This happens because, for example, if the prefix `"re"` matches the subtring ending at position i, then the slightly shorter prefix `"r"` must match the substring ending at position $i - 1$.

The numbers in the prefix array tell us how much of the pattern has to be kept to the left of the mismatch. *Smaller* numbers in the prefix array therefore correspond to *larger* skips.

There are two parts to the code for the Knuth–Morris–Pratt skipping algorithm. The first part, the constructor, produces the prefix array. The second part, the `match()` method, uses the prefix array to search for the pattern within the text.

First consider the constructor, shown in Figure 13–14. Java initializes `prefixArray` to all zeroes. The loop on lines 16–26 works through `prefixArray` from left to right, starting at index 1. Throughout the loop, `matches` is the length of the longest prefix we've matched so far.

```
 1 /**
 2  * String matcher using the Knuth-Morris-Pratt skipping algorithm.
 3  */
 4 public class KnuthMorrisPrattStringMatcher
 5    extends AbstractStringMatcher {
 6
 7    /**
 8     * Length of longest pattern prefix ending at each position in
 9     * pattern.
10     */
11    private int[] prefixArray;
12
13    /** Pattern is the pattern being sought. */
14    public KnuthMorrisPrattStringMatcher(String pattern) {
15       super(pattern);
16       prefixArray = new int[getPattern().length()]; // All zeroes
17       int i = 1;
18       int matches = 0;
```

Figure 13-14: Field and constructor for the KnuthMorrisPrattStringMatcher class. (Part 1 of 2)

```
19    while (i < getPattern().length()) {
20      if (getPattern().charAt(i) == getPattern().charAt(matches)) {
21        matches++;
22        prefixArray[i] = matches;
23        i++;
24      } else if (matches > 0) {
25        matches = prefixArray[matches - 1];
26      } else {
27        i++;
28      }
29    }
30  }
31
32 }
```

Figure 13-14: Field and constructor for the KnuthMorrisPrattStringMatcher class. (Part 2 of 2)

On each pass through the loop, one of three things can happen:

- We find another match (lines 18–20). In this case, we increment `matches`, store that number in `prefixArray[i]`, and move on to the next character.

- We don't find another match, but `matches` is *not* zero (lines 22). This happens right after the end of a sequence of increasing `prefixArray` entries. More on this in a moment.

- We don't find a match and `matches` is zero (line 24). In this case, we leave `prefix-Array[i]` at 0 and move on to the next character.

Let's take a closer look at that second case (Figure 13–15). When we discover that the prefix we were currently working on can't be extended, we have to try some shorter prefix.

How do we know what value to set `matches` to—that is, how big a prefix to try extending next? In Figure 13–15, we've matched 7 characters in a row and then we find a mismatch. Our next try should be the longest prefix that also matches the end of the 7-character prefix.

Handily, *we have already computed this value*. This is the value stored at the seventh (zero-based) position in `prefixArray`—that is, `prefixArray[6]`. Line 22 simply looks up this number. This reuse of already-computed values is another example of dynamic programming, like the `fibo()` algorithm in Figure 9–35.

The `match()` method is very similar to the constructor (Figure 13–16).

The similarity between the constructor and the `match()` method is not surprising, because they do similar things. While the prefix array is initialized in the constructor to answer the question:

How long is the longest prefix of the pattern that can be shifted to the right to match the part of the *pattern* ending here?

the `match()` method answers the question:

Is the longest prefix of the pattern that can be shifted to the right to match the part of the *text* ending here *as long as the pattern*?

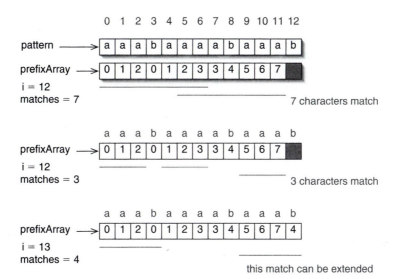

Figure 13–15: The constructor for KnuthMorrisPrattStringMatcher in action. A prefix of length 7 was matched in position 11, and position 12 is now being examined (top). There is a mismatch, so the next entry is not 8. Instead, we consider a shorter prefix matching at position 6 (middle). This prefix *can* be extended (bottom).

```
 1 public int match(String text) {
 2   int i = 0;
 3   int matches = 0;
 4   while (i < text.length()) {
 5     if (text.charAt(i) == getPattern().charAt(matches)) {
 6       matches++;
 7       if (matches == getPattern().length()) {
 8         return i + 1 - getPattern().length();
 9       } else {
10         i++;
11       }
12     } else if (matches > 0) {
13       matches = prefixArray[matches - 1];
14     } else {
15       i++;
16     }
17   }
18   return -1;
19 }
```

Figure 13–16: The match() method for the KnuthMorrisPrattStringMatcher class is very similar to the constructor.

We now analyze the worst-case running time of the Knuth–Morris–Pratt skipping algorithm.

First consider the constructor. On each pass through the loop, either i is incremented or matches decreases. Since matches can only be incremented along with i, each increment of i is responsible for at most two passes through the loop. Since the algorithm stops when i is p (the length of the pattern), there are no more than $2p$ passes through the loop, each of which takes constant time. The constructor therefore takes time in $O(p)$.

By a similar argument (assuming $t > p$), the match() method takes time in $O(t)$. The total running time for the algorithm is therefore in $O(p + t)$. Since merely reading the pattern and the text takes this long, the time is in fact in $\Theta(p + t)$, and we can't hope for an algorithm with better worst-case performance.

Exercises

13.4   Which method from the String class performs String matching?

13.5   What is the prefix array for the String "abracadabra"?

13.6   For which string would the prefix array entries likely be lower: a randomly generated string of 100 lower-case letters or a randomly generated string of 100 ones and zeroes? Explain.

Summary

Because Strings are so widely used, Java provides special syntax for this class: double quotes for instance creation and + for concatenation. Java takes advantage of the immutability of Strings by sometimes creating multiple references to the same instance. This can save space, but it costs time when a String is being built in pieces. The StringBuilder class, which is something like an ArrayList of chars, is a better choice in such situations.

String matching is the problem of determining where, if anywhere, a given pattern String appears within a longer text String. Three algorithms were discussed in this chapter: the naive algorithm, the Rabin–Karp fingerprinting algorithm, and the Knuth–Morris–Pratt skipping algorithm.

The naive algorithm, which simply tries each position, takes time in $O(p \cdot t)$.

The Rabin–Karp fingerprinting algorithm keeps track of a "fingerprint" (something like a hash code) for each section of the text. It is necessary to check for an exact match only when the fingerprint matches. This is no faster than the naive algorithm in the worst case, but since spurious fingerprint matches are extremely rare, the average running time is in $\Theta(p + t)$.

The Knuth–Morris–Pratt skipping algorithm first computes a prefix array for the pattern. It then acts like the naive algorithm, but uses the prefix array to sometimes skip ahead several positions at once. Using dynamic programming to efficiently compute the prefix array, it achieves a worst-case running time of $\Theta(p + t)$, which can't be beat.

Both the Rabin–Karp and Knuth–Morris–Pratt algorithms perform well in practice. More sophisticated versions of these algorithms appear in string matching libraries. They can be adapted to related tasks, such as searching for a pattern of pixels in a two-dimensional image.

Vocabulary

fingerprint. Number associated with a region of text in the Rabin–Karp fingerprinting algorithm.

Knuth–Morris–Pratt skipping algorithm. String matching algorithm that uses a prefix array to avoid redundant character comparisons.

naive string matching algorithm. Obvious string matching algorithm that compares the pattern against the text at each position.

pattern. String being sought in string matching.

prefix. Substring beginning at position 0. For example, `"car"` is a prefix of `"carnauba"`.

prefix array. In the Knuth–Morris–Pratt skipping algorithm, array based on the pattern. The number at position i is the length of the longest pattern prefix that matches the stretch of pattern ending at position i.

radix. Base of a number system, such as 2 for binary or 10 for decimal. Unicode characters can be treated as radix 65536 digits.

Rabin–Karp fingerprinting algorithm. String matching algorithm that generates a fingerprint for the initial pattern-length stretch of text, then incrementally updates it. Where the fingerprints don't match, there is no need to compare the text with the pattern.

string matching. Task of finding where, if anywhere, a pattern string appears within a text string.

substring. Consecutive sequence of 0 or more characters within a string.

suffix. Substring ending at the end of a string. For example, `"ILLZ"` is a suffix of `"L33T SKILLZ"`.

text. String being searched through in string matching.

wild card. Special character in a pattern that is considered equivalent to any character in the text (Project 13.11).

Problems

13.7   Modify AbstractStringMatcher to include an abstract method `allMatches()` which accepts a String text and returns an ArrayList of all positions where the pattern appears within that String. Provide this method for all three subclasses.

13.8   Suppose we have

        `String[] strands;`

containing n Strings, each of which represents a strand of DNA. Each strand is m characters long. Write code which determines if any two strands are identical by comparing each strand to each of the others using `equals()`. What is the running time of this operation? Now read about the `intern()` method of the String class in the API. Write an improved version of your method using `intern()` and give its running time. State any assumptions you make about how `intern()` works. Hint: Comparing two Strings with `==` takes constant time, but comparing them with `equals()` takes time in $\Theta(m)$.

13.9   The constructor for the KnuthMorrisPrattStringMatcher is difficult to understand. A more direct approach would be to check, for each position i, whether each prefix of length $i - 1$ down to 1 matches the part of the pattern ending at position i. Implement this algorithm and analyze its worst-case running time.

Projects

13.10   Write a program which takes two command-line arguments: a pattern and a file to search. The program should print out each line in the file in which the pattern occurs. Hint: Look at the code from the Anagrams constructor (Figure 11–7) to see how to read from a file.

13.11   The string matching problem is more difficult if the pattern may contain *wild cards*. A wild card is a character that can match any character in the text. For example, the pattern `"de?er"`, with `'?'` as a wild card, matches both `"defer"` and `"deter"`.

Modify the comments for AbstractStringMatcher to allow the use of the character `'?'` as a wild card. Modify two of the subclasses to provide this functionality. Explain why this would be difficult for the other subclass.

14

Advanced Trees

This chapter discusses four advanced data structures based on trees. Heaps (Section 14.1) provide an efficient implementation of a new kind of queue, as well as an interesting sorting algorithm. Section 14.2 uses trees to model a cluster of disjoint sets. Digital search trees (Section 14.3) provide a new way to store sets of Strings. Red-black trees (Section 14.4), a variation on binary search trees, are guaranteed to remain balanced, avoiding the linear worst-case time of binary search tree operations.

14.1 Heaps

Note: The term "heap" is used in a completely different way in Chapter 16.

A *heap* is a binary tree of Comparables with the following special properties:

- The value at each node is less than or equal to the values at the children of that node.

- The tree is perfect or close to perfect. It might be missing some nodes on the right end of the bottom level.

An example is shown in Figure 14–1.

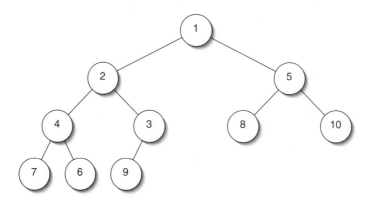

Figure 14-1: In a heap, each node is less than or equal to its children. It follows that the smallest element is at the root. On the other hand, a node may be lower in the tree than a smaller cousin (compare 6 and 8).

We could implement a heap using BinaryNodes (Section 10.1), but there is a more efficient representation. The requirement that a heap is "perfect or close to perfect" lets us use a contiguous representation somewhat analogous to the representation of multidimensional arrays from Section 12.3. We use an ArrayList, with the root at position 0, its children in the next two positions, their children in the next four, and so on (Figure 14–2). The constraint on the shape of the tree ensures that there will be no gaps in this representation.

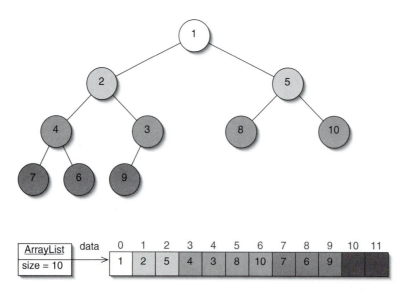

Figure 14-2: A heap can be represented using an ArrayList. The levels of the tree (highlighted by shading) are represented, one after another, in the array.

This representation is more space-efficient than a linked one, but how do we find the relatives of a node? We only have to do a little arithmetic.

The left child of the node at index i is at index $2i + 1$. Take a moment to verify this in Figure 14–2. The right child is at index $2i + 2$. The parent is at index:

$$\left\lfloor \frac{i-1}{2} \right\rfloor$$

The basic outline of the Heap class, including methods to find relatives, is given in Figure 14–3.

```
 1 /**
 2  * A nearly perfect tree where nodes are <= their children.
 3  * Can be used as a priority queue or for heapsort.
 4  */
 5 public class Heap<E extends Comparable<E>> {
 6
 7   /** Contiguous representation of the tree. */
 8   private ArrayList<E> data;
 9
10   /** The tree is initially empty. */
11   public Heap() {
12     data = new ArrayList<E>();
13   }
14
15   /** Return true if this Heap is empty. */
16   public boolean isEmpty() {
17     return data.isEmpty();
18   }
19
20   /** Return the index of the left child of the node at index. */
21   protected static int leftChildIndex(int index) {
22     return (2 * index) + 1;
23   }
24
25   /** Return the index of the parent of the node at index. */
26   protected static int parentIndex(int index) {
27     return (index - 1) / 2;
28   }
29
30   /** Return the index of the right child of the node at index. */
31   protected static int rightChildIndex(int index) {
32     return (2 * index) + 2;
33   }
34
35 }
```

Figure 14-3: Easy parts of the Heap class.

Priority Queues

A heap is a good data structure for implementing a ***priority queue***. Recall that when we remove something from a regular queue (Section 4.4), we get the *oldest* element. In a priority queue, on the other hand, we get the *smallest* element. It's easy to find the smallest element in a heap: it's always at index 0.

If we want to add something to a priority queue, we start by tacking it onto the end of the Array-List. We can't stop there, because the tree represented by this list might not be a valid heap any more. Specifically, the new element might be smaller than its parent. We fix this problem by filtering the offending element up toward the root until it is in a valid position (Figure 14–4).

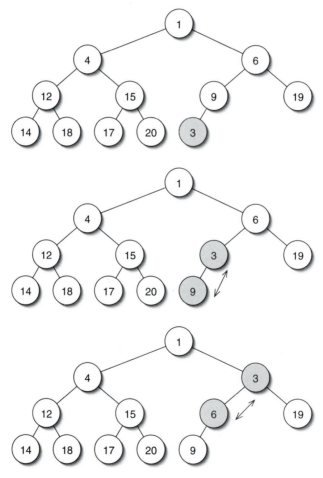

Figure 14–4: Filtering up in a heap. When a new node is added (top), it is compared with its parent. If it is smaller than its parent, they are swapped (middle). This continues until the new element moves up to its proper place (bottom).

Even in the worst case, this takes time proportional to the height of the tree. Since the tree is perfect or close to perfect, this is in O(log n). The code is given in Figure 14–5.

```
 1 /** Add a new element, maintaining the heap properties. */
 2 public void add(E target) {
 3   data.add(target);
 4   filterUp(data.size() - 1);
 5 }
 6
 7 /** Move the element at index up to restore the heap properties. */
 8 protected void filterUp(int index) {
 9   int parent = parentIndex(index);
10   while (parent >= 0) {
11     if (data.get(index).compareTo(data.get(parent)) < 0) {
12       swap(index, parent);
13       index = parent;
14       parent = parentIndex(index);
15     } else {
16       return;
17     }
18   }
19 }
20
21 /** Swap the elements at indices i and j. */
22 protected void swap(int i, int j) {
23   E temp = data.get(i);
24   data.set(i, data.get(j));
25   data.set(j, temp);
26 }
```

Figure 14–5: Adding a new element to a priority queue involves filtering it up to its proper place in the heap.

Removing an element from a priority queue is only slightly more complicated (Figure 14–6). We remember the element at index 0 so we can return it later. The element in the last position is then copied over the root and filtered *down* until it is in a legitimate position. If both children are smaller than their parent, we swap the parent with the smaller of the two.

This operation also takes time in O(log n). The code (Figure 14–7) is somewhat long because of the three-way comparison between a node and its children.

Heapsort

Heaps are also useful for a sorting algorithm called **heapsort**. The algorithm begins by copying the data to be sorted into a heap. The filterDown() method is then invoked several times to make the heap valid. Finally, we remove elements from the heap one at a time. Since each removal from the heap returns the smallest remaining element, they are removed in increasing order.

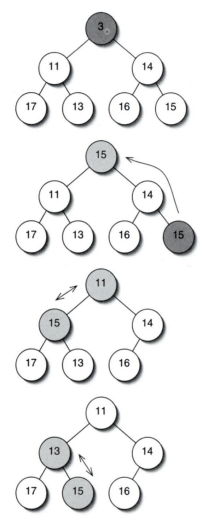

Figure 14-6: When the root is removed from a heap (top), it is replaced by the last element (second from top). This element is then filtered down to a legitimate position.

Since we've already laid most of the groundwork, the code for the `heapsort()` method is remarkably short (Figure 14–8). Lines 7–9 copy `unsortedData`, taking time in $\Theta(n)$. Line 11, which takes time in $O(\log n)$, is run no more than n times, for a total in $O(n \log n)$. The same is true of line 20. The total worst-case time for heapsort is therefore in $O(n \log n)$. Heapsort is a comparison sort (Section 12.4), so we can conclude that the worst-case time is precisely in $\Theta(n \log n)$.

```
1 /** Move the element at index down to restore heap properties. */
2 protected void filterDown(int index) {
3   while (index < data.size()) {
4     int left = leftChildIndex(index);
5     int right = rightChildIndex(index);
6     int smallest = index;
7     if ((left < data.size())
8         && (data.get(left).compareTo(data.get(smallest)) < 0)) {
9       smallest = left;
10    }
11    if ((right < data.size())
12        && (data.get(right).compareTo(data.get(smallest)) < 0)) {
13      smallest = right;
14    }
15    if (index == smallest) {
16      return;
17    }
18    swap(index, smallest);
19    index = smallest;
20  }
21 }
22
23 /** Remove and return the smallest element in the Heap. */
24 public E remove() {
25   E result = data.get(0);
26   E lastElement = data.remove(data.size() - 1);
27   if (data.size() > 0) {
28     data.set(0, lastElement);
29   }
30   filterDown(0);
31   return result;
32 }
```

Figure 14-7: Code for removing an element from a priority queue.

```
1 /**
2  * Copy the elements of unsortedData into the tree, then
3  * rearrange them to make it a heap.
4  */
5 protected Heap(ArrayList<E> unsortedData) {
6   data = new ArrayList<E>();
7   for (E e : unsortedData) {
8     data.add(e);
9   }
10  for (int i = (data.size() / 2) - 1; i >= 0; i--) {
```

Figure 14-8: Heapsort. The constructor on lines 1–13 is a second, overloaded constructor for the Heap class; the other was in Figure 14–3. (Part 1 of 2)

```
11      filterDown(i);
12    }
13 }
14
15 /** Sort data. */
16 public static <E extends Comparable<E>> void
17    heapsort(ArrayList<E> data) {
18    Heap<E> heap = new Heap<E>(data);
19    for (int i = 0; i < data.size(); i++) {
20      data.set(i, heap.remove());
21    }
22 }
```

Figure 14-8: Heapsort. The constructor on lines 1–13 is a second, overloaded constructor for the Heap class; the other was in Figure 14–3. (Part 2 of 2)

The type parameter specified between static and void on line 16 is necessary because heapsort() is a static method; it is not associated with a particular instance of Heap, although it creates one on line 18. Since the type parameter E at the beginning of the Heap class might stand for different things in different instances of Heap, a static method like heapsort() has to specify a new type parameter.

Java's PriorityQueue Class

The java.util package contains a PriorityQueue class. The comments for Java's Queue interface are carefully worded to encompass both FIFO queues (Section 4.4) and priority queues. The LinkedList and PriorityQueue classes therefore both extend this interface (Figure 14–9).

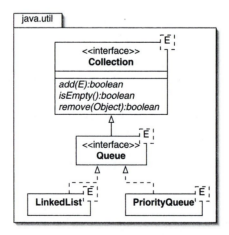

Figure 14-9: The java.util.Queue interface is implemented by both LinkedList and PriorityQueue. The add() and remove() methods inherited from Collection each return a boolean value indicating whether the operation succeeded.

Exercises

14.1   Can a tree ever be *both* a heap and a binary search tree? If so, give an example. If not, explain why not.

14.2   Write methods `leftSiblingIndex()` and `rightSiblingIndex()` for the Heap class.

14.3   On lines 10–12 of Figure 14–8, `filterDown()` is invoked only on the first $\lfloor n/2 \rfloor$ elements of `data`. How can we be sure that the heap is valid at the end of this? Why does i decrease to 0 instead of increasing from 0?

14.4   Java's built-in TreeSet class uses time in O(log *n*) for insertion and deletion. It seems that we could build a $\Theta(n \log n)$ sorting algorithm by simply inserting all of the data into a TreeSet, then traversing the TreeSet inorder (Figure 14–10). The running-time analysis is correct, but this algorithm fails to sort some ArrayLists. Why? (Hint: Think about the definition of a Set.)

```
1 /** Sort data. */
2 public static <E extends Comparable<E>> void
3   sort(java.util.ArrayList<E> data) {
4   java.util.TreeSet<E> tree = new java.util.TreeSet<E>(data);
5   data.clear();
6   for (E item : tree) {
7     data.add(item);
8   }
9 }
```

Figure 14–10: Code for Exercise 14.4.

14.2 Disjoint Set Clusters

This section introduces a data structure for representing a cluster of ***disjoint*** sets. Sets are disjoint if they have no elements in common. Clusters of disjoint sets include the sets of players on different baseball teams, the sets of cities in different countries, and the sets of newspapers owned by different media companies. They also play a crucial role in an algorithm we will see in Section 15.6.

We could use several instances of implementations of the Set interface. The alternate data structure described here allows us to more efficiently perform the following operations:

- Determine whether two elements belong to the same set.

- Merge two sets.

A cluster of sets is represented as a forest of trees (Figure 14–11). If two elements are in the same tree, they are in the same set. Unlike trees we've seen in the past, nodes in these trees keep track of their *parents*, rather than their children. They are therefore sometimes called ***up-trees***.

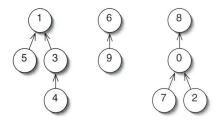

Figure 14-11: A forest of up-trees representing the disjoint sets {1, 3, 4, 5}, {6, 9}, and {0, 2, 7, 8}.

To determine if two elements are in the same set, we follow the arrows up from each element up to a root. If they lead to the same root, the elements are in the same tree.

To merge two sets, we make the root of one tree point to the root of the other tree (Figure 14–12).

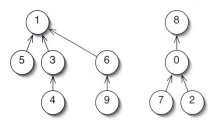

Figure 14-12: After merging, there are only two sets: {1, 3, 4, 5, 6, 9} and {0, 2, 7, 8}.

We could represent the up-trees with linked structures, but if we assume that the elements are ints in the range 0 through $n - 1$, we can use a more efficient contiguous structure (Figure 14–13). At each position, we store the parent of the corresponding element. For example, since 8 is the parent of 0, we store 8 at index 0. The special value −1 is used for roots, which have no parent.

0	1	2	3	4	5	6	7	8	9
8	−1	0	1	3	1	1	0	−1	6

Figure 14-13: Contiguous representation of the up-trees in Figure 14–12. Each position holds the parent of the corresponding element, or −1 if there is no parent.

The code for this implementation is given in Figure 14–14. All of the methods take constant time except for findRoot(). In the worst case (a single, linear tree), this takes time in $\Theta(n)$. The techniques described next ensure that the trees are shallow and wide, making the paths shorter.

```
1  /** A cluster of disjoint sets of ints. */
2  public class DisjointSetCluster {
3
4    /** parents[i] is the parent of element i. */
5    private int[] parents;
6
7    /** Initially, each element is in its own set. */
8    public DisjointSetCluster(int capacity) {
9      parents = new int[capacity];
10     for (int i = 0; i < capacity; i++) {
11       parents[i] = -1;
12     }
13   }
14
15   /** Return the index of the root of the tree containing i. */
16   protected int findRoot(int i) {
17     while (!isRoot(i)) {
18       i = parents[i];
19     }
20     return i;
21   }
22
23   /** Return true if i and j are in the same set. */
24   public boolean inSameSet(int i, int j) {
25     return findRoot(i) == findRoot(j);
26   }
27
28   /** Return true if i is the root of its tree. */
29   protected boolean isRoot(int i) {
30     return parents[i] < 0;
31   }
32
33   /** Merge the sets containing i and j. */
34   public void mergeSets(int i, int j) {
35     parents[findRoot(i)] = findRoot(j);
36   }
37
38 }
```

Figure 14–14: First draft of the DisjointSetCluster class.

Merging by Height

When we merge two up-trees, we have to choose which root becomes a child of the other root (Figure 14–15). Instead of doing this arbitrarily, we can keep the trees shorter by making the root of the shorter tree a child of the root of the taller tree. This is called *merging by height*.

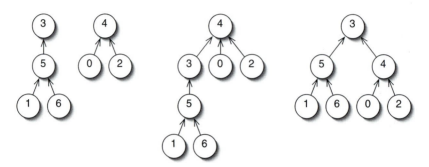

Figure 14-15: The two up-trees at left are to be merged. We could merge the taller one into the shorter one (middle) or vice versa (right). The result on the right is better because it is a shorter tree.

To do this, we need to keep track of the height of each tree. There is a clever way to do this without using any more memory. We need to keep track of heights only for the roots. These are exactly the nodes which don't have parents. We can therefore store the height of each root in the array `parents`.

To avoid confusion between a root with height 3 and a node whose parent is 3, we store the heights as negative numbers (Figure 14–16). We have to subtract one from all of these negative

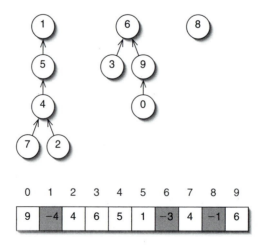

Figure 14-16: For height merging, we must keep track of the height of each tree. The entry in parents for the root of a tree of height *h* is −*h* − 1.

numbers, because a tree might have height 0 and there is no such int as –0. Thus, the entry for the root of a tree of height h is $-h - 1$.

The improved version of `mergeSets()` is shown in Figure 14–17.

```
 1 /** Merge the sets containing i and j. */
 2 public void mergeSets(int i, int j) {
 3    if (parents[i] > parents[j]) {
 4       parents[findRoot(i)] = findRoot(j);
 5    } else {
 6       if (parents[i] == parents[j]) {
 7          parents[i]--;
 8       }
 9       parents[findRoot(j)] = findRoot(i);
10    }
11 }
```

Figure 14–17: The `mergeSets()` method using height merging.

Path Compression

A second improvement to up-trees involves the `findRoot()` method. Suppose we determine that the root of the tree containing 4 is 7. We can make this operation faster next time by making 7 the parent of 4 (Figure 14–18). In fact, we might as well make 7 the parent of *every* node we visit on the way to the root. This technique is called ***path compression***.

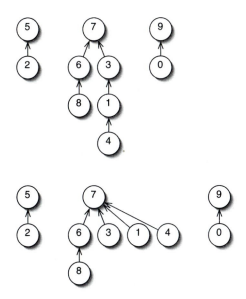

Figure 14–18: The root of the tree containing 4 is 7 (top). Using path compression, we reset the parent of every node visited in determining this to 7, making the tree shorter.

In writing the code for path compression, we realize that we can't alter these parents until *after* we've found the root. Since this involves remembering work we still have to do, this algorithm is most clearly expressed recursively (Figure 14–19).

```
1 /** Return the index of the root of the tree containing i. */
2 protected int findRoot(int i) {
3   if (isRoot(i)) {
4     return i;
5   }
6   parents[i] = findRoot(parents[i]);
7   return parents[i];
8 }
```

Figure 14-19: The findRoot() method with path compression.

Path compression may render the height counts inaccurate, but they are still legitimate upper bounds on the heights of the trees.

The analysis of up-trees with these improvements is beyond the scope of this book, but the result is impressive. The amortized running times of findRoot() and mergeSets() are in $O(\log^* n)$, where $\log^* n$ is the number of times we have to take the logarithm to get down to 1. In other words, $\log^* n$ is to $\log n$ what $\log_2 n$ is to $n/2$. This is an incredibly slowly-growing function (Figure 14–20). For all practical purposes, the amortized running time of up-tree operations is constant.

n	*log* n*
2	1
4	2
16	3
65536	4
2^{65536}	5

Figure 14-20: The log* function (assuming base 2 logarithms).

Exercises

14.5   Which order is higher: $\Theta(\log (\log n))$ or $\Theta(\log^* n)$?

14.6   How could we store a cluster of disjoint sets of Strings? (Hint: Don't modify the DisjointSetCluster class; use an additional data structure.)

14.7 Can we have an empty set in a DisjointSetCluster? If so, how? If not, why not?

14.8 Can we traverse the elements of a DisjointSetCluster? If so, how? If not, why not?

14.3 Digital Search Trees

It's been a while since we've had a game. The rules of Ghost are given in Figure 14–21.

Ghost

Players: 2 or more

Object: To avoid completing a word.

Play: Each player in turn names a letter. There must exist a word which starts with the sequence of letters named so far. If a player completes a word (at least three letters long), he loses.

For simplicity, we play only a single game and omit the scoring system.

Figure 14–21: Ghost is a great game for long road trips. Our implementation pits one player against the computer.

A sample game is shown in Figure 14–22.

```
 1 Welcome to Ghost.
 2
 3 The word so far:
 4 Your letter? a
 5 I choose d.
 6 The word so far: ad
 7 Your letter? v
 8 I choose a.
 9 The word so far: adva
10 Your letter? n
11 I choose t.
12 The word so far: advant
13 Your letter? a
14 I choose g.
15 The word so far: advantag
16 Your letter? e
17 That completes the word 'advantage'.  You lose.
```

Figure 14–22: A sample game of Ghost.

The key problem for the program is to find a word that starts with a given prefix. This could be done by searching a general-purpose Set, but there is a better way. The entire word set can be represented as a ***digital search tree*** (Figure 14–23). Words are represented as paths through the tree. Each child of a node is associated with a letter. If a path corresponds to a word, the node at the end is marked.

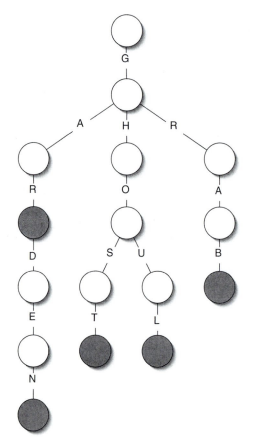

Figure 14–23: A digital search tree containing the words "gar," "garden," "ghost," "ghoul," and "grab." Shaded nodes indicate the ends of words.

As we play Ghost, we keep track of the current node. Whenever the user enters a letter, we descend to the appropriate child. If there is no such child, the user loses. When we need to pick a letter, we randomly choose a child and the corresponding letter. (Better strategy is explored in Project 14.24.)

The digital search tree is implemented in a straightforward linked way (Figure 14–24). A Map is used to associate letters (Characters) with child nodes.

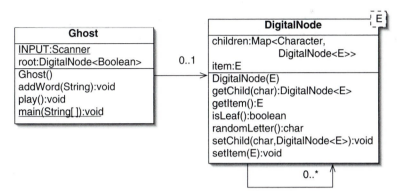

Figure 14-24: UML class diagram of our Ghost program. An instance of the Ghost class contains a DigitalNode, which contains a Map associating Characters with child DigitalNodes.

The code for the DigitalNode class is given in Figure 14–25. General-purpose interfaces like Map and Set pay off handsomely here. On line 37, we give the full name of java.util.Set to distinguish it from our own Set interface, which is likely to be in the same directory. The Digital-Node class is generic, because we will use it in a different way in Section 17.2.

```
1 import java.util.*;
2
3 /** Node in a digital search tree. */
4 public class DigitalNode<E> {
5
6    /** Map associating Characters with child nodes. */
7    private Map<Character,DigitalNode<E>> children;
8
9    /** True if this node is the end of a word. */
10   private E item;
11
12   /** A new node has no children. */
13   public DigitalNode(E item) {
14      children = new HashMap<Character,DigitalNode<E>>(1);
15      this.item = item;
16   }
17
18   /** Return the child associated with c. */
19   public DigitalNode<E> getChild(char c) {
20      return children.get(c);
21   }
22
```

Figure 14-25: The DigitalNode class. (Part 1 of 2)

```
23   /** Return the item stored at this node. */
24   public E getItem() {
25     return item;
26   }
27
28   /** Return true if this node is a leaf. */
29   public boolean isLeaf() {
30     return children.isEmpty();
31   }
32
33   /**
34    * Choose the letter of a random child.
35    */
36   public char randomLetter() {
37     java.util.Set<Character> letters = children.keySet();
38     int i = (int)(Math.random() * letters.size());
39     for (char letter : letters) {
40       if (i == 0) {
41         return letter;
42       }
43       i--;
44     }
45     return '?';                    // This should never happen
46   }
47
48   /** Associate c with child. */
49   public void setChild(char c, DigitalNode<E> child) {
50     children.put(c, child);
51   }
52
53   /** Set the item associated with this node. */
54   public void setItem(E item) {
55     this.item = item;
56   }
57
58 }
```

Figure 14-25: The DigitalNode class. (Part 2 of 2)

The easy parts of the Ghost class are listed in Figure 14–26.

```
1 import java.util.*;
2
3 /** The game of Ghost. */
4 public class Ghost {
5
```

Figure 14-26: Easy parts of the Ghost class. (Part 1 of 2)

```
6   /** For reading from the console. */
7   public static final Scanner INPUT = new Scanner(System.in);
8
9   /** Root of the digital search tree holding the word list. */
10  private DigitalNode<Boolean> root;
11
12  /** Read in the words from the file "words.txt". */
13  public Ghost() {
14    root = new DigitalNode<Boolean>(false);
15    try {
16      Scanner input = new Scanner(new java.io.File("words.txt"));
17      while (input.hasNextLine()) {
18        addWord(input.nextLine());
19      }
20    } catch (java.io.IOException e) {
21      e.printStackTrace();
22      System.exit(1);
23    }
24  }
25
26  /** Create and play the game. */
27  public static void main(String[] args) {
28    Ghost game = new Ghost();
29    System.out.println("Welcome to Ghost.\n");
30    game.play();
31  }
32
33 }
```

Figure 14-26: Easy parts of the Ghost class. (Part 2 of 2)

Of greater interest is the addWord() method (Figure 14–27). As we go through word character by character (lines 4–11), we descend to the appropriate child for each letter. When there is no such child, we create one (lines 6–9). Finally, at the end of the word, we mark the node (line 12).

```
1 /** Add word to the digital search tree. */
2 public void addWord(String word) {
3   DigitalNode<Boolean> node = root;
4   for (char c : word.toCharArray()) {
5     DigitalNode<Boolean> child = node.getChild(c);
6     if (child == null) {
7       child = new DigitalNode<Boolean>(false);
8       node.setChild(c, child);
9     }
10    node = child;
11  }
12  node.setItem(true);
13 }
```

Figure 14-27: Adding a word to a digital search tree.

The last method is play() (Figure 14–28).

```
1 /** Play one game. */
2 public void play() {
3   String word = "";
4   DigitalNode<Boolean> node = root;
5   boolean userTurn = true;
6   char letter;
7   while ((word.length() < 3) || !(node.getItem())) {
8     if (userTurn) {
9       System.out.println("The word so far: " + word);
10      System.out.print("Your letter? ");
11      letter = INPUT.nextLine().charAt(0);
12      word += letter;
13      if (node.getChild(letter) == null) {
14        System.out.println("Sorry, there is no word that starts"
15                           + "with" + word + ".");
16        System.out.println("You lose.");
17        return;
18      }
19    } else {
20      if (node.isLeaf()) {
21        System.out.println("I can't think of anything"
22                           + "-- you win!");
23        return;
24      }
25      letter = node.randomLetter();
26      System.out.println("I choose " + letter + ".");
27      word += letter;
28    }
29    node = node.getChild(letter);
30    userTurn = !userTurn;
31  }
32  System.out.print("That completes the word '" + word + "'.  ");
33  if (userTurn) {                // userTurn has been flipped
34    System.out.println("You win!");
35  } else {
36    System.out.println("You lose.");
37  }
38 }
```

Figure 14–28: The play() method. Use of DigitalNodes is emphasized.

Since it is nothing more than a hash table lookup, getChild() takes constant average time. This makes a digital search tree an excellent choice when searching for Strings containing a prefix that grows one character at a time.

Exercises

14.9   What is the maximum number of children a DigitalNode can have in the context of the Ghost game? Speculate on whether nodes with many children are more common near the root or near the leaves.

14.10   Does a digital search tree have more nodes if the words it contains share many prefixes or if they do not? Explain.

14.11   What would it mean if, in a digital search tree, the root were marked as the end of a word?

14.12   Why, on line 14 of Figure 14–25, do we specify that the new HashMap has a capacity of 1?

14.13   Why would direct addressing be a poor choice for associating characters with children in a digital search tree?

14.14   On line 7 of Figure 14–28, the program checks to make sure that any completed word is at least three letters long. Modify addWord() (Figure 14–27) to make this check unnecessary.

14.15   Add a method containsWord() to the Ghost class that returns true if a specified String is present in the digital search tree. What is the average running time of this method? Does it depend on the length of the word, the number of words in the tree, neither, or both?

14.16   In the game of Ghost, once we hit the end of a word, the game ends. Consequently, words that contain other words as prefixes are irrelevant. Modify the Ghost program to save memory by taking advantage of this fact.

14.4 Red-Black Trees

A plain binary search tree (Section 11.3) performs poorly if the tree is not balanced. In the worst case, which occurs if the elements are inserted in order, the tree is linear, so search, insertion, and deletion take linear time. The variation described in this section, the ***red-black tree***, ensures that the tree cannot become significantly imbalanced, so these operations run in logarithmic time in the worst case. In the Java collections framework, the classes TreeSet and TreeMap use red-black trees.

Properties of Red-Black Trees

A red-black tree (Figure 14–29) is a binary search tree in which each node has a color, either red or black. The tree has the following properties:

  •   The root is black.

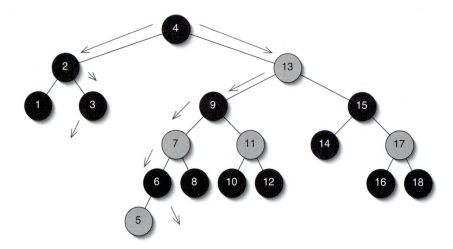

Figure 14–29: In a red-black tree, every path from the root to a null child contains the same number of black nodes (for this tree, three). Lightly shaded nodes are red.

- No red node has a red child.

- Consider each path from the root, through several descendants, down to a null child. These are the paths followed in unsuccessful searches. All such paths must contain the same number of black nodes.

These properties ensure that the tree cannot be significantly imbalanced. Specifically, suppose the shortest path to a null child contains d nodes. The longest path can contain at most $2d$ nodes. This happens when the short path is all black, while the long path alternates between black and red. It is not possible for one side of the tree (or any subtree) to become very tall while the other side remains short.

It can be proven (although we will not bother to do so) that the height of a red-black tree containing n nodes is in $O(\log n)$. The running times of search, insertion, and deletion are proportional to the height of the tree, so these operations run in logarithmic time. The challenge is to maintain the properties of the red-black tree while performing these operations.

Search

Search in red-black trees is identical to search in binary search trees.

Insertion

Insertion in a red-black tree starts out like insertion in a binary search tree. We start at the root and descend until we either find the target or try to descend from a leaf. In the latter case, the target is not present in the tree, so we attach a new, red leaf.

Unfortunately, this may invalidate the red-black tree. Specifically, the new node may be a child of another red node, which is illegal. We fix this by working our way back up the tree, changing colors and rearranging nodes. This repair operation, while complicated, takes time proportional to the height of the tree, so the total running time for insertion is still in O(log *n*).

A key step in tree repair is ***rotation*** (Figure 14–30). When we rotate, we replace a node with one of its children. This is a strictly local operation, affecting only a few nodes. The ordering of the nodes remains valid. In the Figure, the subtree rooted at 5 contains only values between 3 and 7, so it is in the correct position both before and after the rotation.

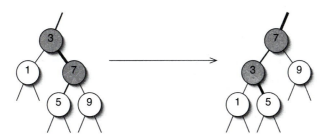

Figure 14–30: Rotation within the subtree rooted at 3. (3's parent, if any, and the proper descendants of 1, 5, and 9 are not shown.) Node 3 moves down to the left, while node 7 moves up. Only the three relationships shown by thick lines are changed; other nodes, such as node 5's proper descendants, are unaffected. Rotation is independent of color.

Color changes and rotations can be used to repair a red-black tree after inserting a new red node. The plan is to work back up the tree in several steps, performing color changes and rotations. Each step either fixes the tree or moves the problem closer to the root. If we get to the root and still have a red node, we can simply color it black. Since each step takes a constant amount of time, the whole repair process takes time proportional to the height of the tree.

Let node be the newly added node. Suppose node is red and has a red parent. How do we fix this? There are three cases to consider, depending on the color of node's parent's sibling (that is, node's aunt) and on whether node is a left or right child. We describe the cases below in order of increasing complexity.

First, if node has a red aunt, we simply change the colors of node's parent, aunt, and grandparent (Figure 14–31). This makes the grandparent red (see Exercise 14.19). Since the great-grandparent may also be red, we may have to do some repair there, too, but we're getting closer to the root.

Second, suppose node has a black aunt. If node and its parent are both left children (or both right children), we call node an ***outer child***. In this case, we change the colors of the parent and grandparent, then rotate the grandparent in the other direction (Figure 14–32). No further work is necessary at this point.

The third case occurs when node has a black aunt and is an ***inner child***—for example, if node is a right child but its parent is a left child (Figure 14–33). A rotation makes the parent an outer child of node. This new outer child is red and has a red parent, so we repair it as before.

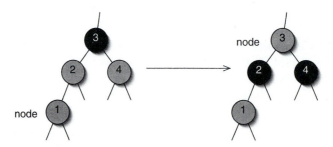

Figure 14-31: Repairing the tree for a node with a red parent and a red aunt. The colors of the parent, aunt, and grandparent are changed. It may be necessary to perform more repairs on the grandparent, which is now red.

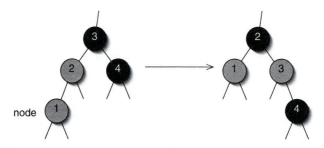

Figure 14-32: Repairing the tree for an outer child with a red parent and a black uncle. This involves two color changes and a rotation.

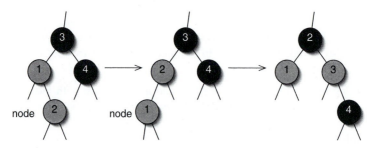

Figure 14-33: Repairing the tree for an inner child with a red parent and a black uncle. A rotation transforms this into the outer child case, which is resolved as in Figure 14–32.

Deletion

We now move on to deletion from a red-black tree. This is even more complicated than insertion, but the idea is the same: perform the operation as usual, then repair the tree if necessary.

Splicing out a red node can never cause any problems. If we splice out a black node, on the other hand, search paths that used to lead through this node now have one fewer black node than other search paths. Let node be the child of the node that was spliced out. If node is red, we can simply color it black to cancel out the problem. Otherwise, we work up the tree looking for a red node. There are four cases to consider this time.

In the first case, if node's sibling is black and has two black children, we color the sibling red (Figure 14–34). Now both the subtree rooted at node and the subtree rooted at its sibling are short a black node. In other words, the subtree rooted at node's parent is short a black node. We may have to make repairs there. That's closer to the root, so we're making progress.

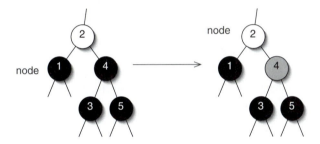

Figure 14–34: Repairing after deletion when node's sibling is black and has two black children. The parent, which may be of either color, becomes the new node.

In the second case, node's sibling is black and the sibling's outer child is red (Figure 14–35). Some color changes and a rotation here completely eliminate the problem.

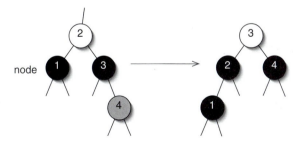

Figure 14–35: Repairing after deletion when node's sibling is black and has a red outer child. The sibling gets the parent's color, the parent and outer child become black, and there is a rotation.

In the third case, node's sibling is black, has a black outer child, and has a red inner child (Figure 14–36). Color changes and a rotation transform this into the red outer child situation just covered.

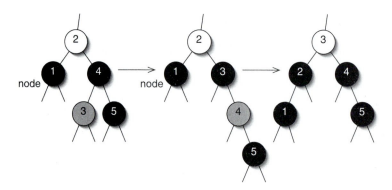

Figure 14–36: Repairing after deletion when node's sibling is black, has a black outer child, and has a red inner child (left). Color changes and a rotation transform this into the red outer child case (middle), which is handled as before (right).

The fourth case occurs when node's sibling is red (Figure 14–37). Color changes and a rotation transform this into one of the other cases.

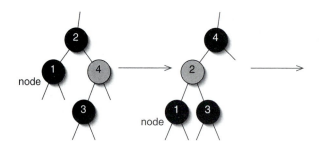

Figure 14–37: Repairing after deletion when node's sibling is red. Color changes and a rotation transform this into one of the other cases, which can be handled appropriately.

Implementation

The code for red-black trees is fairly complicated. In order to simplify things, we employ a couple of special tricks.

First, in place of null, we use references to a special black node called a *sentinel* (Figure 14–38). The sentinel indicates that we can't go any farther, but it is an actual node, so we

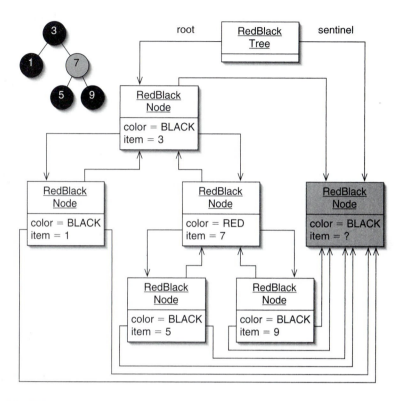

Figure 14–38: A red-black tree (upper left) and its implementation. Each node has references to its children and its parent. Where there is no child or parent, references are to a sentinel node (shaded).

can invoke methods on it. Thus, for example, we can ask for the color of a node's left child and get an answer even if the node doesn't really have a left child. Thus, we can say

```
if (node.getLeft().isBlack()) {
```

instead of:

```
if ((node.getLeft() == null) || (node.getLeft().isBlack())) {
```

To save space, we use a single sentinel instance to represent all nonexistent children.

Second, we keep track of the parent of each node. This is similar to the idea of a doubly linked list (Section 6.1). The root's parent is the sentinel.

The code for the RedBlackNode class is given in Figure 14–39. Some methods, such as isRed() and getColor(), are somewhat redundant, but they make the code in RedBlackTree easier to understand.

```
1  /** Node in a RedBlackTree. */
2  public class RedBlackNode<E extends Comparable<E>> {
3
4    /** Black node color. */
5    public static final boolean BLACK = false;
6
7    /** Red node color. */
8    public static final boolean RED = true;
9
10   /** Color of this node, BLACK or RED. */
11   private boolean color;
12
13   /** Item associated with this node. */
14   private E item;
15
16   /** Left child of this node. */
17   private RedBlackNode<E> left;
18
19   /** Parent of this node. */
20   private RedBlackNode<E> parent;
21
22   /** Right child of this node. */
23   private RedBlackNode<E> right;
24
25   /** Used for constructing a sentinel. */
26   protected RedBlackNode() {
27     color = BLACK;
28     // All other fields are irrelevant
29   }
30
31   /**
32    * The new node is red and both of its children are sentinel.
33    * The node's parent is NOT set by this constructor.
34    */
35   public RedBlackNode(E item, RedBlackNode<E> sentinel) {
36     color = RED;
37     this.item = item;
38     left = sentinel;
39     right = sentinel;
40   }
41
```

Figure 14–39: The RedBlackNode class. (Part 1 of 3)

```
42   /**
43    * Return this node's left (if direction is negative) or right
44    * (otherwise) child.
45    */
46   public RedBlackNode<E> getChild(int direction) {
47     if (direction < 0) {
48       return left;
49     }
50     return right;
51   }
52
53   /** Return the color of this node. */
54   public boolean getColor() {
55     return color;
56   }
57
58   /** Return the item associated with this node. */
59   public E getItem() {
60     return item;
61   }
62
63   /** Return this node's left child. */
64   public RedBlackNode<E> getLeft() {
65     return left;
66   }
67
68   /** Return this node's parent. */
69   public RedBlackNode<E> getParent() {
70     return parent;
71   }
72
73   /** Return this node's right child. */
74   public RedBlackNode<E> getRight() {
75     return right;
76   }
77
78   /** Return true if this node has two black children. */
79   public boolean hasTwoBlackChildren() {
80     return left.isBlack() && right.isBlack();
81   }
82
83   /** Return true if this node is black. */
84   public boolean isBlack() {
85     return color == BLACK;
86   }
87
```

Figure 14–39: The RedBlackNode class. (Part 2 of 3)

```
88    /** Return true if this node is red. */
89    public boolean isRed() {
90       return color == RED;
91    }
92
93    /**
94     * Set this node's left (if direction is negative) or right
95     * (otherwise) child.
96     */
97    public void setChild(int direction, RedBlackNode<E> child) {
98       if (direction < 0) {
99          left = child;
100      } else {
101         right = child;
102      }
103   }
104
105   /** Make this node black. */
106   public void setBlack() {
107      color = BLACK;
108   }
109
110   /** Set the color of this node. */
111   public void setColor(boolean color) {
112      this.color = color;
113   }
114
115   /** Set the item associated with this node. */
116   public void setItem(E item) {
117      this.item = item;
118   }
119
120   /** Set the parent of this node. */
121   public void setParent(RedBlackNode<E> parent) {
122      this.parent = parent;
123   }
124
125   /** Make this node red. */
126   public void setRed() {
127      color = RED;
128   }
129
130 }
```

Figure 14-39: The RedBlackNode class. (Part 3 of 3)

The trivial parts of the RedBlackTree class are given in Figure 14–40. When the tree is empty, the root is the sentinel.

```
 1 /** A red-black tree of Comparables. */
 2 public class RedBlackTree<E extends Comparable<E>>
 3  implements Set<E> {
 4
 5   /** The root node of this tree. */
 6   private RedBlackNode<E> root;
 7
 8   /** All "null" node references actually point to this node. */
 9   private RedBlackNode<E> sentinel;
10
11   /** The tree is initially empty. */
12   public RedBlackTree() {
13     sentinel = new RedBlackNode<E>();
14     root = sentinel;
15   }
16
17    public int size() {
18      return size(root);
19    }
20
21   /** Return the size of the subtree rooted at node. */
22   protected int size(RedBlackNode<E> node) {
23     if (node == sentinel) {
24       return 0;
25     } else {
26       return 1 + size(node.getLeft()) + size(node.getRight());
27     }
28   }
29
30 }
```

Figure 14-40: Easy parts of the RedBlackTree class.

The code for the RedBlackTree version of contains() (Figure 14–41) is somewhat shorter than the binary search tree version, because the RedBlackNode class provides a method get-Child() which accepts a direction as an argument.

```
 1 public boolean contains(E target) {
 2   RedBlackNode<E> node = root;
 3   while (node != sentinel) {
 4     int comparison = target.compareTo(node.getItem());
```

Figure 14-41: The contains() method from the RedBlackTree class. (Part 1 of 2)

```
 5     if (comparison == 0) {
 6       return true;
 7     } else {
 8       node = node.getChild(comparison);
 9     }
10   }
11   return false;
12 }
```

Figure 14-41: The contains() method from the RedBlackTree class. (Part 2 of 2)

Insertion in a red-black tree starts out like insertion in a binary search tree (Figure 14–42). We start at the root and descend until we either find the target or reach the sentinel. We then attach a new, red node at this point.

```
 1 public void add(E target) {
 2   RedBlackNode<E> targetNode
 3     = new RedBlackNode<E>(target, sentinel);
 4   RedBlackNode<E> parent = sentinel;
 5   RedBlackNode<E> node = root;
 6   int comparison = 0;
 7   while (node != sentinel) {
 8     parent = node;
 9     comparison = compare(targetNode, node);
10     if (comparison == 0) {
11       return;
12     }
13     node = node.getChild(comparison);
14   }
15   linkParentAndChild(parent, targetNode, comparison);
16   if (parent == sentinel) {
17     root = targetNode;
18   }
19   repairAfterInsertion(targetNode);
20 }
21
22 /**
23  * Return a negative number if child is to the left of parent,
24  * positive otherwise.
25  */
26 protected int compare(RedBlackNode<E> child,
27   RedBlackNode<E> parent) {
28   if (child == parent.getLeft()) {
29     return -1;
30   }
31   if (child == parent.getRight()) {
32     return 1;
33   }
34   return child.getItem().compareTo(parent.getItem());
35 }
```

Figure 14-42: The add() and compare() methods from the RedBlackTree class. The compare() method makes the code slightly clearer. Lines 26–31 are there so that compare() works even if child is the sentinel, which has a null item.

The linkParentAndChild() method is given in Figure 14–43. The argument dir allows us to specify whether child should become a left or right child of **parent**.

```
 1 /**
 2  * Set child to be the left (if dir is negative) or right
 3  * (otherwise) child of parent.
 4  */
 5 protected void linkParentAndChild(RedBlackNode<E> parent,
 6                                   RedBlackNode<E> child,
 7                                   int dir) {
 8   parent.setChild(dir, child);
 9   child.setParent(parent);
10 }
```

Figure 14–43: The linkParentAndChild() method from RedBlackTree.

The code for repairAfterInsertion() and rotate() is given in Figure 14–44. The loop runs until node has a black parent. If node is the root (whose parent is the black sentinel), we have to color node black, since the root of a red-black tree must be black.

```
 1 /** Restore the tree to validity after inserting a node. */
 2 protected void repairAfterInsertion(RedBlackNode<E> node) {
 3   while (node.getParent().isRed()) {
 4     RedBlackNode<E> parent = node.getParent();
 5     RedBlackNode<E> grandparent = parent.getParent();
 6     RedBlackNode<E> aunt
 7       = grandparent.getChild(-compare(parent, grandparent));
 8     if (aunt.isRed()) {        // Red aunt
 9       parent.setBlack();
10       aunt.setBlack();
11       grandparent.setRed();
12       node = grandparent;
13     } else {
14       int nodeComparison = compare(node, parent);
15       int parentComparison = compare(parent, grandparent);
16       if (nodeComparison != parentComparison) { // Inner child
17         rotate(nodeComparison, parent);
18         node = parent;
19       }
20       node.getParent().setBlack(); // Outer child
21       node.getParent().getParent().setRed();
22       rotate(parentComparison, node.getParent().getParent());
23     }
24   }
25   root.setBlack();
26 }
27
```

Figure 14–44: The repairAfterInsertion() method is aided by rotate(). (Part 1 of 2)

```
28 /**
29  * Move node's left (if dir is negative) or right (otherwise)
30  * child up into its place.  Move node down on the other side.
31  */
32 protected void rotate(int dir, RedBlackNode<E> node) {
33   RedBlackNode<E> child = node.getChild(dir);
34   RedBlackNode<E> parent = node.getParent();
35   if (node.getParent() == sentinel) {
36     root = child;
37   }
38   linkParentAndChild(node, child.getChild(-dir), dir);
39   linkParentAndChild(parent, child, compare(node, parent));
40   linkParentAndChild(child, node, -dir);
41 }
```

Figure 14-44: The `repairAfterInsertion()` method is aided by `rotate()`. (Part 2 of 2)

We now move on to deletion from a red-black tree. This is even more complicated than insertion, but the idea is the same: perform the operation as usual, then repair the tree if necessary. The easy parts are shown in Figure 14–45.

```
 1 /** Return the inorder successor of node. */
 2 protected RedBlackNode<E> inorderSuccessor(RedBlackNode<E> node) {
 3   RedBlackNode<E> descendant = node.getRight();
 4   while (descendant.getLeft() != sentinel) {
 5     descendant = descendant.getLeft();
 6   }
 7   return descendant;
 8 }
 9
10 public void remove(E target) {
11   RedBlackNode<E> node = root;
12   while (node != sentinel) {
13     int comparison = target.compareTo(node.getItem());
14     if (comparison == 0) {
15       if ((node.getLeft() == sentinel)
16           || (node.getRight() == sentinel)) {
17         spliceOut(node);
18       } else {
19         RedBlackNode<E> successor = inorderSuccessor(node);
20         node.setItem(successor.getItem());
21         spliceOut(successor);
22       }
23       return;
```

Figure 14-45: The `remove()` method invokes `spliceOut()`, which may invoke `repairAfterDeletion()`. (Part 1 of 2)

```
24      } else {
25         node = node.getChild(comparison);
26      }
27   }
28 }
29
30 /** Splice node out of the tree. */
31 protected void spliceOut(RedBlackNode<E> node) {
32   RedBlackNode<E> child;
33   if (node.getLeft() != sentinel) {
34     child = node.getLeft();
35   } else {
36     child = node.getRight();
37   }
38   linkParentAndChild(node.getParent(),
39                      child,
40                      compare(node, node.getParent()));
41   if (node == root) {
42     root = child;
43   }
44   if (node.isBlack()) {
45     repairAfterDeletion(child);
46   }
47 }
```

Figure 14–45: The `remove()` method invokes `spliceOut()`, which may invoke `repairAfterDeletion()`. (Part 2 of 2)

The code for `repairAfterDeletion()` is given in Figure 14–46.

```
 1 /** Restore the tree to validity after a deletion. */
 2 protected void repairAfterDeletion(RedBlackNode<E> node) {
 3   while ((node != root) && (node.isBlack())) {
 4     RedBlackNode<E> parent = node.getParent();
 5     int comparison = compare(node, parent);
 6     RedBlackNode<E> sibling = parent.getChild(-comparison);
 7     if (sibling.isRed()) {     // Red sibling
 8       sibling.setBlack();
 9       parent.setRed();
10       rotate(-comparison, parent);
11       sibling = node.getParent().getChild(-comparison);
```

Figure 14–46: The `repairAfterDeletion()` method. (Part 1 of 2)

```
12    }
13    if (sibling.hasTwoBlackChildren()) { // Two black children
14      sibling.setRed();
15      node = node.getParent();
16    } else {
17      if (sibling.getChild(-comparison).isBlack()) {
18        // Red inner child
19        sibling.getChild(comparison).setBlack();
20        sibling.setRed();
21        rotate(comparison, sibling);
22        sibling = parent.getChild(-comparison);
23      }
24      sibling.setColor(parent.getColor()); // Red outer child
25      parent.setBlack();
26      sibling.getChild(-comparison).setBlack();
27      rotate(-comparison, parent);
28      node = root;
29    }
30  }
31  node.setBlack();
32 }
```

Figure 14-46: The `repairAfterDeletion()` method. (Part 2 of 2)

Exercises

14.17   Prove that a red node must have either zero or two children.

14.18   What is the tallest possible linear red-black tree?

14.19   If a newly inserted node's parent is red (before repairing the tree), its grandparent *must* be black. Why?

14.20   The deletion repair case shown in Figure 14–37 makes node lower in the tree. Why is there no danger that this could lead to an infinite loop, where no progress is made toward the root? (Hint: What is the color of node 4's right child?)

Summary

A heap is a binary tree data structure used either to represent a priority queue (in which only the smallest element can be removed) or in the heapsort algorithm. A heap is a perfect binary tree or close to it. The value at each node is less than or equal to the values at the node's children. It follows that the smallest element is at the root, but a node may be lower in the tree than a smaller cousin. When changes are made to a heap, it is repaired by filtering the offending element up or down until it is in the right place. This take logarithmic time.

A cluster of disjoint sets may be represented as a forest of up-trees. Two elements in the same set are in the same tree, which can be detected by following parents up to the root. The up-trees are represented using an ArrayList of Integers, in which the value at each index is the parent of the corresponding element. This data structure supports efficient algorithms for determining whether two elements are in the same set and merging two sets. With merging by height and path compression, these operations take amortized time in $O(\log^* n)$.

A set of strings may be represented as a digital search tree. Each string corresponds to a path through the tree. This is a good data structure for finding all words starting with a certain prefix.

Java's TreeSet and TreeMap classes use red-black trees, which are similar to binary search trees. In a red-black tree, each node is either red or black. The colors in the tree must have certain properties, which guarantee that the tree cannot be badly out of balance. This in turn gives worst-case running time in $O(\log n)$ for search, insertion, and deletion.

To simplify the code, each node in a red-black tree keeps track of its parent as well as its children. A special sentinel node is used in place of absent parents and children, where there would normally be null references. This allows us to invoke methods on a node's parent regardless of whether it really has a parent.

Search in a red-black tree works just as it does in a binary search tree. After the basic insertion and deletion operations, it may be necessary to repair the tree to satisfy the properties. This repair is accomplished by working up the tree, performing color changes and rotations.

Vocabulary

digital search tree. Tree for storing strings. Each string is represented as a path from the root down to some node in the tree.

disjoint. Of two or more sets, having no elements in common.

heap. Perfect or almost-perfect binary tree in which the value at each node is less than or equal to the value at the node's children.

heapsort. Sorting algorithm that places the elements into a heap, then extracts them in order.

inner child. Node in a binary tree that is a child on the opposite side as its parent, such as a left child of a right child.

merging by height. Improvement to up-tree merging algorithm in which the root of the shorter tree becomes a child of the root of the taller tree. Keeps trees wide and shallow.

outer child. Node in a binary tree that is a child on the same side as its parent, such as a left child of a left child.

path compression. Improvement to up-tree merging algorithm in which all nodes visited along the path to a root are made to "point" directly to the root.

priority queue. Queue in which only the smallest element (rather than the oldest element, as in a FIFO queue) can be removed.

red-black tree. Binary search tree variant that is guaranteed to have height logarithmic in the number of nodes. Each node is either red or black. The root is black, no red node has a red child, and the number of black nodes is the same on each path from the root to a null child.

rotation. Local rearrangement of nodes within a tree. Used to maintain the validity of a red-black tree.

sentinel. Special node or value used to delineate the boundary of a data structure. Use of a sentinel can sometimes simplify code by eliminating special cases. In our red-black tree implementation, a sentinel is used as the parent of the root and in place of null children.

up-tree. Representation of a disjoint set. Each node keeps track of its parent rather than its children.

Problems

14.21   Modify the Heap class so that each node has a value *greater* than or equal to its children.

Projects

14.22   Implement a priority queue using an OrderedLinkedList instead of a heap. Give the worst-case running time of each of your methods.

14.23   After doing Problem 14.21, rewrite the Heap class to handle only heaps of doubles. Use an array rather than an ArrayList. Your implementation of heapsort should be in place. (Hint: Recall Figure 8–7.)

14.24   Write a DisjointSetCluster class that uses an ArrayList of Sets instead of the up-tree data structure described in Section 14.2. Provide the methods inSameSet() and mergeSets(). What is the running time of these operation?

14.25   Suppose Figure 14–23 is the entire digital search tree for a game of Ghost. If your opponent starts the game with 'g,' why is 'r' not a wise response? Modify the program to take advantage of this information.

15

Graphs

So far we have dealt only with linear structures and trees. A linear structure can be considered a special case of a tree, where every node (except for the single leaf) has exactly one child. Just as trees generalize linear structures, graphs generalize trees (Figure 15–1). The key difference between trees and graphs is that, in a graph, there may be more than one path between two nodes.

This chapter begins with discussions of graph terminology (Section 15.1), representation (Section 15.2), and traversal (Section 15.3). The remaining sections present several algorithms

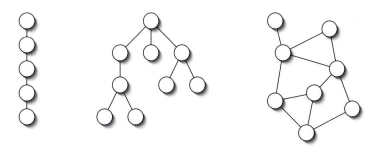

Figure 15–1: A linear structure (left) is a special case of a tree (middle), which is in turn a special case of a graph (right).

related to graphs. An incredible variety of computational problems can be phrased in terms of graphs. For example:

- Consider a set of tasks in a complicated cooking or industrial fabrication process. Some of the tasks have others as prerequisites. In what order can the tasks be performed? This is the topological sorting problem, addressed in Section 15.4.

- What is the shortest driving route from Los Angeles to Chicago? Section 15.5 covers algorithms for finding shortest paths.

- Given a set of computers in various locations in a building, how can they be connected with the least amount of cable? This is the problem of finding a minimum spanning tree, discussed in Section 15.6.

15.1 Terminology

Understanding graphs allows us to create much more elaborate games than we could before. Almost any game board can be treated as a graph. For a concrete example, we present the game of Galaxy (Figure 15–2).

A partial transcript using our implementation is given in Figure 15–3.

This user interface clearly leaves something to be desired; improving it is left as Problem 15.28.

Before writing the code for Galaxy, we introduce some graph terminology.

A **graph** consists of **vertices** (nodes) and **edges**. In a drawing, the vertices are shown as circles and the edges are shown as lines or arrows.

In an **directed** graph, an edge is an arrow going from one vertex to another (Figure 15–4). In some situations, it is meaningful to have a **self-loop**, an edge connecting a vertex to itself. In an **undirected** graph, an edge is simply a line connecting two vertices. Undirected graphs usually do not have self-loops. For every undirected graph there is a corresponding directed graph where each undirected edge is replaced by two directed edges, one in each direction.

The **neighbors** of a vertex are those vertices that can be reached by moving along one edge. In Figure 15–4, the neighbors of N are J, K, and Q. The neighbors of H are E and B, but *not* I—it is illegal to move backward along a directed edge.

A **path** from one vertex to another is a sequence of vertices, each a neighbor of the previous one. In Figure 15–4, the sequence I→H→B→A is a path from I to A. The **length** of the path is the number of edges along the path, one less than the number of vertices. The aforementioned path has length 3. The **distance** between two vertices is the length of the shortest path between them.

A **cycle** is a path (of length one or more) from a vertex back to itself. In Figure 15–4, F→G→D→C→F is a cycle. In an undirected graph, a cycle may not follow the same edge more than once. Thus, J→K→N→J is a cyle, but not Q→N→Q.

Galaxy

Players: 2

Object: To score the most points.

Board: There are twenty stars in the galaxy, connected by lines as shown below. Each player initially controls one star chosen at random

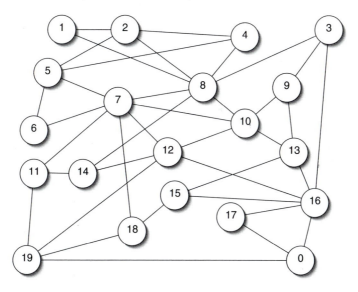

Play: On a turn, choose any unoccupied star and occupy it. Score a point for each adjacent enemy star.

Game End: The game ends when all 20 stars are occupied.

Figure 15-2: The game of Galaxy, by James Ernest. Used with permission of the designer.

```
1 Star   Owner   Neighbors
2 0      0       [ 16 17 19 ]
3 1      0       [ 2 8 ]
4 2      0       [ 1 4 5 8 ]
5 3      0       [ 8 9 16 ]
6 4      0       [ 2 5 8 ]
7 5      1       [ 2 4 6 7 ]
```

Figure 15-3: Sample move in a game of Galaxy. Player 2 scores 2 points occupying star 4, which is adjacent to two stars occupied by player 1: star 5 and star 8. (Part 1 of 2)

```
 8 6        0       [ 5 7 ]
 9 7        2       [ 5 6 8 10 11 12 18 ]
10 8        1       [ 1 2 3 4 7 10 14 ]
11 9        0       [ 3 10 13 ]
12 10       1       [ 7 8 9 12 13 ]
13 11       0       [ 7 14 19 ]
14 12       2       [ 7 10 14 16 19 ]
15 13       0       [ 9 10 15 16 ]
16 14       0       [ 8 11 12 ]
17 15       0       [ 13 16 18 ]
18 16       0       [ 0 3 12 13 15 17 ]
19 17       0       [ 0 16 ]
20 18       0       [ 7 15 19 ]
21 19       0       [ 0 11 12 18 ]
22 Player 1: 2
23 Player 2: 2
24
25 Player 2, pick a star: 4
26 Star      Owner   Neighbors
27 0         0       [ 16 17 19 ]
28 1         0       [ 2 8 ]
29 2         0       [ 1 4 5 8 ]
30 3         0       [ 8 9 16 ]
31 4         2       [ 2 5 8 ]
32 5         1       [ 2 4 6 7 ]
33 6         0       [ 5 7 ]
34 7         2       [ 5 6 8 10 11 12 18 ]
35 8         1       [ 1 2 3 4 7 10 14 ]
36 9         0       [ 3 10 13 ]
37 10        1       [ 7 8 9 12 13 ]
38 11        0       [ 7 14 19 ]
39 12        2       [ 7 10 14 16 19 ]
40 13        0       [ 9 10 15 16 ]
41 14        0       [ 8 11 12 ]
42 15        0       [ 13 16 18 ]
43 16        0       [ 0 3 12 13 15 17 ]
44 17        0       [ 0 16 ]
45 18        0       [ 7 15 19 ]
46 19        0       [ 0 11 12 18 ]
47 Player 1: 2
48 Player 2: 4
```

Figure 15-3: Sample move in a game of Galaxy. Player 2 scores 2 points occupying star 4, which is adjacent to two stars occupied by player 1: star 5 and star 8. (Part 2 of 2)

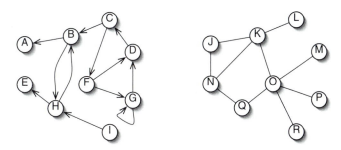

Figure 15-4: Directed (left) and undirected (right) graphs. Vertex G in the directed graph has a self-loop.

A graph with no cycles is called *acyclic*. A directed acyclic graph is sometimes called a *dag* (Figure 15–5).

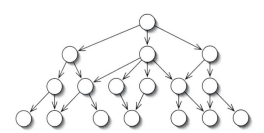

Figure 15-5: A directed acyclic graph or dag.

A graph in which every pair of vertices is connected by a path (not necessarily an edge) is said to be *connected* (Figure 15–6). Not all graphs are connected.

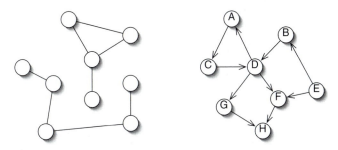

Figure 15-6: The undirected graph at left is not connected. The directed graph at right appears to be connected, but it is not: there is, for example, no path from F to E.

Data are usually associated only with the vertices of a graph. Occasionally, there are also data (usually numbers) associated with the edges (Figure 15–7). Such a number might represent the length of a road between two cities or the price of a cable between two computers. Such graphs are called *weighted* graphs.

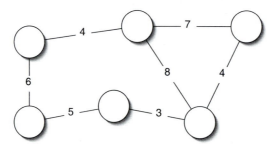

Figure 15–7: In a weighted graph, there are data associated with the edges.

When analyzing graph algorithms, we often give results in terms of v (the number of vertices) and e (the number of edges). In a directed graph, each of the v vertices might have an edge leading to itself and every other vertex, so $e \leq v^2$. In an undirected graph, the first vertex might be connected to each of the others. The second vertex might also be connected to each of the others, but the edge connecting it to the first vertex shouldn't be counted again. This gives a total of:

$$(v-1) + (v-2) + \dots + 1 + 0 \;=\; \sum_{i=0}^{v-1} i \;=\; \frac{v(v-1)}{2}$$

In either case $e \in O(v^2)$. This is an upper limit; many graphs have far fewer edges. For example, consider the network of computers in your building. Every computer or router can be thought of as a node, every ethernet cable as an undirected edge. There is probably not an edge connecting each vertex to each other vertex! A graph with close to the maximum number of edges is called *dense*. A graph with far fewer edges is called *sparse*.

Exercises

15.1   Is the graph for the Galaxy game (Figure 15–2) directed or undirected? Weighted or unweighted? Connected or unconnected?

15.2   Which vertex in the graph for the Galaxy game has the most neighbors?

15.3   Find a cycle of length 6 in the graph for the Galaxy game (Figure 15–2).

15.4   Is a dag always, sometimes, or never connected?

15.5   What is the maximum number of edges in a directed graph with no self-loops?

15.6   What is the minimum length of a cycle in an undirected graph?

15.7   What is the minimum number of edges in a connected, undirected graph?

15.8   What is the minimum number of edges in a connected, directed graph?

15.2 Representation

In representing graphs, we assume that the vertices are numbered 0 through $v - 1$. If it is necessary to associate other data such as city names with the vertices, this can be done with a Map or a direct address table.

In an unweighted graph, we need to keep track only of which vertices are the neighbors of each vertex. The first approach to doing this is the ***neighbor list*** representation (Figure 15–8), also known as the ***adjacency list*** representation. There is an array containing a chain of ListNodes for each vertex. Each list contains the indices of the neighboring vertices. The amount of memory used is in $\Theta(v + e)$. The time to check for a particular edge is in $O(e)$.

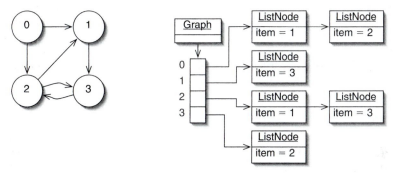

Figure 15–8: A graph (left) and its neighbor list representation (right).

If a graph is dense, it is better to use a ***neighbor matrix*** (Figure 15–9), also known as an ***adjacency matrix***. This is essentially a two-dimensional array of booleans. Element $<i, j>$ of this array is true when there is an edge from vertex i to vertex j. The memory used by this representation is

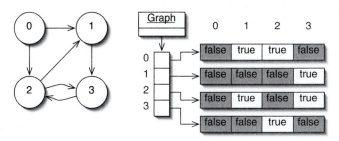

Figure 15–9: A graph (left) and its neighbor matrix representation (right).

in $\Theta(n^2)$, which is more than the neighbor list representation if the graph is sparse. On the other hand, the time to check for a particular edge is constant.

An added advantage of the neighbor matrix representation is that it is easily adapted to handle weighted graphs (Figure 15–10). Instead of storing a boolean at each position, we store the weight of the corresponding edge, or 0 if there is no edge.

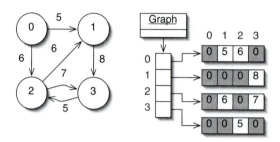

Figure 15–10: A weighted graph (left) and its neighbor matrix representation (right).

Code for the neighbor matrix representation is given in Figure 15–11. It can be used to represent an unweighted graph (with the methods addEdge() and hasEdge()) or a weighted graph (with

```
1 /** A potentially weighted graph. */
2 public class Graph {
3
4    /**
5     * edges[i][j] is the weight of the edge from i to j, or 0 if
6     * there is no such edge.
7     */
8    private double[][] edges;
9
10   /** The argument is the number of vertices in this Graph. */
11   public Graph(int vertices) {
12     edges = new double[vertices][vertices]; // All zero by default
13   }
14
15   /** Add an edge of weight 1 from i to j. */
16   public void addEdge(int i, int j) {
17     edges[i][j] = 1;
18   }
19
```

Figure 15–11: Beginning the Graph class. (Part 1 of 2)

```
20   /** Add edges of weight 1 from i to j and from j to i. */
21   public void addUndirectedEdge(int i, int j) {
22     edges[i][j] = 1;
23     edges[j][i] = 1;
24   }
25
26   /** Return the weight of the edge from i to j. */
27   public double getEdge(int i, int j) {
28     return edges[i][j];
29   }
30
31   /** Return true if there is an edge from i to j. */
32   public boolean hasEdge(int i, int j) {
33     return edges[i][j] != 0.0;
34   }
35
36   /** Set the weight of the edge from i to j. */
37   public void setEdge(int i, int j, double weight) {
38     edges[i][j] = weight;
39   }
40
41   /** Set the weight of the edge from i to j and from j to i. */
42   public void setUndirectedEdge(int i, int j, double weight) {
43     edges[i][j] = weight;
44     edges[j][i] = weight;
45   }
46
47   /** Return the number of vertices in this Graph. */
48   public int size() {
49     return edges.length;
50   }
51
52 }
```

Figure 15–11: Beginning the Graph class. (Part 2 of 2)

the methods setEdge() and getEdge()). The methods addUndirectedEdge() and setUndirectedEdge() allow us to represent undirected edges as well.

It will often prove useful to obtain a List of the neighbors of a vertex, so we provide a method for this (Figure 15–12).

We will add quite a few additional methods to this class, but we have enough now to write the Galaxy program. A UML class diagram is given in Figure 15–13.

The fields and main() method for the Galaxy class are given in Figure 15–14.

The constructor (Figure 15–15) is rather lengthy because it has to specify all of the edges on the board. Line 3 creates a Graph with 20 vertices but no edges. Lines 4–24 add the edges. Specifically, a two-dimensional array of ints is created and the rows are traversed using an enhanced

```
 1 /** Return a List of the neighbors of vertex i. */
 2 public List<Integer> neighbors(int i) {
 3   List<Integer> result = new ArrayList<Integer>();
 4   for (int j = 0; j < size(); j++) {
 5     if (hasEdge(i, j)) {
 6       result.add(j);
 7     }
 8   }
 9   return result;
10 }
```

Figure 15–12: The `neighbors()` method.

`for` loop. Each row contains two numbers, which are passed to `addUndirectedEdge()` on line 23. On line 25, `scores` has length 3 so that we can refer to `scores[1]` and `scores[2]`; `scores[0]` is not used. Line 26 allocates the array `stars`. Line 27 gives a random star to player 1. The loop on lines 28–34 gives a random star to player 2; it usually runs only once, but it is set up to try again if player 2 happens to get the same star as player 1.

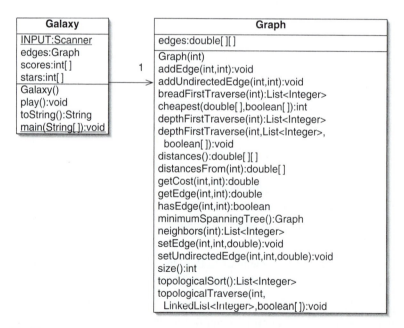

Figure 15–13: UML class diagram showing the Galaxy and Graph classes. For completeness, all of the Graph methods are shown, even those not used in Galaxy.

```
1 import java.util.Scanner;
2
3 /** The game of Galaxy. */
4 public class Galaxy {
5
6    /** For reading from the console. */
7    public static final Scanner INPUT = new Scanner(System.in);
8
9    /** Edges linking the stars together. */
10   private Graph edges;
11
12   /** Points earned so far by each player. */
13   private int[] scores;
14
15   /** Number of player controlling each star, or zero if none. */
16   private int[] stars;
17
18   /** Create and play the game. */
19   public static void main(String[] args) {
20      Galaxy game = new Galaxy();
21      System.out.println("Welcome to Galaxy.\n");
22      game.play();
23   }
24
25 }
```

Figure 15–14: Fields and `main()` method for the Galaxy class.

```
1 /** Build the galaxy and give one star to each player. */
2 public Galaxy() {
3    edges = new Graph(20);
4    for (int[] pair : new int[][]
5       {{0, 16}, {0, 17}, {0, 19},
6        {1, 2}, {1, 8},
7        {2, 4}, {2, 5}, {2, 8},
8        {3, 8}, {3, 9}, {3, 16},
9        {4, 5}, {4, 8},
10       {5, 6}, {5, 7},
11       {6, 7},
12       {7, 8}, {7, 10}, {7, 11}, {7, 12}, {7, 18},
13       {8, 10}, {8, 14},
14       {9, 10}, {9, 13},
15       {10, 12}, {10, 13},
16       {11, 14},
17       {11, 19},
18       {12, 14}, {12, 16}, {12, 19},
```

Figure 15–15: Constructor for the Galaxy class. (Part 1 of 2)

```
19        {13, 15}, {13, 16},
20        {15, 16}, {15, 18},
21        {16, 17},
22        {18, 19}}) {
23      edges.addUndirectedEdge(pair[0], pair[1]);
24    }
25    scores = new int[3];          // Initially all zeroes
26    stars = new int[20];          // Initially all zeroes
27    stars[(int)(Math.random() * 20)] = 1;
28    do {
29      int star = (int)(Math.random() * 20);
30      if (stars[star] == 0) {
31        stars[star] = 2;
32        return;
33      }
34    } while (true);
35 }
```

Figure 15-15: Constructor for the Galaxy class. (Part 2 of 2)

In writing the `toString()` method (Figure 15–16), we opt for a simple table.

```
1 public String toString() {
2   StringBuilder result = new StringBuilder();
3   result.append("Star\tOwner\tNeighbors\n");
4   for (int i = 0; i < 20; i++) {
5     result.append(i + "\t" + stars[i] + "\t"
6             + edges.neighbors(i) + "\n");
7   }
8   for (int p = 1; p <= 2; p++) {
9     result.append("Player " + p + ": " + scores[p] + "\n");
10  }
11  return result.toString();
12 }
```

Figure 15-16: The `toString()` method from the Galaxy class.

The `play()` method (Figure 15–17) is one of the simpler ones we've written. In the loop, lines 6-8 read a star number from the user. Line 9 gives the user control of that star. Lines 10–14 add any points scored. Line 15 toggles whose turn it is.

Exercises

15.9   How can the neighbor list representation (Figure 15–8) be modified to handle weighted graphs?

```
1 /** Play the game. */
2 public void play() {
3    int player = 1;
4    for (int turn = 0; turn < 18; turn++) {
5       System.out.println(this);
6       System.out.print("Player " + player + ", pick a star: ");
7       int star = INPUT.nextInt();
8       INPUT.nextLine();           // To clear out input
9       stars[star] = player;
10      for (int s : edges.neighbors(star)) {
11         if (stars[s] == 3 - player) {
12            scores[player]++;
13         }
14      }
15      player = 3 - player;
16   }
17   System.out.println(this);
18 }
```

Figure 15–17: The `play()` method from the Galaxy class.

15.10 What is the order of the running time of the `neighbors()` method (Figure 15–12)?

15.11 A graph could be represented as a List of edges, with each edge containing the indices of the two vertices connected by the edge. How much memory is used by this representation? How long does it take to check for the existence of a particular edge? How can this representation be modified to handle weighted graphs?

15.3 Graph Traversal

Like a tree, a graph can be traversed in more than one way. We must choose an arbitrary vertex to start from. This is called the *source* vertex. A *depth-first* traversal (Figure 15–18) follows edges until it reaches a dead end, then backtracks to the last branching point to try a different branch. The order in which the different branches are tried is arbitrary.

A *breadth-first* traversal (Figure 15–19) visits one vertex, then its neighbors, then vertices two edges away, and so on.

In either case, vertices that cannot be reached from the source (such as the one at the upper right in Figures 15–18 and 15–19) are never visited. Because there may be more than one path to a given vertex, it is necessary to keep track of which vertices have already been visited. This is done with an array of booleans.

The algorithm for depth-first traversal can be stated using a stack or, more concisely, using recursion (Figure 15–20).

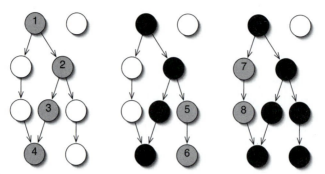

Figure 15-18: Depth-first traversal of a graph. The traversal begins by following edges until a dead end is reached (left). It then backtracks to the last decision point, following a different branch (middle). This continues until all reachable vertices have been visited (right).

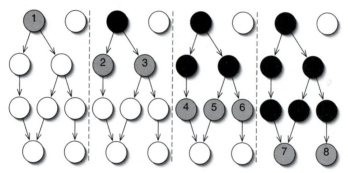

Figure 15-19: In a breadth-first traversal of a graph, vertices closer to the source vertex are visited earlier than more distant vertices. The dashed lines merely separate the four copies of the graph.

```
 1 /**
 2  * Return a list of the vertices reachable from source, in depth-
 3  * first order.
 4  */
 5 public List<Integer> depthFirstTraverse(int source) {
 6   List<Integer> result = new ArrayList<Integer>(size());
 7   boolean[] visited = new boolean[size()];
 8   depthFirstTraverse(source, result, visited);
 9     return result;
10 }
11
```

Figure 15-20: Depth-first traversal of a graph. The second, protected method depthFirstTraverse() is recursive. (Part 1 of 2)

```
12 /**
13  * Visit the vertices reachable from vertex, in depth-first order.
14  * Add vertices to result as they are visited.
15  */
16 protected void depthFirstTraverse(int vertex,
17                                   List<Integer> result,
18                                   boolean[] visited) {
19   visited[vertex] = true;
20   result.add(vertex);
21   for (Integer i : neighbors(vertex)) {
22     if (!visited[i]) {
23       depthFirstTraverse(i, result, visited);
24     }
25   }
26 }
```

Figure 15-20: Depth-first traversal of a graph. The second, protected method depthFirstTraverse() is recursive. (Part 2 of 2)

The algorithm for breadth-first traversal (Figure 15–21) uses a queue, much like the level order traversal of a tree (Section 10.2).

```
1 /**
2  * Return a list of the vertices reachable from source, in
3  * breadth-first order.
4  */
5 public List<Integer> breadthFirstTraverse(int source) {
6   List<Integer> result = new ArrayList<Integer>(size());
7   boolean[] visited = new boolean[size()];
8   Queue<Integer> q = new LinkedList<Integer>();
9   visited[source] = true;
10  q.offer(source);
11  while (!(q.isEmpty())) {
12    int vertex = q.poll();
13    result.add(vertex);
14    for (Integer i : neighbors(vertex)) {
15      if (!visited[i]) {
16        visited[i] = true;
17        q.offer(i);
18      }
19    }
20  }
21  return result;
22 }
```

Figure 15-21: Breadth-first traversal of a graph.

Exercises

15.12   Figure 15–22 shows an undirected graph. In what order might the vertices be visited during a depth-first traversal starting at vertex G? What about a breadth-first traversal? (There is more than one correct answer for each question.)

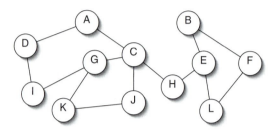

Figure 15–22: Undirected graph for Exercise 15.12

15.13   What bad thing could happen if we removed the test on line 22 of Figure 15–20?

15.4 Topological Sorting

A directed acyclic graph can be used to represent a set of tasks, some of which are prerequisites of others (Figure 15–23). An edge indicates that one task must be performed before another.

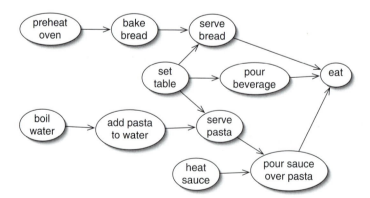

Figure 15–23: Dinner involves a number of different tasks, shown in this directed graph. An edge indicates that one task must be performed before another. For example, the oven must be preheated before the bread can be baked. It should be noted that only a programmer would consider this a complete meal.

A *topological sort* of such a graph is an ordering in which the tasks can be performed without violating any of the prerequisites. There may be more than one topological sort of a given graph. If the graph is redrawn with all of the vertices in topologically sorted order, all of the arrows lead from earlier to later tasks (Figure 15–24).

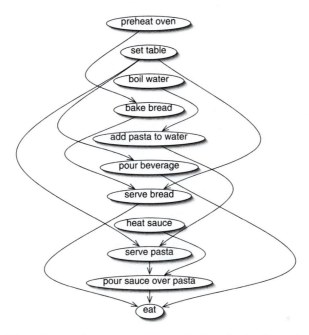

Figure 15–24: When the vertices are arranged in topologically sorted order, all of the edges lead from earlier to later tasks.

For a second example, consider the game of Pick Up Sticks (Figure 15–25).

Pick Up Sticks

Players: 2 or more

Object: To pick up as many sticks as possible.

Setup: Drop a number of long, thin sticks in a disorganized pile on the ground.

Play: In turn, each player picks up a stick. If she successfully extracts a stick without moving any of the others, she wins that stick and gets another turn.

Figure 15–25: Pick Up Sticks requires some dexterity, but the sticks must be picked up in a topologically sorted order.

In practice, this is a game of dexterity. Ignoring this detail, we can phrase it as a topological sorting problem: in what order should the sticks be picked up? Before any stick can be picked up, all of the sticks overlapping it must be picked up. A topological sort is a valid order for picking up the sticks (Figure 15–26).

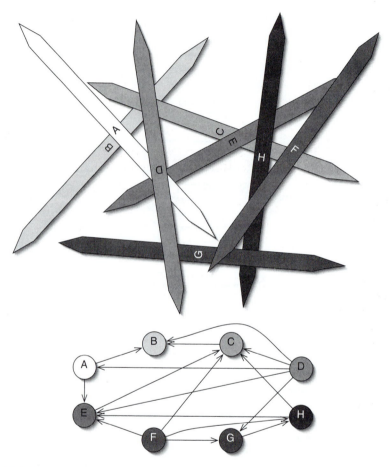

Figure 15-26: A game of Pick Up Sticks and the corresponding directed acyclic graph. An edge indicates that one stick overlaps another. A topological sort of this graph would give a valid order for picking up the sticks.

We would like to write a program that, given the information on which sticks overlap which other sticks, determines an order in which they may be picked up. A transcript is given in Figure 15–27.

The heart of this program is the topological sorting algorithm. This algorithm is similar to a series of depth-first traversals, one starting from each vertex, but all sharing the same `visited` array.

```
 1 Welcome to Pick Up Sticks.
 2
 3 How many sticks are there? 4
 4 Which sticks overlap stick 0 (separate with spaces)?
 5 Which sticks overlap stick 1 (separate with spaces)? 0
 6 Which sticks overlap stick 2 (separate with spaces)? 1 3
 7 Which sticks overlap stick 3 (separate with spaces)? 0
 8
 9 The sticks can be picked up in this order:
10 ( 0 3 1 2 )
```

Figure 15-27: Transcript of the PickUpSticks program.

Suppose we do a depth-first traversal starting from some vertex, such as vertex F in Figure 15–26. When we complete this traversal, we have visited everything that can be reached from this vertex. In other words, we have stick F and everything below it. If we add each vertex to the *end* of the solution list as we visit it, all of the edges will lead backward. If we add these vertices to the *beginning* instead, all of the edges will lead forward, giving us a topological sort.

The code is given in (Figure 15–28).

```
 1 /** Return a topological sort of this directed acyclic Graph. */
 2 public List<Integer> topologicalSort() {
 3   LinkedList<Integer> result = new LinkedList<Integer>();
 4   boolean[] visited = new boolean[size()];
 5   for (int i = 0; i < size(); i++) {
 6     if (!visited[i]) {
 7       topologicalTraverse(i, result, visited);
 8     }
 9   }
10   return result;
11 }
12
13 /**
14  * Visit the vertices reachable from vertex in depth-first
15  * postorder, adding them to result. The array visited
16  * prevents any vertex from being visited more than once.
17  */
18 protected void topologicalTraverse(int vertex,
19                                    LinkedList<Integer> result,
20                                    boolean[] visited) {
21   visited[vertex] = true;
```

Figure 15-28: The topological sort algorithm performs a series of depth-first, postorder traversals. These methods are in the Graph class. (Part 1 of 2)

```
22    for (Integer i : neighbors(vertex)) {
23      if (!visited[i]) {
24        topologicalTraverse(i, result, visited);
25      }
26    }
27    result.setNext(new ListNode<Integer>(vertex, result.getNext()));
28  }
```

Figure 15-28: The topological sort algorithm performs a series of depth-first, postorder traversals. These methods are in the Graph class. (Part 2 of 2)

Each vertex is visited exactly once. It takes time in $\Theta(v)$ to traverse the neighbors of each vertex, so the total running time for `topologicalSort()` is in $\Theta(v^2)$.

The PickUpSticks program is now just a bit of input and output (Figure 15–29).

```
 1 import java.util.Scanner;
 2
 3 /** The game of Pick Up Sticks. */
 4 public class PickUpSticks {
 5
 6    /** For reading from the console. */
 7    public static final Scanner INPUT = new Scanner(System.in);
 8
 9    /**
10     * Directed acyclic graph indicating which sticks overlap which
11     * others.
12     */
13    private Graph overlaps;
14
15    /** The number of sticks is set here, but not any overlaps. */
16    public PickUpSticks(int n) {
17      overlaps = new Graph(n);
18    }
19
20    /** Ask the user which sticks overlap which others. */
21    protected void determineOverlaps() {
22      for (int i = 0; i < overlaps.size(); i++) {
23        System.out.print("Which sticks overlap stick " + i
24                        + " (separate with spaces)? ");
25        Scanner line = new Scanner(INPUT.nextLine());
26        while (line.hasNextInt()) {
27          overlaps.addEdge(line.nextInt(), i);
28        }
29      }
30    }
31
```

Figure 15-29: The PickUpSticks program. (Part 1 of 2)

```
32  /** Print an order in which the sticks can be picked up. */
33  protected void solve() {
34    System.out.println("\nThe sticks can be picked up in
35                          + "this order:");
36    System.out.println(overlaps.topologicalSort());
37  }
38
39  /** Create and solve the game. */
40  public static void main(String[] args) {
41    System.out.println("Welcome to Pick Up Sticks.\n");
42    System.out.print("How many sticks are there? ");
43    PickUpSticks game = new PickUpSticks(INPUT.nextInt());
44    INPUT.nextLine();          // To clear out input
45    game.determineOverlaps();
46    game.solve();
47  }
```

Figure 15-29: The PickUpSticks program. (Part 2 of 2)

We do something unusual on lines 24–26 to read several numbers on one line. We read in a line of text, store it in the String line, and then create a new Scanner that reads from that line instead of from the keyboard. We can read ints from this Scanner until there are none left. It wouldn't work to read these directly from the keyboard, because the Scanner would have no way of knowing when the user was done entering numbers.

Exercises

15.14   Give a topological sort of the graph at the bottom of Figure 15–26.

15.15   Draw the graph described in Figure 15–27.

15.16   In the topological sort algorithm, why is it important that the graph be acyclic? What would our topologicalSort() method do if given a cyclic graph?

15.17   Why is it more efficient for topologicalSort() to use a LinkedList rather than an ArrayList?

15.18   What is the running time of topologicalSort(), assuming a neighbor list representation?

15.5 Shortest Paths

A very common graph problem is finding the shortest path between two vertices. Applications range from finding a way through a maze to finding a route through a computer network.

We address the problem for weighted graphs, since the unweighted version is just a special case of this. For example, suppose we want to drive from one city to another. We want a path with the fewest total miles of driving, not the fewest intermediate cities visited. In graph terms, we want to minimize the *sum of the weights* of the edges on the path, not the *number of vertices* along the path. This is the ***shortest-path*** problem.

It is convenient to talk about the ***cost*** to get directly from one vertex to another. This is zero if the vertices are the same one. If the vertices are connected by an edge, the weight of that edge is the cost. If the vertices are *not* connected by an edge (there is no way to go directly between them), the cost is infinite.

Costs are computed by the method `getCost()` in Figure 15–30. It makes use of the special double value `Double.POSITIVE_INFINITY`. This behaves as we would expect infinity to behave— it is greater than any other double, and:

`Double.POSITIVE_INFINITY + 1 == Double.POSITIVE_INFINITY`

```
 1 /** Return the cost to go directly from i to j. */
 2 public double getCost(int i, int j) {
 3   if (i == j) {
 4     return 0.0;
 5   }
 6   if (edges[i][j] == 0.0) {
 7     return Double.POSITIVE_INFINITY;
 8   }
 9   return edges[i][j];
10 }
```

Figure 15–30: The `getCost()` method returns 0 if `i` and `j` are identical, infinity if there is no edge between them, or the weight of the edge if there is one.

We now present two algorithms for finding shortest paths in a weighted graph. For simplicity, we will find the distances rather than the paths themselves. Both algorithms use dynamic programming (Section 9.5). Dijkstra's single-source algorithm determines the distances from one vertex to all others. (We would have to do just as much work to find the distance to a single destination.) The Floyd–Warshall all-pairs algorithm, which might be used to create a table of distances in a road atlas, determines the distance from each vertex to each other vertex.

Dijkstra's Single-Source Algorithm

Dijkstra's single-source algorithm finds the shortest path from one source vertex to each other vertex. It does this by maintaining an array `result` containing the distance to each vertex. Initially, the distance to the source vertex is 0 and all other distances are infinite (Figure 15–31).

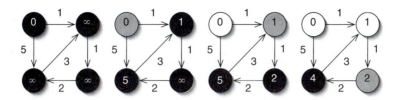

Figure 15-31: Dijkstra's algorithm at work. Black nodes have not yet been visited. Gray nodes have just been visited. The number within each vertex is its estimated distance. Initially (left) all distances are infinity, except for the distance to the source vertex, which is 0. As each vertex is visited, the distances to its neighbors are updated.

As the algorithm runs, it reduces the other distances. By the time each vertex is visited, its distance is correct.

The vertices are visited in order of increasing distance from the source. This guarantees that, by the time we visit a vertex, we have visited all of the vertices along the shortest path to that vertex. This is similar to a breadth-first traversal, but the weights are taken into account. As each vertex i is visited, the distances to its neighbors are updated. Specifically, we compare the current distance of neighbor j (that is, `result[j]`) with the length of the path going from the source to i, then following one edge from i to j:

`result[i] + getCost(i, j)`

If this sum is smaller, we have found a shorter path to j, so we update `result[j]`.

The code for this algorithm is given in Figure 15–32. The main loop on lines 22-29 runs v times. On each pass, it invokes `cheapest()` and runs the inner loop on lines 25–28, each of which take time in $\Theta(v)$. The total running time is therefore in $\Theta(v^2)$.

```
 1 /**
 2  * Return the index of the smallest element of distances,
 3  * ignoring those in visited.
 4  */
 5 protected int cheapest(double[] distances, boolean[] visited) {
 6   int best = -1;
 7   for (int i = 0; i < size(); i++) {
 8     if (!visited[i]
 9         && ((best < 0) || (distances[i] < distances[best]))) {
10       best = i;
11     }
12   }
13   return best;
14 }
15
```

Figure 15-32: Code for Dijkstra's algorithm. (Part 1 of 2)

```
16 /**
17 /* Return an array of the distances from source to each other
18  * vertex.
19  */
20 public double[] distancesFrom(int source) {
21    double[] result = new double[size()];
22    java.util.Arrays.fill(result, Double.POSITIVE_INFINITY);
23    result[source] = 0;
24    boolean[] visited = new boolean[size()];
25    for (int i = 0; i < size(); i++) {
26      int vertex = cheapest(result, visited);
27      visited[vertex] = true;
28      for (int j = 0; j < size(); j++) {
29        result[j] = Math.min(result[j],
30                             result[vertex] + getCost(vertex, j));
31      }
32    }
33    return result;
34 }
```

Figure 15-32: Code for Dijkstra's algorithm. (Part 2 of 2)

The Floyd–Warshall All-Pairs Algorithm

To find the shortest path between each pair of vertices, we could just run Dijkstra's algorithm once from each vertex, using time in $\Theta(v^3)$. The *Floyd–Warshall all-pairs algorithm* takes time in this order, but it is somewhat simpler, so there is a smaller constant factor associated with the asymptotic notation. It is also somewhat easier to write.

Like Dijkstra's algorithm, the Floyd–Warshall all-pairs algorithm uses dynamic programming. Specifically, it maintains a two-dimensional `result` array, where `result[i][j]` is the shortest known distance from vertex i to vertex j.

Initially, all of the elements are initialized to the costs, as computed by `getCost()`. The Floyd–Warshall algorithm updates the `result` by asking the following series of questions:

- What is the shortest distance between each pair of vertices using *vertex 0* as an intermediate point?

- What is the shortest distance between each pair of vertices using *vertices 0 and 1* as intermediate points?

- What is the shortest distance between each pair of vertices using *vertices 0 through 2* as intermediate points?

This continues until all possible intermediate points have been considered, at which point the distances are correct.

To see how the updating works, suppose we have considered vertices 0 through 4 as intermediate points, and we're ready to consider 0 through 5 (Figure 15–33). There are two possibilities for each pair of vertices i and j:

- The shortest path using vertices 0 through 5 as intermediate points *does not* involve vertex 5. It was already correct.

- The shortest path using vertices 0 through 5 as intermediate points *does* involve vertex 5. It must be `result[i][5] + result[5][j]`. Neither of these two subpaths can have vertex 5 as an intermediate point, because it is an endpoint.

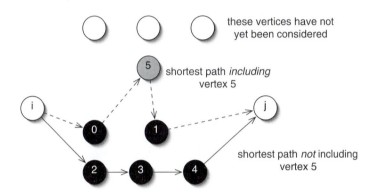

Figure 15–33: Finding the shortest path from vertex i to vertex j, using only vertices 0 through 5 as intermediate points. The shortest distance must be either `result[i][j]` (lower path) or `result[i][5] + result[5][j]` (upper path). This diagram is schematic; many other edges, not shown, are presumed to exist.

Updating `result` consists of taking the minimum of these two possibilities for each pair of vertices.

The code (Figure 15–34) is short, sweet, and to the point. Lines 11–19 are a simple triply nested loop, giving a running time in $\Theta(v^3)$.

```
1 /**
2  * Return a two-dimensional array of the distances from each vertex
3  * to each other vertex.
4  */
5 public double[][] distances() {
6   double[][] result = new double[size()][size()];
```

Figure 15–34: The Floyd–Warshall all-pairs algorithm. (Part 1 of 2)

```
7   for (int i = 0; i < size(); i++) {
8     for (int j = 0; j < size(); j++) {
9         result[i][j] = getCost(i, j);
10    }
11  }
12  for (int midpoint = 0; midpoint < size(); midpoint++) {
13    for (int i = 0; i < size(); i++) {
14      for (int j = 0; j < size(); j++) {
15        result[i][j] = Math.min(result[i][j],
16                                result[i][midpoint]
17                                + result[midpoint][j]);
18      }
19    }
20  }
21  return result;
22 }
```

Figure 15-34: The Floyd–Warshall all-pairs algorithm. (Part 2 of 2)

Exercises

15.19   What is the value of `1 / 0`? What about `1.0 / 0`?

15.20   Write a Graph method which takes two vertex numbers and returns the distance between them.

15.21   What is the order of the running time of the `getCost()` method (Figure 15–30)? What would it be if Graph used the neighbor list representation instead of the neighbor matrix representation?

15.22   Would the algorithms in this section work on unweighted graphs? Explain.

15.6 Minimum Spanning Trees

Our last graph algorithm deals with the situation in which we want to connect a set of vertices while minimizing expenses. For example, we might want to connect a set of computers in a building using as little cable as possible.

We begin by defining a *spanning tree*. Given a connected, undirected graph G, a spanning tree is another graph which has all of G's vertices and a subset of G's edges (Figure 15–35). The spanning tree is also connected, but has only $v - 1$ edges. This is the minimum number of edges required to connect all of the vertices. A spanning tree never contains a cycle. There may be more than one spanning tree for a given graph.

In a weighted graph, a *minimum spanning tree* is a spanning tree in which the sum of the edge weights is as small as possible. In the computer network example, if the edges are the lengths of

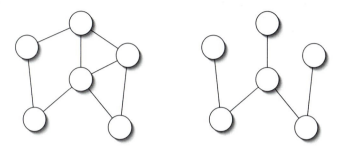

Figure 15-35: A connected, undirected graph (left) and one of several spanning trees for that graph (right).

potential cables, we want to use no more cable than necessary. There may be more than one minimum spanning tree for a given graph.

There are several algorithms for finding minimum spanning trees. We present **Kruskal's minimum spanning tree algorithm**. The idea behind this algorithm is quite simple: begin with an edgeless graph (Figure 15-36), then add edges until we have a minimum spanning tree.

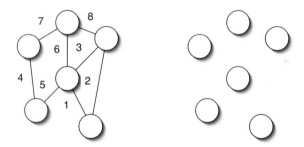

Figure 15-36: Given a weighted graph (left), Kruskal's minimum spanning tree algorithm starts with a new graph having no edges (right).

In each pass through the main loop, we consider adding the cheapest edge that we haven't tried before. If there was not already a path between the vertices at the ends of this edge, we add the edge (Figure 15-37).

This process continues until we have a connected graph, which is a minimum spanning tree (Figure 15-38).

The skeptical reader may wonder, "Is it always best to choose the cheapest edge at each step? Might there be some cheaper path to connect these vertices that involves more edges?" There is nothing to worry about, because any such path would have to be made of *even cheaper* edges that have already been considered. If it existed, we would have found it by now.

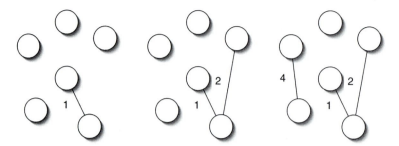

Figure 15-37: Three steps in building a minimum spanning tree. At each step, we add the cheapest edge from the original graph, unless it connects two already-connected vertices. Here, the edge of cost 3 was skipped for this reason.

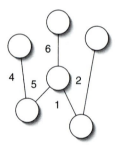

Figure 15-38: When the graph is connected, it is a minimum spanning tree.

An algorithm like this, which always does whatever seems best in the short term, is called a *greedy algorithm*. Ignoring what's over the horizon is not always a good idea, as is known by Chess players, guidance counselors, and global climate change researchers. Sometimes we can prove that there's no danger of missing out on something better, as we have done for this problem.

The minimumSpanningTree() method (Figure 15–39) takes advantage of a couple of data structures from Chapter 14. In order to find the next-cheapest edge, we use a priority queue

```
1 /** Return a minimum spanning tree for this Graph. */
2 public Graph minimumSpanningTree() {
3    DisjointSetCluster partition = new DisjointSetCluster(size());
4    Graph result = new Graph(size());
5    Heap<Edge> edges = new Heap<Edge>();
```

Figure 15-39: Kruskal's algorithm for finding a minimum spanning tree uses some data structures from Chapter 14. (Part 1 of 2)

```
 6    for (int i = 0; i < size(); i++) {
 7      for (Integer j : neighbors(i)) {
 8        edges.add(new Edge(i, j, getEdge(i, j)));
 9      }
10    }
11    while (!(edges.isEmpty())) {
12      Edge e = edges.remove();
13      int i = e.getSource();
14      int j = e.getDest();
15      if (!(partition.inSameSet(i, j))) {
16        partition.mergeSets(i, j);
17        result.setUndirectedEdge(i, j, e.getWeight());
18      }
19    }
20    return result;
21 }
```

Figure 15–39: Kruskal's algorithm for finding a minimum spanning tree uses some data structures from Chapter 14. (Part 2 of 2)

(Section 14.1). On line 12, we extract the cheapest edge from the priority queue of edges. To keep track of which vertices are connected, we use a disjoint set cluster (Section 14.2). On line 15, we check if vertices i and j are in the same set.

As a final detail, the priority queue edges has elements of type Edge. The Edge class is given in Figure 15–40.

```
 1 /** An edge connecting two vertices in a graph. */
 2 public class Edge implements Comparable<Edge> {
 3
 4    /** Index of the destination vertex. */
 5    private int dest;
 6
 7    /** Index of the source vertex. */
 8    private int source;
 9
10    /** Weight associated with this Edge. */
11    private double weight;
12
13    /** Store the given values. */
14    public Edge(int source, int dest, double weight) {
15      this.source = source;
16      this.dest = dest;
17      this.weight = weight;
18    }
19
```

Figure 15–40: The Edge class. (Part 1 of 2)

```
20    public int compareTo(Edge that) {
21      if (weight > that.weight) {
22        return 1;
23      }
24      if (weight == that.weight) {
25        return 0;
26      }
27      return -1;
28    }
29
30    /** Return the destination vertex of this Edge. */
31    public int getDest() {
32      return dest;
33    }
34
35    /** Return the source vertex of this Edge. */
36    public int getSource() {
37      return source;
38    }
39
40    /** Return the weight of this Edge. */
41    public double getWeight() {
42      return weight;
43    }
44
45 }
```

Figure 15-40: The Edge class. (Part 2 of 2)

Analyzing Kruskal's algrithm, we see that line 7 takes time in $\Theta(v)$ and runs v times, for a total in $\Theta(v^2)$. Line 8, on the other hand, only runs e times. Each priority queue insertion takes time in $O(\log e)$, so the total time for line 8 is $O(e \log e)$. The main loop on lines 11–19 is executed at most e times. Each pass involves removing an edge from the priority queue ($O(\log e)$ in the worst case) and a couple of disjoint set cluster operations ($O(\log^* e)$ amortized). The total amortized running time for the algorithm is therefore in:

$$O(v^2 + e \log e + e \log e) = O(v^2 \log e)$$

Exercises

15.23   Under what conditions will the main loop on lines 11–19 of Figure 15–39 run e times?

15.24   Kruskal's algorithm could be made to run faster by keeping track of the number of connected components. What is the initial value of this variable? At what value can the algorithm stop, even if all edges haven't yet been examined? When can this variable be decremented? Does this change the order of the running time of the algorithm?

15.25 What is the amortized running time of Kruskal's algorithm, assuming a neighbor list representation?

15.26 In our representation, each undirected edge is represented by *two* directed edges. Why do these excess edges not cause a problem for Kruskal's algorithm?

15.27 In what sense is Dijsktra's single-source algorithm (Section 15.5) a greedy algorithm?

Summary

A graph is a collection of vertices connected by edges. Graphs may be directed or undirected, weighted or unweighted, and connected or unconnected. A graph with no cycles (roughly, paths leading from a vertex back to itself) is called acyclic. If v is the number of vertices in a graph and e is the number of edges, $e \in O(v^2)$. If e is close to this limit, the graph is dense. Otherwise, it is sparse. An enormous variety of computational problems can be phrased in terms of graphs.

Graphs are normally represented using neighbor lists or neighbor matrices. Neighbor lists use less space for sparse graphs. Neighbor matrices take less time in either case.

A graph may be traversed depth-first or breadth-first, starting from a specified source vertex.

A topological sort of a directed acyclic graph is an ordering of the vertices such that no edges point from a later vertex to an earlier vertex. We have an algorithm for topological sorting that takes time in $\Theta(v^2)$.

We give two algorithms for finding shortest paths in a weighted graph: Dijkstra's single-source algorithm, which takes time in $\Theta(v^2)$, and the Floyd–Warshall all-pairs algorithm, which takes time in $\Theta(v^3)$.

A minimum spanning tree of a connected, undirected, weighted graph eliminates some edges so as to stay connected while minimizing the total edge weight. Kruskal's minimum spanning tree algorithm is a greedy algorithm which takes amortized time in $O(v^2 \log e)$.

Vocabulary

acyclic. Of a graph, having no cycles.

adjacency list. Neighbor list.

adjacency matrix. Neighbor matrix.

breadth-first. Graph traversal in which vertices nearer to the source are visited first.

connected. Of a graph, having a path from each vertex to each other vertex.

cost. Number indicating difficulty of travelling directly from one vertex to another. Zero if the vertices are the same, infinity if there is no edge, or the weight of the edge if there is one.

cycle. Path of length one or more from a vertex back to itself. In an undirected graph, a cycle may not follow the same edge more than once.

dense. Of a graph, having close to the maximum possible number of edges.

depth-first. Graph traversal that follows edges all the way to a dead end before backing up and trying another branch.

Dijkstra's single-source algorithm. Dynamic programming algorithm for finding the shortest path from one vertex to all others in a graph.

directed. Of an edge, leading from one vertex to another, but not vice versa. Of a graph, having only directed edges.

directed acyclic graph (dag). Directed graph with no cycles.

distance. Length of the shortest path from one vertex to another.

edge. Connection between a pair of vertices in a graph.

Floyd–Warshall all-pairs algorithm. Dynamic programming algorithm for finding the shortest path from each vertex to each other vertex in a graph.

graph. Set of vertices and associated set of edges.

greedy algorithm. Any algorithm that does whatever seems best in the short term, such as Kruskal's minimum spanning tree algorithm.

Kruskal's minimum spanning tree algorithm. Algorithm for finding a minimum spanning tree by repeatedly adding the lowest-weight edge from the original graph that does not create a cycle.

length. Number of edges along a path.

minimum spanning tree. Of a weighted, connected, undirected graph, a spanning tree having minimal sum of edge weights.

neighbor. Vertex that can be reached by following an edge from another vertex.

neighbor list. Graph representation consisting of an array of linked lists, each containing the indices of the neighbors of one vertex.

neighbor matrix. Graph representation consisting of a two-dimensional array. Each element specifies the presence (and, if appropriate, weight) of an edge.

path. Sequence of vertices, each a neighbor of the previous one.

self-loop. Directed edge leading from a vertex back to itself.

shortest path. Path between two vertices having, among all such paths, the minimum sum of weights.

source. Vertex at the beginning of an edge or traversal.

spanning tree. Of a connected, undirected graph, another such graph having all the same vertices but only $v - 1$ edges.

sparse. Of a graph, having far fewer than the maximum possible number of edges.

topological sort. Ordering of the vertices in a dag so that all edges point from earlier to later vertices.

undirected. Of an edge, connecting two vertices in both directions. Of a graph, having only undirected edges.

vertex. Node in a graph.

weighted. Of a graph, having data (usually numbers) associated with edges.

Problems

15.28   Write a better `toString()` method for the Galaxy class.

15.29   Add a method `isCyclic()` to the Graph class that returns `true` if and only if the (directed) graph is cyclic. What is the order of the worst-case running time of your algorithm?

15.30   Implement the neighbor list representation of a graph by modifying the Graph class from this chapter. The more complicated methods, such as `distances()` and `topologicalSort()`, should not have to be altered.

15.31   Modify the method `breadthFirstTraverse()` (Figure 15–21) so that it returns an Iterator instead of a List. Your version should *not* simply create a List and then ask it for an Iterator. Instead, create a BreadthFirstGraphIterator class which maintains the queue and the set of visited vertices.

15.32   Modify Dijkstra's single-source algorithm to find the actual paths instead of the distances. Do this by keeping track, for each vertex, of the previous vertex along the shortest known path from the source.

Projects

15.33   Implement the game of Nine Men's Morris (Figure 15–41).

15.34   Implement the game of Aggression (Figure 15–42). Generate the board randomly, so that a city has a 50% chance of being connected to each of the cities next to it horizontally, vertically, or diagonally.

Nine Men's Morris

Players: 2

Object: To either reduce the opponent to two pieces or to leave the opponent with no legal move.

Board: See below. The pieces (merels) are placed on the dots (points) and moved along the lines to adjacent points. Each player gets nine merels in her color. The board is initially empty.

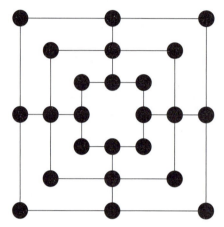

Play: Players take turns. On a turn, a player places a merel on an unoccupied point. If a player has no merels left to place, she instead moves one of her merels to an adjacent point.

Capture: If a player's move causes three of her merels to be in a horizontal or vertical line through adjacent points, she has formed a mill. She gets to remove any one of the opponent's merels from the board. If possible, she must choose a merel which is not currently part of a mill. The removed merel is discarded; the opponent does not get it back.

Game End: The game ends when one player either has only two merels or has no legal move. This player loses.

Figure 15–41: Nine Men's Morris is one of the oldest games in existence.

Aggression

Players: 2, black and white.

Object: To control the most cities at the end of the game.

Board: There are 20 cities and some roads on the board. Two cities are adjacent if they are connected by a single road segment. The board may be different in each game. A typical board is shown below.

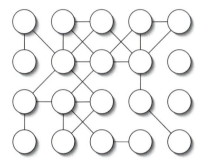

Setup: The board is initially empty. Each player starts with 100 troops. In turns, each player places one or more troops in any unoccupied city to claim it. This continues until all cities have been claimed or both players have deployed all of their troops. An example is shown below.

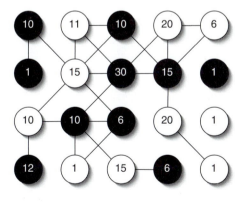

Figure 15–42: Aggression is a simple, abstract wargame. (Part 1 of 2)

Play: Taking turns, each player chooses a city to attack. The attack is successful if the number of troops in the city is less than the number of opposing troops in adjacent cities. After a successful attack, the defending troops are removed and the city becomes neutral. The attacking troops are unaffected. An unsuccessful attack has no effect.

As an example, in the game above, black could successfully attack the upper white 20 (with 45 adjacent troops), but not the lower white 20 (with only 15 adjacent troops).

Game End: The game ends when either one player has no troops left or there are no successful attacks left to make. The player controlling the most cities wins.

Figure 15–42: Aggression is a simple, abstract wargame. (Part 2 of 2)

16

Memory Management

We rely heavily on Java's automatic memory management. When we allocate memory for an object or array using the keyword new, we don't think about where the memory comes from. When an object or array becomes unreachable, it magically disappears.

Some languages, notably C and C++, do not have automatic memory management. Section 16.1 discusses the alternative: explicit memory management. This is worth knowing, because we may be called upon to work in one of these languages some day, and because we can sometimes optimize a Java program by using explicit memory management.

Section 16.2 discusses the algorithms behind automatic memory management systems like Java's.

16.1 Explicit Memory Management

A computer's memory is divided into two sections: the call stack and the *heap*. The call stack, discussed in Section 4.2, is where variables (and arguments) are stored. The rest of memory is the heap. (This has nothing to do with the use of the word "heap" in Section 14.1.)

For each variable, a certain number of bytes are allocated in the call frame where the variable lives. If the variable is of a primitive type, the required number of bytes is known in advance, so the variable's value can be stored directly in the call frame. For reference types, which are often polymorphic, it is not clear how many bytes must be allocated. For example, a variable of type Object might hold a simple object like a Die or or something much more elaborate like a HashTable. Such objects live in the heap, which is effectively a gigantic array. Within the call frame, a reference to the heap object is stored. A reference is actually a number, called the ***address*** of the object, indicating where in the heap the object lives.

An object may take up several positions, or ***cells***, in the heap. For example, an instance of class Card has two fields, so it takes up two cells in the heap. (This is an oversimplification, but it will do for our purposes.) When we initialize a variable

```
Card card = new Card(7, Card.HEARTS);
```

we get the situation shown in Figure 16–1.

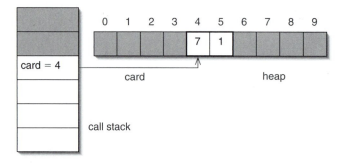

Figure 16-1: The variable `card`, on the call stack, is a reference to an object in the heap. The address of this object is 4. The arrow is redundant; the actual pointer is the number 4 on the call stack. Shaded cells are not in use.

An object can, of course, have fields of reference types. In other words, the heap can contain pointers. A linked list might be represented as in Figure 16–2. Notice that the list can be scattered around memory. Indeed, as we shall see in Section 16.2, the Java system might even move things around in memory without our knowledge! As long as following the pointers gets us to the correct objects, this is not a problem.

A null pointer is represented by a pointer to some invalid address. In Figure 16–2, this is the number –1. This is why we use ==, rather than equals(), to check if an object is null. The == operator directly compares the contents of two locations in memory. In contrast, equals() follows the pointers in those two locations and compares the objects to which they refer.

In languages with explicit memory management, like C and C++, it is possible to determine the address of an object. In Java, we can't see the addresses. This is what people mean when they say that "Java doesn't have pointers." We do have references in Java, so we can build linked structures, but we don't have direct access to the addresses themselves.

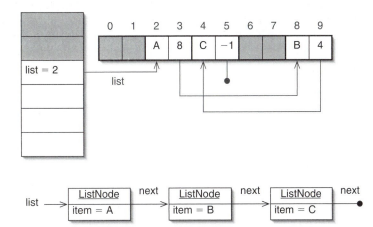

Figure 16–2: A linked list. In the heap (top), the first node is at address 2, the second at address 8, and the last at address 4. Within each node, the second cell is a reference to (that is, gives the address of) the next one. The order in which the elements appear in the list (bottom) is not necessarily the order in which they appear in memory.

Aficionados of various languages will argue at great length about whether or not addresses should be visible. We won't attempt to settle this argument here, but we will illustrate some of the consequences of each approach.

We can't access real addresses in Java, but we can build a simulated memory in which the addresses *are* visible (Figure 16–3).

```
1  /**
2   * A simulated memory for illustrating memory management.  Each
3   * object takes up two cells.
4   */
5  public class Memory {
6
7    /** Number of cells in memory. */
8    public static final int MEMORY_SIZE = 1000;
9
10   /** The null reference. */
11   public static final int NULL = -1;
12
13   /** Data are stored in these locations. */
14   private int[] heap;
15
```

Figure 16–3: A simulated memory. (Part 1 of 2)

```
16   /** Create the heap. */
17   public Memory() {
18     heap = new int[MEMORY_SIZE];
19   }
20
21   /** Return the contents of address. */
22   public int get(int address) {
23     return heap[address];
24   }
25
26   /** Set the contents of address to value. */
27   public void set(int address, int value) {
28     heap[address] = value;
29   }
30
31 }
```

Figure 16-3: A simulated memory. (Part 2 of 2)

Figure 16–4 shows Java statements and the corresponding statements for the simulated memory.

Java	Simulated Memory

`Card card = new Card(7, 1);`	`int card = 4;`
	`set(card + 0, 7);`
	`set(card + 1, 1);`

`int r = card.rank;`	`int r = get(card + 1);`
`card.suit = 2;`	`set(card + 0, 2);`

Figure 16-4: Some Java statements and the corresponding statements for the simulated memory. In the simulated memory, there are no real references; we must handle addresses directly.

The reader with an eye for detail will wonder why the address 4 was chosen. This choice is arbitrary, but it raises a very serious concern: how do we make sure we don't choose a section of the heap that overlaps with one being used for some other object? *Memory management* is the job of keeping track of which addresses are in use.

The Free List

Let us assume, for simplicity, that each object takes up exactly two cells in the heap. We can string all of the unused cell pairs together in a sort of linked list (Figure 16–5). This list of available memory is called the *free list*.

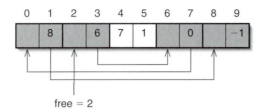

free = 2

Figure 16–5: The free list contains the objects beginning at addresses 2, 6, 0, and 8. As shown here, the free list does not necessarily start at address 0.

When we first create our memory, we have to string all of the cell pairs together to create the free list (Figure 16–6).

```
1 /** Address of the beginning of the free list. */
2 private int free;
3
4 /** Create the heap. */
5 public Memory() {
6   heap = new int[MEMORY_SIZE];
7   for (int i = 0; i < heap.length; i += 2) {
8     set(i + 1, i + 2);
9   }
10   set(heap.length - 1, NULL);
11   free = 0;
12 }
```

Figure 16–6: When the memory is first created, all memory must be put on the free list.

When we need a new object, we just take the first one off the front of the free list (Figure 16–7).

```
1 /**
2  * Return the address of an available object, which is removed from
3  * the free list.
4  */
5 public int allocate() {
6   int result = free;
7   free = get(free + 1);
8   return result;
9 }
```

Figure 16–7: The `allocate()` method returns the address of an available object.

Thus, instead of

```
int card = 4;
```

we would say:

```
int card = allocate();
```

This allocation is similar to what happens in Java when we use new. A more significant difference comes when we're done with an object. In Java, if there are no references to an object, it is
automatically returned to the free list. In a language with explicit memory management, we have
to tell the system that we're no longer using the memory allocated for that object. In our simulated memory, this is accomplished with the method free() (Figure 16–8).

```
1 /** Put the object at address back on the free list. */
2 public void free(int address) {
3   set(address + 1, free);
4   free = address;
5 }
```

Figure 16-8: In explicit memory management, when we're done with an object, we
have to manually put it back on the free list, using this method.

If we are done with a linked structure (Figure 16–9), we must be sure to free each of the objects
in that structure.

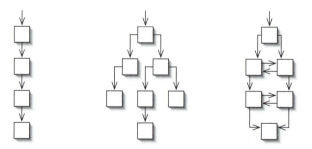

Figure 16-9: Freeing linked structures requires some care. Objects can be linked in
lists (left), trees (middle), and directed graphs (right). Each square here represents an
object, which may occupy many cells in the heap and therefore contain several
pointers.

Freeing a list is fairly easy, but we must take care to store the address of the next object *before*
we free the current one (Figure 16–10). Once we free some memory, any other part of our program (or even another program) may claim it and change its contents.

Freeing a tree is more difficult. We have to have some way of distinguishing cells that contain
pointers from those that don't. In practice, the compiler builds this information into the instruc-
tion part of the program. In our simulated memory, we assume that any value less than NULL is
not a pointer.

```
1 /** Free the linked list starting at address. */
2 public void freeList(int address) {
3   while (address != NULL) {
4     int next = get(address + 1);
5     free(address);
6     address = next;
7   }
8 }
```

Figure 16-10: Freeing a linked list.

To free a tree, we just traverse it, freeing objects as we go (Figure 16–11). Once we free the memory for an object, we can no longer look inside it to find its descendants. It therefore is important to do this traversal postorder.

```
1 /** Free the tree rooted at address. */
2 public void freeTree(int address) {
3   if (address > NULL) {
4     freeTree(get(address));
5     freeTree(get(address + 1));
6     free(address);
7   }
8 }
```

Figure 16-11: A tree can be freed with a postorder traversal.

Notice that freeTree() would also work to free a linked list. If we know that we have a linked list, though, freeList() is more efficient, because it does not involve recursive method invocations.

We will not give a method for freeing a graph just yet, but note that such a method would also work for a tree or a linked list. Again, there would be a price in efficiency for handling a more general case. The automatic memory management techniques described in Section 16.2 address this most general case, so the programmer needn't think about the details of freeing linked structures.

Advocates of explicit memory management emphasize the efficiency cost of always using general-purpose techniques when sometimes a simpler method like freeList() would do. Advocates of automatic memory management point out that insidious bugs that can arise from failure to properly free memory when we're done with it.

Suppose a method allocates memory for a temporary object, but fails to return it to the free list afterward. Every time the method is run, a little bit less memory is available. This kind of bug is called a ***memory leak***. A memory leak is difficult to find, because it does not cause a problem immediately. The program runs perfectly *for a while*, until the computer runs out of memory and the program crashes.

A complementary bug is freeing some memory that we're not really done using. A pointer into memory that we don't really control is called a ***dangling pointer***. A dangling pointer can be caused either by freeing memory and then trying to access it, or by failing to initialize a pointer in the first place. Debugging a program with a dangling pointer is particularly nasty, because the program may behave differently on each run. When we free memory, its contents will probably stay the same for a while, but once someone else grabs that memory, its contents will change in unpredictable ways. Even more bizarre behavior can result from *writing* to the memory on the other end of a dangling pointer, which could alter the data—or even the instructions—of another program.

Barring bugs in the Java compiler, both memory leaks and dangling pointers are impossible in Java. Memory is returned to the free list exactly when we're done with it. We can't even get a dangling pointer by failing to initialize a field of a reference type, because Java automatically initializes such fields to null. If we try to follow such a reference, we get a NullPointerException.

Returning to the other side of the debate, advocates of explicit memory management point out that certain things can be done only with direct access to addresses. For example, consider the method swap() (Figure 16–12).

```
1 /** Swap the data at addresses x and y. */
2 public void swap(int x, int y) {
3    int temp = get(x);
4    set(x, y);
5    set(y, temp);
6 }
```

Figure 16-12: This method works in the simulated memory, in which we have access to addresses, but can't be written for normal Java variables.

We can do this in the simulated memory, but in plain Java, *there is no way to write* a method swap() so that after

```
int x = 1;
int y = 2;
swap(x, y);
```

x will be 2 and y will be 1.

The debate between explicit and automatic memory management is analogous to the debate between manual and automatic transmissions. A manual transmission offers more efficiency and precise control, but requires more attention and responsibility from the driver. An automatic transmission sacrifices a bit of efficiency to let the driver concentrate on other tasks, such as steering. In programming, the tradeoff is between efficiency on the one hand and correctness and rapid development on the other hand.

Using a Node Pool

We can gain some of the efficiency of explicit memory management without switching to another language such as C or C++. In a program which spends a lot of time allocating and freeing memory, we can allocate a bunch of objects—say, list nodes—in advance. These objects comprise a *node pool*. We manage the node pool much like the free list described above (Figure 16–13).

```
 1 /** A pool of ListNodes. */
 2 public class NodePool<E> {
 3
 4   /** Number of nodes in the pool. */
 5   public static final int POOL_SIZE = 1000;
 6
 7   /** First in the linked list of free nodes. */
 8   private ListNode<E> front;
 9
10   /** Create the pool. */
11   public NodePool() {
12     for (int i = 0; i < POOL_SIZE; i++) {
13       front = new ListNode<E>(null, front);
14     }
15   }
16
17   /** Get a node from the pool, set its fields, and return it. */
18   public ListNode<E> allocate(E item, ListNode<E> next) {
19     ListNode<E> result = front;
20     front = front.getNext();
21     result.setItem(item);
22     result.setNext(next);
23     return result;
24   }
25
26   /** Return a node to the pool. */
27   public void free(ListNode<E> node) {
28     node.setNext(front);
29     front = node;
30   }
31
32 }
```

Figure 16–13: A node pool. All of the nodes are created in the constructor.

The node pool improves the efficiency of our program for two reasons. First, we don't have to use Java's general-purpose automatic memory manager to keep track of our nodes. Second, since all of the nodes are allocated at the same time, they probably live near each other in the heap, which improves cache performance.

How much speed do we gain from using a node pool? The answer can vary considerably, depending on the particular Java system being used. We can perform an empirical test by doing some memory-intensive operations both with and without the node pool. The methods in Figure 16–14 grow and shrink a linked stack of 1,000 nodes, repeating the experiment 10,000 times.

```
 1 /** Number of times to run the experiment. */
 2 public static final int RUNS = 10000;
 3
 4 /** Compare memory-intensive operations with and without pool. */
 5 protected void test() {
 6   long before;
 7   long after;
 8   ListNode<E> list;
 9   System.out.print("With node pool: ");
10   list = null;
11   before = System.currentTimeMillis();
12   for (int run = 0; run < RUNS; run++) {
13     for (int i = 0; i < POOL_SIZE; i++) {
14       list = allocate(null, list);
15     }
16     for (int i = 0; i < POOL_SIZE; i++) {
17       ListNode<E> node = list;
18       list = list.getNext();
19       free(node);
20     }
21   }
22   after = System.currentTimeMillis();
23   System.out.println((after - before) + " milliseconds");
24   System.out.print("Without node pool: ");
25   list = null;
26   before = System.currentTimeMillis();
27   for (int run = 0; run < RUNS; run++) {
28     for (int i = 0; i < POOL_SIZE; i++) {
29       list = new ListNode<E>(null, list);
30     }
31     for (int i = 0; i < POOL_SIZE; i++) {
32       list = list.getNext();
33     }
34   }
35   after = System.currentTimeMillis();
36   System.out.println((after - before) + " milliseconds");
37 }
38
39 /** Create a pool and test it. */
```

Figure 16-14: Testing the value of a node pool. (Part 1 of 2)

```
40 public static void main(String[] args) {
41   NodePool pool = new NodePool<Object>();
42   pool.test();
43 }
```

Figure 16-14: Testing the value of a node pool. (Part 2 of 2)

Results will vary from one machine to another. On the author's system, a typical run produces this result:

```
With node pool: 200 milliseconds
Without node pool: 960 milliseconds
```

The use of the node pool appears to speed up this program by a factor of between 4 and 5. This result should be taken with a grain of salt, because this particular program does almost nothing but allocate and free memory.

Like any other optimization, a node pool should be used sparingly. A program should first be made to run correctly. Once this is done, if there is reason to suspect that a lot of time is being spent on memory management, a node pool can offer considerable speedup.

Exercises

16.1   Do arrays live on the call stack or in the heap? Explain.

16.2   What programs have you used that were too slow, and therefore might have benefited from explicit memory management? What programs were either buggy or took too long to develop, and therefore might have benefited from automatic memory management?

16.3   What's wrong with the version of `freeList()` in Figure 16–15?

```
1 /** Free the linked list starting at address. */
2 public void freeList(int address) {
3   while (address != NULL) {
4     free(address);
5     address = get(address + 1);
6   }
7 }
```

Figure 16-15: Broken version of `freeList()` for Exercise 16.3.

16.4   In line 3 of Figure 16–11, what would happen if the > were replaced with >=?

16.5   Does the use of a node pool make it possible to produce a memory leak or a dangling pointer? Explain.

16.6   What happens if we invoke `allocate()` on a NodePool in which all of the nodes are in use?

16.7   Many programs take some time to initialize data structures before they can accept commands from the user. Does the use of a node pool speed this up or slow it down? Explain.

16.2 Automatic Memory Management

In Java, memory is managed automatically. Memory that cannot be reached from a *root* (a variable or argument on the call stack) is called *garbage*. Under explicit memory management, memory leaks occur when garbage is not cleaned up. This section describes several algorithms used to automatically return garbage to the pool of available memory.

Reference Counting

A first approach is to store, along with each object, a number indicating how many pointers point to that object (Figure 16–16). When this *reference count* drops to zero, the object is garbage, so it can be returned to the free list.

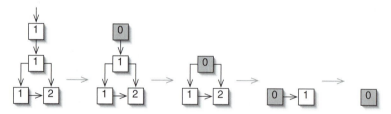

Figure 16–16: With reference counting, each object keeps track of the number of pointers pointing to it. Each square here represents an object, with its reference count shown inside. In the situation at left, a variable points to the top object. When that variable changes, the object's reference count drops to zero, so it can be returned to the free list. This in turn reduces the reference count of other objects, eventually freeing the entire structure.

Reference counting is simple and fast, but it does not work for cyclic graphs (Figure 16–17). Even after all of the incoming pointers are removed, the reference counts within a cyclic island of garbage never drop to zero.

Only *pure* reference counting systems have this problem. Many modern systems use a combination of reference counting and one of the approaches to be described next.

The next two approaches are called *garbage collection*. They wait until the system is running low on memory, then pause to clear out the garbage. This pause was quite noticeable with early garbage collectors but is much shorter in modern systems. Reference counting, in contrast, reclaims the memory from each object as soon as it becomes inaccessible.

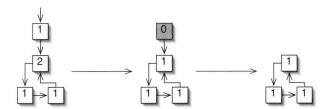

Figure 16-17: Pure reference counting cannot reclaim cyclic structures.

Mark-and-Sweep Garbage Collection

A *mark-and-sweep garbage collector* operates in two phases:

1. Perform a depth-first traversal of the objects in memory, starting from each root. As each object is visited, mark it. (In such a system, each object has a bit set aside for marking.) At the end of this phase, only the reachable objects are marked.

2. Sweep through the heap, reclaiming any space that isn't in a marked object. When a marked object is encountered, unmark it to prepare for the next garbage collection.

This technique works, even when the heap contains cyclic graphs. It is somewhat wasteful because it has to traverse the entire heap. In practice, most objects are discarded shortly after they are created. For example, an object created during a method invocation becomes garbage when the method ends (unless a reference to the object is returned). The consequence is that *the heap consists almost entirely of garbage*. The next technique performs garbage collection without touching the garbage.

Copying Garbage Collection

A second type of garbage collector combines several advantages with one horrendous-sounding disadvantage: the computer can only use half its memory at any given time! A *copying garbage collector* divides the heap into two halves (Figure 16–18). When the garbage collector is not running, only one half can be used. When this half fills up, the garbage collector copies all of the in-use nodes from that half into the other half, leaving the garbage behind. Now, only the *other* half can be used until the next garbage collection.

The half of the heap in which all of the reachable objects start is called *from-space*. When the algorithm finishes, the objects will have been moved into the other half, *to-space*.

The algorithm starts with the objects to which roots point directly. These objects are copied into to-space (Figure 16–19). Whenever an object is copied, a *forwarding address* is left behind. This is the object's new address. It is easy to distinguish forwarding addresses from other pointers, because they point into to-space.

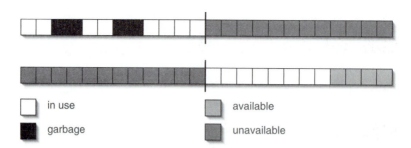

Figure 16-18: A copying garbage collector divides the heap in half. Before garbage collection (top), the right half is unavailable. After garbage collection (bottom), all of the in-use memory has been copied into the right half and the left half is unavailable.

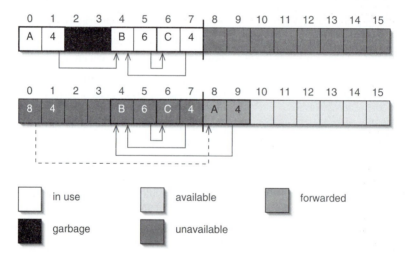

Figure 16-19: Copying garbage collection begins by forwarding the objects to which roots point. Here, assume there is a root pointing to address 0. A forwarding address (dashed arrow) is left in the object's old location.

The algorithm now begins examining the data that have been copied into to-space, cell by cell (Figure 16–20). During this process, additional objects may be copied into to-space. To-space is divided into three regions: data that have been examined, forwarded data that have not yet been examined, and available space.

There are three possibilities for the contents of each cell being examined:

- It's not a pointer. Nothing more has to be done.

- It's a pointer to an object which has not yet been forwarded into to-space. Forward the object and set the current cell to point to the new location.

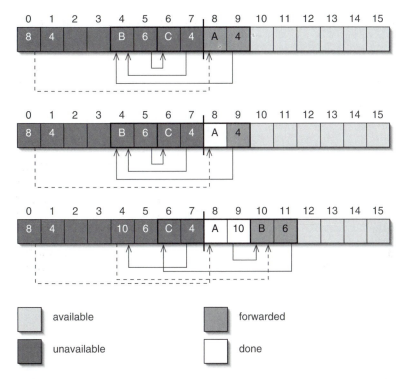

Figure 16–20: The copying garbage collector continues by examining the data that have been copied into to-space. To-space (right half) is divided into three sections: data that have been examined (white), forwarded data that have not yet been examined (medium grey), and available space (light gray). If a cell does not contain a pointer (like cell 8), no change is necessary. If a cell contains a pointer to an object that has not been forwarded (like cell 9), the object is forwarded and the pointer is changed to point to the new location.

- It's a pointer to an object which has already been forwarded. Set the current cell to point to the new location.

This third case, which is the reason for leaving the forwarding addresses, is illustrated in Figure 16–21.

The process continues until all data copied into to-space has been examined. Now all of the reachable objects have been moved. Garbage collection ends. To-space becomes the usable half of memory.

Something rather remarkable has happened during copying garbage collection. Every single reachable object has been moved to a new location in memory, but the programmer (the one invoking `allocate()`) doesn't have to care! As long as following the same pointers leads to the same objects, it doesn't matter where in memory they are located.

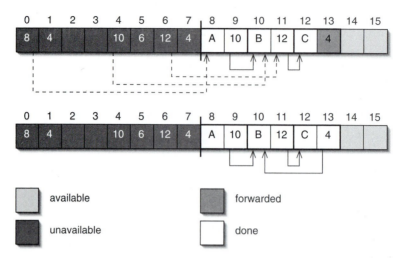

Figure 16-21: When the pointer in cell 13 is examined, it is discovered that the object to which it points (at address 4) has already been forwarded (to address 10). The pointer in cell 13 is updated to point to this new address. At this point in the example, there are no more cells to examine, so the garbage collection is complete.

The copying garbage collector can be illustrated with another simulated memory. The code for this memory assumes that any negative value (including NULL) is not a pointer to be followed. In any experiments with this memory, be sure to use negative numbers for the nonpointer data.

The preliminaries are shown in Figure 16–22. The field `free` indicates the beginning of the region of available memory. The field `end` indicates the end of the half of the heap currently being used (from-space when the garbage collector is running). In `isForwarded()`, `end` is used to determine whether `get(address)` is a pointer into from-space or to-space.

```
 1 /** A simulated memory for illustrating memory management. */
 2 public class MemoryWithGarbageCollection {
 3
 4     // NULL and heap are as in Figure 16-3
 5
 6     /** Number of cells in each half of memory. */
 7     public static final int MEMORY_SIZE = 8;
 8
 9     /** Address of the beginning of the free region. */
10     private int free;
11
```

Figure 16-22: Preliminaries for a memory with copying garbage collection. The constant MEMORY_SIZE is set to an unreasonably small value so that we can print an example later. (Part 1 of 2)

```
12   /** One more than the address of the last free cell. */
13   private int end;
14
15   /** Create the heap. */
16   public MemoryWithGarbageCollection() {
17     heap = new int[MEMORY_SIZE * 2];
18     free = 0;
19     end = MEMORY_SIZE;
20   }
21
22   /**
23    * Return the address of an available object, which is
24    * removed from the free list.
25    */
26   public int allocate() {
27     int result = free;
28     free += 2;
29     return result;
30   }
31
32   // get() and set() are as in Figure 16-3
33
34   /** Forward the two cells at address to destination. */
35   protected void forward(int address, int destination) {
36     set(destination, get(address));
37     set(destination + 1, get(address + 1));
38     set(address, destination);
39   }
40
41   /** Return true if address contains a forwarding address. */
42   protected boolean isForwarded(int address) {
43     return (get(address) > NULL)
44       && ((get(address) > MEMORY_SIZE) == (end == MEMORY_SIZE));
45   }
46
47   // get() and set() are as in Figure 16-3
48
49 }
```

Figure 16–22: Preliminaries for a memory with copying garbage collection. The constant MEMORY_SIZE is set to an unreasonably small value so that we can print an example later. (Part 2 of 2)

The copying garbage collector itself is shown in Figure 16–23. Lines 6–13 set up variables to keep track of the different regions of to-space. Lines 14–15 forward the first object. Lines 16–26 are the main loop that examines each of the cells from head through (but not including) tail. Lines 27–28 set fields to make to-space usable. Line 29 returns the new address of the object that was at root.

```
1  /**
2   * Perform a copying garbage collection, keeping only the objects
3   * reachable from root.  Return the new address of the root object.
4   */
5  public int garbageCollect(int root) {
6    int head; // Beginning of unexamined region of to-space
7    if (end == MEMORY_SIZE) {
8      head = MEMORY_SIZE;
9    } else {
10     head = 0;
11   }
12   int tail = head; // Beginning of unused region of to-space
13   int result = head;
14   forward(root, tail);
15   tail += 2;
16   while (head < tail) {
17     int referent = get(head);
18     if (referent > NULL) {
19       if (!isForwarded(referent)) {
20         forward(referent, tail);
21         tail += 2;
22       }
23       set(head, get(referent));
24     }
25     head++;
26   }
27   free = tail;
28   end = (MEMORY_SIZE * 3) - end;
29   return result;
30 }
```

Figure 16–23: A copying garbage collector.

We can test our garbage collector with the `main()` method in Figure 16–24.

```
1  public String toString() {
2    StringBuilder result = new StringBuilder();
3    for (int i = 0; i < heap.length; i++) {
4      if ((i >= MEMORY_SIZE) == (end == MEMORY_SIZE)) {
5        result.append("X ");
6      } else {
7        result.append(heap[i] + " ");
8      }
9    }
10   return result.toString();
11 }
12
```

Figure 16–24: Methods `toString()` and `main()` to test the garbage collector on the example in Figures 16–19 through 16–21. (Part 1 of 2)

```
13 /** Test the garbage collector. */
14 public static void main(String[] args) {
15    MemoryWithGarbageCollection mem
16       = new MemoryWithGarbageCollection();
17    int a = mem.allocate();
18    mem.set(a, -2);
19    int d = mem.allocate();
20    mem.set(d, -3);
21    mem.set(d + 1, -4);
22    int b = mem.allocate();
23    mem.set(a + 1, b);
24    mem.set(b, -5);
25    int c = mem.allocate();
26    mem.set(b + 1, c);
27    mem.set(c, -5);
28    mem.set(c + 1, b);
29    System.out.println(mem);
30    System.out.println("Moving " + a + " to "
31                          + mem.garbageCollect(a));
32    System.out.println(mem);
33 }
```

Figure 16–24: Methods `toString()` and `main()` to test the garbage collector on the example in Figures 16–19 through 16–21. (Part 2 of 2)

When we run the program, it prints:

```
-2 4 -3 -4 -5 6 -5 4 X X X X X X X X X
Moving 0 to 8
X X X X X X X X -2 10 -5 12 -5 10 0 0
```

We had to use negative numbers instead of letters to represent nonpointer values because heap is of type `int[]`.

The price of copying garbage collection is that only half of memory is available. This price can be reduced by more sophisticated versions of the algorithm which divide the memory into several pieces, all but one of which are usable at any given time. In any case, several advantages make the price worth paying:

- Unlike a mark-and-sweep garbage collector, a copying garbage collector never touches the garbage. Since the heap consists mostly of garbage, this greatly increases the speed of garbage collection.

- After the garbage collector is run, the heap is **compacted**. All of the in-use cells are grouped together at the lower end of the available half of the heap. Consequently, the there is no need for a free list; the available memory can be viewed as an array stack. Whenever memory is needed for a new object, it can be sliced off the front of the single, large chunk of available memory.

- Since objects are near each other in compacted memory, cache performance is improved.

- Using a mark-and-sweep garbage collector with objects of different sizes, we might reach the state shown in Figure 16–25. Memory (or disk storage) which is broken up like this is said to be *fragmented*. In fragmented memory, it may be impossible to allocate a large block of memory, even when the total amount of memory available exceeds the amount needed. When memory is compacted, there is no fragmentation; all available memory is in one long block.

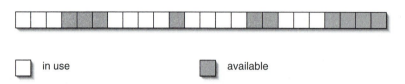

☐ in use	▨ available

Figure 16–25: Fragmented memory. There are 10 cells available, but there is no place to allocate even half this much memory for a single object.

Because of these advantages, many garbage collectors today use some variation of the copying scheme.

Exercises

16.8	Would pure reference counting work on a doubly linked list? Explain.

16.9	In the UNIX operating system (including variants such as Linux and Mac OS X), the ln command creates a hard link to a file. If there is a file source, then after executing the command

ln source target

the file can be referred to by either name. At this point,

rm source

does *not* delete the file from the disk, because it still has another name. Because it is not legal to make a hard link to a directory, the directory structure is a directed acyclic graph. Does reference counting work to determine when a file can be removed from the disk? Explain.

16.10	Suppose the heap has capacity c. When a reference is changed, a reference counter may have to reclaim several objects. What is the worst-case time required for this? What is the amortized time per operation over a sequence of n allocations followed by n deallocations?

16.11	Suppose you have a Java program that controls the landing of an aircraft. It would be very bad for the program to pause for garbage collection just as the plane lands. Find a way to force the garbage collector to run just before this critical moment, so that there will be plenty of memory available. (Hint: Look at the API for the System class.)

16.12   Suppose there are *n* cells in use and *m* cells in the entire heap. How much time is required for mark-and-sweep garbage collection?

16.13   Suppose there are *n* cells in use and *m* cells in the entire heap. How much time is required for copying garbage collection?

16.14   Draw a UML instance diagram of the objects in the heap in Figure 16–19. Assume that each two-cell pair is a ListNode.

16.15   The copying garbage collector traverses all objects reachable from the roots. Is this traversal breadth-first or depth-first?

16.16   Why doesn't the MemoryWithGarbageCollection class have a `free()` method?

16.17   What does the method `isForwarded()` (Figure 16–22) return if `address` is 5 or 11 and if `end` is 8 or 16? (Deal with all four combinations.)

16.18   Which automatic memory management technique would be a bad choice for a palmtop computer with very little memory? Explain.

Summary

Memory is divided into the call stack and the heap. Primitive values may live on the call stack, but objects must live in the heap. A reference to such an object is really just a number, giving the address in the heap where the object lives. Memory management is the task of keeping track of which memory in the heap is in use and which is available for creating new objects.

Memory can be managed explicitly (as in C and C++) or automatically (as in Java). Explicit memory management can be more efficient, but it allows for some exceedingly nasty bugs, including memory leaks and dangling pointers.

While we cannot manage all of our memory explicitly in Java, we can gain some speed using a node pool. In a node pool, we allocate a bunch of objects (such as ListNodes) in advance, then borrow them from this pool as they are needed.

Approaches to automatic memory management include reference counting, mark-and-sweep garbage collection, and copying garbage collection.

Reference counting keeps track of the number of references to each object. When this number drops to zero, the memory used for the object is made available again. In its pure form, reference counting cannot handle cyclic islands of garbage.

Mark-and-sweep garbage collection traverses the reachable objects, then frees everything else.

Copying garbage collection divides the heap into two or more parts, one of which is off limits. The garbage collector copies all reachable objects into the forbidden area, makes this area ready for use, and makes some other area forbidden. Such a system cannot use all of its memory at once. On the other hand, it does not have to touch the garbage (which is most of the heap) and it compacts the heap. Many modern automatic memory management systems are variations on copying garbage collection.

Vocabulary

address. Location of an object (index in the heap).

cell. Position in the heap. An object may occupy multiple cells.

compacted. Of memory or disk storage, having one contiguous in-use region.

copying garbage collector. Garbage collector that copies reachable objects into another part of memory.

dangling pointer. Pointer to memory a program does not control. Can result from failing to initialize a pointer or from freeing memory and then trying to access it.

fragmented. Of memory or disk storage, having the in-use regions scattered about, leaving many small available regions.

free list. Linked list of available areas of the heap.

forwarding address. In a copying garbage collector, a pointer from from-space into to-space indicating the address to which an object has been copied.

from-space. In a copying garbage collector, the area of memory from which objects are being copied.

garbage. Memory that cannot be reached by following one or more pointers from a root.

garbage collection. Any memory management technique that occasionally pauses the program to reclaim garbage.

heap. Area of memory where objects (and arrays live), as opposed to the call stack.

mark-and-sweep garbage collector. Garbage collector that traverses the heap from the roots to see what is reachable, then sweeps through the heap to reclaim anything not visited on the first pass.

memory leak. Bug in which a program fails to free memory it is no longer using.

memory management. Keeping track of which cells are in use.

node pool. Set of frequently used objects (such as list nodes) maintained to avoid creating new instances.

reference counting. Memory management technique in which each object keeps track of the number of references to that object. When this count reaches zero, the object is unreachable.

root. Reference on the call stack pointing into the heap.

to-space. In a copying garbage collector, the area in memory to which objects are being copied.

Problems

16.19 Modify garbageCollect() (Figure 16–23) so that it accepts an array of roots, rather than just a single root.

16.20 Define an exception class SegmentationFaultException. In the MemoryWithGarbage-Collection class, modify get() and set() so that they throw such an exception if the specified address is not in the usable portion of memory.

16.21 Modify the MemoryWithGarbageCollection class to handle objects of different sizes. (Hint: For an objects of size s, use $s + 1$ cells. The first cell indicates the size of the object.)

16.22 Add a field root, giving the address of the current root, to the MemoryWithGarbage-Collection class. Modify the allocate() method so that, if there is no available memory, the garbage collector runs. Assuming that there was some garbage, memory can now be allocated.

Projects

16.23 Write a simulated memory that uses mark-and-sweep garbage collection.

17

Out to the Disk

This chapter deals with data stored on disk rather than in memory. There are two main reasons for using disk storage. First, information on disk persists even when the electricity goes out or the computer is rebooted. Second, some applications involve so much data that it does not fit in memory. For example, a search engine that examines 10 billion web sites, averaging 10 kilobytes each, would have to handle 100 terabytes of data!

Section 17.1 deals with the basics of interacting with files in Java. The remaining sections address special data structures and algorithms used with data stored on disk. Two algorithms for compressing data, so that it takes up less space on disk, are described in Section 17.2. In Section 17.3, we look at an algorithm for sorting data which does not fit in memory. Finally, in Section 17.4, we discuss B-trees, a binary search tree variant especially suited for data stored on disk.

17.1 Interacting with Files

The built-in java.io package contains dozens of classes for reading and writing data in memory, on disk, and over networks. These relatively simple components can be strung together in a huge variety of ways. The intent of this design is to give experienced programmers a good deal of control over input and output. Unfortunately, the vast collection of classes is confusing and intimidating to the new programmer. In this section, we will concentrate on a few particularly useful classes, demonstrating how to read and write text and data.

Text Files

We begin with the simple task of writing text to a file. We can do this using the java.io.Print-
Writer class (Figure 17–1).

```
 1 import java.io.*;
 2
 3 /** Class to demonstrate text file output. */
 4 public class Ozymandias {
 5
 6   /** Print a string to a file. */
 7   public static void main(String[] args) throws IOException {
 8     PrintWriter out = new PrintWriter("ozymandias.txt");
 9     out.println("Look on my works, ye mighty, and despair!");
10   }
11
12 }
```

Figure 17-1: This program almost works.

The PrintWriter class has a constructor which accepts a file name as a String. Invoking this constructor might throw an IOException (specifically, a FileNotFoundException) if the file in question does not exist and cannot be created. There's nothing our program can do if such an
exception occurs, so we pass it on by declaring that main() might throw an IOException.

Once we have a PrintWriter, we can invoke the methods print() and println(), which work
just like the ones provided by System.out.

When we run this program, it almost works. It creates a file called ozymandias.txt in the current directory (the directory from which we ran the program). If we examine the file, however,
we discover that it is empty! What happened?

The problem is that the PrintWriter is **buffered**. In other words, it doesn't write to the file every
time we invoke println(). Instead, it saves up its output until it has a large amount, then
writes all of it to the disk. This is a reasonable thing to do, because accessing the disk is an
extremely time-consuming operation. Because a disk involves physical moving parts, a disk
access can take roughly a million times as long as a memory access. On the other hand, once the
disk's read/write head is in the right place, reading or writing more data at the same place is
practically free. Thus, it is more efficient to make a few large disk accesses than many small
ones.

In order to get our program to work properly, we must **flush** the buffer—that is, tell the Print-
Writer, "You can really send that stuff to the disk now." We could do this by invoking the

flush() method, but since we're done with the file, we might as well close the file completely (Figure 17–2).

```
1 /** Print a string to a file. */
2 public static void main(String[] args) throws IOException {
3    PrintWriter out = new PrintWriter("ozymandias.txt");
4    out.println("Look on my works, ye mighty, and despair!");
5    out.close();
6 }
```

Figure 17–2: Closing the PrintWriter flushes the buffer.

A more elaborate way to write this program would be to explicitly create an instance of the File class, then attach a PrintWriter to that file (Figure 17–3). The File object handles interaction with the disk, while the PrintWriter object provides the print() and println() methods.

```
1 /** Print a string to a file. */
2 public static void main(String[] args) throws IOException {
3    File file = new File("ozymandias.txt");
4    PrintWriter out = new PrintWriter(file);
5    out.println("Look on my works, ye mighty, and despair!");
6    out.close();
7 }
```

Figure 17–3: Explicitly creating a File object.

There is no particular reason to use this more complicated version here, because PrintWriter has a constructor that lets us specify the file name directly. This example does demonstrate the philosophy of the java.io package: provide many simple components which can be combined to produce the desired behavior. Later, we'll attach a different "filter" to a File to write something other than text.

Before moving on, let's look at some of the classes involved in what we've done so far (Figure 17–4).

A PrintWriter both is a Writer and contains one. Specifically, when we hook one up to a File, it contains a FileWriter (Figure 17–5). Fortunately, we don't have to keep track of all of these intermediate objects; the constructors in PrintWriter do the work for us.

The object System.out, incidentally, is an instance of the class PrintStream.

We would also like to read text in from files. Oddly enough, there is no such thing as a Print-Reader. Instead, we can use the java.util.Scanner class. As we have seen, this class has several constructors. One constructor takes an InputStream, such as System.in. Another, used in the Pick Up Sticks program in Figure 15–29, takes a String. Yet another takes a File.

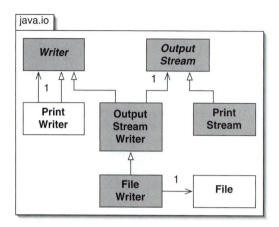

Figure 17-4: Classes involved in writing text to a file. The shaded classes have not been discussed previously.

Figure 17-5: A PrintWriter can contain a FileWriter, which in turn contains a File. Each object in this chain offers some additional functionality.

As an example, let's write a program that reads a Java program and prints the lines containing the substring "public" (Figure 17–6).

```
 1 import java.io.*;
 2 import java.util.Scanner;
 3
 4 /** Print all lines containing the substring "public". */
 5 public class PrintPublicMembers {
 6
 7   /** Run on the file specified as args[0]. */
 8   public static void main(String[] args) throws IOException {
 9     File file = new File(args[0]);
10     Scanner in = new Scanner(file);
```

Figure 17-6: This program prints all lines of a file containing the substring "public". (Part 1 of 2)

```
11      while (in.hasNextLine()) {
12        String line = in.nextLine();
13        if (line.contains("public")) {
14          System.out.println(line);
15        }
16      }
17    }
18
19  }
```

Figure 17-6: This program prints all lines of a file containing the substring `"public"`. (Part 2 of 2)

Running this program allows us to see all of the public methods of a class. For example, if we run our program with the command

```
java PrintPublicMembers ArrayList.java
```

we get:

```
public class ArrayList<E> implements List<E> {
  public ArrayList() {
  public void add(E target) {
  public boolean contains(E target) {
  public boolean isEmpty() {
  public java.util.Iterator<E> iterator() {
  public E get(int index) {
  public E remove(int index) {
  public boolean remove(E target) {
  public void set(int index, E target) {
  public int size() {
  public String toString() {
```

Incidentally, this program touches on one of the deepest ideas in computer science: *it is possible to write programs that treat other programs as data*. We have been dealing with one such program throughout this book: the Java compiler. It reads a program (as Java source code) from a file and writes another program (as compiled Java byte code) to another file.

As with text output, there's more going on behind the scenes than is apparent in the code we've written (Figure 17–7).

A Scanner is associated with an instance of some class implementing the Readable interface. Different things happen, depending on which Scanner constructor we use:

- If the argument is a String, the Scanner contains a StringReader, which in turn contains the String.

- If the argument is a File, the Scanner contains a FileReader, which in turn contains that File.

- If the argument is a BufferedInputStream (such as System.in), the Scanner contains an InputStreamReader, which in turn contains that BufferedInputStream.

Once again, we are thankful that we don't have to keep track of all of this!

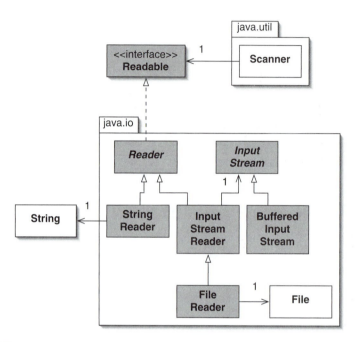

Figure 17-7: Classes and interfaces involved in reading text from a file. The shaded classes have not been discussed previously.

Data Files

Information in files need not be stored in text. If it is not necessary for humans to read files directly, text is somewhat inefficient. For example, suppose we want to store nine-digit Social Security numbers. As text, each digit is a character, occupying one byte in the ASCII encoding. (Java actually uses the more comprehensive Unicode encoding. The way Unicode characters are represented on disk is complicated; we ignore these details.) A nine-digit number can also be stored in a four-byte int, using less than half the space. If hundreds of thousands of such numbers are being stored, this can be a significant savings.

To interact with data stored in this **binary format**, we use the classes ObjectInputStream and ObjectOutputStream. These are subclasses of InputStream and OutputStream, respectively (Figure 17–8).

As a simple example, the program in Figure 17–9 takes an optional command-line argument. If an argument is provided, it is stored in a file (lines 13–16). Otherwise, the first int in the file is read and printed to the screen (lines 18–20).

In addition to `readInt()` and `writeInt()`, there are corresponding methods for all of the other primitive types.

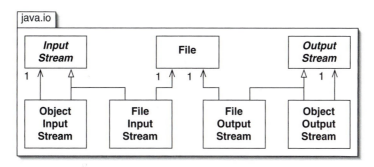

Figure 17-8: Classes involved in reading from and writing to a binary data file.

```
 1 import java.io.*;
 2
 3 /** Example of storing data in binary format. */
 4 public class DataFileExample {
 5
 6   /**
 7    * If an int is provided on the command line, store it in
 8    * number.data. Otherwise, read an int from number.data
 9    * and print it.
10    */
11   public static void main(String[] args) throws IOException {
12     File file = new File("number.data");
13     if (args.length > 0) {
14       ObjectOutputStream out
15         = new ObjectOutputStream(new FileOutputStream(file));
16       out.writeInt(Integer.parseInt(args[0]));
17       out.close();
18     } else {
19       ObjectInputStream in
20         = new ObjectInputStream(new FileInputStream(file));
21       System.out.println(in.readInt());
22     }
23   }
24
25 }
```

Figure 17-9: Reading and writing data in binary format.

There are also methods readObject() and writeObject(). When we write an object to an ObjectOutputStream, Java automatically writes the contents of the object's fields. If these are references to other objects, those objects are written as well. The observant reader, recalling Chapter 16, will see a problem here. We need to write all of the objects reachable from the original root object. Each object must be written exactly once: we don't want to miss any, and we don't want to write two copies of an object just because there are two references to it.

Handily, this is exactly the problem solved by the copying garbage collector described in Section 16.2. Java uses this algorithm to convert a directed graph of objects into a linear file, a process called *serialization*. All we have to do is make every object we are saving serializable. We do this by implementing the java.io.Serializable interface. This interface has no methods; we merely have to state that we are implementing it. Many built-in classes, including String and all of the wrapper classes, are Serializable.

As an example, recall the game of Questions from Section 10.1. A major drawback of the program was that, when we quit the program, the decision tree was lost. It would be much better to store the tree in a file. We can accomplish this by adding Serializable to the list of interfaces implemented by the BinaryNode and Questions classes, and by updating the main() method for Questions, as shown in Figure 17–10.

```
 1 /** Create and repeatedly play the game. */
 2 public static void main(String[] args) throws IOException {
 3   Questions game = new Questions();
 4   System.out.println("Welcome to Questions.");
 5   do {
 6     System.out.println();
 7     game.play();
 8     System.out.print("Play again (yes or no)? ");
 9   } while (INPUT.nextLine().equals("yes"));
10   // Save knowledge to a file
11   ObjectOutputStream out
12     = new ObjectOutputStream(new FileOutputStream("questions.data"));
13   out.writeObject(game);
14   out.close();
15 }
```

Figure 17-10: Once BinaryNode and Questions implement Serializable, we can store the decision tree in a file. Questions must also import java.io.*.

Running this program once produces a file questions.data, but we have no way to read it. We have to modify the main() method so that, when it starts, we read the tree from the file (Figure 17–11).

The program now works properly, but there's something fishy going on. The original decision tree, containing just the leaf node "a giraffe", does not appear anywhere in the program. That knowledge exists only in the data file. If we were ever to lose the data file, we would have no way to start over.

We want to start over *only if the file does not already exist*. The next subsection discusses how to determine this.

```
 1 /** Create and repeatedly play the game. */
 2 public static void main(String[] args)
 3   throws ClassNotFoundException, IOException {
 4   // Read knowledge from a file
 5   ObjectInputStream in
 6     = new ObjectInputStream(new FileInputStream("questions.data"));
 7   Questions game = (Questions)(in.readObject());
 8   // Play the game
 9   System.out.println("Welcome to Questions.");
10   do {
11     System.out.println();
12     game.play();
13     System.out.print("Play again (yes or no)? ");
14   } while (INPUT.nextLine().equals("yes"));
15   // Save knowledge to a file
16   ObjectOutputStream out
17     = new ObjectOutputStream(new FileOutputStream
18                                    ("questions.data"));
19   out.writeObject(game);
20   out.close();
21 }
```

Figure 17–11: Reading the Questions data from a file.

Directories

We begin with the anticlimactic answer to the question posed in the previous paragraph. To determine whether a file exists, we use the `exists()` method of the corresponding File object (Figure 17–12).

```
 1 /** Create and repeatedly play the game. */
 2 public static void main(String[] args)
 3   throws ClassNotFoundException, IOException {
 4   // Read knowledge from a file
 5   Questions game;
 6   File file = new File("questions.data");
 7   if (file.exists()) {
 8     ObjectInputStream in
 9       = new ObjectInputStream(new FileInputStream(file));
10     game = (Questions)(in.readObject());
11   } else {
12     game = new Questions();
13   }
14   // Play the game
15   System.out.println("Welcome to Questions.");
```

Figure 17–12: Improved version of the `main()` method from the Questions class. If there is no data file to read from, it creates a new instance of Questions. (Part 1 of 2)

```
16  do {
17    System.out.println();
18    game.play();
19    System.out.print("Play again (yes or no)? ");
20  } while (INPUT.nextLine().equals("yes"));
21  // Save knowledge to a file
22  ObjectOutputStream out
23    = new ObjectOutputStream(new FileOutputStream(file));
24  out.writeObject(game);
25  out.close();
26 }
```

Figure 17-12: Improved version of the `main()` method from the Questions class. If there is no data file to read from, it creates a new instance of Questions. (Part 2 of 2)

The `exists()` method seems strange. Doesn't every object exist? Yes, the object `file`, which is an instance of class File, does exist. It contains the name of a hypothetical file on disk. The question answered by `exists()` is whether there really is a file with that name.

We don't have to put all files in the current directory. A File object can specify the entire path of a file. For example, if the current directory has a subdirectory `lib`, then we could have a file corresponding to `lib/questions.data`. If we simply replace the name of the file in line 6 in Figure 17–12, however, we'll have a couple of problems.

One problem is that not all operating systems use "/" to separate directories in a path. Specifically, Windows uses "\" instead. For platform independence, instead of

`"lib/questions.data"`

we should use:

`"lib" + File.separator + "questions.data"`

A second problem is that, if the `lib` directory doesn't exist, opening `lib/questions.data` for output won't create it. A directory must be explicitly created using the `mkdir()` method. In this case:

`new File("lib").mkdir();`

A third problem is that `lib` is a subdirectory of the current working directory. It would be better to use an absolute path, so that the location of the data file is independent of the directory from which Questions is invoked. This is particularly important in modern graphic development environments and operating systems. If a program is invoked by selecting it from a menu or clicking on an icon, it may not be clear what the current working directory is.

We can find the name of the directory containing the Questions program with the following arcane incantation, which we make no attempt to explain:

`Questions.class.getProtectionDomain().getCodeSource()`
`  .getLocation().getFile();`

The final version of `main()` is given in Figure 17–13.

```
 1 /** Create and repeatedly play the game. */
 2 public static void main(String[] args)
 3    throws ClassNotFoundException, IOException {
 4    // Read knowledge from a file
 5    Questions game;
 6    String home = Questions.class.getProtectionDomain().getCodeSource()
 7      .getLocation().getFile() + File.separator();
 8    File file = new File(home + "lib"
 9                          + File.separator + "questions.data");
10    if (file.exists()) {
11      ObjectInputStream in
12        = new ObjectInputStream(new FileInputStream(file));
13      game = (Questions)(in.readObject());
14    } else {
15      game = new Questions();
16      new File(home + "lib").mkdir();
17    }
18    // See lines 14-25 of Figure 17-12
19 }
```

Figure 17–13: The file `questions.data` now lives in the `lib` subdirectory of the directory containing the Questions program.

Exercises

17.1   What is printed if we run the PrintPublicMembers program on itself?

17.2   Write a program that prints its own source code.

17.3   Explain why, in Figure 17–6, we couldn't replace lines 9–10 with:

```
Scanner in = new Scanner(args[0]);
```

17.4   Look up the API for the File class. How can we determine if a file refers to a directory?

17.2 Compression

Files can often be *compressed*—that is, represented using fewer bytes than the standard representation. This technique is useful for saving disk space and for reducing network traffic. The total time required to compress a file, send the compressed file, and uncompress it at the other end is often less than the time required to send the uncompressed file. This explains why software made available for download over the Internet is usually compressed.

In this section, we discuss two algorithms for compressing data. The discussion is in terms of text, but these algorithms can be adapted to work for any kind of data.

Huffman Encoding

In an ASCII text file, each character is represented by the same number of bits. Such a *fixed-length encoding* is somewhat wasteful, because some characters are more common than others. If a character appears frequently, it should have a shorter representation. *Huffman encoding* produces such an efficient representation.

Consider the String "beekeepers_&_bees". Eight different characters appear in this String, so we could have a 3-bit code for each character (Figure 17–14). (ASCII works like this, using 7 bits to encode 128 different characters.) In a Huffman encoding, common characters such as 'e' have shorter codes than rare characters such as '&'.

Character	Fixed-Length Code	Huffman Code
b	000	110
e	001	0
k	010	11110
p	011	11111
r	100	1011
s	101	100
_	110	1110
&	111	1010

Figure 17–14: In a Huffman encoding, more frequent characters are represented by shorter codes.

Representing the String "beekeepers_&_bees" using the fixed-length encoding requires 51 bits:

         000 001 001 010 001 001 011 001 100 101 110 111 110 000 001 001 101

Using the Huffman encoding, this takes only 45 bits:

         110 0 0 11110 0 0 11111 0 1011 100 1110 1010 1110 110 0 0 100

The savings can be considerably greater on a long String, such as the entire text of a novel.

We included spaces above to make it clear where one code begins and another ends. In practice, there is only a sequence of bits. It is easy to detect the end of a code in a fixed-length encoding, because each code uses the same number of bits. We might worry that, in a Huffman encoding, we might incorrectly conclude that we've read the code 100 when we've really only read the first three characters of the code 10011. To avoid this danger, Huffman encodings are designed so that no code is a prefix of another code. For example, the code for 'b' is 110, and no other code starts with 110.

A Huffman encoding can be automatically generated from a table of character frequencies. These should be drawn from a string typical of those being compressed. For example, when compressing English text, character frequencies on the front page of the *New York Times* will do nicely. To keep our example small, however, we will use the frequencies in the message being compressed (Figure 17–15).

Character	Count
b	2
e	7
k	1
p	1
r	1
s	2
_	2
&	1

Figure 17–15: Frequencies of different characters in the String "beekeepers_&_bees".

To generate a Huffman encoding, we first construct a binary tree. When we are done, leaves in this tree corresponds to characters. Deeper leaves have longer codes.

One node is created for each character, holding both that character and its count (Figure 17–16). This is a forest of trees, each containing one node. On each pass through the main loop, we choose the two lowest-count roots and merge them. (It doesn't matter how we handle ties.) The count for the new parent is the sum of its children's counts.

This continues until there is only one tree (Figure 17–17). The code for each character is determined by the path from the root to the corresponding leaf. Each right descent is represented by a 1, each left descent by a 0. For example, the path to 'b' is right-right-left, so its code is 110.

To translate these ideas into Java, we first need a class HuffmanNode (Figure 17–18). This is almost identical to a BinaryNode<Character>, but it has an additional field count. It also implements Comparable<HuffmanNode>, so that we can find the lowest-count root. Inheritance pays off handsomely here.

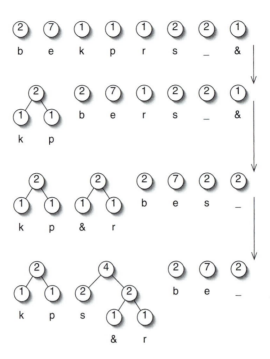

Figure 17-16: Building a Huffman tree. Initially, each node is in a separate tree (top). On each pass through the main loop, we combine the two roots with the lowest counts.

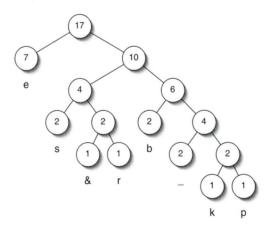

Figure 17-17: Final Huffman tree. The code for each character is determined by the path from the root to the corresponding leaf.

```
 1 /** Node in a Huffman tree. */
 2 public class HuffmanNode extends BinaryNode<Character>
 3   implements Comparable<HuffmanNode> {
 4
 5   /** Frequency of this letter or set of letters. */
 6   private int count;
 7
 8   /** Create a node with no children. */
 9   public HuffmanNode(char letter, int count) {
10     super(letter);
11     this.count = count;
12   }
13
14   /**
15    * Create a node with two children.  Its count is the sum of
16    * its children's counts.
17    */
18   public HuffmanNode(HuffmanNode left, HuffmanNode right) {
19     super('?', left, right);
20     this.count = left.count + right.count;
21   }
22
23   /** The comparison is based on the counts of the nodes. */
24   public int compareTo(HuffmanNode that) {
25     return count - that.count;
26   }
27
28 }
```

Figure 17-18: The HuffmanNode class extends BinaryNode<Character>.

An instance of the Huffman class contains a tree of such nodes and a direct addressing table mapping characters to their codes (Figure 17–19). The codes are given as Strings of ones and zeroes for readability. In practice, the program would really read and write bits from a file; this is left as Project 17.20.

```
 1 /** Huffman encoder/decoder. */
 2 public class Huffman {
 3
 4   /** The root of the Huffman tree. */
 5   private HuffmanNode root;
 6
```

Figure 17-19: The constructor for the Huffman class first generates a tree, then uses the tree to generate a table of codes. (Part 1 of 2)

```
 7   /** Direct addressing table mapping characters to Strings. */
 8   private String[] table;
 9
10   /** The frequency distribution is in the code for this method. */
11   public Huffman() {
12     char[] letters = "bekprs_&".toCharArray();
13     int[] counts = {2, 7, 1, 1, 1, 2, 2, 1};
14     root = generateTree(letters, counts);
15     table = new String[128];
16     generateCodes(root, "");
17   }
18
19 }
```

Figure 17–19: The constructor for the Huffman class first generates a tree, then uses the tree to generate a table of codes. (Part 2 of 2)

In generating the tree, we need to keep track of a set of roots. In each pass through the main loop, we need to grab the two roots with the smallest counts. This is a job for a priority queue (Figure 17–20).

```
 1 /** Generate the Huffman tree. */
 2 protected HuffmanNode generateTree(char[] letters, int[] counts) {
 3   Heap<HuffmanNode> q = new Heap<HuffmanNode>();
 4   for (int i = 0; i < letters.length; i++) {
 5     q.add(new HuffmanNode(letters[i], counts[i]));
 6   }
 7   while (true) {
 8     HuffmanNode a = q.remove();
 9     if (q.isEmpty()) {
10       return a;
11     }
12     HuffmanNode b = q.remove();
13     q.add(new HuffmanNode(a, b));
14   }
15 }
```

Figure 17–20: A priority queue is used in building a Huffman tree.

This tree will be useful in decoding, but to encode a String we'll need a way to quickly get from a character to its code. This is accomplished using a direct-addressing table, which is populated by the elegant recursive method generateCodes() (Figure 17–21).

Once we have this table, encoding a String is just a matter of concatenating the codes for the characters making up the String (Figure 17–22).

Now, for example, if we

encode("beekeepers_&_bees")

```
 1 /** Generate the table of codes. */
 2 protected void generateCodes(BinaryNode<Character> root,
 3                              String code) {
 4   if (root.isLeaf()) {
 5     table[root.getItem()] = code;
 6   } else {
 7     generateCodes(root.getLeft(), code + "0");
 8     generateCodes(root.getRight(), code + "1");
 9   }
10 }
```

Figure 17-21: As generateCodes() recurs more deeply into the tree, **code** gets longer.

```
 1 /**
 2  * Return the bits of the encoded version of message, as a
 3  * human-readable String.
 4  */
 5 public String encode(String message) {
 6   StringBuilder result = new StringBuilder();
 7   for (char c : message.toCharArray()) {
 8     result.append(table[c] + " ");
 9   }
10   return result.toString();
11 }
```

Figure 17-22: The code for each character can be looked up in the table.

the result is:

"110 0 0 11110 0 0 11111 0 1011 100 1110 1010 1110 110 0 0 100"

To decode a message, we start at the root of the tree and use the incoming bits to steer left and right (Figure 17–23). When we hit a leaf, we add a character to the result and go back to the root.

```
 1 /** Return the original version of a String encoded by encode(). */
 2 public String decode(String encodedMessage) {
 3   StringBuilder result = new StringBuilder();
 4   BinaryNode<Character> node = root;
 5   for (char c : encodedMessage) {
 6     if (c == '0') {
 7       node = node.getLeft();
 8     } else if (c == '1') {
 9       node = node.getRight();
10     }
```

Figure 17-23: The Huffman tree is used in decoding a String. (Part 1 of 2)

```
11    if (node.isLeaf()) {
12        result.append(node.getItem());
13        node = root;
14    }
15 }
16 return result.toString();
17 }
```

Figure 17-23: The Huffman tree is used in decoding a String. (Part 2 of 2)

Now, for example,

```
decode(encode("beekeepers_&_bees"))
```

returns "beekeepers_&_bees".

Lempel–Ziv Encoding

It is possible to prove that Huffman encoding is the best possible character-by-character encoding. We can do even better by creating codes for frequently occurring substrings. For example, when compressing Java programs, it could be useful to have special codes for substrings such as "public" and "for (int i = 0; i <". *Lempel–Ziv encoding* uses this idea.

The set of codes used in Lempel–Ziv encoding is not created in advance, but generated during encoding or decoding. Each code is an int corresponding to a String of one or more characters. Originally, there is a code for each single character.

As an example, consider encoding the String "beekeepers_&_bees" (Figure 17–24). We begin by reading the character 'b' and outputting the code for 'b'. On each subsequent step, we *output a code* and *create a new code*. As we work through the text, we eventually encounter substrings for which we have already created codes.

We output the code corresponding to the longest prefix of the remaining text for which there is a code. For example, when the remaining text is "eepers_&_bees", there is a code for "ee" but not for "eep", so the code for "ee" is output.

When a new code is created, it represents a String constructed from the Strings represented by the last two codes emitted. Specifically, it is the concatenation of the older string and *the first character of* the newer string. For example, when the last two codes emitted represented "k" and "ee", the new code represents "ke".

To implement this algorithm, we need two data structures to keep track of the codes. The first structure is a direct-addressing table mapping ints to Strings. The second structure is a digital search tree (Section 14.3) with codes stored at the nodes.

These data structures are declared in Figure 17–25. The constructor initializes them by creating one child of root for each of the 128 ASCII characters.

Our encode() method (Figure 17–26) reads from a Scanner and writes ints to an ObjectOutput-Stream. In the main loop on lines 8–20, we work down the digital search tree, using characters from the input to choose a child. When we can't go any further, we've found the longest prefix, so we emit a code and create a new one (lines 11–15).

Output Code	New Code
b	–
e	be
e	ee
k	ek
ee	ke
p	eep
e	pe
r	er
s	rs
–	s_
&	_&
–	&_
be	_b
e	bee
s	–

Figure 17-24: Lempel–Ziv encoding generates new codes as it works. Each code represents the concatenation of the string represented by the previous code and the first character of the string represented by the current code.

```
1 import java.io.*;
2 import java.util.Scanner;
3
4 /** Lempel-Ziv compression of text. */
5 public class LempelZiv {
6
7    /** Root of the digital search tree. */
8    private DigitalNode<Integer> root;
9
```

Figure 17-25: Data structures and constructor for the LempelZiv class. (Part 1 of 2)

```
10   /** Direct-addressing table mapping codes to Strings. */
11   private ArrayList<String> strings;
12
13   /** Initialize the codes with ASCII values. */
14   public LempelZiv() {
15     root = new DigitalNode<Integer>(null);
16     strings = new ArrayList<String>();
17     for (char i = 0; i < 128; i++) {
18       root.setChild(i, new DigitalNode<Integer>((int)i));
19       strings.add("" + i);
20     }
21   }
22
23 }
```

Figure 17-25: Data structures and constructor for the LempelZiv class. (Part 2 of 2)

```
 1 /** Read text from in, write ints to out. */
 2 public void encode(Scanner in, ObjectOutputStream out)
 3     throws IOException {
 4   DigitalNode<Integer> parent = null;
 5   DigitalNode<Integer> node = root;
 6   while (in.hasNextLine()) {
 7     String line = in.nextLine() + "\n";
 8     for (int i = 0; i < line.length(); ) {
 9       DigitalNode<Integer> child = node.getChild(line.charAt(i));
10       if (child == null) {
11         int code = node.getItem();
12         out.writeInt(code);
13         addNewCode(parent, code);
14         parent = node;
15         node = root;
16       } else {
17         node = child;
18         i++;
19       }
20     }
21   }
22   out.writeInt(node.getItem());
23   out.close();
24 }
```

Figure 17-26: Lempel–Ziv encoding.

The protected method addNewCode() adds a node to the tree and an entry to the direct-addressing table (Figure 17–27).

```
 1 /**
 2  * Add a new code.  It represents the concatenation of the String
 3  * for the code at parent and the first character of the String for
 4  * code.
 5  */
 6 protected void addNewCode(DigitalNode<Integer> parent, int code) {
 7   if (parent != null) {
 8     char firstChar = strings.get(code).charAt(0);
 9     parent.setChild(firstChar,
10                     new DigitalNode<Integer>(strings.size()));
11     strings.add(strings.get(parent.getItem()) + firstChar);
12   }
13 }
```

Figure 17–27: Adding a new code to both data structures.

Now, for example, to compress the file words into the file words.lz, we could do this:

```
Scanner in = new Scanner(new File("words"));
ObjectOutputStream out
  = new ObjectOutputStream(new FileOutputStream("words.lz"));
new LempelZiv().encode(in, out);
```

Surprisingly, we don't need to keep the data structures around to decode a string. They can be generated on the fly during the decoding process, just as during the encoding process (Figure 17–28).

```
 1 /** Read ints from in, write text to out. */
 2 public void decode(ObjectInputStream in, PrintWriter out)
 3   throws IOException {
 4   DigitalNode<Integer> parent = null;
 5   while (in.available() > 0) {
 6     int code = in.readInt();
 7     DigitalNode<Integer> node = root;
 8     String s = strings.get(code);
 9     for (char c : s.toCharArray()) {
10       out.print(c);
11       node = node.getChild(c);
12     }
13     addNewCode(parent, code);
14     parent = node;
15   }
16   out.close();
17 }
```

Figure 17–28: Lempel–Ziv decoding.

To uncompress the previously compressed file, we could do this:

```
ObjectInputStream in
  = new ObjectInputStream(new FileInputStream("words.lz"));
PrintWriter out = new PrintWriter("words");
new LempelZiv().decode(in, out);
```

Since each int takes up four bytes, Lempel–Ziv encoding provides no compression until the encoder starts emitting codes representing strings longer than four characters. On long files, however, it can provide significant compression.

Java provides several classes that perform a variation on Lempel–Ziv encoding, including java.util.zip.ZipInputStream, java.util.zip.GZIPInputStream, and java.util.jar.JarInputStream. We won't discuss these in detail.

Exercises

17.5   Can any compression algorithm guarantee that *every* String becomes shorter when compressed? Explain. (Hint: Recall the pigeonhole principle.)

17.6   Discuss how these algorithms might be adapted to work on files containing binary data rather than text.

17.7   Why can't line 8 of Figure 17–23 be a simple else?

17.8   If we use our Lempel–Ziv encoding algorithm on a sufficiently large file, the code table will become too large. It might become so large that an int is not sufficient to specify an index, or it might simply become too large to fit in memory. In practice, a limit is set on the table size. Discuss how the algorithm might reasonably proceed when the table is full.

17.3 External Sorting

We occasionally need to sort collections of data so large that they do not fit in memory. The algorithms we've explored previously, such as heapsort, do not work efficiently for external sorting. While the ith element of an array can be accessed very quickly, accessing the ith object stored in a file on disk is horrendously slow. As mentioned previously, any action involving the moving physical parts of a disk drive can take a million times as long as accessing memory. Worse, if the objects in the file are of different sizes, or if the data are stored on a sequential access device like a magnetic tape drive, finding the ith element can take time linear in the size of the file.

The process of sorting data too big to fit in memory is called ***external sorting***. This section presents an external sorting algorithm based on merge sort (Section 9.3). We begin by dividing the data into many short ***runs***. Each run is small enough to fit into memory, so we can sort the individual runs. The runs are then repeatedly merged into longer and longer runs, until there is only one run left.

Let c be the number of data that can fit in memory. We initially make runs of length c (Figure 17–29). (The last run, containing any "spare change," may be shorter than this.) These are then merged into runs of length $2c$, then $4c$, and so on, until all of the data are in the same run.

Original Data	Split		First Merge		Second Merge		Result
t	g	c	c	e	c	a	a
g	m	j	g	f	e	b	b
m	t	q	j	i	f	d	c
j	*e*	*f*	m	l	g	h	d
q	*l*	*i*	q	n	i	k	e
c	*n*	*s*	t	s	j	o	f
n	a	b	*a*	*h*	l	p	g
e	d	k	*b*	*r*	m	r	h
l	o	p	*d*		n		i
i	*h*		*k*		q		j
f	*r*		*o*		s		k
s			*p*		t		l
a							m
d							n
o							o
p							p
k							q
b							r
r							s
h							t

Figure 17–29: External sorting. The original data file is split into two files, each consisting of sorted runs. Bold, italic type is used to emphasize where one run ends and another begins. In the initial split, runs are short enough to fit in memory; in this example, the initial runs are of length 3 or less. These are merged into runs of length 6 or less, then 12 or less, and finally 24 or less. This final run is long enough to contain all of the data, which are now sorted.

The code we now present sorts the lines of a text file. There are several places in the algorithm where we have to determine whether there is another line left in a run. A run limited to length $4c$, for example, might run out either because we've taken $4c$ lines from it or because we've hit the end of the file. To simplify the main code, these details are encapsulated in the ExternalSortRun class (Figure 17–30).

```java
1 import java.util.Scanner;
2
3 /** A run of lines used by the ExternalSort program. */
4 public class ExternalSortRun {
5
6   /** Number of lines left in this run, possibly an overestimate. */
7   private int count;
8
9   /** The next available line, if any. */
10   private String next;
11
12   /** The Scanner from which the lines are drawn. */
13   private Scanner scanner;
14
15   /** Up to maxLength lines will be drawn from scanner. */
16   public ExternalSortRun(Scanner scanner, int maxLength) {
17     count = maxLength;
18     this.scanner = scanner;
19     if (scanner.hasNext()) {
20       next = scanner.nextLine();
21     } else {
22       count = 0;
23     }
24   }
25
26   /** Return true if there is another line in this run. */
27   public boolean hasNext() {
28     return count > 0;
29   }
30
31   /** Return the next available line and advance the run. */
32   public String next() {
33     String result = next;
34     count--;
35     if (count > 0) {
36       if (scanner.hasNext()) {
37         next = scanner.nextLine();
38       } else {
39         count = 0;
40       }
41     }
42     return result;
43   }
44
```

Figure 17-30: The ExternalSortRun class manages the details of each run. (Part 1 of 2)

```
45    /** Return the next available line but do not advance the run. */
46    public String peek() {
47      return next;
48    }
49
50 }
```

Figure 17-30: The ExternalSortRun class manages the details of each run. (Part 2 of 2)

We describe the ExternalSort class (Figure 17–31) in a top-down fashion. The `main()` method invokes `sort()` on Files corresponding to `args[0]` and `args[1]`. Thus, to sort the file `poetry.txt` and put the output in `sorted.txt`, we would invoke our program as:

```
java ExternalSort poetry.txt sorted.txt.
```

```
 1 import java.io.*;
 2 import java.util.Scanner;
 3
 4 /** Externally sort the lines of a text file. */
 5 public class ExternalSort {
 6
 7    /** Maximum number of lines stored in memory at any one time. */
 8    public static final int CAPACITY = 3;
 9
10    /** Sort the file in and write the output to out. */
11    public static void sort(File in, File out) throws IOException {
12      File[][] files = {{new File(in.getPath() + ".a0"),
13                         new File(in.getPath() + ".a1")},
14                        {new File(in.getPath() + ".b0"),
15                         new File(in.getPath() + ".b1")}};
16      split(in, files[0]);
17      int runLength = CAPACITY;
18      int i = 0;
19      while (merge(files[i], files[1 - i], runLength)) {
20        i = 1 - i;
21        runLength *= 2;
22      }
23      files[1 - i][0].renameTo(out);
24      for (i = 0; i < 2; i++) {
25        for (int j = 0; j < 2; j++) {
26          files[i][j].delete();
27        }
28      }
29    }
30
```

Figure 17-31: Top-level methods in the ExternalSort class. (Part 1 of 2)

```
31    /**
32     * Sort the file args[0] and write the output to args[1].
33     */
34    public static void main(String[] args) throws IOException {
35      sort(new File(args[0]), new File(args[1]));
36    }
37
38  }
```

Figure 17-31: Top-level methods in the ExternalSort class. (Part 2 of 2)

Lines 12–15 create four new files. If `in` is the file `poetry.txt`, these are `poetry.txt.a0`, `poetry.txt.a1`, `poetry.txt.b0`, and `poetry.txt.b1`. These files are used during the repeated mergings. On line 16, `in` is split into the two files in `files[0]`—that is, those with `'a'` in their final extension. The bulk of the work—the merging—happens on lines 19–22. The invocation of `merge()` on line 19 both performs one round of merging and returns a boolean telling us whether there is more work to do. The variable i toggles back and forth between 0 and 1, so the output of the first merging goes to `files[1]`, the next merging overwrites `files[0]` (which are no longer needed), the next merging uses `files[1]` again, and so on. Only four temporary files are needed now no matter how many rounds of merging there are. Line 23 renames the first temporary file to contain all of the data. Lines 24–28 delete the temporary files.

The `split()` method (Figure 17–32) uses the same trick with the variable i. On each pass through the loop on lines 10–19, the method reads up to CAPACITY lines from input, storing them in a SortableArrayList. This ArrayList is internally sorted on line 15. (In a professional implementation, we would use a faster internal sorting algorithm than insertion sort.) Since the size of the ArrayList is no more than CAPACITY, it's okay to sort it internally. Once sorted, the lines are printed to one of the output files.

```
1  /**
2   * Split in into runs of maximum length CAPACITY and write them
3   * to out[0] and out[1].
4   */
5  protected static void split(File in, File[] out)
6    throws IOException {
7    Scanner input = new Scanner(new FileInputStream(in));
8    PrintWriter[] output = {new PrintWriter(out[0]),
9                            new PrintWriter(out[1])};
10   int i = 0;
11   while (input.hasNext()) {
12     SortableArrayList<String> run = new SortableArrayList<String>();
13     for (int j = 0; (input.hasNext()) && (j < CAPACITY); j++) {
14       run.add(input.nextLine());
15     }
```

Figure 17-32: Splitting a file into two files of sorted runs. (Part 1 of 2)

```
16      run.insertionSort();
17      for (String s : run) {
18        output[i].println(s);
19      }
20      i = 1 - i;
21    }
22    output[0].close();
23    output[1].close();
24 }
```

Figure 17-32: Splitting a file into two files of sorted runs. (Part 2 of 2)

The merge() method (Figure 17–33) is similar to the one from the internal merge sort algorithm (Section 9.3), but it uses the ExternalSortRun class. This class encapsulates certain details, including the situation in which the last run in a file contains less than runLength lines.

```
 1 /**
 2  * Merge runs, of maximum length runLength, in the files in[0] and
 3  * in[1], into runs twice this length in out[0] and out[1].
 4  * Return true if both output files are needed.
 5  */
 6 protected static boolean merge(File[] in, File[] out, int runLength)
 7    throws IOException {
 8    boolean bothOutputsUsed = false;
 9    Scanner[] input = {new Scanner(new FileInputStream(in[0])),
10                       new Scanner(new FileInputStream(in[1]))};
11    PrintWriter[] output = {new PrintWriter(out[0]),
12                            new PrintWriter(out[1])};
13    int i = 0;
14    while (input[0].hasNext() || input[1].hasNext()) {
15      ExternalSortRun[] runs
16        = {new ExternalSortRun(input[0], runLength),
17           new ExternalSortRun(input[1], runLength)};
18      if (i == 1) {
19        bothOutputsUsed = true;
20      }
21      while ((runs[0].hasNext()) || (runs[1].hasNext())) {
22        if ((!runs[1].hasNext())
23            || ((runs[0].hasNext())
24                && (runs[0].peek().compareTo(runs[1].peek()) < 0))) {
25          output[i].println(runs[0].next());
26        } else {
27          output[i].println(runs[1].next());
28        }
```

Figure 17-33: The core of the merge() method is very similar to the one from the internal merge sort algorithm discussed in Section 9.3. (Part 1 of 2)

```
29      }
30      i = 1 - i;
31   }
32   output[0].close();
33   output[1].close();
34   return bothOutputsUsed;
35 }
```

Figure 17-33: The core of the `merge()` method is very similar to the one from the internal merge sort algorithm discussed in Section 9.3. (Part 2 of 2)

There is no external sorting algorithm built into Java, but the UNIX utility `sort` provides similar functionality.

Exercises

17.9   If there is enough memory, will increasing the length of each run in the initial split make the external sorting algorithm run more quickly? Explain.

17.10   Modify the ExternalSort program so that the sorted data are printed to System.out rather than stored in a file if no second command-line argument is given.

17.4 B-Trees

It is sometimes necessary to store a set of data so large that it cannot fit in memory. This section introduces **B-trees** (B for balanced), which are commonly used in database programs. A B-tree is similar to a red-black tree (Section 14.4), but it goes to great lengths to minimize the number of disk accesses needed to find, insert, or delete an element.

A typical B-tree is shown in Figure 17–34.

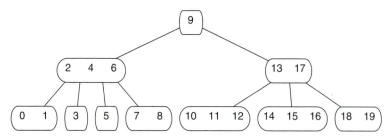

Figure 17-34: A B-tree.

A B-tree is defined as follows:

- A node can hold more than one element. There are upper and lower limits on the number of elements, to be explained shortly.

- The number of children that an internal node has is always one more than the number of elements it has.

- The children are interlaced with the elements. All of the elements in the subtree rooted at a child are greater than the element to the left of that child and less than the element to the right.

- All of the leaves are on the same level. This ensures that the tree is balanced.

The limit on node sizes depends on a constant m. In Figure 17–34, m is 2. No internal node has more than $2m$ children. No internal node (except possibly the root) has fewer than m children. The number of elements in a node (other than the root) is between $m - 1$ and $2m - 1$. We define the *size* of a node to be one more than the number of elements it has. For an internal node, the size is the number of children. A node of size m is called **minimal**. A node of size $2m$ is called *full*.

We use $m = 2$ in our diagrams so that they'll fit on the page. In practice, m is much larger, per-haps 200. This is because it is not much more expensive to read (or write) a bunch of data than a single element. We'd like a node to be as large as possible, but still small enough that we can read it in one disk access.

Having large nodes also makes the tree extremely shallow. This reduces the number of nodes examined in a search, which in turn reduces the number of disk accesses. The number of elements on each level increases exponentially with depth (Figure 17–35). If $m = 200$, then level 2 alone could contain nearly 64 million elements—and we can find any of them in only three disk accesses! This fabulous performance justifies the complicated coding required for B-trees.

Level	Minimum # of elements	Maximum # of elements
0	1	$2m - 1$
1	$2(m - 1)$	$2m(2m - 1)$
2	$2m(m - 1)$	$4m^2(2m - 1)$
d	$2md^{-1}(m - 1)$	$(2m)d(2m - 1)$

Figure 17–35: The number of elements on each level increases exponentially with depth.

Each of the Set operations (search, insertion, and deletion) is accomplished in one downward pass through the tree. In the worst case, therefore, each operation makes a number of disk accesses proportional to the height of the tree. The height of a B-tree is proportional to $\log_m n$. When m is large, the tree is very short.

Search

Searching a B-tree is much like searching a binary search tree. We first examine the root to see if the element in question is there; if not, we descend to the appropriate child. This continues until either we find the target or we try to descend from a leaf (in which case we give up).

Insertion

As with a red-black tree, we have to do some acrobatics when inserting an element into a B-tree to make sure we still have a B-tree when we're done. Specifically, every node has to have an acceptable number of elements, and all of the leaves have to be at the same level.

In the simplest case, the tree consists of a single nonfull node. We just insert the new element in the right place (Figure 17–36).

Figure 17-36: When a B-tree consists of a single nonfull node (left), a new element can be inserted directly into this node.

In general, the root is not a leaf, so we have to descend to another node (Figure 17–37).

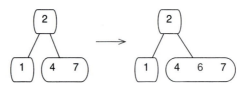

Figure 17-37: Inserting 6 in a B-tree. The target is not present in the root, we have to descend to a leaf.

What if we now want to insert 5? It belongs in the right leaf, but there's no room. In this case, we first **split** the leaf into two nodes, moving the middle element up into the parent (Figure 17–38). A full node has exactly enough elements to remove one and leave enough elements to make two minimal nodes.

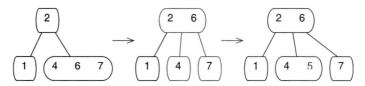

Figure 17-38: Inserting 5 into a B-tree. The right leaf is full, so we have to split it (middle) before we can insert the target.

Notice that the parent node gains an element as a result of the splitting. To make sure that this does not cause a further overflow, we *always split a full node before descending into it to insert.* If the root splits, the tree becomes taller. Binary search trees, in contrast, become taller by adding new leaves.

Deletion

Removing an element from a leaf is trivial (Figure 17–39).

Figure 17–39: Deleting 2 from a leaf.

What if the leaf is minimal? This isn't a problem, because we *always make sure a node is non-minimal before descending into it to delete.* The root is an exception, because it is allowed to have fewer elements than other nodes.

Splicing an element out of an internal node is not so simple. Our first approach is similar to the deletion algorithm for binary search trees: we remove either the inorder successor or the inorder predecessor of the target and copy it into the target's old location (Figure 17–40).

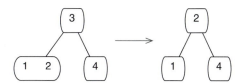

Figure 17–40: Deleting 3 from a B-tree. The target is present in an internal node, so we replace it with (in this case) its inorder predecessor.

Sometimes it is not possible to remove a predecessor or successor, because they are both in minimal nodes. In this case, we have to *merge* the two children (Figure 17–41). Merging is like splitting in reverse.

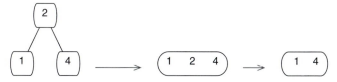

Figure 17–41: Deleting 2 from a B-tree. It cannot be replaced by a predecessor or successor, so its children are merged.

When two siblings are merged, their parent loses an element. The elements from the two minimal siblings, plus one element from their parent, just barely fit into a full node. If (as in Figure 17–41) the root loses its last element, the tree becomes shorter.

There are still more cases to handle. If the target is not present in the current node, we have to descend to a child. If that child is minimal, we have to make it larger before descending. If the child has a nonminimal sibling, we can enlarge the child with a rotation (Figure 17–42), which is similar to the rotations used in red-black trees (Section 14.4).

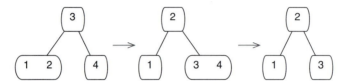

Figure 17–42: Deleting 4 from a B-tree. The node containing the target is minimal, so we can't descend into it (left). We make it larger by performing a right rotation, moving 2 up into the parent and 3 down into the right child (middle). Now we can descend into the node and delete 4 (right).

If the child has no nonminimal siblings, we can't rotate in another element. In this case, we merge the child with one of its siblings.

Implementation

We now provide a working implementation of B-trees storing ints. This code demonstrates the key ideas and complexities of B-trees. A professional implementation would store more general objects, such as employee records.

We begin with the BTreeNode class. Each node has elements and (unless it is a leaf) children. In any other data structure, we would have references to child objects. We don't want to do that here, because we want each BTreeNode stored in a separate file. We keep an id number for each node. The node with id 37, for example, is stored in the file `b37.node`. Each node knows its own id and the ids of its children.

In our representation, each BTreeNode contains an int `id` and two `ArrayList<Integer>`s, `data` and `children` (Figure 17–43). In a leaf, `children` is `null`.

Before we get to the code for the BTreeNode class, we have to address the question of how we will generate these id numbers. It seems clear that we want a counter that keeps track of the next available id. Whenever we get a new id, we increment the counter. If this counter is a variable in a method, we'll get the same id every time we run the method, which is no good. A nonstatic field isn't much better, because each instance will generate its own sequence of ids. A static field almost does the trick, but it will start from scratch every time we start the program, causing us to overwrite files we saved previously.

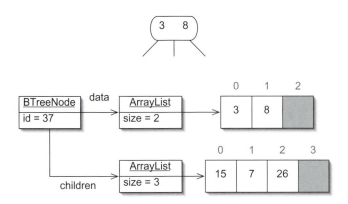

Figure 17-43: A B-tree node (top) is represented by an instance of the BTreeNode class (bottom). This node has size 3. Note the indices of the arrays.

The only way we can make this work is to save the counter in a file. This way, when the program starts, it can read the value of the counter from the file and pick up where we left off. The class IdGenerator (Figure 17–44) uses a tiny file `id` to store this single int. The constant `BTree.DIR` specifies the directory where all of the files will live.

```
1 import java.io.*;
2
3 /** Generates unique id numbers, even across multiple sessions. */
4 public class IdGenerator {
5
6   /** File in which the next available id is stored. */
7   public static final File FILE = new File(BTree.DIR + "id");
8
9   /** Return the next available id number. */
10  public static int nextId() {
11    try {
12      int result;
13      if (FILE.exists()) {
14        ObjectInputStream in
15          = new ObjectInputStream(new FileInputStream(FILE));
16        result = in.readInt();
17      } else {
18        result = 0;
19      }
20      ObjectOutputStream out
21        = new ObjectOutputStream(new FileOutputStream(FILE));
```

Figure 17-44: Every time we invoke `IdGenerator.nextId()`, we get a new id number, even if we have restarted our program since the last time we invoked it. (Part 1 of 2)

```
22        out.writeInt(result + 1);
23        out.close();
24        return result;
25      } catch (IOException e) {
26        e.printStackTrace();
27        System.exit(1);
28        return 0;
29      }
30    }
31
32 }
```

Figure 17-44: Every time we invoke `IdGenerator.nextId()`, we get a new id number, even if we have restarted our program since the last time we invoked it. (Part 2 of 2)

Now we can get started on the BTreeNode class (Figure 17–45). Since we'll be writing BTreeNodes to disk, the class implements Serializable. The constant HALF_MAX is the number *m* mentioned previously. There is no field for size; the size of a node is computed by invoking `size()` on `data` and adding one (line 32).

```
 1 import java.io.*;
 2
 3 /** Node in a BTree. */
 4 public class BTreeNode implements Serializable {
 5
 6   /** Minimum number of children.  Max is twice this. */
 7   public static final int HALF_MAX = 2;
 8
 9   /** Items stored in this node. */
10   private java.util.ArrayList<Integer> data;
11
12   /** Ids of children of this node. */
13   private java.util.ArrayList<Integer> children;
14
15   /** Number identifying this node. */
16   private int id;
17
18   /**
19    * The new node has no data or children yet.  The argument
20    * leaf specifies whether it is a leaf.
21    */
22   public BTreeNode(boolean leaf) {
23     this.id = IdGenerator.nextId();
24     data = new java.util.ArrayList<Integer>((HALF_MAX * 2) - 1);
```

Figure 17-45: Beginning of the BTreeNode class. We use the version of ArrayList from java.util because we need its constructor accepting a capacity (lines 24 and 26) and one of its **add()** methods (used later in this section). (Part 1 of 2)

```
25      if (!leaf) {
26        children = new java.util.ArrayList<Integer>(HALF_MAX * 2);
27      }
28    }
29
30    /** Return one plus the number of items in this node. */
31    public int size() {
32      return data.size() + 1;
33    }
34
35 }
```

Figure 17–45: Beginning of the BTreeNode class. We use the version of ArrayList from java.util because we need its constructor accepting a capacity (lines 24 and 26) and one of its **add()** methods (used later in this section). (Part 2 of 2)

The methods for reading and writing BTreeNodes to disk are given in Figure 17–46. Because they involve the disk, these methods (and any others that invoke them) are extremely expensive. If any exception occurs, we catch it and crash, because it's almost certainly an IOException about which we can't do anything.

```
 1 /** Delete the file containing this node from the disk. */
 2 public void deleteFromDisk() {
 3    try {
 4      File file = new File(BTree.DIR + "b" + id + ".node");
 5      file.delete();
 6    } catch (Exception e) {
 7      e.printStackTrace();
 8      System.exit(1);
 9    }
10 }
11
12 /** Read from disk and return the node with the specified id. */
13 public static BTreeNode readFromDisk(int id) {
14    try {
15      ObjectInputStream in
16        = new ObjectInputStream
17        (new FileInputStream(BTree.DIR + "b" + id + ".node"));
18      return (BTreeNode)(in.readObject());
19    } catch (Exception e) {
20      e.printStackTrace();
21      System.exit(1);
22      return null;
23    }
24 }
25
```

Figure 17–46: BTreeNode methods for disk access. (Part 1 of 2)

```
26 /** Write this node to disk. */
27 public void writeToDisk() {
28   try {
29     ObjectOutputStream out
30       = new ObjectOutputStream
31       (new FileOutputStream(BTree.DIR + "b" + id + ".node"));
32     out.writeObject(this);
33     out.close();
34   } catch (Exception e) {
35     e.printStackTrace();
36     System.exit(1);
37   }
38 }
```

Figure 17-46: BTreeNode methods for disk access. (Part 2 of 2)

Some additional convenience methods are given in Figure 17–47.

```
1 /**
2  * Read the ith child of this node from the disk and return it.
3  * If this node is a leaf, return null.
4  */
5 public BTreeNode getChild(int index) {
6   if (isLeaf()) {
7     return null;
8   } else {
9     return readFromDisk(children.get(index));
10   }
11 }
12
13 /** Return the id of this node. */
14 public int getId() {
15   return id;
16 }
17
18 /** Return true if this node is full. */
19 public boolean isFull() {
20   return size() == HALF_MAX * 2;
21 }
22
23 /** Return true if this node is minimal. */
24 public boolean isMinimal() {
25   return size() == HALF_MAX;
26 }
27
```

Figure 17-47: More methods from the BTreeNode class. (Part 1 of 2)

```
28 /** Make this node a leaf if value is true, not a leaf otherwise. */
29 public void setLeaf(boolean value) {
30   if (value) {
31     children = null;
32   } else {
33     children = new java.util.ArrayList<Integer>(HALF_MAX * 2);
34   }
35 }
```

Figure 17-47: More methods from the BTreeNode class. (Part 2 of 2)

We will need more methods in BTreeNode, but let's look at the BTree class (Figure 17–48). A BTree has only one field: the id of the root node. The BTree object is stored in the file btree. Our implementation supports only a single B-tree at any one time, although it could be easily modified to store each tree in a different directory.

```
1 import java.io.*;
2
3 /** BTree storing many ints on disk. */
4 public class BTree implements Serializable {
5
6   /** Directory where files are stored. */
7   public static final String DIR
8     = BTree.class.getProtectionDomain().getCodeSource()
9     .getLocation().getFile() + File.separator;
10
11   /** Id number of the root node. */
12   private int rootId;
13
14   /** A new BTree is initially empty. */
15   public BTree() {
16     BTreeNode root = new BTreeNode(true);
17     rootId = root.getId();
18     root.writeToDisk();
19     writeToDisk();
20   }
21
22   /** Read a previously saved BTree from disk. */
23   public static BTree readFromDisk() {
24     try {
25       ObjectInputStream in
26         = new ObjectInputStream
27         (new FileInputStream(DIR + "btree"));
```

Figure 17-48: Easy parts of the BTree class. (Part 1 of 2)

```
28        return (BTree)(in.readObject());
29      } catch (Exception e) {
30        e.printStackTrace();
31        System.exit(1);
32        return null;
33      }
34    }
35
36    /** Write this BTree to disk. */
37    public void writeToDisk() {
38      try {
39        ObjectOutputStream out
40          = new ObjectOutputStream
41          (new FileOutputStream(DIR + "btree"));
42        out.writeObject(this);
43        out.close();
44      } catch (Exception e) {
45        e.printStackTrace();
46        System.exit(1);
47      }
48    }
49
50 }
```

Figure 17–48: Easy parts of the BTree class. (Part 2 of 2)

There are two parts to searching. We have to be able to find an element within a node, and we have to be able to find an element within an entire tree.

To search for an element within a node, we use the indexOf() method from the BTreeNode class (Figure 17–49). If target is present in the node, indexOf() returns its index in the node's data ArrayList. If not, indexOf() returns a noninteger indicating which subtree to search next. For example, if target belongs in subtree 1, indexOf() returns 1.5.

```
 1 /**
 2  * Return the index of target in this node if present.  Otherwise,
 3  * return the index of the child that would contain target,
 4  * plus 0.5.
 5  */
 6 public double indexOf(int target) {
 7   for (int i = 0; i < data.size(); i++) {
 8     if (data.get(i) == target) {
 9       return i;
10     }
```

Figure 17–49: The indexOf() method from the BTreeNode class returns a double. (Part 1 of 2)

```
11    if (data.get(i) > target) {
12    return i + 0.5;
13    }
14  }
15  return size() - 0.5;
16 }
```

Figure 17–49: The `indexOf()` method from the BTreeNode class returns a double. (Part 2 of 2)

To search the entire tree, we use the `contains()` method in the BTree class (Figure 17–50), which invokes `indexOf()`. On line 6, the result d is converted to an int i. If d is an integer, i is the index of `target` in `data`. Otherwise, i is the index of the child to which we want to descend.

```
 1 /** Return true if this BTree contains target. */
 2 public boolean contains(int target) {
 3   BTreeNode node = BTreeNode.readFromDisk(rootId);
 4   while (node != null) {
 5     double d = node.indexOf(target);
 6     int i = (int)d;
 7     if (i == d) {
 8       return true;
 9     } else {
10       node = node.getChild(i);
11     }
12   }
13   return false;
14 }
```

Figure 17–50: The `contains()` method from the BTree class.

For insertion, we begin with the `add()` method from the BTree class (Figure 17–51).

```
 1 /** Add target to this BTree and write modified nodes to disk. */
 2 public void add(int target) {
 3   BTreeNode root = BTreeNode.readFromDisk(rootId);
 4   if (root.isFull()) {
 5     BTreeNode parent = new BTreeNode(root);
 6     rootId = parent.getId();
 7     writeToDisk();
 8     parent.add(target);
 9   } else {
10     root.add(target);
11   }
12 }
```

Figure 17–51: The `add()` method from the BTree class.

If the root is full, add() invokes a second constructor for BTreeNode, which splits the root and returns the new parent (Figure 17–52). Recall that the statement this(false), on line 6, invokes the constructor from Figure 17–45.

```
1 /**
2  * Create a new node that has two children, each containing
3  * half of the items from child.  Write the children to disk.
4  */
5 public BTreeNode(BTreeNode child) {
6   this(false);
7   children.add(child.getId());
8   splitChild(0, child);
9 }
```

Figure 17–52: A second constructor for the BTreeNode class.

We now look at our first complicated method, add() from BTreeNode (Figure 17–53). This method descends to the proper node and adds target locally to that node. On lines 34 and 36, addToLocally() invokes a version of the add() method from the java.util.ArrayList class that inserts an element at a particular location, shifting all subsequent elements to the right.

```
1  /**
2   * Add target to the subtree rooted at this node.  Write nodes
3   * to disk as necessary.
4   */
5  public void add(int target) {
6    BTreeNode node = this;
7    while (!(node.isLeaf())) {
8      double d = node.indexOf(target);
9      int i = (int)d
10     if (i == d) {
11       return;
12     } else {
13       BTreeNode child = node.getChild(i);
14       if (child.isFull()) {
15         node.splitChild(i, child);
16       } else {
17         node.writeToDisk();
18         node = child;
19       }
20     }
21   }
22   node.addLocally(target);
23   node.writeToDisk();
24 }
25
```

Figure 17–53: The add() and addLocally() methods from BTreeNode. (Part 1 of 2)

```
26 /**
27  * Add target to this node, which is assumed not to be full.
28  * Make room for an extra child to the right of target.
29  */
30 protected void addLocally(int target) {
31   double d = indexOf(target);
32   int i = (int)d; // Because d might be negative
33   if (i != d) {
34     data.add(i, target);
35     if (!isLeaf()) {
36       children.add(i + 1, 0);
37     }
38   }
39 }
```

Figure 17–53: The add() and addLocally() methods from BTreeNode. (Part 2 of 2)

Splitting a child is handled by the splitChild() method (Figure 17–54). On line 7, this method removes the middle element from child (shifting all subsequent elements to the left) and adds it to the parent.

```
 1 /**
 2  * Split child, which is the full ith child of this node, into
 3  * two minimal nodes, moving the middle item up into this node.
 4  */
 5 protected void splitChild(int i, BTreeNode child) {
 6   BTreeNode sibling = child.createRightSibling();
 7   addLocally(child.data.remove(HALF_MAX - 1));
 8   child.writeToDisk();
 9   children.set(i + 1, sibling.getId());
10 }
11
12 /**
13  * Create and return a new node which will be a right sibling
14  * of this one.  Half of the items and children in this node are
15  * copied to the new one.
16  */
17 protected BTreeNode createRightSibling() {
18   BTreeNode sibling = new BTreeNode(isLeaf());
19   for (int i = HALF_MAX; i < (HALF_MAX * 2) - 1; i++) {
20     sibling.data.add(data.remove(HALF_MAX));
21   }
```

Figure 17–54: The splitChild() and createRightSibling() methods from BTreeNode. (Part 1 of 2)

```
22   if (!isLeaf()) {
23     for (int i = HALF_MAX; i < HALF_MAX * 2; i++) {
24       sibling.children.add(children.remove(HALF_MAX));
25     }
26   }
27   sibling.writeToDisk();
28   return sibling;
29 }
```

Figure 17-54: The `splitChild()` and `createRightSibling()` methods from BTreeNode. (Part 2 of 2)

The two loops on lines 19–21 and 23-25 of `createRightSibling()` are not as efficient as they could be. Since each invocation of `remove()` on an ArrayList takes linear time, the total time for each of these lists is quadratic. This is not too big a problem, because it is quadratic in the *size of a node* (which is limited to 2 * HALF_MAX) rather than the *number of elements in the B-tree*. More importantly, this work is all being done in memory, so it is dwarfed by the cost of a disk access. A professional implementation would probably improve the efficiency of this method at the expense of code clarity.

Finally, we turn to the really nasty part: deletion. The `remove()` method from BTree (Figure 17–55) seems innocent enough.

```
 1 /** Remove target from this BTree. */
 2 public void remove(int target) {
 3   BTreeNode root = BTreeNode.readFromDisk(rootId);
 4   root.remove(target);
 5   if ((root.size() == 1) && (!(root.isLeaf()))) {
 6     BTreeNode child = root.getChild(0);
 7     root.deleteFromDisk();
 8     rootId = child.getId();
 9     writeToDisk();
10   }
11 }
```

Figure 17-55: The `remove()` method from BTree.

This invokes the `remove()` method from BTreeNode (Figure 17–56). There are three possibilities here: `this` is a leaf (lines 8–12), `target` is present but `this` is not a leaf (lines 13–14), or `target` belongs in a subtree (lines 15–16). The first case is trivial; we just have to remove `target` from `data`. The other two cases are somewhat hairier, so they are delegated to other methods.

We have to make sure every node is nonminimal before we descend into it. This is accomplished with rotation and merging. These operations are complicated, because there are so many special cases. To find a sibling from which we can rotate an element, we have to examine the left and right siblings; if they are both minimal, we have to merge. Worse yet, the leftmost child has no

```
 1 /**
 2  * Remove target from the subtree rooted at this node.
 3  * Write any modified nodes to disk.
 4  */
 5 public void remove(int target) {
 6   double d = indexOf(target);
 7   int i = (int)d
 8   if (isLeaf()) {
 9     if (i == d) {
10       data.remove(i);
11       writeToDisk();
12     }
13   } else if (i == d) {
14     removeFromInternalNode(i, target);
15   } else {
16     removeFromChild(i, target);
17   }
18 }
```

Figure 17-56: The `remove()` method from BTreeNode.

left sibling and the rightmost child has no right sibling, so we need special code to avoid Array-IndexOutOfBoundsExceptions in these cases.

We first address `removeFromInternalNode()` (Figure 17–57). As in a binary search tree, our plan is to replace `target` with its inorder predecessor or successor. We'd like to take something from a subtree with a nonminimal root, which might be to the left or to the right of `target`. If both of the children next to `target` are minimal, we have to merge them.

```
 1 /**
 2  * Remove the ith item (target) from this node.
 3  * Write any modified nodes to disk.
 4  */
 5 protected void removeFromInternalNode(int i, int target) {
 6   BTreeNode child = getChild(i);
 7   BTreeNode sibling = getChild(i + 1);
 8   if (!(child.isMinimal())) {
 9     data.set(i, child.removeRightmost());
10     writeToDisk();
11   } else if (!(sibling.isMinimal())) {
12     data.set(i, sibling.removeLeftmost());
13     writeToDisk();
14   } else {
15     mergeChildren(i, child, sibling);
16     writeToDisk();
```

Figure 17-57: The `removeFromInternalNode()` and `mergeChildren()` methods from BTreeNode. (Part 1 of 2)

```
17      child.remove(target);
18    }
19 }
20
21 /**
22  * Merge this node's ith and (i+1)th children (child and sibling,
23  * both minimal), moving the ith item down from this node.
24  * Delete sibling from disk.
25  */
26 protected void mergeChildren(int i, BTreeNode child,
27                             BTreeNode sibling) {
28    child.data.add(data.remove(i));
29    children.remove(i + 1);
30    if (!(child.isLeaf())) {
31      child.children.add(sibling.children.remove(0));
32    }
33    for (int j = 0; j < HALF_MAX - 1; j++) {
34      child.data.add(sibling.data.remove(0));
35      if (!(child.isLeaf())) {
36        child.children.add(sibling.children.remove(0));
37      }
38    }
39    sibling.deleteFromDisk();
40 }
```

Figure 17–57: The removeFromInternalNode() and mergeChildren() methods from BTreeNode. (Part 2 of 2)

Removing the leftmost element in a subtree sounds easy enough, so the length of the method (Figure 17–58) may be surprising. The problem is that we might encounter a minimal node on the way down. If so, we make it larger by rotating in an element from its sibling (line 14) or, if the sibling is also minimal, merging it with its sibling (line 12).

```
 1 /**
 2  * Remove and return the leftmost element in the leftmost descendant
 3  * of this node.  Write any modified nodes to disk.
 4  */
 5 protected int removeLeftmost() {
 6   BTreeNode node = this;
 7   while (!(node.isLeaf())) {
 8     BTreeNode child = node.getChild(0);
 9     if (child.isMinimal()) {
10       BTreeNode sibling = node.getChild(1);
11       if (sibling.isMinimal()) {
```

Figure 17–58: The removeLeftmost() and rotateLeft() methods from BTreeNode. (Part 1 of 2)

```
12              node.mergeChildren(0, child, sibling);
13          } else {
14              node.rotateLeft(0, child, sibling);
15          }
16      }
17      node.writeToDisk();
18      return child.removeLeftmost();
19   }
20   int result = node.data.remove(0);
21   node.writeToDisk();
22   return result;
23 }
24
25 /**
26  * Child is the ith child of this node, sibling the (i+1)th.
27  * Move one item from sibling up into this node, one from this
28  * node down into child.  Pass one child from sibling to node.
29  * Write sibling to disk.
30  */
31 protected void rotateLeft(int i, BTreeNode child,
32                          BTreeNode sibling) {
33   child.data.add(data.get(i));
34   if (!(child.isLeaf())) {
35     child.children.add(sibling.children.remove(0));
36   }
37   data.set(i, sibling.data.remove(0));
38   sibling.writeToDisk();
39 }
```

Figure 17-58: The removeLeftmost() and rotateLeft() methods from BTreeNode. (Part 2 of 2)

Removing the rightmost element involves the same issues (Figure 17–59).

```
 1 /**
 2  * Remove and return the rightmost element in the rightmost
 3  * descendant of this node.  Write any modified nodes to disk.
 4  */
 5 protected int removeRightmost() {
 6   BTreeNode node = this;
 7   while (!(node.isLeaf())) {
 8     BTreeNode child = node.getChild(size() - 1);
 9     if (child.isMinimal()) {
10       BTreeNode sibling = node.getChild(size() - 2);
```

Figure 17-59: The removeRightmost() and rotateRight() methods from BTreeNode. (Part 1 of 2)

```
11        if (sibling.isMinimal()) {
12          node.mergeChildren(size() - 2, sibling, child);
13          child = sibling;
14        } else {
15          node.rotateRight(size() - 2, sibling, child);
16        }
17      }
18      node.writeToDisk();
19      return child.removeRightmost();
20    }
21    int result = node.data.remove(size() - 2);
22    node.writeToDisk();
23    return result;
24 }
25
26 /**
27  * Sibling is the ith child of this node, child the (i+1)th.
28  * Move one item from sibling up into this node, one from this
29  * node down into child.  Pass one child from sibling to node.
30  * Write sibling to disk.
31  */
32 protected void rotateRight(int i, BTreeNode sibling,
33                             BTreeNode child) {
34    child.data.add(0, data.get(i));
35    if (!(child.isLeaf())) {
36      child.children.add(0,
37                         sibling.children.remove(sibling.size() - 1));
38    }
39    data.set(i, sibling.data.remove(sibling.size() - 2));
40    sibling.writeToDisk();
41 }
```

Figure 17-59: The removeRightmost() and rotateRight() methods from BTreeNode. (Part 2 of 2)

Good news: now that we've laid all the groundwork for rotation and merging, only the remove-FromChild() method (Figure 17–60) remains. This one is so long because we have to handle the special cases where target belongs in the first child, the last child, or one in between. In any case, we might be able to rotate an element in from a sibling, or we might have to merge.

It goes without saying that B-trees are difficult to implement and debug. Their ability to find any element in a database of billions with a handful of disk accesses justifies this effort.

```
1 /**
2  * Remove target from the subtree rooted at child i of this node.
3  * Write any modified nodes to disk.
4  */
5 protected void removeFromChild(int i, int target) {
6   BTreeNode child = getChild(i);
7   if (child.isMinimal()) {
8     if (i == 0) {                    // Target in first child
9       BTreeNode sibling = getChild(1);
10      if (sibling.isMinimal()) {
11        mergeChildren(i, child, sibling);
12      } else {
13        rotateLeft(i, child, sibling);
14      }
15    } else if (i == size() - 1) { // Target in last child
16      BTreeNode sibling = getChild(i - 1);
17      if (sibling.isMinimal()) {
18        mergeChildren(i - 1, sibling, child);
19        child = sibling;
20      } else {
21        rotateRight(i - 1, sibling, child);
22      }
23    } else {                         // Target in middle child
24      BTreeNode rightSibling = getChild(i + 1);
25      BTreeNode leftSibling = getChild(i - 1);
26      if (!(rightSibling.isMinimal())) {
27        rotateLeft(i, child, rightSibling);
28      } else if (!(leftSibling.isMinimal())) {
29        rotateRight(i - 1, leftSibling, child);
30      } else {
31        mergeChildren(i, child, rightSibling);
32      }
33    }
34  }
35  writeToDisk();
36  child.remove(target);
37 }
```

Figure 17-60: The removeFromChild() method from BTreeNode.

Exercises

17.11   Are the nodes of a B-tree always, sometimes, or never full when the root is split?

17.12   Explain why 1 is not a legitimate value for HALF_MAX.

17.13   Draw a UML instance diagram of an empty BTree.

17.14   Write an isEmpty() method for the BTree class.

17.15 Modify indexOf() (Figure 17–49) to use binary search rather than linear search.

17.16 Write a useful toString() method for the BTree class.

Summary

Disk storage has two advantages over memory storage: it persists between program runs, and it has greater capacity. On the other hand, accessing data on disk can take a million times as long as accessing data in memory. When the disk is accessed, it is not much more expensive to read many elements than to read one.

Java provides many classes for reading from and writing to disk. These include Scanner and PrintWriter for text and ObjectInputStream and ObjectOutputStream for binary data. Most of these classes are in the java.io package. We can write an instance of any class to disk if the class implements the Serializable interface.

Strings (and hence files) can be compressed by defining short codes for frequently occurring text. Huffman encoding takes advantage of the frequencies of individual characters. Lempel–Ziv encoding creates codes for longer substrings.

Data too big to fit in memory can be sorted externally using an algorithm based on merge sort.

The B-tree data structure is useful for maintaining a set of data too large to fit in memory. Each node in a B-tree can contain many elements. The associated algorithms ensure that the tree stays balanced and very shallow, minimizing the number of disk accesses needed to find, insert, or delete an element.

Vocabulary

B-tree. Data structure used to represent a very large set.

binary format. Format of files stored as data rather than text.

buffered. Of an input or output stream, waiting until it has a large chunk of data before actually sending it.

compressed. Of a file, stored in a format that uses fewer bits. Compressing or uncompressing a file takes time but saves space on disk or transmission time over a network.

external sorting. Sorting performed using files, for use when the data set is too large to fit in memory.

fixed-length encoding. Any encoding, such as ASCII, in which each character is represented by the same number of bits.

flush. Force a buffered stream to send data.

full. Of a B-tree node, having the largest allowable number of elements (one more than twice as many as in a minimal node).

Huffman encoding. Encoding in which more frequent characters are represented by shorter bit sequences.

Lempel–Ziv encoding. Encoding in which each code may represent a long string of characters.

merge. Join two minimal B-tree nodes, plus an element pulled down from the parent, into a full node.

minimal. Of a B-tree node, having the smallest allowable number of elements.

run. Sorted sequence of elements used in external sorting.

serialization. Process of storing a directed graph of objects in memory in a linear file on disk.

size. Of a B-tree node, one more than the number of elements in the node.

split. Divide a full B-tree node into two minimal nodes and one extra element, which is moved up into the parent.

Problems

17.17 Write a program that, given a directory, lists the contents of that directory and any sub-directories. The output should be nicely formatted, with files deeper in the directory structure indented farther. (Hint: Look at the API for the File class.)

17.18 Modify the ExternalSort program so that it sorts files of ints (in binary format) rather than lines of text.

17.19 There is a subtle flaw in the IdGenerator class (Figure 17–44): if we use it many times, the counter in the file will "wrap around" to negative numbers, and then back to 0. Eventually it will begin handing out ids that have been generated before and that might still be in use. Modify the class to keep a set of in-use ids in the file. The nextId() method should never return an in-use id. Modify the deleteFromDisk() method of the BTreeNode class to inform the IdGenerator when an id number is no longer in use.

Projects

17.20 Modify the Huffman program so that it can encode and decode actual ASCII text files. Encoding a typical large file should actually compress it. Use the text being encoded to find the character frequency and store the Huffman tree as the first object in the compressed file.

17.21 Create a class IntList which acts like an ArrayList<Integer>, but uses raw ints instead of Integers. Modify the BTree and BTreeNode classes to use this class. How does this affect the amount of space used on disk for each node?

VI

Appendices

IV

Appendices

Review of Java

A

This appendix is intended as a review of basic Java. While it is not possible to stuff an entire CS1 course into one appendix, this should get the reader up to speed on material that may have been glossed over, omitted, or forgotten since the first course. It should be enough for anyone who has taken a first course in C/C++ to make the transition to Java. Object-oriented programming is not addressed here—that is the subject of the first three chapters of this book.

A.1 The First Program

When a computer scientist sets out to learn a new programming language, one of the first steps is to write a "Hello, world" program. Among other things, this ensures that the compiler and other development tools have been installed correctly.

Before you can run this program, you will need to install a Java system such as Sun's J2SE (Java 2, Standard Edition) Software Development Kit, available for free at java.sun.com. The code in this book was tested on version 1.5.0 and should work with any later version. (Confusingly, version 1.5.0 is also known as version 5.0.) You can check your Java version with the command:

```
java -version
```

Our first program is shown in Figure A–1.

```
1 /** The standard "Hello, world" program. */
2 public class Hello {
3
4   /** Print a friendly greeting. */
5   public static void main(String[] args) {
6     System.out.println("Hello, world!");
7   }
8
9 }
```

Figure A-1: The Hello program.

Type it into a file called `Hello.java`, save it, and compile it with the command:

`javac Hello.java`

Finally, run the program with the command:

`java Hello`

Some common bugs to watch out for:

- The program *must* be saved in a file called `Hello.java`. This is case sensitive— `hello.java` is not good enough.

- The command to compile is `javac`, but the command to run is `java`.

- `javac` needs an extension (.java) for the filename, but `java` does not. (In fact, `java` won't accept a filename with an extension.)

Let's examine the program line by line. (The line numbers are only for our convenience when discussing programs—don't type them.)

Line 1 is a comment, as is line 4. Comments make the program more readable to humans. They are ignored by the Java system.

Line 2 names the program Hello. The program must be saved in an appropriately named file. The keyword `public` is discussed in Section 3.3. Classes are covered in Chapter 1. The curly brace at the end of the line opens a block of code which ends at the matching brace on line 9. The entire program must be within this block.

This program has one **method** (similar to a function or procedure in another language). This is the `main()` method. When we run a class, we are really running the `main()` method. The method occupies lines 5 through 7.

Line 5 is the **signature** of the method, indicating various aspects of the way the method behaves. The signature includes the following facts:

- The method is *public*, meaning that any program can see it. More on this in Section 3.3.

- The method is *static*. All methods in this appendix are static. We will explain what this means, and introduce nonstatic methods, in Chapter 1.

- The method does not return a value. Put another way, the ***return type*** of the method is void. Some methods return values. Others, like this one, only print things or have other side effects. Still other methods both have side effects and return values.

- The *name* of the method is `main()`. When we refer to method names in the text, we will include empty parentheses behind the name to emphasize that it is a method, rather than a variable or something else.

- The method takes one *argument*, which is of type String[] and named `args`. We ignore this argument here, but it is necessary because the `main()` method always has the same signature. Programming language theorists distinguish between a method's ***parameters*** (its own names for the values it receives) and its ***arguments*** (the values themselves). We will ignore this distinction and always refer to them as arguments.

Two other things might appear in a method signature: a list of exceptions thrown (Section 4.3) and any generic type parameters (Section 4.1).

The body of the method is line 6. This is the part that actually does something! It invokes another method by passing an argument to it. The method is called `System.out.println()`. More precisely, the method is named `println()`, and `System.out` indicates where the method can be found. This will be explained in more detail in Section A.7.

Not surprisingly, this method prints out its argument, followed by a newline character.

Exercises

A.1   Change the message in the Hello program, recompile it, and run it again.

A.2   What error message do you get if you leave off the closing curly brace?

A.3   What error message do you get if the method is outside of the class—that is, if you move the final curly brace from line 9 to line 3?

A.4   What error message do you get if you save the program as `Howdy.java`?

A.2 Variables and Types

Our program will be more interesting if it can store some information. We do this using ***variables***, as shown in Figure A–2.

Line 3 ***declares*** a variable called `name`, which is of ***type*** String. We cannot use a variable until it has been declared.

The next thing we must do with a variable is ***initialize*** it—that is, give it a value. The variable `name` is initialized on line 4.

```
1 /** Print a friendly greeting. */
2 public static void main(String[] args) {
3     String name;
4     name = "Bob";
5     System.out.println("Hello, " + name + "!");
6 }
```

Figure A-2: This improved `main()` method for the Hello program greets the user by name.

It is legal to declare and initialize a variable on the same line. We could combine lines 3 and 4 of Figure A–2 into the single line:

```
String name = "Bob";
```

Now that **name** has a value, we can use it to stand for that value. On line 5, we build a longer String by concatenating together three Strings: `"Hello, "`, the value of name, and `"!"`.

A few special Strings are given in Figure A–3.

String	Meaning
"\n"	newline
"\t"	tab
"\""	quotation marks
"\\"	backslash

Figure A-3: Special Strings.

The most common types for variables are listed in Figure A–4. The first four types are called *primitive types*, because they cannot be broken down into smaller pieces. A String, in contrast, can be broken down into chars. There are four other primitive types: short, long, byte, and float. These are rarely used.

We can convert between primitive numeric types (including chars) by *casting*. For example, if we want to convert the double 3.14159 into an int, the syntax is:

```
(int)3.14159
```

This conversion throws away any fractional part. In this case, the result is 3.

If we want to assign a variable of type int a value of type double, we must do this casting:

```
int n = (int)3.14159;
```

Type	Range	Example
boolean	`true` or `false`	`true`
char	Unicode characters	`'a'`
double	roughly $\pm 1.8 \times 10^{308}$	`3.14159`
int	roughly ± 2 billion	`23`
String	sequences of characters	`"Hello"`

Figure A-4: Commonly used types. Unicode is a character-encoding scheme similar to ASCII, but it encompasses characters from many languages.

When converting from a less precise to a more precise type, we don't have to cast explicitly. For example:

```
double x = 3;
```

Arithmetic operations automatically convert to the most precise type involved, so the result of

```
3 * 2.0
```

is of type double.

As we will see in Chapter 1, it is possible (and quite useful) to define new types. It is *not* possible to define new primitive types.

We can also have an *array* of any type. To specify an array type, add `[]` to the end of another type name. For example, the argument to the `main()` method is an array `args`, which is of type String[]. When we run a Java program, any additional command-line arguments are placed into this array. If we run the program as

```
java Hello Akiko Bob Carlos
```

then `args[0]` is `"Akiko"`, `args[1]` is `"Bob"`, and `args[2]` is `"Carlos"`. The length of the array, `args.length`, is 3.

The *scope* of a variable or argument is the part of the program in which we can refer to the variable or argument. Without going into too much detail, the scope of a variable or argument is generally the code between a pair of curly braces. Specifically, an argument like `args` or a variable like `name` is visible only within the current method.

Exercises

A.5   What happens if you declare two variables or arguments with the same name in the same scope? Specifically, what if you declare a variable `args` within the `main()` method?

A.6   What error message do you get if you declare a variable of type int and initialize it to 10,000,000,000?

A.7   What happens if you print `args`?

A.3 Loops

Loops allow us to write a program which does something many times in a row with only a few lines of code. There are three ways to write loops in Java. We can always use any one of them, but there are circumstances in which one is clearer than another.

The first loop is the `while` loop (Figure A–5). This consists of the keyword `while`, a test (boolean expression) in parentheses, and then a body in curly braces. Java first evaluates the test expression. If it evaluates to true, the body of the loop is then executed. The test is then evaluated again, and so on.

```
1 /** Print a friendly greeting. */
2 public static void main(String[] args) {
3   int index = 0;
4   while (index < args.length) {
5     System.out.println("Hello, " + args[index] + "!");
6     index = index + 1;
7   }
8 }
```

Figure A–5: Saying hello to each person named on the command line using a `while` loop.

Very similar to the `while` loop is the `do` loop (Figure A–6). This is almost the same, except that the body of the loop is executed once *before* the test is evaluated. For this program, the `do` loop actually introduces a subtle bug, which we will fix in Section A.5.

```
1 /** Print a friendly greeting. */
2 public static void main(String[] args) {
3   int index = 0;
4   do {
5     System.out.println("Hello, " + args[index] + "!");
6     index = index + 1;
7   } while (index < args.length);
8 }
```

Figure A–6: This `do` loop is not exactly equivalent to the `while` loop in Figure A–5. It guarantees that the body of the loop is executed at least once.

Finally, there is the `for` loop (Figure A–7). While a bit cryptic, it allows for a very concise statement of the loop. It consists of the keyword `for`, a loop header in parentheses, and then a body in curly braces. The loop header has three parts, separated by semicolons: an initialization statement, a test, and an update. Java first evaluates the initialization statement and then the test. If the test is false, the loop ends. Otherwise, the body and the update are both executed, the test is evaluated again, and so on.

```
1 /** Print a friendly greeting. */
2 public static void main(String[] args) {
3   int index;
4   for (index = 0; index < args.length; index = index + 1) {
5     System.out.println("Hello, " + args[index] + "!");
6   }
7 }
```

Figure A-7: This for loop is exactly equivalent to the while loop in Figure A–5.

For loops like this are extremely common. Programmers typically take advantage of a few shortcuts to make the loop even more concise:

- The loop variable can be declared as part of the initialization statement. If this is done, the variable disappears as soon as the loop ends.

- If the loop variable is an index into an array, it is almost invariably named i.

- The loop variable can be incremented with the shorter statement i++.

The resulting method (Figure A–8) behaves exactly like the previous version.

```
1 /** Print a friendly greeting. */
2 public static void main(String[] args) {
3   for (int i = 0; i < args.length; i++) {
4     System.out.println("Hello, " + args[i] + "!");
5   }
6 }
```

Figure A-8: Cosmetic changes produce a more typical-looking for loop.

Java 1.5 introduces an enhanced for loop which allows us to loop through the elements of an array in an even more concise manner. In Figure A–9, line 3 can be read, "For each String name in args...." On the first pass through the loop, name is short for args[0]. On the next pass, name is short for args[1], and so on.

```
1 /** Print a friendly greeting. */
2 public static void main(String[] args) {
3   for (String name : args) {
4     System.out.println("Hello, " + name + "!");
5   }
6 }
```

Figure A-9: The enhanced for loop in Java 1.5 makes looping through an array even easier.

The enhanced for loop can also be used on iterable data structures (Section 5.4).

Exercises

A.8 What is the scope of `index` in Figure A–7? What is the scope of `i` in Figure A–8? (Hint: Try printing the variable after the loop ends.)

A.9 Using each kind of loop, print the numbers 1 through 10.

A.10 Using two nested `for` loops, print a multiplication table for the numbers 1 through 10.

A.4 Interacting with the User

Accepting arguments from the command line is helpful, but our programs would be very limited if we had no other way to interact with the user. We also need to be able to print text to the screen and read input from the keyboard.

Printing text is accomplished with the `System.out.println()` method, as used previously. There is a related method `System.out.print()`, which does not move on to the next line.

Before Java 1.5, reading from the keyboard was fantastically awkward. The introduction of the new Scanner class makes it reasonable. Before reading from the keyboard, a program must create a Scanner with the following incantation:

```
java.util.Scanner input = new java.util.Scanner(System.in);
```

This may seem somewhat cryptic at this point, but we have seen this kind of statement already. This is a declaration and initialization of a variable `input`. The type of the variable is java.util.Scanner, which will make more sense after we discuss packages (Section 3.3). The part to the right of the equals sign gives `input` its initial value. Specifically, it is the invocation of a constructor (Section 1.2). It doesn't matter that we don't understand these things just yet.

Now that we have input, we can read from the keyboard. If we store the next line typed by the user in a variable `answer`, we do this:

```
String answer = input.nextLine();
```

We can also ask for `input.nextInt()` to get an int from the user, `input.nextDouble()` to get the next double, and so on. A technical detail is that these methods only "use up" the number in question, not the entire line of input. If we want to go on to ask the user for non-numeric input, we should invoke `nextLine()` to clear out the rest of the line. In a program that *only* asks for numbers, this can be ignored. We will do more elaborate things with the Scanner class over the course of the book.

Exercises

A.11 Modify the Hello program in Figure A–2 so that it asks the user for her name and then greets her by name.

A.5 Branching

We often want our programs to make decisions based on the value of some variable. Java has two statements for this: `if` and `switch`.

The `if` statement allows us to execute a body only if some test evaluates to true. In Figure A–6, we wrote a `do` loop which was not exactly equivalent to the `while` and `for` loop examples from the same section. The difference is that, if `args.length` happens to be exactly zero (that is, no command-line arguments are provided), the `do` loop executes its body once anyway. This causes the program to crash, because line 5 tries to refer to `args[0]`, and there is no such element. We can fix this with an `if` statement (Figure A–10).

```
 1 /** Print a friendly greeting. */
 2 public static void main(String[] args) {
 3   if (args.length > 0) {
 4     int index = 0;
 5     do {
 6       System.out.println("Hello, " + args[index] + "!");
 7       index = index + 1;
 8     } while (index < args.length);
 9   }
10 }
```

Figure A-10: With an added `if`, the `do` loop becomes exactly equivalent to the `while` and `for` loops.

Optionally, an `if` statement can end with the keyword `else` followed by another body. This body is executed if the test evaluates to false. We can deal with several different possibilities with a statement of this form:

```
if (...) {
  ...
} else if (...) {
  ...
} else if (...) {
  ...
} else {
  ...
}
```

This is illustrated in the Guess program (Figure A–11). The `if` statement beginning on line 15 first tests whether the variable `comparison` is the char `'<'`. If so, the program adjusts the range of numbers it will consider for its next guess.

```
1 /** Game where the computer guesses a number. */
2 public class Guess {
3
4   /** Play the game. */
5   public static void main(String[] args) {
6     java.util.Scanner input = new java.util.Scanner(System.in);
7     System.out.println("Think of an integer between 1 and 100.");
8     int min = 1;
9     int max = 100;
10    char comparison;
11    do {
12      int guess = min;
13      System.out.print("Is it <, =, or > than " + guess + "? ");
14      comparison = input.nextLine().charAt(0);
15      if (comparison == '<') {
16        max = guess - 1;
17      } else if (comparison == '=') {
18        System.out.println("I win!");
19      } else {
20        min = guess + 1;
21      }
22    } while (comparison != '=');
23  }
24
25 }
26
```

Figure A-11: A first draft of the Guess program. A `do` loop is appropriate here, because the program always has to make at least one guess. The statement on line 14 reads the next line from the user, extracts the first character, and stores it in the variable `comparison`.

Otherwise, the program tests whether `comparison` is `'='`. If so, the program declares victory. Otherwise, it assumes that `comparision` must be `'>'`.

An equivalent way to write this program is using a `switch` statement (Figure A–12). This checks for various possible values of one variable. The code from the first matching case up to the next `break` statement (or the end of the `switch` statement) is executed.

```
1 do {
2   int guess = min;
3   System.out.print("Is it <, =, or > than " + guess + "? ");
4   comparison = input.nextLine().charAt(0);
```

Figure A-12: The same loop using a `switch` statement. (Part 1 of 2)

```
 5   switch (comparison) {
 6     case '<':
 7        max = guess - 1;
 8        break;
 9     case '=':
10        System.out.println("I win!");
11        break;
12     default:
13        min = guess + 1;
14   }
15 } while (comparison != '=');
```

Figure A-12: The same loop using a `switch` statement. (Part 2 of 2)

A handy feature of the `switch` statement is that, if we don't put a `break` statement at the end of a case, Java will keep right on going to the next one. For example, suppose that while running the program we keep accidentally typing a comma when we mean to type a less-than sign. We can add an extra case for this which prints a message and then treats the comparison as `'<'` (Figure A–13).

```
 1 switch (comparison) {
 2   case ',':
 3      System.out.println("I assume you meant '<'.");
 4   case '<':
 5      max = guess - 1;
 6      break;
 7   case '=':
 8      System.out.println("I win!");
 9      break;
10   default:
11      min = guess + 1;
12 }
```

Figure A-13: After executing its own code, the top case falls through to the following one.

Exercises

A.12   Modify the program in Figure A–11 so that it behaves the same way, but does not contain the keyword `else`. (Hint: The first occurrence of `else`, on line 17, can simply be replaced with a newline. Why doesn't this work for the one on line 19?)

A.6 Methods and Breaking Out

Unless a program is very tiny, breaking it down into several methods can make it easier to understand. For example, in the Guess program, we could shove the task of choosing a guess off onto a separate method (Figure A–14). This method is invoked using its name followed by a left parenthesis, any arguments (separated by commas), and a right parenthesis. The value of this expression is whatever is returned by the method.

```
 1 /** Game where the computer guesses a number. */
 2 public class Guess {
 3
 4   /** Guess a number between min and max, inclusive. */
 5   public static int makeGuess(int min, int max) {
 6     return min;
 7   }
 8
 9   /** Play the game. */
10   public static void main(String[] args) {
11     System.out.println("Think of an integer between 1 and 100.");
12     int min = 1;
13     int max = 100;
14     char comparison;
15     do {
16       int guess = makeGuess(min, max);
17       // See Figure A-12, lines 3-14, for the rest of the loop body
18     } while (comparison != '=');
19   }
20
21 }
```

Figure A-14: The choice of a guess can be moved to a separate method.

Within the method, a `return` statement causes the method to end immediately and (unless the method has a return type of void) return a value. Enough people miss this point that it is worth repeating: *once a `return` statement is executed, the method invocation is over, and any subsequent code is skipped.*

A `return` statement is not the same as a break statement. We saw the `break` statement in the discussion of the `switch` statement. It can also be used in any kind of loop. It tells Java, "Okay, I'm done with this loop, let's go do whatever comes after the loop." A `return` statement is stronger, because it exits the entire method, no matter how deep in loops and `switch` statements it is.

In the event that we want an even stronger statement, use the `exit()` method from the built-in System class. This takes one int as an argument. By convention, this is 0 if the program is exiting normally, some other number if it is exiting due to some kind of error. When a statement such as

`System.exit(0);`

is executed, the entire program ends. This drastic measure is rarely used.

Dividing a program into methods has a number of advantages, as will be discussed in Chapter 1. One is that it makes the program easier to modify. For example, if we want to make our program smarter, we can have it guess the number in the *middle* of the possible range, rather than at the bottom. To make this improvement, we don't even have to look at the `main()` method. We just have to change `makeGuess()` (Figure A–15).

```
1 /** Guess a number between min and max, inclusive. */
2 public static int makeGuess(int min, int max) {
3   return (min + max) / 2;
4 }
```

Figure A-15: A change to the `makeGuess()` method makes the program smarter.

Exercises

A.13   Write a method which behaves exactly like the one in Figure A–5, but in which line 4 is:

        while (true) {

A.14   Write a method which accepts an int n as an argument and returns the square of n.

A.15   Write a method which accepts an int n as an argument, prints out the numbers 1 through n, and does not return a value.

A.7 Constants

The program in Figure A–16 computes the circumference and radius of a circle. Two of the methods make use of the mathematical constant π. This program works, but it is bad style for an unidentified *magic number* like this to appear in several places in the code. If we have to type it several times, we might make a mistake. If we later want to change the value (for example, to specify more digits of precision), we have to find every occurrence of the number in the file. Finally, it might not be obvious to someone reading the code what this number means.

```
1 /** Compute the circumference and area of a circle. */
2 public class Circle {
3
4   /** Return the area of a circle with the specified radius. */
5   public static double area(double radius) {
6     return 3.14159 * radius * radius;
7   }
8
```

Figure A-16: The number 3.14159 appears in several places in the code. It is best to replace such a magic number with a constant. (Part 1 of 2)

```
 9   /** Return the circumference of a circle with the specified
     radius. */
10   public static double circumference(double radius) {
11      return 3.14159 * 2 * radius;
12   }
13
14   /**
15    * Read the radius from the user and print the circumference and
16    * area.
17    */
18   public static void main(String[] args) {
19      java.util.Scanner input = new java.util.Scanner(System.in);
20      System.out.print("Enter the radius of the circle: ");
21      double radius = input.nextDouble();
22      System.out.println("Circumference: " + circumference(radius));
23      System.out.println("Area: " + area(radius));
24   }
25
26 }
```

Figure A-16: The number 3.14159 appears in several places in the code. It is best to replace such a magic number with a constant. (Part 2 of 2)

A better solution is to declare a ***constant***, a variable which cannot change. In Java, this is done with the keyword `final`:

`final` double pi = 3.14159;

Where should we put this line? If we put it in `circumference()`, it will not be visible in `area()`, and vice versa. If we put it in `main()`, neither of the other methods will be able to see it.

The solution is to put it in the class, but not inside any particular method. Like a method, we declare it public and static (Figure A–17). A variable like this is called a ***class field***, ***static field***, or ***class variable***. This is different from an instance field, which is not declared static and will be discussed in Chapter 1.

Just as we can invoke a method from another class, we can refer to a class field from another class. Two particularly useful constants appear in the built-in Math class: `Math.PI` (roughly 3.14159, the ratio of the circumference to the diameter of a circle) and `Math.E` (roughly 2.71828, the base of the natural logarithms).

We can now understand `System.out.println()` slightly more precisely. `System` is a class. There is a constant `out` within that class. The method `println()` is invoked on the object `System.out`. This is a nonstatic method, as will be explained in Section 1.2.

```
 1 /** Compute the circumference and area of a circle. */
 2 public class Circle {
 3
 4   /** Ratio of the circumference to the diameter of a circle. */
 5   public static final double PI = 3.14159;
 6
 7   /** Return the area of a circle with the specified radius. */
 8   public static double area(double radius) {
 9     return PI * radius * radius;
10   }
11
12   /**
13    * Return the circumference of a circle with the specified
14    * radius.
15    */
16   public static double circumference(double radius) {
17     return PI * 2 * radius;
18   }
19
20   // See Figure A-16, lines 14-21, for the main() method
21
22 }
```

Figure A-17: The magic number has been replaced with a constant.

It is often a good idea to create a single constant instance of the java.util.Scanner class:

```
public static final java.util.Scanner INPUT
  = new java.util.Scanner(System.in);
```

Exercises

A.16   Define a constant String specifying your favorite color.

A.8 Operators

Operators are built-in functions for manipulating (usually primitive) values. In Java, we can define new methods, but we cannot define new operators.

Arithmetic Operators

Arithmetic operators are summarized in Figure A–18.

These generally behave as one would expect, but we must remember the following:

- It is legal to do arithmetic with chars. For example 'c' - 'a' is 2. This is particularly useful when converting between alphabetic and numeric indices. If we are given a char letter, then letter - 'a' is 0 if letter is 'a', 1 if letter is 'b', and so on.

Operator	Description	Notes
+	addition	chars can be added with Strings, this is the concatenation operator
–	subtraction	can be applied to a single value (for example, -x) chars can be subtracted
*	multiplication	
/	division	with ints, remainder is discarded
%	remainder	behaves like modulo with positive numbers

Figure A-18: Arithmetic operators.

- Adding two Strings together concatenates them into one longer String.

- When working with ints, division discards any remainder.

- The % operator, sometimes called modulo, returns the remainder of a division. For example, 27 % 10 is 7. (It is not exactly the same as the mod operator as used by mathematicians. For example, -2 % 10 is –2, but –2 mod 10 is 8.)

- There is an operator precedence hierarchy specifying that multiplication happens before addition and so on. Since Java has so many operators, the complete hierarchy has 14 levels. Rather than trying to memorize it and expecting anyone reading our code to do the same, we use parentheses to ensure that operations happen in the correct order.

Assignment Operators

Assignment operators are used to set or change the value of a variable. They are summarized in Figure A–19.

Things to watch out for:

- The = operator returns the value of its right-hand operand. One consequence is that it is legal to assign the same value to several variables like this:

  ```
  x = (y = (z = 3));
  ```

  It is okay to omit the parentheses in this case:

  ```
  x = y = z = 3;
  ```

  A second consequence is that if we accidentally type

  ```
  if (love = true) { ... }
  ```

  when we mean to type

  ```
  if (love == true) { ... }
  ```

Operator	Description	Notes
=	assignment	returns a value
++	increment	returns a value, but the value should not be used
--	decrement	returns a value, but the value should not be used
+=	increment by	x += y is equivalent to x = x + y
-=	decrement by	x -= y is equivalent to x = x - y
*=	multiply by	x *= y is equivalent to x = x * y
/=	divide by	x /= y is equivalent to x = x / y
%=	remainder by	x %= y is equivalent to x = x % y

Figure A-19: Assignment operators.

then the test will always be passed, because `love = true` is an assignment statement that returns `true`. We can avoid this issue by using the equivalent code:

```
if (love) { ... }
```

- Suppose x is 2 and we evaluate the statement:

```
y = x++;
```

Now x is 3, but what is y? There is an answer, but it's not immediately obvious whether it's 2 or 3. Worse, the answer is different for:

```
y = ++x;
```

Rather than ask anyone reading our programs to perform these mental gymnastics, we'll just avoid using the return value of a ++ or -- expression.

Comparison Operators

These operators, used to compare values, are summarized in Figure A–20.

The only thing to watch out for here is that == and != should be used only to compare primitive values. If they are used to compare (for example) Strings, strange things can happen. This is explained in much more detail in Chapter 2.

Logical Operators

Figure A–21 shows some operators for manipulating boolean values.

The && and || operators are *short-circuited*, meaning that Java stops as soon as it knows the answer. In addition to saving computation time, this is particularly useful for expressions such as:

Operator	Description	Notes
==	equality	use only with primitive values
!=	inequality	use only with primitive values
<	less than	
<=	less than or equal to	
>	greater than	
>=	greater than or equal to	

Figure A-20: Comparison operators.

Operator	Description	Notes
&&	and	short-circuited
||	or	short-circuited
!	not	

Figure A-21: Logical operators.

```
(bears.length > 10) && (bears[10] == "hungry")
```

If the left side evaluates to false, the entire expression must evaluate to false, so Java does not bother evaluating the right side. Since the right side is not evaluated, it does not cause a problem if there is no such element as `bears[10]`.

Perversely, if you accidentally type & instead of && (or | instead of | |), the Java compiler won't complain—but you'll get a non-short-circuited version.

Java has a few other operators, but they are fairly obscure. The only other ones we will use in this book are the bitwise operators discussed in Section 12.1.

Exercises

A.17   What is the value of 3 / 4? How about 3.0 / 4.0?

A.18   What is the value of 123 % 20?

A.19   Which assignment operators (Figure A–19) can be used to initialize a variable?

A.20   Change line 15 of Figure A–11 to read:

```
if (comparison = '<') {
```

Why is this an error? Does the compiler catch it?

A.21   Write a program which contains the erroneous expression `args[-1] == args[0]` but still compiles and runs. (Hint: Use a short-circuited logical operator.)

A.9 Debugging

Professional programmers use sophisticated development environments to debug their programs. While these are beyond the scope of this book, we will mention three useful techniques: compiler error messages, `System.out.println()` statements, and assertions.

Compiler Error Messages

The Java compiler tries to catch as many errors as possible when compiling our programs. It can be annoying to battle the compiler, but it is much better to find errors at this point than to find them when the program is running. We don't have room to discuss all of the different error messages that arise, but there are a few things to keep in mind:

- Sun's widely used Java compiler indicates the file and line number on which an error occurs. Find out how to go to a specific line in your text editor.

- The compiler may report several errors on a single compilation attempt. Always fix the first error first. If the first error is something like a missing close bracket, the compiler may become deeply confused when reading the rest of the program, reporting errors that aren't really there. Fixing the first error may resolve many of the later "errors."

- A successful compilation does *not* mean your program is correct! You must test your program to make sure it does what it is supposed to do in every situation.

System.out.println() statements

A common question in debugging is, "What's going on at this line?" We may wish to verify that the program reached a certain line or to examine the values of variables at that point. This is easily done by inserting a `System.out.println()` statement:

```
System.out.println("Got to point B. x = " + x);
```

These statements can often produce far too much output. If this becomes a problem, it may be better to print a message only when something unusual happens:

```
if (x < 0) {
  System.out.println("Hey, x is negative!");
}
```

Be sure to remove these debugging statements before turning in your program.

Assertions

Assertions are a debugging feature which first appeared in Java 1.4. They provide a way of formalizing assumptions that we make in our programs. For example, suppose we assume that some variable x is positive. We can add this statement to our program:

```
assert x >= 0 : "Hey, x is negative!";
```

This is just like the previous bit of code, except that:

- It is considerably shorter. The syntax is the keyword `assert`, a boolean statement expressing what is supposed to happen, a colon, and then a message to be printed if the assertion fails.

- If any assertion fails, the program crashes immediately, printing the message we supplied and indicating where it occurred. This saves us time in sifting through debugging messages.

- Assertions can be turned on and off at run time. A program is easier to debug with assertions turned on, but has less work to do (and therefore runs faster) with assertions turned off.

  To enable assertions, we must pass the `-ea` command-line option to Java when we run the program.

  ```
  java -ea OurProgram
  ```

  It is common to enable assertions while developing a program, but to disable them once we are fairly confident that the assertions are never violated.

Exercises

A.22   Add an assertion to the Circle program (Figure A–17) so that the program crashes if the user enters a negative radius.

A.10 Coding Conventions

This section describes the standard coding style we will use in this book. You or your instructor may have slightly different preferences. Since coding style exists to make programs easier for humans to read, it is only important that we are consistent and stay fairly close to what most of the Java community does.

Identifiers

Names of constants are in all caps, with words separated by underbars:

```
PI
SCREEN_WIDTH
```

Type parameters (Section 4.1) have one-letter upper-case names. Typical names include E for element, K for key, and V for value.

Names of classes, constructors (Section 1.2), and interfaces (Section 2.3) have words run together, with the first letter of each word capitalized:

```
Hello
PolyhedralDie
```

All other identifiers are formatted the same way, but the first word is *not* capitalized:

```
args
bestSoFar
```

A few standard identifiers are given in Figure A–22.

Identifier	Use
i, j, k	loop variable, index into array
m, n	integer in mathematical function
tally	running count of something
target	element being searched for in, removed from, or added to a data structure
that	object being compared with `this`
result	value to be returned
x, y	double in mathematical function

Figure A–22: Widely used identifiers.

Blocks

We *always* use curly braces for the bodies of loops and if statements. It is technically legal to leave these out if the body consists of a single statement, but it is a very bad idea. If we later go back and add another line (for example, an invocation of `System.out.println()` to print a debugging message), we might run into the problem shown in Figure A–23.

```
1 for (int i = 0; i < 5; i++) {
2     System.out.println("i is " + i);
3     System.out.println("I'm in the loop!");
4 }
5
6 for (int i = 0; i < 5; i++)
7     System.out.println("i is " + i);
8     System.out.println("I'm in the loop!");
```

Figure A–23: These two `for` loops are *not* equivalent.

Despite the deceptive indentation, these loops are not equivalent. In the second loop, the body of the loop is only line 7. Line 8 is not in the loop, so it is executed only once.

Comments

We include a javadoc comment before each class, interface, field, and method, with the exception of some methods which are merely implementing a method from an interface (Section 2.3) or overriding a method from a superclass (Section 3.1). A javadoc comment begins with /** and ends with */.

The wonderful thing about javadoc comments is that they can be used to generate automatic documentation.

Warning: Do not perform this next step if you have any .html files in the same directory as your .java files. The javadoc program may overwrite them!

By this point you presumably have several .java files in your directory. To generate documentation for all of them, use the command:

```
javadoc -public *.java
```

This generates a number of .html files. Open the file `index.html` in your web browser. Click on the name of a class to see its documentation. Part of the documentation for the Circle class (Figure A–17), in the file `Circle.html`, is shown in Figure A–24.

A second type of comment is the C++-style comment which begins with // and goes to the end of the line. We occasionally use this to point out the major sections of a method, explain a particularly cryptic line, or note that some code has been left out of a figure for brevity.

Access Levels

Access levels are discussed in Chapter 3. We adopt the following conventions:

All fields are private, except for constants, which are public.

Methods are either public or protected.

All classes and interfaces are public.

Arrangement of Class Members

The elements of a class appear in the following order:

1.   Static fields

2.   Non-static fields

3.   Constructors

4.   Other methods

5.   The `main()` method

Class Circle

```
java.lang.Object
  |
  +--Circle
```

public class **Circle**
extends java.lang.Object

Compute the circumference and area of a circle.

Field Summary	
static double	**PI** Ratio of the circumference to the diameter of a circle.

Constructor Summary
Circle()

Method Summary	
static double	**area**(double radius) Return the area of a circle with the specified radius.
static double	**circumference**(double radius) Return the circumference of a circle with the specified radius.
static void	**main**(java.lang.String[] args) Read the radius from the user and print the circumference and area.

Figure A-24: Part of the automatically-generated javadoc documentation for the Circle class.

Within each section, members appear in alphabetical order, unless some other order (particularly for fields) would be clearer.

Exercises

A.23 Discuss the advantages and disadvantages of establishing coding conventions for a group project.

A.24 In what way does the method name `println()` violate the standards?

Unified Modeling Language

The *Unified Modeling Language (UML)* is a widely used set of notations for diagramming many aspects of software development, from user interactions to relationships between methods. Most of the UML is beyond the scope of this book, but we make extensive use of two types of UML diagrams. A class diagram (Section B.1) summarizes the features of a class, its relation to other classes, or both. An instance diagram (Section B.2) provides a snapshot of a data structure.

This appendix summarizes the UML features used in this book. The same information is introduced gradually in the main text.

B.1 Class Diagrams

A *UML class diagram* summarizes features of a class, its relation to other classes, or both. Beginning with an example, Figure B–1 shows the Starship class.

The diagram of a class is divided into three sections. The top section shows the name of the class in bold type. The middle section shows the fields of the class. The bottom section shows the methods of the class.

The name and type of each field are given, separated by a colon. A static field, such as SPEED_OF_LIGHT, is underlined.

```
              Starship
SPEED_OF_LIGHT:double
heading:int
mass:double
speed:double
Starship(double)
accelerate(double,int):void
getHeading():int
getMass():double
getSpeed():double
main(String[]):void
```

Figure B-1: UML class diagram summarizing the Starship class.

In the methods section, the name, argument types, and return type of each method are given. In Figure B–1, the method `accelerate()` takes a double and an int as argument, but has a return type of `void`. Constructors have no return type. Static methods, like `main()`, are underlined.

UML class diagrams can also be used to show the relationships between classes. In Figure B–2, a Fleet contains zero or more Starships. If a Fleet always contained three to six Starships, the notation `0..*` would be replaced with `3..6`.

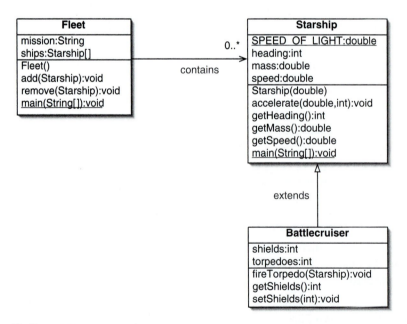

Figure B-2: UML class diagram showing the relationships between the Fleet, Starship, and Battlecruiser classes. The notation `0..*` indicates any number that is at least zero.

Figure B–2 also shows that the class Battlecruiser extends the class Starship. In other words, Battlecruiser is a direct subclass of Starship. This is explained in much more detail in Chapter 3. In a UML class diagram, any fields or methods present in the superclass are normally not listed in the subclass.

The words "contains" and "extends" are not normally included in UML class diagrams. Instead, the different arrow styles indicate the relationship in question. A line arrowhead indicates a "contains" or "has-a" relationship. A hollow arrowhead indicates an "is-a" relationship, such as "extends."

When there are many classes involved, it is sometimes clearer to leave out some or all of the fields and methods (Figure B–3).

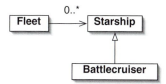

Figure B-3: Fields and methods are sometimes omitted in UML class diagrams.

Interfaces (Section 2.3) can also be shown in UML class diagrams (Figure B–4). An interface name is labeled with the notation <<interface>>. A dashed arrow with a hollow head indicates an "implements" relationship, which is another kind of "is-a" relationship.

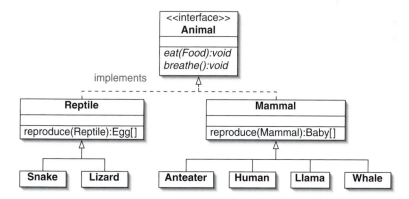

Figure B-4: The interface Animal is implemented by the classes Reptile and Mammal, which are extended by other classes.

The methods in an interface are in italics to indicate that they are abstract. In other words, only the method signatures are specified in the interface; it is up to subclasses to provide concrete implementations. An abstract class (Section 5.5) can contain both abstract and concrete methods. In a UML class diagram, the name of an abstract class is italicized (Figure B–5).

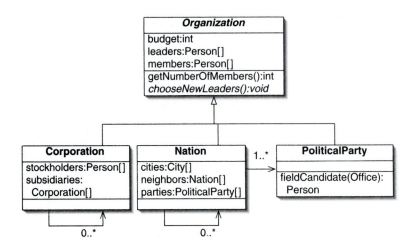

Figure B-5: The class Organization is abstract, as is its method `chooseNewLeaders()`. A Corporation may have other corporations as subsidiaries. A Nation has at least one PoliticalParty, and may have other Nations as neighbors.

Java 1.5 introduces the notion of generic types (Section 4.1). A generic type has one or more other types as parameters. For example, a generic List type allows us to distinguish between a List of Integers and a List of Strings. In a UML class diagram, a type parameter is shown as a small, dashed box at the upper right of a class or interface (Figure B–6). This may contain either a type variable (such as E for element) or the name of a specific class.

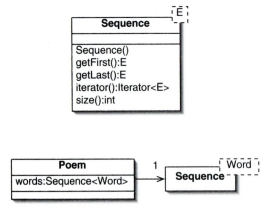

Figure B-6: The Sequence class (top) is generic. A Poem (bottom) contains a Sequence of Words.

In very large programs, classes are often grouped into packages (Section 3.3). In a UML class diagram, a package looks something like a file folder drawn behind the classes it contains (Figure B–7).

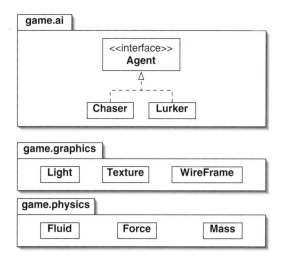

Figure B-7: The game.ai package contains an interface and two classes. Each of the other two packages contains three classes.

B.2 Instance Diagrams

A *UML instance diagram*, also known as a *UML object diagram*, shows a snapshot of the state of one or more objects. These diagrams are used extensively in Part I of this book, and are crucial to understanding the linked structures introduced in Chapter 6.

More than one instance of a class may be shown in an instance diagram (Figure B–8). Static fields and all methods are omitted, as they are the same for every instance. The name of the class of each instance is underlined, but not bold. A specific value is given for each primitive field.

Starship
heading = 45
mass = 1013.6
speed = 245.72

Starship
heading = 180
mass = 484.0
speed = 113.22

Figure B-8: UML instance diagram showing two instances of the Starship class.

References are shown as arrows. In Figure B–9, the instance of class Outfit has four fields: `price`, `top`, `bottom`, and `feet`. Technically speaking, fields of type String are references to instances of the String class, but we omit this detail for clarity.

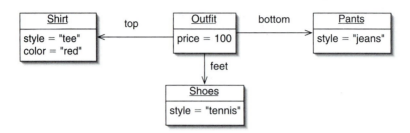

Figure B-9: An instance of class Outfit with references to three other objects.

A number of minor extensions to standard UML instance diagrams are used in this book.

First, a null reference is sometimes shown as a line ending in a large dot (Figure B–10). If including such lines would complicate the diagram excessively, null references are simply omitted.

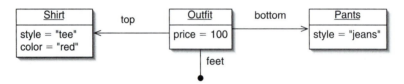

Figure B-10: In this instance of class Outfit, the `feet` field contains a null reference.

Second, arrays are shown as rows of boxes (Figure B–11). Each box may contain a primitive value or a reference to an object or array.

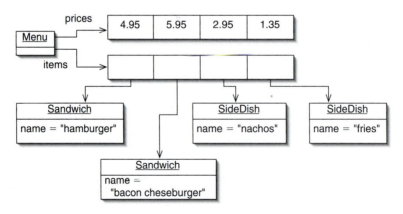

Figure B-11: This instance of Menu contains two arrays, `prices` and `items`.

Third, variables, arguments, and constants are sometimes included in UML instance diagrams (Figure B–12).

Figure B-12: The variable `target` has the value 17. The constant `ORIGIN` is a reference to an instance of Point.

We end this appendix by noting that some special notation is used in Chapter 16, which deals with references in great detail.

C

Summation Formulae

The algebra of sums is useful when analyzing algorithms (Chapter 7). This appendix reviews some basic summation formulae. Proofs are omitted, but we provide a diagram for each formula to aid in memory.

C.1 Sum Notation

Sums can be concisely written using the upper-case Greek letter sigma. For example,

$$\sum_{i=1}^{4} 2i^2$$

is read, "The sum, for i from 1 to 4, of $2i^2$." This is:

$$2 + 8 + 18 + 32 = 60$$

Often the upper limit of the index (written above the sigma) is some other variable involved in the analysis, such as n. For example, in Section C.3, we will see a formula for the sum of the first n positive integers:

$$\sum_{i=1}^{n} i = \frac{n(n+1)}{2}$$

In order to wrangle an expression into a form for which we have a formula, it is often useful to add or remove terms. For example:

$$\sum_{i=1}^{n+1} i = \left(\sum_{i=1}^{n} i\right) + (n+1)$$

Substitution of variables is another useful technique. For example, to evaluate the sum

$$\sum_{i=1}^{2m} i$$

we define $n = 2m$. Then:

$$\sum_{i=1}^{n} i = \frac{n(n+1)}{2}$$

$$= \frac{2m(2m+1)}{2}$$

Sum notation is sometimes used more casually. For example, to describe the total value of all of the cars on a sales lot, we might write:

$$\sum_{car} \langle\text{price of car}\rangle$$

C.2 Sum of Constants

Our first formula is for a sum of n copies of a constant c.

$$\sum_{i=1}^{n} c = cn$$

This is fairly obvious, but for completeness we present Figure C–1.

C.3 Sum of First _n_ Integers

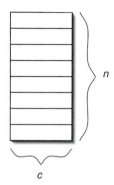

Figure C–1: If each small rectangle has width _c_ and height 1, the total area of the large rectangle is _cn_.

Here is the formula for the sum of the first _n_ integers.

$$\sum_{i=1}^{n} i = \frac{n(n+1)}{2}$$

This is slightly more than $n^2/2$, as illustrated in Figure C–2.

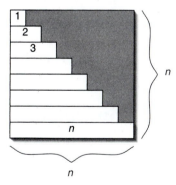

Figure C–2: The sum of the first _n_ integers occupies just over half of an $n \times n$ square.

C.4 Sums of Halves and Doubles

In the next formula, each term is half as large as the previous term.

$$\sum_{i=1}^{n} \left(\frac{1}{2}\right)^i = 1 - \frac{1}{2^n}$$

Even when we don't know the exact number of terms, we can still say:

$$\sum_{i=1}^{n} \left(\frac{1}{2}\right)^i < 1$$

It may be somewhat surprising that the sum is less than 1 no matter how many terms there are. Figure C–3 shows why this is true.

Figure C–3: When the terms of a sum of halves are rearranged, they don't quite fill up a 2 × 1/2 rectangle. The missing piece is precisely the size of the last term: 1/2n.

It is sometimes more convenient to write a sum in which each term is twice (rather than half) the previous term.

$$\sum_{i=0}^{n} 2^i = 2^{n+1} - 1$$

C.5 Upper Limit on Sum of a Function

We often deal with monotonically nondecreasing functions, such as running-time functions for algorithms. It is easy to state an upper limit on a sum of applications of such a function.

$$\sum_{i=1}^{n} f(i) \leq n \cdot f(n)$$

Figure C–4 shows why this is true.

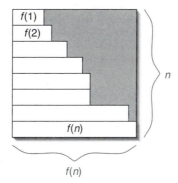

Figure C-4: Since $f(n) \geq f(i)$ for any $i < n$, the sum falls within an $f(n) \times n$ rectangle.

C.6 Constant Factors

A constant factor can be moved to the outside of a sum.

$$\sum_{i=1}^{n} c \cdot f(i) = c \cdot \sum_{i=1}^{n} f(i)$$

This is illustrated in Figure C–5.

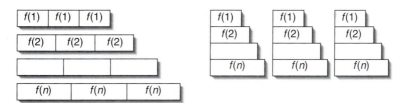

Figure C-5: On the left, we multiply each term by a constant (3) before adding. On the right, we evaluate the sum and then multiply by the constant. The area is the same.

Further Reading

This appendix mentions a few places where the interested reader might turn next.

D.1 Data Structures and Algorithms

Cormen, Thomas H. et al., *Introduction to Algorithms, 2d ed.*, Cambridge, MA: MIT Press, 2001.

  This large but very clear book deals with algorithm analysis. Most of the proofs that were omitted as being "beyond the scope of this book" can be found in Cormen *et al*.

Lewis, Harry R., and Denenberg, Larry, *Data Structures and Their Algorithms*, Boston: Addison-Wesley Longman, 1997.

  A bit denser than this book, Lewis and Denenberg goes into more detail on optimizations and covers more data structures.

D.2 Java

Horstmann, Cay S., and Cornell, Gary, *Core Java 2, 7th ed., Vols. 1 and 2*, Upper Saddle River, NJ: Prentice Hall PTR, 2005.

This is an invaluable reference for any serious Java programmer. A reader interested in, for example, graphic user interfaces in Java should turn here next. Be sure to get the latest edition.

D.3 Games

Mohr, Merilyn Simonds, *The Games Treasury*, Snelbourne, VT: Chapters Publishing Ltd., 1993.

A solid collection of traditional games with some interesting historical information.

Pritchard, David, *The Family Book of Games*, London: Sceptre Books, Time-Life Books/ Brockhampton Press, 1994.

Another anthology which includes some obscure games.

James Ernest publishes his own games through his company, Cheapass Games. They are available in fine game stores everywhere and through his web site:

`http://www.cheapass.com`

Index